MW01093283

Meredith,

Thank you so
much for all your
great support of Honolulu
& [illegible]

[signature]

NORTH PACIFIC TEMPERATE RAINFORESTS

NORTH PACIFIC TEMPERATE RAINFORESTS

Ecology & Conservation

Edited by
GORDON H. ORIANS *and*
JOHN W. SCHOEN

AUDUBON ALASKA *and*
THE NATURE CONSERVANCY OF ALASKA

in association with

UNIVERSITY OF WASHINGTON PRESS
Seattle and London

AUDUBON ALASKA
441 West Fifth Ave., Suite 300
Anchorage, AK 99501
ak.audubon.org

THE NATURE CONSERVANCY IN ALASKA
715 L Street, Suite 200
Anchorage, AK 99501
www.nature.org

UNIVERSITY OF WASHINGTON PRESS
PO Box 50096, Seattle, WA 98145, USA
www.washington.edu/uwpress

LIBRARY OF CONGRESS CATALOGING-IN-PUBLICATION DATA
North Pacific temperate rainforests : ecology and conservation /
edited by Gordon Orians and John Schoen.
pages   cm
ISBN 978-0-295-99261-7 (hardback)
1. Temperate rain forest ecology—British Colombia.   2. Temperate
rain forest conservation—British Colombia.   3. Temperate rain
forest ecology—Alaska.   4. Temperate rain forest conservation—
Alaska.   I. Orians, Gordon H., editor of compilation.   II. Schoen,
John W., editor of compilation.
SD146.B7N67 2013   577.34—dc23   2013007835

The paper used in this publication is acid-free and meets the mini-
mum requirements of American National Standard for Information
Sciences—Permanence of Paper for Printed Library Materials,
ANSI Z39.48 1984.∞

TO JOHN CAOUETTE

IT IS RARE INDEED WHEN A SCIENTIST OVERTURNS A WIDELY HELD paradigm, but John Caouette did. John transformed the dominant method of describing and mapping coastal forests in southeastern Alaska from an industrial inventory of timber volume to an ecological framework of tree size and stand density that more accurately reflects the variety of key ecological functions, habitat associations, and locations of rare forest types across the landscape. In his methodical way, John's work focused our attention on characteristic patterns of forest structure that illustrated underlying ecological processes and provided a very pragmatic approach to forest management and conservation planning. He was a skilled statistician with the uncommon eye of a naturalist, ever helpful in providing insightful discussion, guidance, and support. John was a valued colleague with tremendous dedication to his work, yet even higher dedication to his family, friends, and community. John is and will continue to be missed greatly, and this book is dedicated to him.

Dave Albert
The Nature Conservancy

CONTENTS

PREFACE AND ACKNOWLEDGMENTS

THIS PROJECT WAS FIRST CONCEIVED IN 2007 TO EXPAND SCIEN-
tific awareness and understanding of the North Pacific temperate rainforest ecosystem and the Tongass National Forest by inviting key scientists
to participate in a science cruise through a portion of the Tongass. The goal
of the expedition (completed in May 2008) was to conduct a field-based
peer review of the Audubon Alaska–The Nature Conservancy (TNC) conservation assessment and resource synthesis for southeast Alaska and
the Tongass National Forest. J. Schoen (Audubon) and D. Albert (TNC)
hosted eight scientists (P. Alaback, University of Montana; J. Cook, University of New Mexico; M. Kirchhoff, Alaska Department of Fish and
Game; A. MacKinnon, British Columbia Forest Service; M. Nie, University
of Montana; B. Noon, Colorado State University; G. Orians, University of
Washington; and D. Secord, Wilburforce Foundation) on a cruise around
northeastern Chichagof Island.

This group of scientists also served as a steering committee for a science workshop that was held in Juneau, Alaska, in February 2009. It was
sponsored jointly by Audubon Alaska and The Nature Conservancy, with
agency cooperation from the Alaska Department of Fish and Game, USDA
Forest Service, US Fish and Wildlife Service, and the Alaska Chapter of
The Wildlife Society. The purpose of the workshop and public conference
was to discuss opportunities for incorporating fundamental concepts of
conservation biology into management strategies for conserving the biodiversity and ecological integrity of the Tongass National Forest. The two-
day workshop featured eight invited papers with focused discussions
under the "Dahlem Conference" framework, which consisted of a small
group of participants invited to thoroughly discuss several agreed-upon
issues and themes. Each paper was provided to all invited participants four
weeks prior to the workshop, and two invited commentators (for each

FIGURE 0.01. Members of the Tongass science cruise sitting under a nearly 3 m diameter Sitka spruce tree (one of the 10 largest known to occur in Alaska) in Tenakee Inlet on Chichagof Island, May 2008. *Left to right, bottom row*: Dave Secord, Barry Noon, John Schoen, Dave Albert. *Top row*: Andy MacKinnon, Martin Nie, Paul Alaback, Gordon Orians, Joe Cook, Matt Kirchhoff. Photo by John Schoen.

paper), with expertise on that topic, also provided written comments. The presenters included seven senior authors (P. Alaback, W. Beese, J. Cook, L. Crone, K. Lertzman, B. Marcot, and D. Person) of the focal papers included in this book and D. D'Amore (a coauthor with senior author R. Edwards). In addition, the following scientists provided written commentary on each of the presented papers: D. Albert, S. N. Dawson, J. Franklin, S. Gende, T. Hanley, K. Hastings, K. Koski, A. MacKinnon, M. McClellan, J. Nichols, M. Nie, B. Noon, G. Nowacki, K. Petersen, D. Policansky, T. Reimchen, S. Saunders, J. Schoen, and L. Suring. G. Orians moderated the workshop. The workshop was attended by 60 scientists and managers with experience in forest ecology, conservation biology, and research and management in the North Pacific rainforests. We thank all those scientists who participated in the detailed discussion of each of the eight focal topics. During the workshop, plans were formalized to use the eight focal topics as the foundation for a book that would be expanded in scope from the Tongass to include the North Pacific temperate rainforest from the central British Columbia coast through southeast Alaska. Special appreciation is extended to D. Albert and M. Kirchhoff, who provided extensive support in planning, organizing, and participating in both the science cruise and workshop. M. Smith assisted with the workshop, and N. Walker prepared graphics for the book.

Appreciation is extended to D. Albert, G. Fay, M. Hunter, J. Kenagy, J. Kimmins, M. Kirchhoff, M. Nie, B. Noon, P. Paquet, M. Smith, T. Spies, and F. Swanson for their helpful reviews of individual chapters. D. Della-Sala and an anonymous reviewer provided invaluable criticisms and editorial suggestions for the entire book.

Audubon Alaska and The Nature Conservancy provided significant support for the science cruise, workshop, and publication of this book. The primary funders of the science cruise and workshop that underpinned this book were the Gordon and Betty Moore Foundation; David and Lucile Packard Foundation; Turner Foundation, Inc.; and Wilburforce Foundation. In addition, the Wilburforce Foundation underwrote a major portion of the publication costs. Funders of the Audubon and TNC conservation work in the Tongass National Forest have included (in addition to those above) the Alaska Conservation Foundation, Brainerd Foundation, Campion Foundation, ConocoPhillips Alaska, Conservation Alliance, William and Flora Hewlett Foundation, Leighty Foundation, True North Foundation, and The Wilderness Society. Classification and mapping of terrestrial ecosystems was supported by a State Wildlife Grant from the Alaska Department of Fish and Game.

Gordon Orians and John Schoen

NORTH PACIFIC TEMPERATE RAINFORESTS

1

Introduction

Gordon H. Orians, John W. Schoen,
Jerry F. Franklin, and Andy MacKinnon

THE MAGNIFICENT COASTAL NORTH PACIFIC TEMPERATE RAINFOR-
est, blanketing a glacially carved landscape of precipitous mountains and
dashing rivers, fragmented by thousands of islands, surrounds the eastern
Pacific Rim from southern Alaska to northern California. Rainforests and
islands have been a major focus of ecological and evolutionary study over
the last century and a half. Today they are a core concern of forest ecologists, conservation biologists, and others.

The purpose of this book is to provide a multidisciplinary overview of
key issues related to the management and conservation of the portion of the
coastal North Pacific rainforests in southeast Alaska and northern coastal
British Columbia. This region (fig. 1.01), with its thousands of islands and
millions of hectares of relatively pristine temperate rainforest, is home to
nearly all the species it harbored before people arrived in North America.
It thus provides a valuable opportunity to compare the ecological functioning of a largely intact forest ecosystem with the significantly modified
ecosystems that typify the Earth's temperate zone. A broader understanding of the conservation challenges and opportunities that scientists, managers, and conservationists face in this region should be of interest and
value to practitioners seeking to balance economic sustainability with
conservation and ecosystem integrity across the globe.

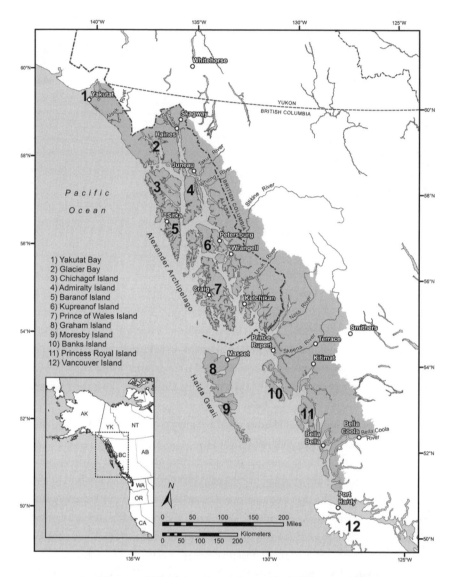

FIGURE 1.01. The coastal North Pacific rainforest (shaded area on map) extends from Yakutat Bay in southeast Alaska to Cape Caution along the central coast of British Columbia.

COASTAL TEMPERATE RAINFORESTS
ARE OF GLOBAL IMPORTANCE

In contrast to the more famous and intensely studied tropical rainforests, coastal temperate rainforests have never been widespread globally. They constitute only 2% to 3% of the area of the world's temperate forests. Coastal temperate rainforests are confined to a handful of relatively small areas, primarily on the northern Pacific coast of North America and the coasts of southern Chile and Argentina, Japan and Korea, and Tasmania and New Zealand (Alaback 1995; Schoonmaker *et al.* 1997; DellaSala, Alaback, *et al.* 2011). Although temperate rainforests once occurred in northwestern Europe, most have been eliminated or dramatically altered by millennia of high-intensity human occupation. Approximately half of the world's coastal temperate rainforest is located on the northwestern maritime margin of North America (Ecotrust *et al.* 1995). DellaSala (2011) inventoried and described the world's relatively rare temperate and boreal rainforests and provided a scientific catalyst for global and regional conservation.

Humans did not occupy the cool, coastal temperate rainforests of the Americas until less than 30,000 years ago. These ecosystems were largely unsuitable for agriculture, so people only lightly modified them after their arrival. However, the coastal temperate rainforest of North America south of Cape Caution on the British Columbia (BC) coast has been extensively modified by recent human activities, particularly clear-cut logging and road construction, sometimes followed by agricultural or urban development. Although most of the forests logged in this area have been regenerated to younger forests, these younger forests differ strikingly from the original forests they replaced (Alaback *et al.*, this volume, chapter 4; Person and Brinkman, this volume, chapter 6). Fortunately, large amounts of the northern half of this forest are similar to what they were when people arrived in the region about 10,000 years ago, following the Wisconsin glacial period.

This area thus offers unusual opportunities for understanding recent ecological changes and learning how to develop and apply methods to sustain the ecological processes that yield the goods and services provided by those ecosystems. In addition, rich opportunities exist to restore the natural composition, structure, and functioning of portions of these forests that have been clear-cut and managed as even-aged timber plantations.

Ecological research on the temperate rainforests of the northern Pacific coast of North America has greatly increased both scientific and societal appreciation of the unusual features and complexity of the region's natural forest ecosystems, especially its older forests (Franklin *et al.* 1981). Extensive and important faunal studies, particularly of flagship species such as the northern spotted owl, marbled murrelet, and Sitka black-tailed deer, were coupled with ecosystem-level research. The degree to which traditional forest practices, which created highly simplified systems in pursuit of efficient wood production, have reduced other forest values has been made clear by other scientific studies (Puettmann *et al.* 2009). The importance of managed lands (the semi-natural matrix) and limitations of protected areas as the only focus in conserving biodiversity and critical ecosystem processes has also become apparent (Lindenmayer and Franklin 2002; Franklin and Lindenmayer 2009).

Judged on taxonomic uniqueness, unusual ecological or evolutionary phenomena, and global rarity, coastal temperate rainforests are globally important ecoregions of the world (Olson and Dinerstein 1998; DellaSala 2011). The lowland, productive sites are among the terrestrial ecosystems with the greatest standing biomass. Hence, they may have a significant potential role in future carbon sequestration strategies (Fitzgerald *et al.* 2011). Even though the forests are dominated by a small number of tree species, the trees tend to be large, with multiple canopy layers. An abundant growth of shrubs, herbs, and cryptogams characterizes the understory. The biological richness of the forests resides in the forest canopies (arthropods and lichens) and the soils (rich animal and microbial communities).

Coastal temperate rainforests are found in regions that have undergone extensive climate changes over recent millennia; some were ice covered during the most recent glacial advances. They are expected to experience significant climatic changes in the near future as well. The coastal temperate rainforests of North and South America contain hundreds to thousands of islands, some of which were connected to the mainland in the recent past. They are still being colonized by new species in response to climate change and are not currently in species richness equilibrium (Cook and MacDonald, this volume, chapter 2). Because these forests occur in regions with high rainfall and complex topography, the interactions between their terrestrial and marine components are especially complex and important (Gende *et al.* 2002; Edwards *et al.*, this volume, chapter 3).

Life on Earth has survived repeated dramatic changes generated by physical forces and by life itself. The productivity and richness of Earth's biota expanded and contracted over the nearly four-billion-year course of life's evolution, but the general trend has been an increase in biological diversity. Humans have caused extinctions of species for thousands of years. When people first crossed the Bering Land Bridge to North America about 20,000 years ago, they exterminated—possibly by overhunting—many species of a rich fauna of large mammals (Ripple and van Valkenburgh 2010). Extermination of large animals also followed the human colonization of Australia. At that time, about 40,000 years ago, Australia had 13 genera of marsupials larger than 50 kg, a genus of gigantic lizards, and a genus of heavy, flightless birds. All of the species in 13 of those 15 genera became extinct. When Polynesian people settled in Hawaii about 2,000 years ago, they exterminated at least 39 species of endemic land birds. More recently European colonists caused the extinction of the Labrador duck (*Comptorhynchus labradorius*), great auk (*Pinguinus empennis*), Carolina parakeet (*Conuropsis carolinensis*), and passenger pigeon (*Ectopistes migratorius*), the most abundant land bird in North America when they arrived.

Although a long-term historical perspective might suggest complacency about current human-caused changes, today the major environmental changes are being caused by a single species. We are becoming acutely aware that our efforts to maximize the delivery of a few of the many goods and services potentially provided by ecosystems (e.g., timber, minerals, food) has greatly diminished their ability to supply many other goods and services (e.g., biodiversity conservation, flood control, water quality) (Millennium Ecosystem Assessment 2003).

Efforts to protect Earth's rich array of habitats and ecological communities and to conserve species have a long history. Early conservation efforts concentrated on species of special economic or social importance, but gradually, as people became aware of the manifold consequences of the activities of Earth's dramatically increasing human population, the scope of their research broadened to include habitat destruction and fragmentation, environmental contamination, spread of diseases, and loss of biodiversity. As Earth's human population has grown rapidly and individual wealth has increased substantially in some nations, pressures to extract goods and services from ecosystems have dramatically increased.

At the same time, we recognize that people have lived in North Pacific temperate rainforests for a long time—since at least the last glacial retreat—and continue to live here today. Our aboriginal peoples—generally referred to as First Nations in British Columbia and Alaska Natives in Alaska—have always had a close relationship with the landscapes they inhabit. But nonaboriginal residents of this region are also more closely tied to their environments than most other North Americans, whether for hunting and fishing, employment in resource industries, or just generally enjoying their magnificent surroundings. Healthy human communities in the North Pacific temperate rainforest depend on vibrant ecosystems.

Two developing fields of scientific inquiry—conservation biology and island biogeography—are particularly relevant to efforts to understand and manage North America's coastal temperate rainforests.

Conservation Biology

The rapid development of the discipline of conservation biology is a response of the scientific community and resource professionals to the accelerating loss of biodiversity. Its practitioners apply principles, data, and concepts from ecology, biogeography, population genetics, economics, sociology, anthropology, economics, and philosophy, in an effort to greatly reduce the current high rates of extinction of species. As the field developed, conservation biologists came to realize that concentrating their efforts on small areas and individual species, although it has conserved local habitats and ecosystems, has failed to stem the loss of Earth's biological diversity. They recognized that they needed to plan and execute conservation strategies at greater spatial and temporal scales, that is, the scales at which the ecological and evolutionary processes that generate and maintain biological diversity operate (Olson and Dinerstein 1998). Conservation biologists have also recognized that management interventions, in addition to creating reserves, need to incorporate biodiversity concerns in the semi-natural landscapes that are being managed for commodity production (Lindenmayer and Franklin 2002).

These insights led to the recognition that large terrestrial areas, characterized by a distinctive climate and dominant vegetation, would be appropriate management units. They need to be large enough to potentially maintain viable populations of the species with the largest spatial requirements, large enough to enable the ecological and evolutionary processes that generate and maintain new species to continue, and extensive enough to include the great variety of Earth's habitats and ecological communities.

Driven in part by the increasing fragmentation of mainland habitats and the extinctions that it may be contributing to, ecologists and conservation biologists are devoting much attention to extrapolating their research insights to large spatial and long temporal scales. What processes become most important at different spatial scales? Are different scales nested hierarchically? Which species have the largest area requirements for long-term persistence of their populations? What new concepts must be developed for the emerging field of landscape ecology?

Island Biogeography

Archipelagoes have long played a key role in helping scientists to recognize the importance of long temporal scales and large spatial scales for the evolution of life and for the structure and functioning of Earth's ecosystems. Insights from the field of island biogeography, which began with the pioneering work of Alfred Russel Wallace (1869, 1876, 1880), help us understand the role of the history of physical changes and movements of organisms across the landscape in generating the current biota of coastal North Pacific temperate rainforests (Cook and MacDonald, this volume, chapter 2).

For more than 100 years, biogeography was primarily a descriptive field, but during the 1960s three major advances changed it into the dynamic multidisciplinary field it is today (Brooks 2004). The first was the publication of the equilibrium theory of island biogeography by Robert MacArthur and Edward O. Wilson (1967). The second, acceptance of the theory of continental drift, provided ways to explain many otherwise puzzling patterns in the distribution of organisms. The third, the development of phylogenetic systematics (Hennig 1966), provided the first phylogenies that were rigorously based on quantitative analyses.

Recognition that patches of habitat types on continents resemble islands in many respects stimulated the use of concepts of island biogeography to explore the dynamics of species on mainland "virtual islands." One result has been the development of hypotheses of nonequilibrium island biogeography, the investigation of patterns of faunal relaxation on recently isolated habitats. Low mammal species richness in montane habitats in the Great Basin of North America (Brown 1971) and in the tropical rainforests of northern Queensland, Australia (Moritz 2005), are prime examples of nonequilibrium island biogeographic patterns.

As a consequence of dramatic sea level changes that accompanied the expansion and contraction of Pleistocene glaciers, many areas of the coastal temperate rainforests of North America that were formerly connected to the mainland have recently become islands. Studies of organisms on some of those islands, in Barkley Sound, on the west coast of Vancouver Island (Cody 2006), for example, have yielded important insights into floral relaxation. The biota of the coastal rainforests of North America is definitely not currently in equilibrium.

MANAGEMENT CHALLENGES OF THE TWENTY-FIRST CENTURY

One of the primary challenges facing residents of coastal North Pacific temperate rainforests as we enter the twenty-first century is how to redesign our land allocation and management strategies to address the goals of maintaining vibrant and dynamic ecosystems and healthy human communities. There are numerous examples around the world (and farther south on our coast) where the ability of ecosystems to sustainably provide the full array of goods and services has been seriously compromised by resource development. Because of the largely undeveloped nature of North Pacific coastal landscapes—an increasingly rare commodity globally—we have an opportunity to work diligently to better understand the complex interrelationships among the different types of goods and services these ecosystems provide so that we can obtain some valuable resources (e.g., forest products) without diminishing other services (e.g., water quality, biodiversity).

To achieve these goals, it would be helpful to focus on ecosystems and not on political boundaries. The ecosystems and species in our region don't recognize the BC–Alaska international border. Yet almost every inventory and mapping effort, and every management plan, has that border as its southern boundary (for Alaskan plans) or its northern boundary (for BC plans). There is little coordination in things like protected areas planning between BC and Alaska. If we want to properly protect this area, there must be.

Another border that needs bridging is the one between terrestrial, freshwater, and marine realms. There are few places on earth where marine and terrestrial realms are so closely linked as in coastal temperate rainforests. Yet terrestrial and marine managers generally work for different agencies and conduct their research, inventory, and planning in isolation from each other. Although this book is primarily about managing terrestrial and freshwater realms, many of the ideas and recommendations it contains must be implemented in cooperation with marine scientists and managers.

On the Canadian side of the border, almost all (>95%) of the land is Provincial Crown land (owned by the province). (Land claims negotiations currently underway with a number of coastal First Nations will likely result in considerable amounts of this land being transferred to First Nations ownership.) Land use plans were developed for BC's central and northern coast in 2006, and in Haida Gwaii in 2010. These plans designate approximately one-third of the central and northern BC coast, and one-half of Haida Gwaii, as protected areas and set out management practices for the rest of the landscape.

In southeast Alaska, about 90% of the land area is federal land. The Tongass National Forest—at 6.8 million ha—encompasses nearly 80% of the land area; Glacier Bay National Park covers 12% of the region. The rest of the land base is managed primarily by the state of Alaska and private land holders including Native corporations. The Tongass Land and Resource Management Plan (USDA Forest Service 2008a) is the guiding document for most of the lands of southeast Alaska.

The objectives, profession, and practice of forestry, the most important modifiers of North America's coastal temperate rainforests, have undergone major changes during the last 30 years as a consequence of fundamental changes in societal perceptions, the domestic and global wood products industry, and scientific understanding of forest ecosystems and landscapes. Changes continue to be driven by new public priorities, new scientific information, and changing economic conditions, combined with the recognition that we need to, and can, learn from past mistakes.

New Priorities

Since its origin, the profession of forestry focused on the efficient and sustainable production of timber (Puettmann *et al.* 2009), firmly grounded in tenets that explicitly considered wood to be the most important product of forests. Broader perspectives on the value of forests began to emerge in the 1960s with increased societal awareness and concern for the environment. This was expressed by adoption of many significant environmental laws during the 1960s and 1970s, several of which had profound consequences for the management of public forest lands. Examples include the Wilderness Act of 1964, the National Environmental Policy Act of 1969, the Endangered Species Act of 1973, and the National Forest Management Act of 1976 in the United States; and the Canadian Forestry Act (1985), the Canadian Environmental Protection Act (1999), and the Federal Fisheries Act of Canada (1985). One major difference between the two countries is that Canada did not introduce federal legislation to protect endangered species until 2002 (Species at Risk Act). In both countries, these laws and regulations reflected society's increased environmental concerns.

New Science

Significant advances in scientific understanding of forest ecosystems and landscapes developed in parallel with societal awakening regarding the environment; in fact, scientific studies made a significant contribution to the shift in societal interest in the environment. Most previous forest research had focused on regeneration and growth of commercial tree species and on silvicultural practices that optimized the production of wood (Puettmann *et al.* 2009). In the 1960s, research was initiated on forests as ecosystems; this research received a significant boost with the US International Biological Program in 1968, which was followed by establishment of an ecosystem studies program in the National Science Foundation (1973). The US Forest Service research program contributed significantly to many of these projects. In BC, formal independent science panels were established to guide development of land use plans for Clayoquot Sound (southwestern Vancouver Island; Scientific Panel for Sustainable Forest Practices in Clayoquot Sound 1995), and the central and northern coast and Haida Gwaii (e.g., Coast Information Team 2004).

The combination of environmental legislation and research had significant impacts on forest management on all forest lands, public and private. These effects were applied differently in the United States—where coastal temperate rainforests are held by a combination of federal and state governments and private entities—than in British Columbia, where forest lands are almost entirely owned by the provincial government. In the US, the laws and regulations were particularly profound on federal forests where the environmental obligations were both most extensive and clearly defined. In BC, the important legislation governing forest practices is provincial legislation, such as the *Forest and Range Practices Act* (2002). In both countries, this combination of environmental legislation and research represented an immense challenge to the forestry profession—both to their fundamental tenets and to traditional silvicultural practices. Ultimately they required the development of a new paradigm based upon modern ecosystem science, including the complex and profound roles of natural disturbances (Franklin *et al.* 2007; North and Keeton 2008).

New Economics

Globalization of the wood products industry late in the twentieth century brought yet another challenge to forestry in North America. With globalization of trade in wood products and of capital markets, corporations moved to invest in areas where economic production was most efficient—primarily in forested regions in the southern hemisphere (Franklin and Johnson 2004). Development of fiber farms—short rotation plantations of exotic pines and eucalypts—was clearly an economically superior approach for growing the large volumes of wood needed to feed the global markets for common wood-based products. Investments flowed to New Zealand, Chile, and Australia. In southeast Alaska and northern coastal BC, the timber industry will increasingly be at a competitive disadvantage with more productive, less isolated forested areas in the production and milling of large volumes of commodity lumber or pulp.

Today society increasingly values forest ecosystems for the broad variety of services and goods that they provide, including watershed protection, carbon sequestration, habitat for a large array of organisms, and recreation and inspiration as well as wood. Currently, the provision of a well-regulated flow of high-quality water may be the most highly valued service provided by undisturbed forest ecosystems. Given the surfeit of efficiently produced wood available from tree plantations, timber production from older forests in North America is declining in value. However, forests may have continued significance for local communities as sources of raw materials.

The challenges these social, environmental, and economic changes pose for forest management in the next century are immense. Goals that give primacy to efficient production of wood are no longer viable. Rather, management approaches that seek to restore and sustain complex forest ecosystems and the full array of goods, services, and organisms they provide are required. Fortunately, the substantial scientific information that has accumulated during the last several decades provides tools for helping meet this goal. Unfortunately, the profession has only recently incorporated such science into management philosophies and practices (Franklin *et al.* 2007; Puettman *et al.* 2009; Bunnell and Dunsworth 2009).

Changes in the economics of the forest industry, however, create significant difficulties as well as conservation opportunities. Although the reduction in the large-scale extraction industry from large regions in North America lessens pressures for timber harvest, it also leaves areas without skilled workers needed to carry out forest stewardship and without processing facilities that can help subsidize the restoration and other forest management activities that need to be undertaken. This lack of skilled professionals is of concern because society is unlikely to expend large amounts of money for forest restoration and stewardship. Climate change adds another dimension of uncertainty that society and professional resource managers must deal with. Managing to maintain future options and ecological resiliency have become important elements in natural resource management.

OPPORTUNITIES AND CHALLENGES WITHIN COASTAL NORTH PACIFIC TEMPERATE RAINFORESTS

New World coastal temperate rainforests offer unusual opportunities for people to apply the latest concepts developed by researchers in the environmental sciences at an ecoregion scale. This knowledge can guide efforts to plan for long-term ecological integrity and sustainable use of these mostly intact native forest ecosystems. A significant body of information exists upon which to base future research, restoration, and management strategies. Information on the rainforests of the North Pacific coast of North America has been summarized by Ecotrust *et al.* (1995) and Della-Sala, Moola, *et al.* (2011). Alaback (1991) and Tecklin *et al.* (2011) detailed the rainforests of Chile and Argentina.

Recognizing the potential for innovative conservation strategies in the cool temperate rainforests of North America, scientists with Audubon Alaska (AA) and The Nature Conservancy, Alaska (TNC), carried out an intensive analysis of the composition and distribution of biological resources in southeast Alaska (Albert and Schoen 2007a, 2007b; Schoen and Albert 2007). In May 2008, AA and TNC hosted a visit by eight scientists who assessed the analysis, observed the array of natural vegetation types in the area, and viewed the effects of commercial timber harvests on aquatic and terrestrial habitats. The consensus of the group was that a continuation of past management practices would likely have significant adverse effects on regional biodiversity and that further in-depth discussions and analyses would be useful to inform management decisions.

This book is a product of that effort. Building upon the extensive background provided by ecological research in the region, we focus on the data and insights derived from recent research in the coastal rainforests of British Columbia and Alaska. This body of work will help inform efforts to develop and implement effective management strategies for these rainforests. Many compelling issues are associated with the ecology and conservation of the North Pacific temperate rainforest. In selecting the scope of this book and choosing the topics for its eight papers, we carefully considered what constitutes the fundamental ecological processes and human behaviors that drive the dynamic behavior of this forest and how managers can use this information to make decisions that will result in sustainable ecosystems and human communities. Authors of the chapters demonstrate how cutting edge concepts in ecology, biogeography, and conservation biology are informing, and can continue to inform, management actions on the ground.

To understand why an ecosystem has its current properties, one needs to know something of its history. Therefore we devote the first portion of the book to chapters that explore the current functioning of the region's ecosystems and describe how they have been influenced by the region's recent history. An overview of the region's biogeographic history was needed to set the stage for understanding the current biota and how it got there. Accordingly, the second chapter, "Island Life: Coming to Grips with the Insular Nature of Southeast Alaska and Adjoining Coastal British Columbia," by Joe Cook and Stephen MacDonald, describes how the advances and retreats of glaciers, major changes in sea levels, and complex patterns of recolonization by plants and animals following the last glacial retreat have yielded what we see today.

The ecological dynamics of the region are driven by its rugged topography and high rainfall. The third chapter, "Riparian Ecology, Climate

Change, and Management in North Pacific Coastal Rainforests," by Rick Edwards, Dave D'Amore, Erik Norberg, and Frances Biles, was commissioned to describe the dominant features of this dynamic landscape, how they have changed, and to explore their ecological consequences. A major feature of the region is that its rivers discharge great amounts of sediments and nutrients to adjacent waters. Conversely, salmon carry large amounts of nutrients upriver, where they feed a variety of animals and enrich vegetation near the rivers. Understanding these massive nutrient interchanges, which are more powerful in this region than elsewhere on Earth, is of vital importance for managing these systems.

Not surprisingly, disturbances of varying intensity and frequency occur in this rugged landscape. Therefore, we commissioned a chapter dealing with the nature and consequences of the current and historically recent patterns caused by windstorms, fire, pest outbreaks, landslides, and other disturbances that frequent the region. In chapter 4, "Natural Disturbance Patterns in the Temperate Rainforests of Southeast Alaska and Adjacent British Columbia," Paul Alaback, Gregory Nowacki, and Sari Saunders analyze these disturbances and describe the complex mosaic of plant communities that they create in space and time. The requirements of many of the region's species have evolved in response to those conditions. Many species may not persist in the region without the full variety of existing habitat types.

We commissioned the chapters for the next part of the book to explore how humans have interacted with and changed the region's rainforests. The current patterns of disturbance generated by human activity differ in some important ways from historical patterns. To understand how and why humans use the region today, and to provide information to guide future human use of the region's natural resources, we need to know the history of human occupation and use.

Chapter 5, "Indigenous and Commercial Uses of the Natural Resources of the North Pacific Rainforest with a Focus on Southeast Alaska and Haida Gwaii," by Lisa Crone and Joe Mehrkens, describes how the first humans to arrive in the region used its resources and how the commercial use of the region's forest, which began seriously only during the twentieth century, has left a legacy of highly modified habitats. It also explores how understanding the policies that supported those activities and their economic and social legacies can help guide a transition to a different and more sustainable use of the region's natural resources and yield conditions that support rich and rewarding human lives.

Constructing roads to enable a region's resources to be accessed, harvested, and exported is a dominant component of modern exploitation of natural environments. Therefore, we judged that a chapter that explored the direct and indirect consequences of road building and timber harvesting would be an essential component of our analysis. Chapter 6, "Succession Debt and Roads: Short- and Long-Term Effects of Timber Harvest on a Large-Mammal Predator-Prey Community in Southeast Alaska," by Dave Person and Todd Brinkman, explores those issues and also explains how transitioning from old growth to second growth affects forest habitats. The unique legacy of road-building efforts in North Pacific rainforests is also discussed in this chapter.

The rapidly expanding field of conservation biology, an applied science that uses theories and data from a broad range of disciplines to conserve, maintain, and restore the biological diversity and resilience of ecosystems, provides a rich array of concepts and tools for managers. Chapter 7, "Concepts of Conservation Biology Applied to Wildlife in Old-Forest Ecosystems, with Special Reference to Southeast Alaska and Northern Coastal British Columbia," by Bruce Marcot, describes how these concepts and tools have been used and can be used in the future to creatively address the complex issues that confront today's managers.

Watersheds have been proposed and widely used as units to guide thinking about managing landscapes. However, an in-depth analysis of when and how to use watersheds as management units had not been conducted. Therefore we commissioned chapter 8, "Why Watersheds: Evaluating the Protection of Undeveloped Watersheds as a Conservation Strategy in Northwestern North America," in which Ken Lertzman and Andy MacKinnon describe the advantages and disadvantages of using watersheds as planning units. They also show under which conditions the advantages of using watersheds are likely to outweigh the disadvantages, and vice versa. Their insightful analyses should be of value to managers operating in a wide variety of ecosystems.

Given that timber harvest has been the most important modifier of North Pacific rainforests, we decided that learning from past and current efforts to manage those forests to maintain the full array of ecosystem goods and services could help forest managers in this and other forest ecosystems. Therefore we commissioned a chapter that would describe the experiences of forest managers with alternative harvesting techniques in the coastal rainforests and their effects on forest succession and biodiversity conservation. Chapter 9, "Variable Retention Harvesting in North Pacific Temperate Rainforests," by Bill Beese, performs that vital service.

The book would not be complete without a final "Synthesis" (chapter 10) that brings together and interprets the general perspectives that emerge from the previous chapters (importance of historical perspectives at multiple scales, importance of variability, virtual versus real islands, importance of clearly specifying conservation and management goals, when and why should we try to mimic nature, etc.). The synthesis also shows how attempts to apply general theories from the environmental sciences have led to useful, rational, and justifiable recommendations for modifying management and conservation strategies in the region. It emphasizes how opportunities and challenges can be used to conserve biological diversity and ecological integrity while also sustaining local economies and quality of human life, both in the region and elsewhere. Although we know a great deal about North Pacific temperate rainforest ecosystems, important gaps in knowledge remain. The concluding chapter highlights uncertainties in our understanding and suggests how these uncertainties might be reduced.

Although this book concentrates on research and its management implications in a specific region, the insights gained from experiences in North Pacific rainforests should be useful to researchers and managers in other temperate rainforests, as well as in other places where the composition, structure, and functioning of natural ecosystems is being modified by human endeavors. Unlike many regions of the world, the northern portion of the coastal North Pacific temperate rainforest provides unusual opportunities for studying processes and management alternatives in both modified and unmodified ecosystems. Researchers and managers in other regions, particularly in forest and island ecosystems, should gain from reading about the experiences of scientists and managers in North Pacific rainforests. Both the forests themselves and the quality of life experienced by people living there will benefit from such efforts.

2

Island Life

COMING TO GRIPS WITH THE INSULAR NATURE OF SOUTHEAST ALASKA AND ADJOINING COASTAL BRITISH COLUMBIA

Joseph A. Cook and Stephen O. MacDonald

> *Island environments have been generally misunderstood, misinterpreted, and mismanaged. . . . Islands are not simply miniature continents and . . . continental solutions do not simply need to be scaled down in order to be successful.*
> —P. D. Nunn, "Through a Mist on the Ocean: Human Understanding of Island Environments"

INTRODUCTION

Southeast Alaska (fig. 2.01), with its remarkable temperate rainforest, extends from Icy Bay southward to the international border at Dixon Entrance. Across this 800 km expanse, more than 1,000 named islands of the Alexander Archipelago extend along the coastline. The adjoining mainland is narrow and bordered to the east by the Coast Mountains and towering Wrangell-St. Elias ranges. These mountains rise to over 5,400 m in elevation, are capped by alpine glaciers and extensive ice fields, and form a substantial barrier to the movement of organisms into the coastal region. Hence, two physiographic features, the precipitous coastal mountains and the highly fragmented Alexander Archipelago, overwhelmingly contribute to the current geographic structure of this terrestrial biota. Although southeast Alaska is the primary focus of this chapter, to the south the coast of British Columbia and archipelago of Haida Gwaii (Queen Charlotte

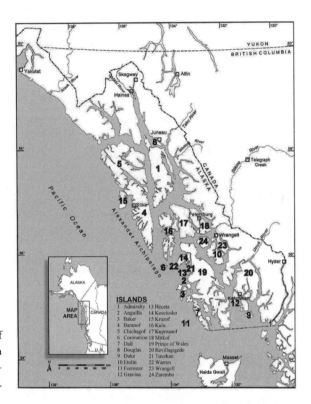

FIGURE 2.01. Map of southeast Alaska with major islands identified (see table 2–2).

ISLANDS
1 Admiralty	13 Heceta
2 Anguilla	14 Kosciusko
3 Baker	15 Kruzof
4 Baranof	16 Kuiu
5 Chichagof	17 Kupreanof
6 Coronation	18 Mitkof
7 Dall	19 Prince of Wales
8 Douglas	20 Revillagigedo
9 Duke	21 Tuxekan
10 Etolin	22 Warren
11 Forrester	23 Wrangell
12 Gravina	24 Zarembo

Islands) are equally significant components of the North Pacific temperate rainforest. The dominant influence of geography throughout the entire region suggests that a comprehensive view of the coastal biome will require critical appraisal of the role of physiographic features in species existence and persistence, community assembly, and ecosystem functioning. At both ecological and evolutionary time scales, a host of environmental perturbations combined with topographic changes due to glacial rebound and sea level fluctuation characterize the Alexander Archipelago and Haida Gwaii. A fundamental understanding of these crucial processes is critical for sound management under the concept of adaptive management (Walters 1997). Biological processes throughout this region are shaped by the isolation of islands and dynamic biogeographic history that included multiple waves of colonization along the coast following the retreat of the glaciers. Moreover, recognition of the peculiar processes associated with island life provides a powerful framework for devising effective strategies for management agencies such as the Tongass National Forest, the largest national forest in the United States.

DEEPER HISTORY: REGIONAL COLONIZATION FOLLOWING DEGLACIATION

The geologic history of the Pacific Northwest coast was dynamic and heavily influenced in the Quaternary by large-scale climatic change (Heusser 1960; Mann and Hamilton 1995; Hebda and Whitlock 1997; Barrie *et al.* 2005). During the Late Pleistocene (fig. 2.02), most of southeast Alaska and coastal British Columbia was covered by the Cordilleran ice sheet (Mann and Hamilton 1995; Carrara *et al.* 2003, 2007; Mandryk *et al.* 2001; Hetherington *et al.* 2004; Baichtal *et al.* 2008; Baichtal and Carlson 2010), hence glacial dynamics played a primary role in shaping historic and contemporary biotic communities (Klein 1965; Heaton *et al.* 1996; Conroy *et al.* 1999; Burles *et al.* 2004; Reimchen and Byun 2005; Wigen 2005; MacDonald and Cook 2007). Two ice-adapted species (arctic fox, *Vulpes lagopus*; and ringed seal, *Pusa hispida*), present during the height of the last glaciation (28–16.5 thousand years BP), no longer occur in the region (Heaton and Grady 2003). Phylogeographic studies, combined with insight from fossils recovered from the extensive karst system on Prince of Wales Island (and more recently on Haida Gwaii: Ramsey *et al.* 2004; Fedje and Mathewes 2005; Erlandson *et al.* 2008), however, suggest that other terrestrial species also persisted nearby in coastal ice-free refugia during glacial advances. About 12,000 years ago, ice retreated eastward into the coastal mountains, exposing a clean slate that allowed widespread recolonization of the deglaciated territory during the Holocene. Species colonized from a variety of distinct sources and they arrived at different times. Species distributions, community composition, and other fundamental attributes of this highly productive coastal region, therefore, have been dynamic due to extensive glacial cycling and associated sea level changes that characterized the last several thousand millennia (fig. 2.02).

Because some of the oldest lineages occur on the more western islands of the Alexander Archipelago and on Haida Gwaii, extant organisms may have persisted in glacial refugia on the outer continental shelf, or they may have first colonized this region of the coast along a tidewater route. Strong molecular genetic signals suggest that a suite of periglacial species persisted in coastal refugia during the last glacial maximum and then recolonized outer islands early in the Holocene. Later in the Holocene, corridors through the Coast Mountains were opened from the interior and allowed the westward colonization of the coastal mainland and eventually the

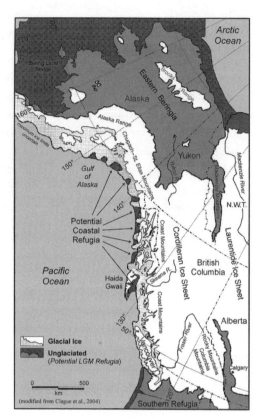

FIGURE 2.02. Map of the extent of glaciation in northwestern North America at the last glacial maximum (LGM), about 20,000 years before the present. Lowered sea levels create the possibility of the existence of glacial refugia to the west of contemporary exposed land.

nearshore islands of the archipelagos. This backdrop is essential to interpreting distributions and variable rates and patterns of evolutionary change so far uncovered in the region (Cook *et al.* 2006, MacDonald and Cook 2007). Nelson (1887) recognized that the biota of this portion of the North Pacific coast was distinctive from the remainder of North America (his "Sitkan District"). Later, Swarth (1936) and Klein (1965) provided overviews of vertebrate diversity and concluded that the region was isolated from the remainder of North America by the coastal range. A series of subsequent studies have corroborated that view.

PATTERNS OF INTRASPECIFIC VARIATION PROVIDE INSIGHT INTO MANAGEMENT UNITS

The DNA of contemporary coastal organisms (i.e., genetic structure of populations) has a tell-tale signature of this dynamic biogeographic history and provides a rigorous framework for implementing future efforts to sustain ecosystem processes and conserve the biota. Molecular genetic investigations of a variety of mammals have identified common patterns of geographic differentiation and genetic structure of populations that reflect common responses to large scale geologic events in southeast Alaska (Cook *et al.* 2006). Some species originated from a single refugium and expanded into southeast Alaska (e.g., Lessa *et al.* 2003; Frances 2008). Single origin species (summarized in Cook *et al.* 2006) arrived from the northern Beringian refugium (e.g., moose, *Alces alces gigas*; wolverine, *Gulo gulo*; northern red-backed vole, *Myodes rutilus*; root vole, *Microtus oeconomus*; arctic ground squirrel, *Spermophilus parryii*; collared pika, *Ochotona collaris*; and brown lemming, *Lemmus trimucronatus*); from a southern coastal refugium (e.g., cinereus shrew, *Sorex cinereus*; northwestern deermouse, *Peromyscus keeni*; wolf, *Canis lupus*; Sitka black-tailed deer, *Odocoileus hemionus sitkensis*; mountain goat, *Oreamnos americanus*; and Pacific marten, *Martes caurina*); or from eastern (continental) refugia located south of the Laurentide ice sheet (e.g., northern flying squirrel, *Glaucomys sabrinus*; southern red-backed vole, *Myodes gapperi*; and meadow vole, *Microtus pennsylvanicus*).

In contrast, several mammal species now found in southeast Alaska are represented by more than one lineage. Multiple lineages indicate multiple colonization events from independent source populations or refugia. Substantial genetic divergence within several species (e.g., dusky shrew, *Sorex monticolus*; long-tailed vole, *Microtus longicaudus*; and black bear, *Ursus americanus*) indicates that diversification was initiated in the mid-Pleistocene with differences persisting through repeated cycles of glacial advance and retreat. Most of these species are represented by lineages originating from a combination of southern coastal (termed Coastal) and southern continental (Continental) refugia (Cook *et al.* 2001, 2006).

OVERVIEW OF ISLAND BIOGEOGRAPHY

Island biogeography, essentially the study of the distribution and dynamics of insular species, provides a theoretical and operational foundation for the design of research and conservation plans in southeast Alaska and along the North Pacific coast of British Columbia. Over the past 150 years, studies of island systems played a fundamental role in the formation of ecological and evolutionary theory (Darwin 1859; Wallace 1902; MacArthur and Wilson 1967), including advances in our understanding of processes related to colonization, extinction, and speciation. Today, new technology combined with intensive studies of organisms on a series of island systems worldwide are proving detailed and often novel views of the history and contemporary dynamics of species (Ricklefs and Bermingham 2008; Trewick and Cowie 2008). To date, the Alexander Archipelago has played a limited role in the published literature on evolution, ecology, and conservation biology, although this system is one of the largest temperate archipelagos worldwide, with 7 of the 15 largest islands in US possession. In this regard, Haida Gwaii has fared better with a series of seminal papers and books focused on the fauna and flora of that archipelago (e.g., Scudder and Gessler 1989; Burles *et al.* 2004; Fedje and Mathewes 2005). Thus far, however, only a small proportion of the more than 7,000 islands that constitute the four major island groups of southeast Alaska and coastal British Columbia has ever been rigorously surveyed. Despite this, a large number of endemic taxa of both animals and plants have been described from these islands (e.g., 50 mammals), suggesting that substantial new diversity will be discovered in the future. There remains much to be learned about the region, and it could emerge as a model system for testing fundamental hypotheses related to environmental and biological change.

CONTINENTAL ARCHIPELAGO?

Alfred Russel Wallace (1902) identified a fundamental dichotomy between islands based on their geologic origin by proposing that archipelagos could be classified as either oceanic or continental (also known as land bridge). Oceanic islands are formed over oceanic plates and have never been connected to continental landmasses. These islands typically are devoid of life at the outset but gradually accumulate species from distant mainland source populations. In contrast, continental (land bridge) islands are found on the continental shelf and were directly connected to the mainland during the Pleistocene ice advances when sea level dropped as much as 130 m (Whittaker and Fernández-Palacios 2007).

Because of their proximity to the mainland, land bridge islands are more heavily dominated by repeated colonization than are distant island archipelagoes, resulting in a relatively high diversity of lineages. Some groups also have diversified within the islands, providing an opportunity to study both intrinsic and extrinsic processes responsible for the buildup of diversity.

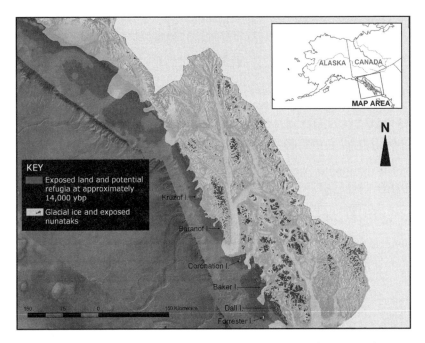

FIGURE 2.03. Predicted extent of glacial advance and ice-free refugia in southeast Alaska about 14,000 years before the present. Map is modified from Carrara *et al.* (2007), Baichtal and Carlson (2010), and James Baichtal (unpublished data).

Although technically considered land bridge islands, the Alexander Archipelago differs in two fundamental ways: the Clean Slate Hypothesis and the Coastal Refugia Hypothesis. These can only be understood within the context of the geologic history of the Pacific Northwest coast.

During the last glacial maximum about 18,000 years ago, cordilleran ice overrode most of this coastal region, essentially erasing terrestrial biota except in glacial refugia. Following the retreat of the Cordilleran ice sheet, the region was essentially a clean slate with regard to terrestrial life, so the contemporary biota is derived from organisms that colonized the North Pacific coastal rainforest from elsewhere. This clean slate scenario suggests that subsequent assembly of species on the islands of the Alexander Archipelago more closely resembles dynamics on oceanic islands rather than land bridge islands (Whittaker and Fernández-Palacios 2007). This cataclysmic event, which was likely repeated on multiple occasions through the Pleistocene, did not encompass all available terrestrial areas (fig. 2.03), since falling sea level exposed substantial sections of the continental shelf

to the west (Carrara *et al.* 2007). Therefore, hypothesized sources for colo-
nizers included not only multiple mainland locations, but also coastal
refugia to the west of the archipelago. These distinct sources likely supported populations that were diverged from the mainland sources.

EVOLUTIONARY EXPECTATIONS OF ISLAND LIFE
Potential for Rapid Morphological Evolution

Millien (2006) showed that rates of morphological evolution are much
higher for island mammal populations than for mainland populations,
with significant changes evident over time scales as short as a few decades.
Cardini *et al.* (2007) further investigated Vancouver Island marmots (*Marmota vancouverensis*) and reported limited genetic differentiation from
mainland populations of hoary marmots (*M. caligata*), but substantial
morphological differences. They concluded that the Vancouver Island marmot is a morphospecies; essentially the other side of the coin of the many
"cryptic" species that have been recently uncovered via molecular genetic
studies (Bickford *et al.* 2007). Cardini *et al.* (2007) suggested rapid morphol-
ogic variation of this island population (Millien 2006), noting that insular
populations may be distinctive due not only to temporally deep separation,
but also due to peculiarities that may arise rapidly from island life (e.g.,
changes in size, fecundity, population density, behavior, survival, aggres-
siveness, and so forth). Rapid morphological change on a Pacific Northwest
island drives home the point that each insular population is potentially
distinctive. Differences may arise not only from deeper temporal evolution, but also from changes that occur at ecological time scales. Similarly,
dwarfism of the now-extinct Dawson caribou (*Rangifer tarandus dawsoni*)
of Haida Gwaii is hypothesized to have occurred within less than 1,500
years (Wigen 2005).

Potential for Rapid Molecular Evolution

Lucid and Cook (2004) assessed levels of genetic variability across 23
island populations of the northwestern deermouse in the Alexander
Archipelago. Populations of this ubiquitous species showed highest levels
of variability on the mainland and on larger islands while lowest levels of
variability were recorded on the smallest and most distant islands. Other
island endemics show extremely low levels of variability (e.g., Prince of

Wales Island flying squirrel and the western pine marten). Hence, insular faunas show not only reduced species richness; individual species also have a characteristic signature of lower genetic variability which may increase the probability of local extirpation (Frankham 1995). Lower genetic variability decreases the ability of organisms to meet novel environmental challenges (Sgro et al. 2010), but the relationship between genetic variability and the process of extinction is complex (Aguilar et al. 2004). The few mammals examined on the Alexander Archipelago to date exhibit low genetic variability (e.g., Bidlack and Cook 2002; Small et al. 2003; Cook et al. 2006; Dawson 2008), so the generality of this trend and its implications for persistence of other North Pacific insular organisms should be examined. Populations with limited ability to disperse with changing conditions, such as island populations, are at much higher risk of loss (Thomas et al. 2004).

ENDEMISM ON ISLANDS IN SOUTHEAST ALASKA AND COASTAL BRITISH COLUMBIA

There are likely a number of parallels between the Alexander Archipelago and other glaciated nearshore archipelagos of midlatitudes, such as Haida Gwaii (Reimchen and Byun 2005), the Japanese Archipelago (Millien-Parra and Jaeger 1999; Conservation International 2012), and the British Isles (Vincent 1990). Natural resource managers should identify collaborative projects with research and management initiatives underway in other archipelagos to meet the peculiar challenges associated with managing insular biotas (e.g., Gaston et al. 2008; BC Integrated Land Management Bureau 2007, 2009). For example, limited effort has focused on threats to the endemic fauna and flora of the Pacific Northwest coast (Cook et al. 2001), primarily because the status of these insular biotas remains poorly documented (Cook and MacDonald 2001; Nagorsen 2004). Few intensive surveys of island organisms have been completed along the coast of British Columbia (Nagorsen 1994, 2004; Shank 1999). For those groups that have been surveyed, such as small mammals (McCabe and Cowan 1945, Foster 1965) and birds (Cannings 1998), there is a tremendous opportunity for specimen-based resurveys to provide an extraordinary assessment of change in these ecosystems on a decadal basis. Much of British Columbia's coastal region has never been properly surveyed for amphibians and reptiles (Matsuda et al. 2006). Knowledge of the vascular plants for many

TABLE 2.1. Extinctions of recent mammals from islands in southeast Alaska and coastal British Columbia (AA, Alexander Archipelago; HG, Haida Gwaii; VAN, Vancouver Island; LGM, last glacial maximum).

	ISLANDS	TIME PERIOD PRESENT	REMARKS
RODENTS			
hoary marmot	AA	pre-LGM→LGM[1]	
brown lemming	AA	pre-LGM[1]	
western heather vole	AA	pre-LGM[1]	(*Phenacomys intermedius*)
CARNIVORES			
arctic fox	AA	pre-LGM→ early postglacial[1]	
red fox	AA	LGM[1]	(*Vulpes vulpes*)
brown bear	AA	pre-LGM; early postglacial→early Holocene[1]	
	HG	early postglacial[1]	
Pacific marten	AA	unknown	former presence on Island inferred from genetic signature of parasite[2]
cf. wolverine	AA	early postglacial	based on molar fragment from a cave on Prince of Wales Island[3]

islands also remains limited or nonexistent (Roemer 1994). Nonvascular plants—the bryophytes (Schofield 1994; Ryan 1996), lichens (Goward 1994), and fungi (Redhead 1994)—remain poorly documented. Terrestrial and freshwater invertebrates, perhaps the richest of the region's biodiversity, are the least known (Cannings 1994; Scudder 1996; Forsyth 2004; Ovaska *et al.* 2010).

Studies based on fossil or molecular genetic evidence have documented extinctions on islands in southeast Alaska and coastal British Columbia (table 2.1). Other studies provided evidence of high endangerment of insular species (e.g., Vancouver Island marmot, <50 individuals; see Bryant 2002). In British Columbia, two-thirds of 74 endemic taxa are restricted to

TABLE 2.1. *(continued)*

		TIME PERIOD	
	ISLANDS	PRESENT	REMARKS
UNGULATES			
Caribou	AA	pre-LGM; early post-glacial→early Holocene[3]	
	HG	pre-LGM; present up until early 1900s early postglacial→recent[1]	
mountain goat	VAN	early postglacial[4]	
	AA	pre-LGM	horn core and molars from Prince of Wales Island tentatively identified as either this species or saiga[1]

1   Fedji *et al.* 2004
2   Koehler 2006; Hoberg *et al.*, in press
3   Heaton and Grady 2003
4   Nagorsen and Keddie 2000

islands, among which over half (56%) are forest dwelling (Bunnell *et al.* 2005). Less than 45% of endemic taxa, however, are listed provincially or nationally (4 of 6 endemic plants are listed; 29 of 35 endemic mammals are not listed) (Bunnell 2005). Management plans in British Columbia and southeast Alaska (e.g., USDA Forest Service 2008a; BC Integrated Land Management Bureau 2007, 2009) still are not tuned to the special attributes of island life (Paquet *et al.* 2004; DellaSala, Moola, *et al.* 2011).

TEMPORAL SCALE OF ENDEMISM

The Coastal Refugia Hypothesis has been accumulating support over the past four decades (Foster 1965; Rogers *et al.* 1991; Heaton *et al.* 1996; Byun *et al.* 1999), and two summary volumes have focused on this issue as it relates to the natural history of Haida Gwaii (Scudder and Gessler 1989; Fedje and Mathewes 2005). A mammalian example that potentially reflects the signature of persistence in a coastal refuge is the discovery of three distinctive lineages of ermine that were detected with molecular techniques in southeast Alaska and adjoining British Columbia (fig. 2.04). Two of these

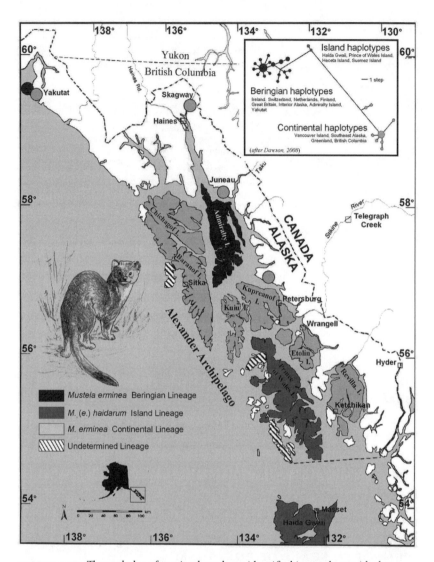

FIGURE 2.04. Three clades of ermine have been identified in southeast Alaska.
The Beringian clade is widely distributed from Europe, through Asia, and into far
northwestern North America (and Admiralty Island). The Continental clade is distributed elsewhere in northern and temperate North America with the exception
of Haida Gwaii and the Prince of Wales archipelagos, where the third (Island) clade
is endemic (Fleming and Cook 2002; Dawson 2008).

lineages also occur widely outside of the coastal region, whereas the third lineage is restricted to Prince of Wales Island, nearby outer islands, and on Haida Gwaii (Fleming and Cook 2002). This island-restricted ermine represents a periglacial relict or paleoendemic that persisted in the region since before the last glacial maximum (LGM). Examples such as this have led to a significant reassessment of the temporal horizon over which elements of this coastal fauna diversified. These paleoendemics also have important implications for the human colonization of North America along a coastal route. Because the LGM apparently did not wipe the slate completely clean along the entire coast, the existence of Pacific Northwest coastal refugia raises the possibility of a suite of other highly divergent coastal taxa that have not yet been detected, and these may require special management status under laws such as the Endangered Species Act.

A review of endemic mammals for North America north of Mexico concluded that the Pacific Northwest coast supports high levels of endemism (Cook and MacDonald 2001; Reimchen and Byun 2005). Subsequent molecular phylogeographic studies largely supported this finding (Cook *et al.* 2006). Indeed, endemic lineages of the northwestern deermouse, northern flying squirrel (Bidlack and Cook 2002), spruce grouse (*Falcipennis canadensis isleibi*) (Dickerman and Gustafson 1996; Barry and Tallmon 2010), chum salmon (*Oncorhynchus keta*) (Kondzela *et al.* 1994), and subalpine fir (*Abies lasiocarpa*) (Carrara *et al.* 2003) have also been identified on the Prince of Wales Archipelago. Likely numerous other endemic organisms occur there that have yet to be discovered, but the baseline samples necessary to complete those analyses are lacking.

ISLAND COMMUNITIES

Consistent with classic island biogeography theory (MacArthur and Wilson 1967), size and distance from the mainland have played a prominent role in shaping diversity across the Alexander Archipelago (Table 2.2). Larger islands (e.g., Revillagigedo, on which Ketchikan is located) close to the mainland have higher species richness, while small distant islands (e.g., Forrester, to the west of Prince of Wales) have lower species richness (MacDonald and Cook 1996). Nonetheless, when the factors of size, distance, and greatest elevation for each of 20 islands are regressed against species richness, only island distance is significant (fig. 2.05). Conroy *et al.* (1999) used species lists for each island to explore factors responsible for

TABLE 2.2. List of 24 major islands in the Alexander Archipelago. Map numbers refer to figure 2.01. Island area, distance to the mainland, maximum elevation, and species richness of mammals are reported for each island.

MAP NUMBER	ISLAND	AREA (HA)	DISTANCE TO MAINLAND (KM)	MAXIMUM ELEVATION (M)	NUMBER OF NATIVE SPECIES
1	Admiralty	431,309	5	1,418	14
2	Anguilla	1,210	9	198	8
3	Baker	13,512	13	697	9
4	Baranof	424,016	6	1,644	9
5	Chichagof	545,317	5	1,192	9
6	Coronation	9,120	11	598	7
7	Dall	65,869	7	949	12
8	Douglas	20,274	1	1,018	20
9	Duke	15,538	5	503	8
10	Etolin ·	88,995	2	1,135	18
11	Forrester	1,013	34	409	3
12	Gravina	23,307	3	833	14
13	Heceta	18,916	9	761	11
14	Kosciusko	48,259	7	947	12
15	Kruzof	44,680	7	976	9
16	Kuiu	193,455	3	1,080	19
17	Kupreanof	282,415	2	1,091	20
18	Mitkof	54,753	1	1,012	26
19	Prince of Wales	578,202	6	1,219	16
20	Revillagigedo	302,659	2	1,401	24
21	Tuxekan	8,523	7	320	11
22	Warren	5,067	11	710	8
23	Wrangell	56,948	1	991	26
24	Zarembo	47,263	5	777	13

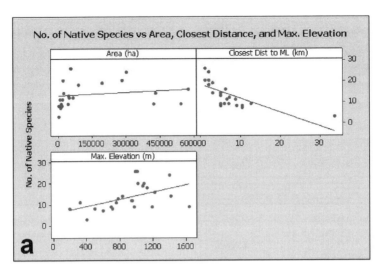

FIGURE 2.05. Plots of species richness for mammals by island area (ha), island maximum elevation (m), and closest distance to the mainland (km) for the 24 islands reported in table 2.1. Only island distance from the mainland is a significant (p < 0.05) factor in explaining differences in species richness. Island distance remains the only significant factor when the outlier (Forrester Island) is removed from the regression analyses (not shown).

community assembly of mammals across the archipelago and showed that mammalian communities on smaller islands were nested within communities on larger islands. They concluded that, across all species, colonization ability (not extinction probability) has been the most important determinant of current community composition on islands, a result that is consistent with the history of heavy glaciations. That study, however, was unable to consider endemism that has since been documented based on molecular analyses. Reanalysis based on estimates of lineage richness rather than species richness (unpublished data) indicates that endemic lineages are not nested; those older forms instead appear to be structured by extinction processes (i.e., island size rather than island distance is important in explaining their presence).

Despite the overall nested pattern found in the archipelago (Conroy *et al.* 1999), species assemblages vary spatially (i.e., from island to island) and temporally (Heaton and Grady 2003). For example, cinereus shrews

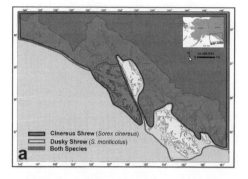

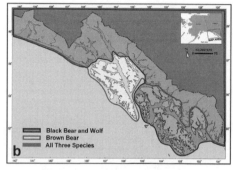

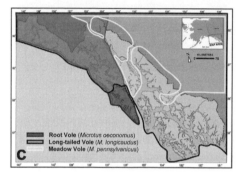

FIGURE 2.06. Series of maps showing the general pattern of insular allopatry among ecologically or functionally equivalent (*a*) shrews, (*b*) large carnivores, and (*c*) arvicoline rodents.

are found on Baranof and Chichagof islands, but not Admiralty or Prince of Wales islands (fig. 2.06a), while dusky shrews show the opposite pattern of occurrence. Both species are sympatric on the mainland, on nearshore islands (e.g., Revillagigedo, Wrangell) and on the peninsula-like islands of Mitkof, Kupreanof, and Kuiu (fig. 2.06b). Historically, brown and black bears coexisted on Prince of Wales Island and Haida Gwaii, but in the last 10,000 years brown bears have ceased to occupy these islands (Heaton and Grady 2003; Wigen 2005). Now, black bears (and wolves) occupy islands south of Frederick Sound, whereas brown bears (and no wolves) occur on northern islands of the Alexander Archipelago. All three of these top predators are sympatric on the mainland. Patterns of exclusion also are seen in rodents of the genus *Microtus* (voles) (fig. 2.06c).

INTERISLAND CONNECTIVITY

MacDonald and Cook (2007) identified the need to document linkages or connections between islands that facilitate metapopulation structure and movement of organisms within the Alexander Archipelago. Linkage sites should be priorities for conservation because gene flow is a critical process with benefits ranging from persistence of small populations to introduction of traits necessary to adapt to fluctuating environments (Templeton *et al.* 2001; Manel *et al.* 2003). These hypothesized connections among islands (MacDonald and Cook 2007) should be assessed, and likely they could be improved as they fail to account for potentially crucial factors, such as oceanic currents or similarity of habitat on either end of the crossing. Reconstruction of sea level fluctuations and the related influence of underwater topography on historic connections among islands also should factor into our understanding of linkages. Sites that may facilitate connectivity among islands should be identified and protected by establishing disturbance buffers and associated wildlife corridors for movement of organisms between islands. Proposed connections should be viewed as hypotheses that can be tested; they also serve to raise awareness of the complex interactions and metapopulation dynamics that may occur among islands. Molecular studies across a number of species have provided preliminary tests of linkages (Cook *et al.* 2006; MacDonald and Cook 2007). The endemic Prince of Wales Island flying squirrel (*Glaucomys sabrinus griseifrons*), for example, has diverged from mainland squirrels (Demboski *et al.* 1998; Bidlack and Cook 2001), but not from other populations of squirrels within the Prince of Wales Archipelago (e.g., Prince of Wales, Heceta, Suemez, Dall; see Bidlack and Cook 2002). Such a pattern, also shared in northwestern deermice, ermine, and potentially southern and northern dusky shrews (Demboski and Cook 2001), suggests high historic or contemporary levels of connectivity among islands of the Prince of Wales Archipelago (Fleming and Cook 2002; Lucid and Cook 2004).

ISLANDS WITHIN ISLANDS

Temporal and spatial scale must be considered as management actions are initiated that further fragment habitats. In addition to the dynamic geologic history and natural fragmentation of the archipelago, industrial logging has recently produced a patchwork of habitats within many islands. Maintaining connectivity or corridors among patches to help mitigate important processes such as dispersal and gene flow should be a goal of management plans along the Pacific Northwest coast. Nevertheless, hypotheses of how landscape corridors will reduce the negative effects of fragmentation are largely untested (Damschen *et al.* 2006; Dixon *et al.* 2006) and predictions are especially uncertain in the face of climate change (Thomas *et al.* 2004). Highly vagile birds, carnivores, and ungulates may disperse among islands more easily than flightless arthropods and small mammals. Preliminary molecular perspectives on mammals (Cook *et al.* 2006) indicate differential connectivity across taxonomic groups. With regard to assessing barriers throughout the archipelago, ubiquitous species are good candidates for identifying overall levels of connectivity, while less vagile species with more limited distributions or narrow habitat requirements may provide finer-scale views of connectivity.

Faunal exchange among islands may be asymmetrical, with some islands acting as source populations while others act as sink populations. Kuiu Island has had high black bear densities (e.g., 1.5 bears/km^2), and a larger number of migrant bears per generation move from Kuiu to Kupreanof Island than vice versa (Peacock 2004; Peacock *et al.* 2007). Unequal rates of immigration and emigration illustrate the distinctive microevolutionary dynamics that populations in close proximity, but on different islands, may be experiencing, as is the case with the Kermode bear (*Ursus americanus kermodei*) among the islands of the northern British Columbia coast (Klinka and Reimchen 2009). Peacock (2004) also recorded little exchange of black bears between Kuiu and Prince of Wales islands. With heavy harvest pressures on these two islands, these new perspectives on connectivity in black bears provide an important framework for maintaining viable populations. Furthermore, the consequences of habitat fragmentation within islands on complex landscapes such as that found on Kuiu Island has been little studied.

CONSERVATION OF ISLAND ECOSYSTEMS

Logging, mining, human sprawl, tourism, hunting and trapping, and introductions of exotic and domesticated species present significant challenges to the maintenance of viable and well-distributed wildlife populations. Each of these impacts may be magnified in insular endemics (Steadman 2006; Whittaker and Fernández-Palacios 2007). All are present, to varying degrees, in southeast Alaska and coastal British Columbia. Several islands have experienced significant impacts from one or more of these threats (e.g., central Prince of Wales, Long, Revillagigedo, Kuiu, Heceta), and the future will likely see a shift from one set of impacts to others. For example, logging has substantially converted old-growth forest habitat on northern Chichagof and central Prince of Wales islands to even-aged second-growth plantations. Increased accessibility and forest fragmentation resulting from the associated high-density network of roads has significantly impacted some wildlife species (Person *et al.* 1996). In most cases, these challenges have not been rigorously evaluated or monitored. Now added to this mix of potential threats is anthropogenic climate change, which is predicted to substantially increase extinction risk for populations and species with limited ability to disperse (Thomas *et al.* 2004), such as many of those found on islands. Inability of insular species to respond (e.g., disperse to new islands) as conditions change raises the possibility that anthropogenic climate change could become a major cause of extirpation of species from islands in southeast Alaska or even extinction for the insular endemic forms.

Inventory programs should be tied to permanent archives (i.e., museums) and research laboratories that would be interested in investigations of selected species. An example is the recent series of papers on northwestern martens that established a molecular framework for understanding geographic variation in these economically important furbearers. This framework, if it had been available earlier, would have demonstrated the folly of the introduction of mainland marten (*Martes americana)* onto several islands in the Alexander Archipelago where the other species (*M. caurina*) may have been endemic (Hoberg *et al.*, in press). Active management of marten and marten habitat over the last 50 years has likely hastened the extirpation of Pacific marten (*M. caurina*) on several islands in the region through introduction of the exotic sister species combined with a substantial reduction in old-growth forest by industrial-scale logging on several islands (e.g., Kuiu Island), but the overall impact remains unknown (MacDonald and Cook 1996, 2007). Koehler *et al.* (2009) uncovered significant phylogeographic structure in a nematode that is parasitic on marten across a number of locations in southeast Alaska. Molecular genetic variation in these worms from marten on Chichagof correspond to two independent introductions of American marten (*M. americana*) from the southeast mainland and Anchorage area, as noted by historic records of introductions of this species. In addition, Koehler *et al.* (2009) found an endemic lineage of worm on Chichagof that is more closely allied with worms from Pacific marten on Admiralty Island and Haida Gwaii. This signal from the parasite is consistent with the recent extirpation of *M. caurina* on Chichagof Island, perhaps hastened by the introduction of *M. americana* (Hoberg *et al.*, in press).

MANAGEMENT RECOMMENDATIONS AND RESEARCH NEEDS

Preliminary investigations of mammals clearly indicate inadequacies in our current understanding of diversity. Outdated taxonomic designations still are used for characterizing diversity and fail to identify forms unique to the region (i.e., endemics). These investigations also show that past logging efforts are strongly correlated with the occurrence of hot spots of endemism (Cook *et al.* 2006). In the future, a well-annotated set of natural history collections could provide the basis for assessing the status and distribution of Pacific Northwest coastal endemics. Assessing biotic change begins with modern inventory studies that are conducted hand in hand with long-term monitoring programs in an effort to develop rigorous databases related to the status of Tongass wildlife and ecosystems. These data should be accessible via the internet and linked to other online databases, GIS applications, research programs, and management initiatives (fig. 2.07). A baseline for wildlife and their associated parasites, especially the pathogens that may impact wildlife (and human) health, is essential to evaluate emerging threats on federally managed lands. The relationship between climate change and emerging pathogens, for example, has recently been explored in high-latitude ungulate populations (Kutz *et al.* 2005; Jenkins *et al.* 2006; Hoberg *et al.* 2008). Because these large mammals play a critical role in subsistence economies, efforts to monitor their health are essential to persistence of northern indigenous cultures. The list of potential studies is primarily limited by the availability of specimens and the creativity of investigators.

WHAT IS NEEDED NOW?

1. Interagency, intergovernmental (i.e., for southeast Alaska, the USDA Forest Service, US Fish and Wildlife Service, Alaska Department of Fish and Game, Native Sovereign Nations, National Marine Fisheries,

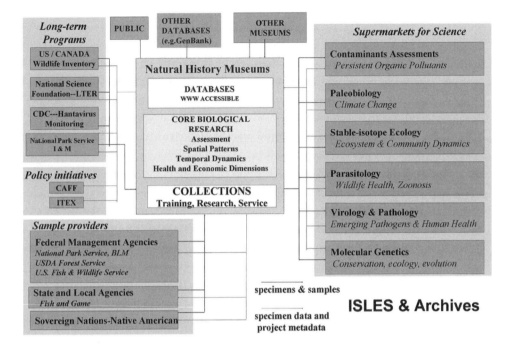

FIGURE 2.07. Schematic of a multiagency effort on the Tongass National Forest called Island Surveys to Learn about Endemic Species (ISLES). Examples of other collaborators or users of the archival observatory include Long Term Ecological Research (LTER) sites, Conservation of Arctic Fauna and Flora (CAFF), International Tundra Experiment (ITEX), Bureau of Land Management (BLM), and Centers for Disease Control (CDC). http://www.msb.unm.edu/mammals/ISLES _website_final_2009/isles_home.html.

National Park Service, universities, and natural history museums), and new international agreements and specialized working groups should focus on establishing a comprehensive management plan aimed at preserving the endemic biota and natural ecosystems of areas such as the Alexander Archipelago and Haida Gwaii. Substantial physical and personnel infrastructure already exists, but coordinated action on island issues is lacking. Because agencies are mandated to manage resources wisely, this infrastructure could be used to implement island-centered management plans. Resource managers are grappling with a number of issues in archipelagos (e.g., Golumbia 2000; Sherley 2000; McNeely *et al.* 2001; Wittenberg and Cock 2001; BC Integrated Land Management Bureau 2007), but they have yet to develop guiding principles that fully address management goals and objectives unique to island systems. An international conference focused on island management along the North Pacific coast would be one productive outcome of such a working group.

2. Rigorous, integrated inventories should be conducted on all islands over 500 ha. There is a pressing need for specimen-based, all-taxa inventories of these islands. Work on Haida Gwaii provides examples of taxonomic groups that could also be the focus of more intensive studies in southeast Alaska. Prior work along the Pacific Northwest coast opens productive opportunities to engage international collaborators and expand seminal studies on mosses (Schofield 1989), flowering plants (Calder and Taylor 1968), ground dwelling beetles (Kavanaugh 1992; Clarke *et al.* 2007), birds (Martin *et al.* 1995; Topp and Winker 2008), and fish (Moodie and Reimchen 1973; Reimchen 1989, 1994). Spatially extensive and site-intensive archives of insular organisms are critical to stimulating investigations that will form the basis for careful management (Chapman 2005). Sophisticated and varied technologies (e.g., stable isotopes, molecular genetics, biotoxin assays) have transformed wildlife management recently and can be employed through truly integrated investigations (Hoberg *et al.* 2003; Reimchen *et al.* 2003; Wilson *et al.* 2009). Specimen archives are fundamental to the development of multidisciplinary views of diversity, because all of these studies can be tied together through individual voucher specimens.

3. Monitoring efforts should be designed to provide information necessary to assess environmental change. Elements to be monitored should include species that (a) are most susceptible to impacts such as fragmentation (e.g., endemics), (b) are introduced and exotic to the region, (c) span multiple trophic levels, (d) have complex lifecycles, (e) are sensitive to climate change and have limited ability to move, or (f) are key to human subsistence.

4. Partnerships to investigate and monitor the region should be actively sought and then built, perhaps modeled after the long-running and highly successful program by the Laskeek Bay Conservation Society on Haida Gwaii (http://www.laskeekbay.org). Subsistence hunters, trappers, resource agencies, rural K–12 schools, citizen scientists, and academia are examples of potential partners that could have powerful and last-

ing impacts on resource management in southeast Alaska and coastal British Columbia.

5. Introduction of exotic species should be thoroughly regulated, since there are a growing number of introduced species in the region (Mac-Donald and Cook 2007; Gaston *et al.* 2008). This is a looming issue for resource managers and one that already has been experienced in southeast Alaska (Heutte and Bella 2003; Schrader and Hennon 2005; McClory and Gotthardt 2008) and Haida Gwaii (Golumbia 2000). The best way to manage introduced species is to implement laws that will help to slow their entry. If exotics become established, detect and eradicate them quickly, or manage them at acceptably low densities to prevent significant negative effects (Simberloff 2002).

Given the complexity of issues facing resource managers working in the extensive island systems of southeast Alaska and coastal British Columbia, a diverse set of approaches is needed to effectively administer wildlife management plans and monitor potential threats to native biotas, including strong, coordinated efforts that include local communities and that cut across agencies and international boundaries. Several steps can be taken immediately that will lessen costs associated with impacts and facilitate swift responses to perturbations in the future, but lack of available baseline materials has become the primary limitation to understanding the magnitude and complexity of change and ultimately applying effective new technologies. Now is the time to develop proactive strategies, rather than waiting until our efforts are entirely consumed by restoration actions.

ACKNOWLEDGMENTS

We first thank the large cast of stimulating colleagues who have participated in field, museum, and/or laboratory work on Tongass wildlife since 1991. We also acknowledge the tireless efforts of personnel of the USDA Forest Service (Tongass Forest and Pacific Northwest Laboratory), Alaska Department of Fish and Game, US Fish and Wildlife Service, and National Science Foundation (0415668) for providing logistics or funding our investigations along the Pacific Northwest coast. We thank Yadeeh Sawyer for technical assistance; Natalie Dawson and Kim Hastings for their critical input, high energy levels, and enthusiasm for island research; and Bill Hanson, Kim Hastings, Carol Seitz-Warmuth, Jim Baichtal, Rod Flynn, Tricia O'Connor, and Tom Hanley for generous support of a series of graduate students whose dissertations focused on North Pacific mammals and their associated parasites over the past two decades. Josh Donlan, Jim Kenagy, and an anonymous reviewer improved the manuscript.

3

Riparian Ecology, Climate Change, and Management in North Pacific Coastal Rainforests

Rick T. Edwards, David V. D'Amore,
Erik Norberg, and Frances Biles

INTRODUCTION

The North Pacific coastal temperate rainforest of North America is the largest and least modified of Earth's temperate rainforests (DellaSala 2011; Wolf *et al.* 1995). A defining characteristic of a rainforest is the abundant flow of water from the atmosphere through the terrestrial and aquatic environments. An important ecotone in this system is the nexus of terrestrial and aquatic ecosystems known by the familiar name *riparian zone*. The riparian zone is the focus of a great deal of attention in most parts of the world, but an understanding of many of the important functions of this ecotone in the coastal temperate rainforest is just emerging, and indeed the definition of the riparian area in coastal temperate rainforests is subject to much debate.

The concepts and applications presented herein are relevant to the perhumid temperate rainforest that encompasses the coastal forests of northern British Columbia and southeast Alaska from the central British Columbia coast north of Vancouver Island to Yakutat, Alaska (fig. 1.01; Kellogg 1992). Data for various subsections of the coastal temperate rainforest come from a variety of sources, and boundaries are defined differently in different sources. We will be specific about what locations summary data are based on, unless the concept illustrated applies across the entire region. For our discussion of riparian zones, we include the entire terrestrial surface, whether it contains forest or not.

Southeast Alaska encompasses over 1,000 islands and has over 29,000 km of coastline (Chadwick 2007), about 20% of the coastline of the entire United States. On average, a square kilometer of southeast Alaska is associated with 0.42 km of shoreline, emphasizing the size of the marine interface. To the south, the coast of British Columbia contains another 25,000 km of convoluted shoreline. Glacial carving and erosion have left a rugged, highly dissected landscape with thousands (>10,000) of small, steep streams running rapidly to the nearby marine ecosystem. Although the total number of streams and the combined length of associated riparian zones cannot be calculated accurately at this time, a look at maps of the region makes it clear that the ratio of freshwater and marine margin to terrestrial surface area is enormous, making the interaction between water and land a defining characteristic of this region.

The riparian zone has been variously defined as the strip of land immediately adjacent to a stream or river channel, or more broadly as the land adjacent to a stream or river that is influenced by, or influences, stream processes (National Academy of Sciences 2002). Riparian zones are sometimes defined by the presence of riparian vegetation and delineated by plant community composition. Proximity to a river (or lake) is inherent to most definitions, but the past two or three decades of stream and wetland research have shown that interactions between land and rivers extend laterally, well past the active channel banks, and vertically into groundwater aquifers and saturated sediments beneath and beside the river channel (Edwards 1998).

The National Academy of Sciences (2002) discusses various definitions used by land management agencies, as well as the contrast between definitions of riparian areas and wetlands and the jurisdictional implications of that distinction. The 2008 Tongass National Forest Land and Resource Management Plan (TLMP) defines riparian as "areas that encompass the zone of interaction between aquatic and terrestrial environments associated with streamsides, lakeshores, and floodplains, and display distinctive ecological conditions characterized by high species diversity, wildlife value, and resource productivity." Important in this definition is the recognition of "interaction" and "productivity" as key riparian characteristics. Common usage of the term *riparian* by the public and managers typically associates riparian zones with proximity to a river; many recognize the importance of influence passing from the terrestrial portion to the aquatic and back.

This chapter focuses on the terrestrial–aquatic interface within the thousands of watersheds in the temperate coastal fringe of southeast Alaska and northern British Columbia. The data presented in this review focus on experience in riparian zones and ecosystems of southeast Alaska, which is dominated by the administrative boundaries of the USDA Forest Service's Tongass National Forest (Tongass). We will not explicitly address riparian zones associated with the large rivers draining the interior of the continent and then penetrating the coastal rainforest, except insofar as their lower riparian zones reflect rainforest conditions. Although these rivers are important to Pacific salmon (*Oncorhynchus* spp.) and contribute to the outwelling of water and nutrients important to the estuarine and coastal marine ecosystem (Simenstad *et al.* 1997), their greater discharge and physical size and the origin of their water make them distinct from the small rivers that lie wholly within the coastal temperate rainforest. In the small, steep rainforest watersheds, water and nutrients are rapidly transported to nearby estuaries. Thus, riparian zones are not just the interface through which the land interacts with streams and lakes; they are tightly connected to the sea as well.

THE COASTAL TEMPERATE RAINFOREST

Rugged coastal mountain ranges intercept moisture-laden Pacific storms and generate abundant year-round precipitation in the coastal temperate rainforest. Rainfall records within southeast Alaska are sparse, and most are at sea level, where precipitation is lowest. Because rainfall in the coastal temperate rainforest is generated by orographic uplift of marine air masses, more precipitation falls at higher elevations, requiring modeling approaches to estimate its distribution. Using the PRISM rainfall model (Daly *et al.* 1994) we estimated rainfall distribution across southeast Alaska based on the 30-year average from 1971 to 2000 and calculated a mean annual area-weighted precipitation of 3 m. This volume of precipitation falling on impermeable glacial till and shallow bedrock is not routed through soils quickly enough on shallow slopes to prevent intermittent or permanent soil saturation; therefore wetlands are abundant and widely distributed.

These widespread wetlands are connected hydrologically to streams through intermittent or permanent surface drainage features and subsurface flow pathways. Wetlands occur from mountain ridge tops down to the intertidal zone, on slopes ranging from flat to over 20%. According to the

National Wetland Inventory (USFWS), 22% of southeast Alaska is classed as wetland. Among individual watersheds in the Alexander Archipelago, the percentage of wetland varies from less than 2% to over 95% cover (D'Amore et al. 2012). Precipitation accumulates in several wetland types, including fens and bogs, by direct atmospheric deposition or lateral flow through adjacent soils. Bogs and fens dominated by peat are commonly referred to in the region as *muskegs*, but the term *peatlands* is more descriptive.

Whether they are located immediately adjacent to stream channels or not, wetlands are functionally connected to channels through their output of water, organic matter, and nutrients (Fellman, Hood, Edwards, and Jones 2009). Wetlands are sources of bioavailable dissolved organic carbon (DOC) and organic nitrogen and phosphorus (DON, DOP) to adjacent streams (Fellman, D'Amore, et al. 2008). The magnitude of the material fluxes and rapid uptake of nutrients by stream communities demonstrate the important aspect of functional connectivity between wetlands and streams (e.g., Brinson 1993; Powell et al. 2003) and highlight the role of nutrient export in support of aquatic habitat productivity (Fellman, Hood, Edwards, and Jones 2009). The influence of materials exported from wetlands extends far from the stream corridor, due to the connectivity of flow paths and large contributing areas of wetlands in coastal temperate rainforest watersheds (Gibson et al. 2000; Fitzgerald et al. 2002; Emili et al. 2006; D'Amore et al. 2010; fig. 3.01). Therefore the distinction between riparian zone and wetland is less useful in the coastal temperate rainforest than nonrainforest regions.

The short average stream length, predominance of wetlands and streams, and close proximity to the ocean give terrestrial–aquatic interactions intensity exceeded nowhere else in the world. Southeast Alaskan rivers discharge about 370 km^3 of fresh water annually (Neal et al. 2010), comparable to the annual discharge of the Mississippi River. We calculated that the Tongass alone generates 200 km^3 of fresh water annually, not including discharge of the larger interior rivers or mass wasting of glaciers. This discharge is similar to the Yukon or Columbia rivers, which have drainage basins over 12 times larger. Export of dissolved organic carbon from the carbon-rich Tongass is about 36 times larger per unit area than that from the average Earth's surface (Edwards et al. 2007).

Accordingly, we will use a general, functionally relevant definition of riparian zone as "the area outside of the active river channel that is influenced by or influences the adjacent terrestrial ecosystem." This definition

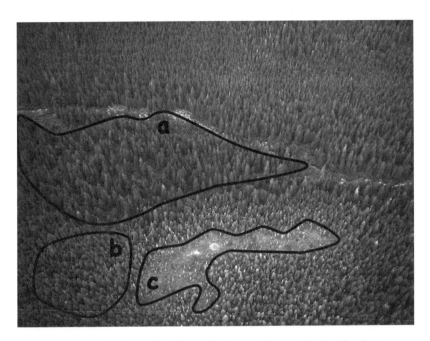

FIGURE 3.01. Aerial photo of McGinnis Creek, near Juneau, Alaska. The photo illustrates the distribution of (*a*) a riparian zone adjacent to the stream channel, (*b*) a forested wetland, and (*c*) a peat bog connected to the stream via subsurface and intermittent surface channels. Only the high-volume riparian floodplain stand outlined in (*a*) would be considered riparian by existing definitions, but the two wetlands dominate the biogeochemistry of the creek.

emphasizes process over structure or location and is not based on legal delineation. If we wish to manage riparian zones in the region, restore them, or understand the impact of management activities or natural disturbances on their future, a definition that explicitly recognizes influence, or functionally significant linkages, is essential. Much of the current discussion on riparian areas within the forest centers on a restricted suite of attributes of the relatively small area adjacent to streams that has been directly impacted by timber harvest. The broader extent of riparian zones and key functions are little acknowledged.

HEADWATER RIPARIAN ZONES

Because ecological processes in the riparian zone and the structures they generate change with location along the drainage (Richardson and Danehy

2007), approaches to management and protection and techniques for study must be tailored to specific locations. In high-gradient upland streams it is commonly assumed that the terrestrial–aquatic influence flows from the surrounding upland forest and soils to the stream. This ignores the obvious fact that the surrounding topography is usually a function of the erosive action of the stream, which influences the overall slope morphology, soil development, and amount of channel incision. Moreover, the small size and low energy of headwater streams allow the development of streamside vegetation that is barely distinguishable from the upland forest around it, making it easy to overlook the existence of a riparian zone and the processes that influence the terrestrial–aquatic interface. The ubiquity of wetlands in the coastal temperate rainforest means that even high-gradient headwater streams are likely to have substantial interactions with wetlands or even originate within wetlands. Within the framework of most management activities, the long-term history of the stream's impact on the riparian zone is ignored and the focus is on more immediate phenomena such as litter input, large wood input, and water temperature. Management agencies typically view riparian zones in the context of impacts of riparian activities on stream biota, most often fish. Therefore high-gradient headwater streams, which often are not fish bearing, receive little or no formal protection under most current management practices. Fortunately, headwater streams are finally receiving greater scrutiny and protection in watershed planning (USDA Forest Service 2008b).

Increasing appreciation of the importance of headwaters to lower stream reaches (Gomi *et al.* 2002) and the discovery of fish higher in drainages than previously reported (Bryant *et al.* 2004) have focused new attention to the structure and function of riparian zones of headwater streams. Headwaters are now recognized for their important functional role in supporting primary and secondary productivity in forested ecosystems through inputs of litter, invertebrates, and nutrients (Johnson and Edwards 2002; Wipfli *et al.* 2007). Wipfli and Musslewhite (2004) demonstrated that fishless headwater streams on Prince of Wales Island supply large amounts of food to downstream, fish-bearing reaches in the form of invertebrates drifting in the water column. A significant proportion of the drift was terrestrial individuals from the riparian zone. Production of aquatic invertebrates is also enhanced by riparian litter and inputs. Peatlands, which include bogs and forested wetlands, may be found in any location within a watershed and often act as headwaters for streams draining even the steepest terrain (Neiland 1971). Activities in headwater streams that increase sediment inputs to downstream reaches may also affect fish and other stream biota significantly (Johnson *et al.* 2000). More recent research on riparian inputs of bioavailable DOC to headwater, fishless reaches (Fellman, Hood, D'Amore, *et al.* 2008; Fellman, Hood, Edwards, and Jones 2009) is consistent with the concept that low-order streams provide important resources to habitats downstream through their influence on energy and organic matter input, food webs, and productivity.

DOWNSTREAM DEPOSITION ZONES

The reciprocal influence between streams and riparian zones is more widely recognized in low-gradient reaches where fluvial deposition and reworking of sediment deposited within the reach have obviously impacted the structure of the terrestrial and aquatic systems. This reciprocity is most obvious in large floodplain reaches, where channel migration and overbank flooding have created complex habitats wherein aquatic and terrestrial species mingle in a dynamic manner, punctuated by large disturbances of varying, but generally, low frequency. Streams are classified by functional attributes related to physical features and modes of formation (USDA Forest Service 1992). Larger rivers that support mass spawning salmon runs are dominated by floodplain stream classes of varying size. These floodplain channels are closely associated with two different alluvial soils adjacent to the stream that are not recognized in many existing soil maps. The delineation of these alluvial soils reveals differences in the underlying physical and chemical structure that influence vegetation communities and material fluxes. Distinguishing between the two soils enhances the ability to study and manage these habitats (D'Amore *et al.* 2011; fig. 3.02).

Within the Alexander Archipelago, lower-gradient and floodplain reaches support multiple species of salmonids, making the connection between riparian areas and fish a dominant concern of management and restoration (Albert *et al.* 2008). Overbank floods, hyporheic flows, and carnivorous animals transfer salmon carcasses and byproducts into the terrestrial realm, with potentially important consequences for tree growth (Helfield and Naiman 2001), nutrient cycling, and habitat quality. Direct effects of road building and timber harvest within floodplains interact with impacts on main channel processes to degrade, eliminate, or isolate

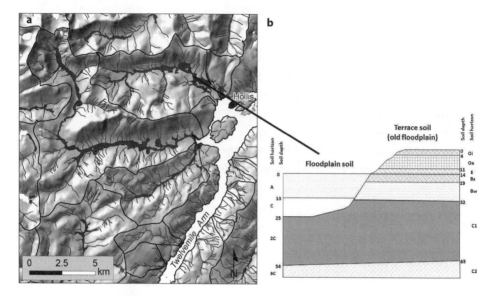

FIGURE 3.02. *(a)* Distribution of alluvial soils, shown as shaded areas along stream channels on Prince of Wales Island, Alaska. *(b)* Cross section of alluvial soils that are mapped as one unit, but actually consist of two distinct soil types, a floodplain soil *(left)* and a terrace soil *(right)*. The two soils differ in their chemistry, structure, and function. Redrawn from D'Amore *et al.* (2011).

floodplain aquatic habitats critical to fish such as coho salmon (*Oncorhyn-chus kisutch*). Restoring connectivity and high-functioning off-channel salmon habitat is a daunting task that requires expensive manipulations of the larger streams that form floodplains, along with thinning and channel improvements within the riparian floodplain itself. Further, a limited understanding of the fundamental processes that maintain the functions that support diverse and productive communities in stream channels reduces our ability to design effective implementation and monitoring of restoration activities.

ESTUARINE INTERFACE

The estuarine ecotone is recognized as a place of intense physical, chemical, and biological interactions (Simenstad *et al.* 1997). The lower watershed boundaries of riparian zones are difficult to distinguish within the small streams of the coastal temperate rainforest, where watersheds are so closely coupled to coastal estuaries. Estuaries were more extensive during the early Holocene and have left remnants of their marine influence along current freshwater reaches (Swanston 1969; Miller 1973; Josenhans *et al.* 1997; Baichtal and Carlson 2010). Although glaciation has left steep shore contours in many locations, sediments filling fiords and estuarine channels create broad tidal flats at river mouths and the end of fiords. The littoral zone is the area at the margin of lakes and the sea analogous to the riparian zone. Lake littoral zones are considered riparian zones by the Forest Service (USDA Forest Service 2008b), but the estuarine littoral zone deserves special attention as a seaward extension of the riparian zone. The high tidal amplitude of over 6 m within the region can make long stretches of the lower river tidal—well above the obvious change in streamside vegetation. Somewhere within the tidally influenced lower channel, the riparian zone grades into the littoral zone, with replacement of riparian trees by grasses and sedges. The lower limit of alluvial stream channels and the estuarine fringe, although distinct in many respects, create a continuum of structure and functioning from riparian to marine. Intertidal areas contain sediments recognized as soils due to the accumulation of plant life and carbon (Osher and Flannagan 2007). Therefore the interaction of the lower riparian, intertidal, and estuarine zones creates a functional linkage between terrestrial and aquatic systems that extends below the high tide line into the near-shore estuarine zone.

Water and dissolved and particulate materials pass through these transitional reaches at the distal end of streams. Animals also move back and forth as seasonal conditions influence habitat quality. Strong gradients in light, algal community composition, and productivity were found along a freshwater–estuarine ecotone in Porcupine Creek on Etolin Island, Alaska (Walter 1984), suggesting that riparian vegetation regulates stream productivity through its influence on light (fig. 3.03). Primary production in the estuarine end of the lower riparian zone exceeded that in the upper stream reaches (Walter 1984), perhaps because river nutrients allow increased primary production where streams received more light. Estuarine uptake of riverine DOC derived from riparian sources exceeds that within the freshwater reaches (Fellman *et al.* 2010). Thus, river organic and inorganic nutrient inputs may support estuarine production, but little has been done to assess the influence of riverine nutrient inputs in subsidizing productivity in the estuary. Salmon utilize the estuaries fringing the terrestrial margin during summer and move among river basins seasonally, further demonstrating the connectedness of these transitional estuaries (Koski

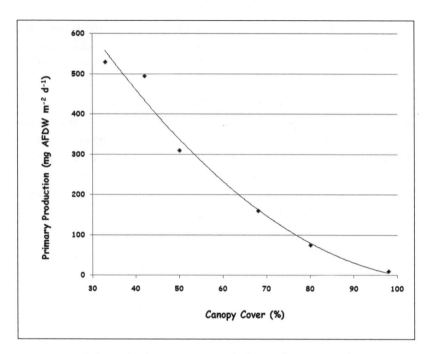

FIGURE 3.03. Relationship between riparian shading and primary production in Porcupine Creek, Alaska. Production units are the ash-free dry weight of organic matter accumulated per square meter per day. Redrawn from Walter (1984).

2009). The American dipper (*Cinclus mexicanus*) ranges seasonally across the stream–estuary gradient, utilizing the intertidal zone for feeding during winter and foraging on stream benthic invertebrates farther inland during other seasons (Willson and Hocker 2008). There are numerous other examples, but these areas at the interface between streams and estuaries are not well understood. They deserve further study because the Tongass shoreline is about 25,000 km long, and there are over 10,000 streams draining into a 35,500 km² estuarine system, making for a very large number of riparian–littoral transition zones.

TERRESTRIAL–MARINE INTERACTIONS

The magnitude of the reciprocal interactions between the coastal temperate rainforest and the marine ecosystem is large, with millions of kilograms of carbon, nitrogen, and phosphorus passing between the two ecosystems (table 3.1). The distal portions of riparian zones are gateways for tidal fluxes

TABLE 3.1. Salmon-derived nutrient (SDN) inputs compared to terrestrial outputs (metric tons) for southeastern Alaska.

NUTRIENTS	SALMON INPUTS[12]	TERRESTRIAL FLUX[2]	RATIO SALMON/FOREST
Carbon (C)	7,900	790,000	0.01
Nitrogen (N)	1,931	46,078	0.04
Phosphorus (P)	281	6,200	0.04

1   Salmon inputs based on total escapement, mean size by species, and mean water C, N, and P content (Carter *et al.* 1992; Gardiner and Geddes 1980; Geiger and McPherson 2004; Gende *et al.* 2004; Pahlke 2005; Shaul *et al.* 2008; Shearer *et al.* 1994).
2   Terrestrial outputs calculated using mean concentrations in watersheds sampled for five years and total annual water flux. Terrestrial output does not include flux from glacial wasting or rivers draining the mainland interior.

and the pulse of ocean nutrients from anadromous fish to infiltrate the freshwater aquatic and terrestrial ecosystem (Gende *et al.* 2004). These areas also receive massive terrestrial nutrient subsidies that are transferred to the marine system from upper watersheds, exceeding the supply from the ocean by about 20 to 100 times (table 3.1). Marine inputs, termed marine-derived nutrients (MDN) or salmon-derived nutrients (SDN), come in the form of fish tissue rich in protein and fat, some of which is transferred to the adjacent riparian zone by the feeding activities of the many animals that depend upon salmon for survival, or by floods or subsurface flows of water (Reimchen *et al.* 2003; Quinn *et al.* 2009). The watershed export is primarily in organic forms (i.e., DOC and DON) and is a pathway of nutrient loss from terrestrial ecosystems (e.g., Perakis and Hedin 2002).

The input of SDN has received much attention as an important subsidy from the marine ecosystem to the generally low-productivity streams of the northeastern Pacific coast (Naiman *et al.* 2002; Willson *et al.* 1998). The population densities and production of many important species depend on the annual return of salmon throughout the North Pacific rainforest (Naiman *et al.* 2002). Often considered a critical "fertilizing" process that sustains aquatic and terrestrial productivity, SDN must be understood in terms of the two fundamental pathways by which it enters forest food webs (Gende *et al.* 2002). The most obvious and best-documented impact of SDN is the support of populations of important species like brown and black bears (*Ursus arctos, Ursus americanus*), mink (*Neovison vison*), otters

(*Lontra canadensis*), bald eagles (*Haliaeetus leucocephalus*), and other emblematic animals that contribute to the diversity and wilderness character of the region (Reimchen *et al.* 2003) and attract visitors from all over the world. The riparian zone is one of the primary locations where animals and salmon interact and is a gateway for the introduction of SDN into the forest.

A second pathway for SDN entry into the forest can be termed the *recycling* or *bottom up* pathway (sensu Gende *et al.* 2002), wherein organic carbon, nitrogen, phosphorus, and other materials within salmon carcasses are delivered to soils and vegetation through excretion by predators and scavengers or decomposition of carcasses carried into the riparian zone by animals or by overbank flooding (Fellman, Hood, Edwards, and D'Amore 2008; Quinn *et al.* 2009). The stimulating effect of the primary plant nutrients (N, P, and K) inspires the "fertilizing" analogy that has been hypothesized to increase growth of riparian vegetation and impact species composition. It has been speculated that increased growth of riparian trees from fertilization by salmon increases habitat quality by increasing the abundance and stability of large wood structures in rivers, thereby increasing salmon production and creating a positive feedback loop (Helfield and Naiman 2001). Whereas the value of spawning salmon as food to birds, mammals, and rearing fish is obvious and incontrovertible (Reimchen *et al.* 2003), evidence for widespread and significant increases in riparian vegetation growth is limited. Much more research is needed to confirm the magnitude of the enhancement of vegetation growth and diversity. Some of the largest conifers in the region are found on alluvial soils dominated by large-stature, widely spaced trees. However, these types of stands are not restricted to areas receiving SDN additions. Alluvial sites above barriers to salmon runs and trees growing on alluvial fans or limestone soils have similar stature and growth.

The potential transfer of nitrogen or phosphorus from fish to riparian zone has been estimated from observations of feeding by bears and other species, and input budgets have been calculated (see Quinn *et al.* 2009; Gende *et al.* 2007). Although experimental application of fish carcasses or leachates to riparian soils may result in measurable salmon-derived nitrogen in foliage, plants would be expected to take up any fertilizer applied to the rooting zone, and it is unclear whether a significant increase in tree growth or production is widespread or common. A more thorough understanding of soil nutrient availability and storage is needed to link plant uptake with soil nutrient pools. The commonly used isotope of nitrogen (^{15}N) has been employed as a tracer for SDN, but it has been shown to be subject to soil (D'Amore *et al.* 2011) and vegetation (Scott *et al.* 2008) influences that affect the enrichment and cycling of this N pool. Even in the absence of marine N inputs, riparian soil types differ widely in microbial nitrogen cycling and the consequent ^{15}N signatures, making conclusions based on nitrogen isotope data questionable. A more detailed understanding of the impact of SDN on terrestrial ecosystems requires careful controls for inherent soil properties and comprehensive measurements of nutrient cycling through vegetation.

We do not dismiss the importance of marine inputs to the region's terrestrial ecosystems. Rather we emphasize the need to integrate studies of marine inputs with those that measure the whole watershed terrestrial subsidy to the marine ecosystem. Rarely are SDN effects interpreted in an ecosystem context, much less a regional one. To understand the interactions between the riparian zone and the estuarine and marine ecosystems, the nature and magnitude of the reciprocal exchanges must be explicitly recognized, since each provides context for the other. Although reductions in the magnitude of salmon escapements caused by climate change could clearly influence riparian organisms, climate warming, by changing hydrology and material transport, will also affect riparian zone nutrient cycling and estuarine and marine ecosystems downstream.

LINKAGE TO GULF OF ALASKA

Coastal waters carrying freshwater runoff and nutrients from the land margin and estuarine plankton are entrained within marine currents and drift for years, traveling up to 1,000 km into the Gulf of Alaska (Whitney and Robert 2002). These marine eddies, named the Haida, Sitka, or Yakutat eddies, contain unusually high concentrations of chlorophyll and nutrients derived from the shelf and coastal watersheds, and they create hotspots of ocean productivity that attract pelagic fish and marine mammals (Johnson *et al.* 2005; Crawford *et al.* 2007). At any time, about 10% of the surface of the Gulf of Alaska is covered by these eddy systems, but between 50% and 80% of the chlorophyll in the sea surface is associated with the eddies (Crawford *et al.* 2007). Outwelling of macro- and micro-nutrients from the land margin to Gulf of Alaska via eddy transport may subsidize marine productivity in the Alaskan Gyre. Thus one of the most significant processes in coastal rainforest riparian zones may be to influence nutrient fluxes to the Gulf of Alaska and support marine production. This poorly recognized phenomenon is revealed by analyses of ecological processes in riparian zones and material fluxes rather than the more usual focus on physical structure. Given the physical and climatic conditions that form the rainforest ecosystems of the North Pacific coast, our concept of a riparian zone needs to be adjusted in recognition that most of the landscape is actually a functional part of a riparian zone and an estuary.

MANAGEMENT HISTORY OF THE TONGASS NATIONAL FOREST RIPARIAN ZONES

Riparian harvest on the Tongass National Forest was most intense prior to 1990 (fig. 3.04; USDA Forest Service 2008d), at which time riparian protection was mandated by the Tongass Timber Reform Act (1990). It is difficult to find data on riparian harvest that have detailed descriptions of how riparian areas were delineated. Various sources report statistics for riparian harvest, but the methods used to delineate the extent of the area are not consistent, making comparisons difficult. As of 2008, about 14,200 ha of young, even-age forests lay within riparian management areas (USDA Forest Service 2008d), presumably the legacy of past riparian logging. Low-elevation forests in the Tongass (<260 m), an area of about 1,500,000 ha, contain about 263,000 ha of riparian zone (Bryant and Everest 1998). Therefore the impacted riparian stands identified by the Tongass young-growth strategy account for about 5.4% of the riparian zones estimated to exist below 250 m (Bryant and Everest 1998) and a much smaller percent of all riparian zones when areas above 250 m are considered.

The low-elevation forest is thought to include the most productive forest and much of the best fish habitat. Many reports distinguish a subset of the low-elevation forest that contained the largest riparian stands, calling them "riparian productive old growth." Assuming that most riparian harvest occurred within that smaller area, estimates of impact are higher. From 1954 to 1995 about 25,000 ha of "riparian productive old growth" were harvested within the 198,000 ha of "riparian productive old growth outside wilderness areas" in the Tongass (USDA Forest Service 1997b), for a total of about 13% of nonwilderness productive riparian habitat. About 34% of the 68,000 km^2 Tongass National Forest is designated wilderness. Assuming that the same proportion of productive old-growth riparian forest occurs

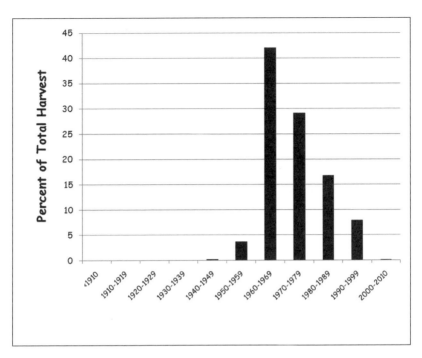

FIGURE 3.04. Chronology of riparian timber harvest on the Tongass National Forest, not including riparian zones within beach fringe (USDA 2008d). Data are percent of total Tongass National Forest timber harvest that occurred within riparian areas for each decade. Riparian zones were delineated for this analysis using floodplain maps or proximity to stream channel and were modified using data layers from the National Wetland Inventory and wetland or riparian soil classification GIS layers to better define riparian boundaries.

within wilderness areas, the total harvest of productive riparian forest within the Tongass would be about 8%. Current plans for the Tongass National Forest call for harvesting up to a total of 1,800 additional km² (USDA Forest Service 2008a), for a total of about 24% of low-elevation forest under active timber management. Current timber harvest practices include riparian buffers for anadromous stream channels; therefore impacts to riparian zones will be far less than prior to 1990. Given the relatively small proportion of riparian zone impacted by past logging and increased protection under current federal management, the future of riparian zones within the national forest, absent any unprecedented changes in federal policy, is largely under the direct control of natural processes.

As of 2000, state and private forest lands within southeast Alaska totaled about 2,400 km^2, with 1,100 km^2 and 1,300 km^2 in state and private ownership respectively (Van Hees 2000). Although stream buffer requirements on state and private land (Alaska Department of Natural Resources 2003) are not as strong as on federal lands, anadromous streams are protected from clear-cutting for distances that vary depending upon stream class. Including all land within southeast Alaska in active timber management, Albert and Schoen (2007a) estimate that 20% of "floodplain forests associated with anadromous fish" have been logged since 1954. These forests include productive old-growth forest documented to be occupied by anadromous fish, which is a smaller subset of the productive old growth forest (2,400,000 ha) or large tree productive old-growth forest (240,000 ha) they report.

Although the total area of riparian zone across southeast Alaska is unknowable, it is clear that only a small proportion of riparian area in the 92,700 km^2 of southeast Alaska has been impacted directly by management or will be actively managed under current land management plans. The area of combined timberlands of federal, state and private ownership is only about 6% of the land area of southeast Alaska, and only a portion of that lies within riparian zones. Thus, in contrast to forests in other parts of North America, southeast Alaskan riparian zones have experienced less direct human disturbance with little likelihood of more in the future. About 95% of temperate rainforest in southeast Alaska is federally owned (USDA Forest Service 1997a) and is therefore spared many of the impacts of agriculture, urbanization, or water withdrawal present in more populated regions that have diverse riparian ownerships.

RIPARIAN RESTORATION

Management of riparian zones within the Tongass has varied widely since the onset of timber harvest (Bryant and Everest 1998). Riparian areas originally received little protection. Timber was cut to the stream banks, and heavy equipment operated within streams that were even used as corridors to move logs and equipment. As logging continued, streams and riparian zones received progressively greater protection, culminating in the Tongass Timber Reform Act of 1990, which mandated riparian buffers on fish-bearing streams. Current practices require buffers and consideration of maintenance of natural stream functioning (USDA Forest Service 2008a). Thus future prospects for riparian areas within the Tongass are good, but significant areas remain that were harvested before riparian safeguards were instituted. Although the percentage of affected riparian areas is low, a disproportionate amount lay within productive old-growth floodplain riparian forest, which has great potential for salmon production (Nickelson *et al.* 1992). Depending upon location within the Tongass, the amount of productive riparian forest that has been harvested ranges up to 41% (Albert and Schoen 2007a). Therefore there are significant areas of riparian habitat that are likely candidates for restoration.

Current riparian restoration approaches prioritize these potentially high-value but degraded reaches for thinning and channel improvements. Six thousand ha of forest within riparian management areas that lie within 75 m (horizontal distance) of anadromous streams are identified as high priority for restoration by thinning to increase future stream recruitment of large conifers (USDA Forest Service 2008a). Interest in restoring riparian zones has increased among many different stakeholders. An encouraging trend is active cooperation among agencies, nongovernmental organizations, and grassroots citizen organizations to prioritize and initiate restoration projects (e.g. Albert *et al.* 2008). Primary restoration efforts have been focused on restoring natural drainage passages, augmenting large wood accumulations to create channel complexity and enhance stream habitats, and restoring off-channel habitat quality and access. Thinning programs implemented by the US Forest Service aim to increase the rate of growth and size of riparian trees to accelerate natural recruitment of large woody debris (LWD) to stream channels and increase plant diversity. However, the application of silvicultural prescriptions is difficult, due to widely varying stand conditions caused by irregular distribution of soil geomorphic assemblages in the riparian zone. The thinning prescriptions can accelerate stand growth and diversification, but large wood additions to streams through natural disturbance will not be realized for decades. Therefore, the investment in riparian stand treatments must be viewed with great scrutiny in order to realize the greatest benefit from riparian vegetation manipulation.

Additional kilometers of impacted stream reach are identified for channel restoration in addition to riparian manipulations. Where road building or harvest have altered channel flows and impeded fish access, restoration within active channels and adjacent floodplains is aimed at stabilizing stream channels to improve access by spawning and rearing salmon. These areas include channels and riparian zones devoid of large wood with low

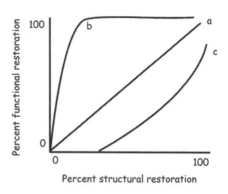

FIGURE 3.05. Possible relationships between restoration of riparian structure and function: *curve a*, implicit assumption that "every little bit helps"; *curve b*, rapid functional recovery with small structural improvements; *curve c*, threshold recovery lagging structural improvements. Many other relationships are possible, but the underlying functional relationships are rarely quantified or monitored.

potential for early recovery of natural wood recruitment. Wood loss resulted in simplified, planar channel beds with measurably different bedforms and processes (Tiegs 2008). Road building and lack of road maintenance have created problems in riparian zones that have persisted decades after harvest. Problems in riparian areas associated with roads include obstruction of fish movements, alterations in drainage patterns, ponding behind collapsed log culverts, and changes in groundwater flow beneath road prisms. The effects of roads on fish and streams are discussed by Person and Brinkman in chapter 6 of this volume. Removal of vegetation by timber harvest destabilizes slopes, creating landslides that become intermittent or perennial drainage channels and sediment sources for long periods. These numerous impacts from past management on riparian form and function offer many opportunities for restoration.

Although past management has impaired the structural and functional attributes of riparian zones, the emphasis on structural manipulations and physical monitoring metrics in riparian restoration plans ignores the effect of restoration on many critical processes and services, such as nutrient cycling or food web productivity. Maintaining key ecological processes in riparian zones is often listed as an important management consideration, but actions on the ground generally manipulate forest and channel structure, and most implementation and monitoring measurements quantify structural rather than functional changes. The relationship between structure and function is often assumed to be linear (fig. 3.05, curve a). However, few quantitative studies have tested this relationship; alternative curves are equally possible depending upon the function chosen. For example, if stream primary production is limited by a dense young conifer canopy, photosynthesis rates could be restored soon after thinning, long before the structural recovery of tree basal area, resulting in a curve much like curve b in figure 3.05.

As we have previously highlighted, a functional consideration leads to an appreciation of the role of riparian zones in controlling the input and export of a variety of materials that support productivity in stream communities and marine systems. The picture is even more complicated because the structure and functioning of riparian zones will likely change dramatically with global warming. Areas that meet our current restoration ideals will likely undergo significant change independent of active management.

CLIMATE CHANGE

Changes in temperature predicted by the end of the century (IPCC 2007) will alter riparian soil processes and geomorphic and hydrologic processes in watershed and stream channels. Reductions in precipitation storage as snow and ice and changes in evapotranspiration will have serious consequences for rivers and riparian zones. Current estimates for maximum temperature increases suggest that the mean snow level will increase by about 900 m by 2100. Under this scenario, about 85% of the northern coastal temperate rainforest will no longer receive large proportions of precipitation as snow, and spatial redistribution of vegetation will be common (Hamann and Wang 2006).

At present, watershed hydrologic responses fall into three classes controlled by elevation and slope (fig. 3.06a). Lower-elevation watersheds (fig. 3.06a, rainfall), which now discharge 20% of the region's water, currently exhibit little snow storage; their hydrographs rise and fall with precipitation. These watersheds tend to be flatter and have high coverage of peat bogs and other wetlands. Intermediate-elevation watersheds (fig. 3.06a, snowmelt), which generate about 50% of annual discharge, will transition from snowmelt systems to predominantly rainfall ones. The hydrographs of those watersheds currently have two peaks: a spring snowmelt peak and an autumnal peak associated with the fall increase in rain and reduction in evapotranspiration. With much less snow, the spring peak will be shifted into winter months, creating a single fall to winter peak in discharge with reduced spring flows. Highest-elevation watersheds, including those with glaciers and perennial snow fields, will lose snow over about half of their

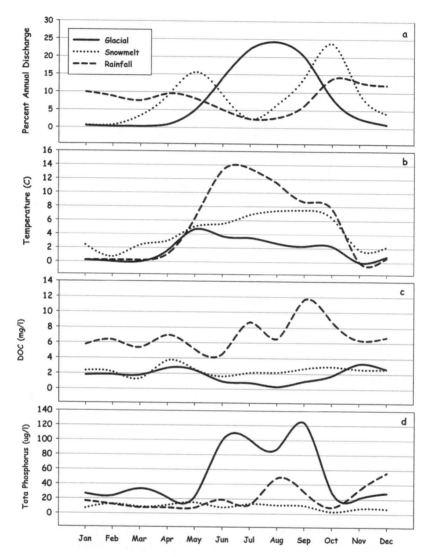

FIGURE 3.06. Monthly mean data for three watersheds from the northern Alexander Archipelago that illustrate systematic differences among watershed type (glacial, snowmelt, and rainfall). Data are (*a*) percent total annual discharge during each month, (*b*) mainstem temperature, (*c*) dissolved organic carbon (DOC) concentrations, and (*d*) total phosphorus concentrations.

area, and many glaciers are predicted to progressively disappear. At present, glacial watersheds exhibit strong discharge during the warm summer months with little output during the winter (fig. 3.06a, glacial). Aggregated discharge from the region is evened out by the different seasonal discharge patterns of the watershed types. When one watershed type is at its annual low, one or more of the other types is in a high discharge period, leading to a sustained input into estuaries.

Although efforts to model the coming hydrologic shifts are only just beginning, it is clear that the shift from a hydrology dominated by ice and rain-on-snow events to a purely rain-dominated response may have regional-scale influences across much of the North Pacific rainforest. As the glacial watersheds take on the discharge pattern of snowmelt watersheds, and snowmelt watersheds transition into a rain-driven hydrograph, overall freshwater discharge will become more seasonal, with lower discharge during summer and higher discharge during winter. The three watershed types presently differ widely in physical and chemical character (fig. 3.06b, c, d). Changes in those characteristics, combined with timing of discharge, may have unexpected consequences not widely considered. By comparing present patterns among the watershed types we can develop scenarios based on the assumption that glacial and snowmelt watersheds will gradually trend toward the hydrologic and chemical properties currently exhibited by rainfall watersheds as climate change proceeds. This space-for-time substitution is imperfect (e.g., glacial watersheds will always be a little cooler than rainfall watersheds because they have more area at higher altitudes) but allows the development of future scenarios that highlight critical research needs.

At the regional scale, widespread shifts in hydrology could affect estuarine and marine production through its effect on the amount and timing of carbon and nutrient export. As we have described, dissolved organic carbon is exported to the ocean in massive amounts. The low-elevation, wetland-dominated watersheds have the highest DOC concentrations (fig. 3.06c). Concentrations of DOC in snowmelt watersheds increase during heavy rains and floods. DOC generation and transport in nonglacial watersheds are controlled by a combination of soil processing and hydrologic transport (D'Amore *et al.* 2012; Fellman, Hood, Edwards, and D'Amore 2009), both of which will change in response to temperature. The Tongass contains one of the largest stores of carbon in any forest in the United States (Leighty *et al.* 2006), and it is likely that the northern BC coast and

Haida Gwaii forest have similar or greater carbon stores, but the fate of that carbon under a warming climate is uncertain. Large increases in DOC export will have mixed effects on North Pacific temperate rainforest rivers and estuaries. A significant component of riverine DOC is biologically active and rapidly taken up by freshwater and marine food webs (Hood *et al.* 2009). Increased DOC export could result in increased productivity in freshwater and estuarine systems but could also decrease habitat quality in nearshore coastal waters through acidification (Orr *et al.* 2005).

DOC export from glacial watersheds is under different controls, but that too will change with climate. Hood *et al.* (2009) found that although glacial watersheds contained low concentrations of DOC, its bioavailability was very high, and it is rapidly taken up by estuarine food webs. In fact, the marine system incorporated glacial DOC more efficiently than did the freshwater community. Paradoxically, the most labile organic matter came from watersheds with the greatest glacial coverage and contained the oldest carbon (up to 4,000 years old). Microbial growth on organic matter produced during the previous interglacial period is thought to be the source of this DOC (Hood *et al.* 2009). Because glacial watersheds are larger than other watershed types and melting of stored ice is increasing their discharge above the annual precipitation input, they are discharging larger amounts of labile DOC than their lower DOC concentrations would suggest. For now, this discharge of high-quality DOC augments the DOC exported by the other watershed types to provide a mixture of readily available organic matter to stimulate estuarine production. As low-elevation glaciers melt and recede, we expect the output of glacial-derived DOC to drop off and the quality of the DOC remaining to become more comparable to that in other rivers. Nearshore coastal waters and estuaries are metabolically active hotspots on regional and national carbon budgets, and it is widely recognized that more data are needed to understand the role of nearshore waters in marine and atmospheric carbon cycles (Chavez *et al.* 2007). The dearth of data and enormous estuarine area in the region are strong reasons to support a major effort to quantify and model these variables.

Changing hydrographs will also affect other material export patterns, with potentially large consequences. Glaciers are continually releasing fresh phosphorus by grinding bedrock into glacial flour. Figure 3.06d illustrates the contrast in total phosphorus concentrations among the three watershed types. Overall phosphorus (P) concentrations are higher year round in glacial watersheds and peak during summer at concentrations up to 10 times higher than other watershed types. This peak in P concentrations coincides with the peak in water discharge, creating a large flux of P into estuaries during the peak of the growing season. Phosphorus is frequently limiting to primary production within estuaries, although little work has been done in the region to understand the impact of this nutrient subsidy. As glaciers disappear, the weathering of rock that releases phosphorus will decrease and water will no longer be discharged primarily during the summer. Whether this will result in decreased estuarine production is unknown, but is a question worth considering. The watershed types exhibit other distinct differences in nitrogen and other ions, with similar potential effects on downstream communities.

Iron is abundant in some Tongass watersheds containing intrusive volcanics; iron seeps are common. Primary production in the northern Gulf of Alaska is limited by iron and silicon availability (Boyd *et al.* 2004). Increased winter discharge and reduced summer discharge caused by damming of the Columbia River are hypothesized to reduce silica and iron nutrient inputs to the Gulf of Alaska and reduce productivity (Whitney *et al.* 2005).We might predict that iron fluxes from regional watersheds differ with hydrology and catchment type, both of which are projected to change with climate. Given that total freshwater discharge from coastal temperate rainforest streams equals that of the Columbia River, and the eddies that form off the coast transport large amounts of iron into the Gulf of Alaska (Johnson *et al.* 2005), similar shifts in riverine output from the eastern coast of the Gulf of Alaska might also result in reductions of primary production within coastal and eddy waters.

Stream temperature alterations alone will have serious biological consequences because of the strong control temperature exerts on aquatic organisms. Glacial watersheds in the Alaskan coastal temperate rainforest are from 8°C to 10°C cooler in the summer than rainfall watersheds, and both glacial and snowmelt watersheds warm later in the spring and cool earlier in the fall (fig. 3.06b). Larval development times of aquatic invertebrates and fish are controlled by the number of degree-days (DD) experienced by growing larvae (Neuheimer and Taggart 2007). The current rate of accumulation of degree-days after the autumn salmon spawning season varies widely in streams of each of the three types (fig. 3.07). Both the rainfall and snowmelt watersheds accumulate significantly more DD before winter sets in. The low-elevation rainfall watersheds continue to accrete DD throughout the winter, whereas the other two types remain flat with

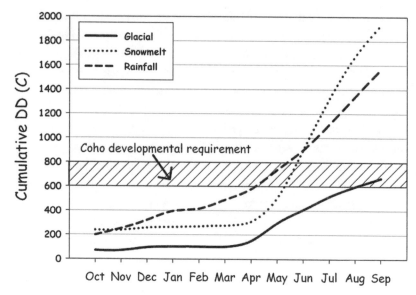

FIGURE 3.07. Cumulative degree-days (DD) in rivers of three watershed types (glacial, snowmelt, and rainfall). Degree days were calculated by multiplying the average daily temperature (degrees Celsius) above zero by the number of days that temperature was reached. For example, if the average stream temperature was 6 degrees Celsius for a month, the total DD would be 180 (6 x 30).

water temperatures near zero. By the end of winter, rainfall watersheds have accumulated significant DD, whereas snowmelt systems lag. In the spring, snowmelt rivers rapidly accumulate degree-days, exceeding the value for rainfall watersheds by May or June. Glacier watersheds presently develop one-third the total degree-days of the other types, and do so over a much longer time period.

Differences in degree-day accumulation may have serious consequences for aquatic species and the animals that rely on them. As temperatures change with warming, we predict that life histories of aquatic invertebrates will adjust, with consequences for availability of prey for fish, birds, and bats. For example, American dippers (*Cinclus mexicanus*) move seasonally from intertidal to stream habitats in search of small fish and aquatic invertebrates (Willson and Hocker 2008). Earlier pupation and emergence of their stream invertebrate prey might cause seasonal shifts in food availability with unknown results. Bats and birds often rely on emerging insects within riparian corridors for food; changes in the timing of emergence will require adaptation. For migratory birds, changes in emergence of insect prey driven by warming can have detrimental consequences by altering the availability of food during critical nesting periods (Both *et al.* 2006).

Salmon life cycles are also sensitive to temperature. The cumulative DD experienced by developing eggs and larvae affect emergence times and size at emergence (Neuheimer and Taggart 2007). The effect of temperature variations on development times for coho is greatest at lower temperatures (2°C to 6°C), with a one-degree increase in temperature shortening the time to emergence by 53 days (McCullough 1999). Coho require 600 to 800 DD from fertilization to emergence (McCullough 1999; interpreted from fig. 4). Assuming development starts in October, rainfall watersheds cross the 600 degree-day threshold by mid-May, with snowmelt rivers a month later. Glacial rivers do not accumulate 600 DD until midsummer. Changes in the timing of emergence, coupled with changes in the life histories of terrestrial and aquatic invertebrates that serve as food, have large implications for life history adaptations and survival of salmon. Combined with decreased summer flows and potentially increased respiratory oxygen demand, freshwater habitats may undergo serious decreases in habitat quality as climate warms and discharge shifts.

Although regional shifts in discharge and chemistry are important, individual rivers will experience even more extreme changes as alterations in discharge change daily patterns in the magnitude, frequency, and duration of floods. To illustrate what might happen as watersheds transition from glacial to snowmelt to rainfall character we have plotted the daily mean discharge over a year in three representative watershed types taken from USGS records (fig. 3.08). It is clear in this simple example that the variation in discharge and flood severity varies widely throughout the year among the three watershed types. Rainfall and snowmelt watersheds exhibit much larger floods during the critical post-spawning autumnal period, and snowmelt rivers vary widely in the magnitude of floods during winter and spring. As changing discharge alters sediment input and transport regimes, channel morphology will adjust along with discharge, with potentially serious consequences for fish habitat (McKean *et al.* 2008) and riparian vegetation.

Along with changing sediment distribution and morphology, larger or more frequent floods may scour out developing salmon eggs, thereby reducing survival. Ocean acidification may reduce the size of pink salmon (*Oncorhynchus gorbuscha*) adults returning to spawn because of a reduction in their food supply (Fabry *et al.* 2008). Smaller fish deposit eggs at shallower depths, making their redds more vulnerable to increased flood

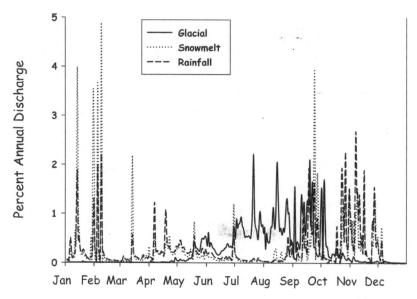

FIGURE 3.08. Daily hydrographs from three rivers within southeast Alaska, representing the three classes of watershed type (glacial, snowmelt, and rainfall). Data are the percent of total annual discharge on a given day.

scour depths. Salmonids will be affected in other ways by the combined effects of shifting floodplain structure and river conditions. Changes in winter flows will alter connectivity to off-channel rearing habitats, and seasonal movements among different habitats may be reduced. Floodplain vegetation may also be affected. For example Pollock et al. (1998) found that the high plant species diversity in riparian wetlands in southeast Alaska was related to flood frequency, with highest diversity at intermediate levels of disturbance. To the extent that the hydrologic changes wrought by warming will alter flood frequencies and magnitude, riparian plant biodiversity could be dramatically changed during coming decades.

Further upstream in high-gradient areas, climate change will likely alter decomposition and carbon cycling within riparian soils, with presently unpredictable effects on the seasonality, quantity, and quality of organic matter and nutrients exported to streams and estuaries. Changes in riparian vegetation may alter the amount, quality, and timing of inputs of leaf litter and terrestrial invertebrates to downstream food webs. Predictions of earlier plant emergence in ecosystems due to earlier spring warming will change the flush of nutrients associated with the release of stored plant material. Smaller tributaries, many of which are intermittent under current conditions, may experience reduced summer flows. The change in soil water storage will lead to shifts in the hydrologic regulation of nutrient cycling, with potential impacts to stream systems. Increased soil temperatures may lead to a shift from export through dissolved pathways to gaseous losses, such as respiration and denitrification. Methane is an important greenhouse gas, and wetlands are hotspots of methane release (Matthews and Fung 1987). Changes in soil saturation and associated redox potentials may alter methane release from the extensive wetlands within coastal rainforest watersheds.

Presently, brownwater streams, which have high loads of dissolved organic matter (DOC), can suffer reduced dissolved oxygen concentrations, sometimes becoming anoxic and killing adult and juvenile fish within the channel and in off-channel floodplain habitats. DOC concentrations have been increasing in many areas of the world (Worrall *et al.* 2004), and it is unclear whether carbon stored within riparian and wetland soils will be mobilized to streams under warmer, wetter conditions. With increased stream temperatures, reduced spring flows, and potentially increased concentrations of DOC, habitat quality and productivity in critical low-gradient riparian zones may be reduced.

Stream and riparian restoration efforts currently underway do not explicitly acknowledge the changing state of the region's watersheds. Restoration goals are based on the premise that some ideal old-growth forest condition, based on current conditions and from which past management has created departures, can be used as the target for restoring the affected area. Current efforts at restoring riparian forests and stream habitat are designed to accelerate return to this idealized pattern of old-growth conditions, but changing climate will alter the nature of unmanaged old-growth conditions through changes in forest structure, tree growth rates, and channel adjustments to changing hydrology. Although there is rarely an explicit description of the time course for convergence with desired future conditions in current restoration projects, the time it will take for trees released by thinning to grow large enough to begin to recruit to channels is of the same order as predicted temperature changes (i.e., 50 to 100 years). That being the case, restoration goals are a moving target, since even the present reference watersheds are unlikely to meet current numerical standards by the end of the century. Therefore, current restoration goals may not be met due to changing baseline conditions induced by climate change rather than failure of the restoration design. Further research and modeling of specific impacts of climate change on stream discharge and channel morphology will be required to better predict how flow changes will impact floodplain dynamics.

FORM VERSUS FUNCTION AND IMPLICATIONS FOR THE FUTURE

Focusing on riparian structure and defining riparian areas in physical terms has led to an emphasis on restoration of structural aspects of relatively small areas while overlooking the functioning of vast riparian areas that have not been directly managed. In an unchanging world we could assume that the goods and services this huge, unmanaged riparian ecosystem provides will not change and so can be ignored. However, predictions about climate change and extrapolations from what information we currently have strongly suggest that massive changes will occur within both managed and unmanaged riparian zones, irrespective of management activities and probably overriding them. If we are focused on manipulating riparian structure in a small, albeit important, portion of the forest, we run the risk of being blindsided by unmanaged changes that result in widespread and extensive ecological impacts, undoing our best intentions and leaving us unprepared for problems as they present themselves. These consequences, although not always preventable, should be anticipated and planned for so that managers can make decisions to maximize the ability of humans, ecosystems, and biota to adapt.

MANAGING FOR FUTURE UNCERTAINTIES

Given the complexity of the terrestrial and aquatic interface in the riparian systems we have described and the uncertainty of climate changes, the risk of unanticipated consequences from restoration measures is increasing. A clear answer for how riparian zones should be treated is not readily available, but it is certain that the current situation requires a broad vision, collaboration among disparate disciplines, and cooperation among agencies and other stakeholders. An integrated approach will require better information about present functioning and controlled variables for the creation of robust models that can be projected into the future.

A cornerstone of any management or rehabilitation of an ecological system should be to maintain its ability to adjust in the face of changing natural conditions. Classically, the ability of an ecosystem to rapidly return to its previous state after a disturbance has been called resilience. Streams and riparian zones are considered resilient because their structure and function depend upon repeated disturbance in the form of floods and erosion. Maintenance of biological diversity is essential to maintaining ecosystem resilience, but biodiversity alone is not sufficient (Elmqvist *et al.* 2003). Functional diversity of abiotic processes and components should also be maintained. The fundamental terrestrial and aquatic ecological processes need to be identified and placed in the context of how they maintain the biodiversity of the system. This approach is usually done as an iterative process that employs adaptive management. However, this approach is not often used in rehabilitation projects that include major channel alterations. The adaptive management approach also needs to include a clear and effective feedback mechanism in the form of monitoring of the project implementation measures and an experimental approach to restoration, including defensible statistical design and adequate replication.

Monitoring provides a way to derive information about the system and can serve as a platform for the interaction of research and management. However, despite recognition of their importance, monitoring efforts rarely receive the attention, budgets, or respect that they deserve and need for true adaptive management to occur. The rapid changes in store for all ecosystem components require renewed commitment to monitoring of ecosystem structure and functioning. Consideration should be given to actively managing for future structural and biological functions of systems rather than "reference conditions," because the rate of change over the next several decades may exceed the ability of organisms and ecosystems to adapt in ways that continue to provide the goods and services that humans desire and require. Maintaining high levels of fish production may require more intrusive, active management.

An important approach to dealing with rapid change is to integrate the key foundation of ecosystem resilience with active management through long-term adaptive management experiments and monitoring projects designed to be sensitive to expected changes. New working relationships among agencies to coordinate management activities for quick response to changing conditions could streamline institutional reactions where impacts span jurisdictions. In much of the northern coastal temperate rainforest, the simplified land ownership and the control it provides, as well as the lower impact of logging compared to agriculture, urban sprawl, and dams, make it more likely that climate change signals can be separated from other impacts to inform management responses.

SUMMARY

The tendency to fragment the landscape into upland, freshwater, estuarine, and marine components, without recognizing and integrating the reciprocal exchanges of water and nutrients, leads to management discontinuities. Riparian zones are both important habitats and sources and transformation conduits for material and energy that flow through the entire array of coupled ecosystems of the coastal temperate rainforests. The combination of physical habitat availability, strong biochemical gradients, biodiversity, and the simple fact that riparian zones are often the flattest and most readily accessed land surface make them centers of ecological and human action. All riparian zones, regardless of past or current management, are undergoing changes due to global warming that will change their physical structure and way of functioning. Human outdoor recreation is expected to increase (Hall *et al.* 2009), and with it human impacts on riparian zones, putting an additional stress on these critical habitats. Adjusting silvicultural practices to reduce undesirable effects on riparian zones has been a simple task compared to the challenges to come. A new management approach is needed that combines coordinated rehabilitation and expanded monitoring with an aggressive program to encourage development of regional models to better predict climate change effects on ecosystem functioning that will serve as key components of adaptive management strategies.

ACKNOWLEDGMENTS

The authors would like to thank Jim Baichtal, Dom Chaloner, Chelsea Crenshaw, Jason Fellman, Eran Hood, Di Johnson, Mike Marshall, and Rick Woodsmith for many animated conversations on new ways of viewing terrestrial–aquatic linkages and their influences.

4

Natural Disturbance Patterns in the Temperate Rainforests of Southeast Alaska and Adjacent British Columbia

Paul Alaback, Gregory Nowacki, and Sari Saunders

INTRODUCTION

Temperate rainforests are characterized by their distinctive climate of high annual rainfall and cool growing season temperatures (Alaback 1991; DellaSala, Alaback, *et al.* 2011). Consequently, species that live there have adaptations to a low-energy and nutrient-poor environment. The forests also have a pattern of disturbance, which results in a complex, patchy structure that characterizes them (Deal 2007; Kramer *et al.* 2001; Veblen and Alaback 1996). Although most temperate trees are adapted to drought stress and to fire disturbances, trees of temperate rainforests lack those adaptations because of the relative rarity of drought and fire (Gavin *et al.* 2003a; Agee 1993; Gutierrez *et al.* 2004). The disturbance ecology of temperate rainforests is of particular interest since it helps explain many aspects of their ecological functions and also helps explain why forest management practices such as clear-cut logging have had such a profound and long-lasting impact. As we outline in this chapter, the manner in which logging has been conducted over the past several decades contrasts significantly with natural disturbance patterns. The contrast between the ecological response to natural patterns of disturbance and logging impacts provides many insights for how to best enhance ecological functioning in these critically important ecosystems. These issues are of global signifi-cance because the temperate rainforests of British Columbia and southeast Alaska comprise the largest and most intact examples of temperate rainforest (DellaSala 2011). Sustainable management of these rainforest land-scapes will require careful attention to details of how to best emulate or maintain natural patterns of disturbance to promote resiliency in the face of climate change and other forms of stress from human activities.

BIOGEOGRAPHICAL CONTEXT

The coastal temperate rainforests of southeast Alaska and adjacent British Columbia are unusual in their biogeographical setting (Nowacki *et al.* 2001), which provides an important context for understanding the ecological responses to disturbances generated by physical, climatic, and biological agents, as well as contemporary human activities. As is true for most coastal temperate rainforests, these forests are nestled between the ocean and a major mountain cordillera fostering orographic precipitation. This region has been strongly affected by Pleistocene and Holocene glaciations and hence fosters youthful landscapes. During warmer periods it has been repeatedly connected to bioregions in Japan and Siberia (Cook and Mac-Donald, this volume, chapter 2; DellaSala 2011). Concurrently, this region is isolated as a result of its many islands and the harsh barrier of the heavily glaciated British Columbian Coast Mountains.

The only other coastal temperate rainforest region comparable in size and physiographic complexity is the temperate rainforest of southern Chile and adjacent Argentina. Both regions share similarities in the importance of wind and rainstorms in creating a fine-scale mosaic of forest conditions and in the isolation created by the interactions of mountains with the dynamics of large ice sheets and the ocean. But they differ dramatically in evolutionary history and connections to adjacent temperate bioregions (e.g., Lawford *et al.* 1996). The northern Pacific coastal rainforest abuts the fire-adapted boreal forest zone to the north and west and via large breaks in the BC coastal ranges, such as along the Skeena and Taku rivers. As a result the biota is dominated by wide-ranging species (Alaback 1996). In South America, by contrast, there are only ancient connections (>30 million years) to other temperate regions, such as the Antarctic continent and New Zealand. Therefore, most species that live there are Gonwana-specific (shared with New Zealand or southern Australia) or endemic to the region (Arroyo *et al.* 1996).

The diverse physiography of the northern Pacific coastal region helps explain wide differences in disturbance ecology, particularly in terms of insect and disease outbreaks, mass wasting, flooding, complex glacial history, topography, and the relatively high frequency of intense windstorms (Nowacki *et al.* 2001; Kramer *et al.* 2001; Mitchell 1995). Coastal rainforests in southern Chile are subjected to intense winds, whose effects are amplified by intense tectonic activity in the Andes that causes widespread mass-wasting events. Mass movements are a major disturbance type in many northern coastal rainforests as well, particularly in terrain with steep, unstable slopes and thin soils. Heavily glaciated and dissected terrain on the mainland, and some rugged island chains, such as Haida Gwaii, provide notable examples of the impacts from mass-wasting events (Gimbarzevsky 1988). These mass-wasting events can be greatly amplified by logging and road building activities (A. Johnson *et al.* 2000; D'Odorico and Fagherazzi 2003) and appear to be increasing in frequency, perhaps due to climate change (Geertsema *et al.* 2006).

Avalanches play a greater role in coastal northern Pacific rainforests due to cooler winter temperatures, and large accumulations of wet, heavy snow (Nowacki *et al.* 2001; Veblen and Alaback 1996). Owing to their shallow, youthful soils, high annual rainfall, and rugged topography, both Pacific rainforest regions are subject to periodic intense flooding events that influence the structure and dynamics of larger river systems (Naiman *et al.* 2000). Tsunamis might also be an important influence in these forests, but the highly irregular and long return intervals make it unlikely that there are specific ecological adaptations to these events.

Interestingly, although riparian systems in South America are mostly dominated by tree species such as *Nothofagus* spp. that also grow on upland sites, in northern rainforests many species, such as willows, cottonwoods, and alders (families Salicaceae and Betulaceae), are specialists in the riparian zone. The lack of riparian specialists has implications for the disturbance ecology of southern riparian systems, including effects on channel morphology and slower rates of vegetation succession following disturbances. For example, northern riparian systems are vulnerable to overexploitation by introduced herbivores, such as the severe reduction in understory vegetation following the introduction of Sitka black-tailed deer (*Odocoileus hemionus sitkensis*) to the islands of Haida Gwaii in British Columbia, but they appear relatively resilient to disturbances such as frequent flooding and river impoundments created by ecosystem engineers such as beavers (*Castor canadensis*). Southern rainforests are much slower to recover, and, as happened following introduction of beavers, may suffer profound transformations in structure and function, as long as beavers and the unique habitats that they create persist in the ecosystem (Anderson *et al.* 2009). Disturbance by beavers can promote tree regeneration and species diversity in the north, but in Patagonia it actually reduces forest cover and promotes invasions of exotic species. This contrast in ecological response underscores the importance of considering biogeographical isolation when comparing these rainforest regions.

GAP DYNAMICS

A general consequence of the lack of coarse-scale fire disturbances in upland high latitude coastal rainforests is the dominance of fine-scale mosaics at the landscape scale (Daniels and Gray 2006; Veblen and Alaback 1996). The dominant pattern of gap dynamics is driven by a combination of disease, insect outbreaks, variable exposure to major storms, edaphic conditions, and species characteristics, all of which interact with larger-scale patterns of ocean to land interactions that govern the intensity and frequency of exposure to storms (Kramer *et al.* 2001, Mitchell 1995). Preliminary studies of gap dynamics in the North Pacific coastal region suggest that most gaps are quite small (<100 m^2) and are formed mostly by the stem breakage of one to two dominant trees (fig. 4.01; Ott and Juday 2002; Hennon and McClellan 2003; Lertzman *et al.* 1996). Such gaps occupy an average of 9% (5.8%–12.6%) of local forest landscapes and persist for at least 80 years. Assuming no changes in climate or wind patterns, they may persist from 200 to 900 years (Ott and Juday 2002). In subalpine or wet forests in British Columbia, gaps may persist even longer (Lertzman and Krebs 1991; Lertzman *et al.* 1996). This proportion of canopy gap is comparable across the region, south to the Oregon Coast Range (Arsenault 1995; Lertzman and Krebs 1991; Lertzman *et al.* 1996; Taylor 1990; range 14.9%–38%).

Canopy gaps are formed in three different ways that correspond to causes of tree death: stem breakage, root throw, and mortality while standing. In the Ott and Juday (2002) study, most gap makers were killed by stem breakage (69%–95%), a significantly higher percentage than reported for similar forests in British Columbia (31%–43%; Lertzman and Krebs 1991; Lertzman *et al.* 1996). In southeast Alaska, a high proportion of old western hemlock trees (*Tsuga heterophylla*), which dominate the upper canopy layers, are infected with heart rot decay fungi that weakens them (Hennon 1995; Hennon and McClellan 2003). The interaction between

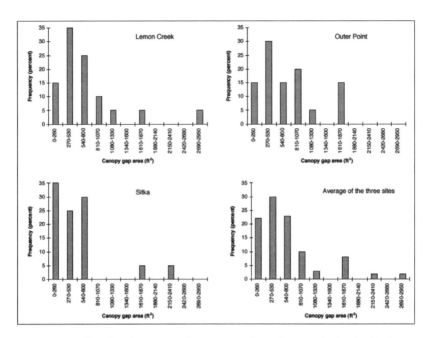

FIGURE 4.01. Size class frequency of canopy gaps from three study sites in Alaska. Modified from Ott and Juday (2002).

stem decay and gap formation in these forests appears to explain the high proportion of gap formation by stem breakage. In many cases, trees with stem breakage died standing, then decayed and broke. In the most detailed study of tree mortality, trees mostly fell in the direction of mountain slopes, not in the direction of wind exposure, further suggesting a key role of decay fungi (Hennon and McClellan 2003).

The less frequent but more intense storms that topple whole trees result in very different ecological consequences than the frequent but dispersed events causing small gaps. Root throw mixes organic and mineral fractions of the soil, thus accelerating decomposition and creating complex forest microtopography, which results in greater nutrient availability and long-term forest productivity (Bormann *et al.* 1995; Kramer *et al.* 2004). Recent investigations have helped clarify the patterns and scale of these disturbances (Kramer *et al.* 2001; DeGayner *et al.* 2005; Harcombe *et al.* 2004). The strongest winds in southeast Alaska generally occur in the fall and winter and come from a southeasterly direction (Nowacki and Kramer 1998).

Larger scale windthrow disturbances generally occur on very specific topographic positions (e.g., in southeast Alaska these are steep slopes that are directly exposed to southeasterly winds), so they can be estimated with a simple model that considers elevation, slope, aspect, soils, and overall wind exposure (Kramer *et al.* 2001; Mitchell *et al.* 2008). In general approximately 15% to 33% of productive forest land in southeast Alaska is susceptible to this form of disturbance, and about one third of the land is topographically protected from these windstorms; the remaining area is a mixture of the two disturbance regimes. In the most wind-exposed sites, stand-replacing storms occur every one to two centuries, so that the forests have younger, smaller trees and higher tree densities than in wind-protected sites (DeGayner *et al.* 2005; Kramer *et al.* 2001). Similar patterns occur in British Columbia (BC), but wind may be less important as a large-scale disturbance agent. These large-scale events (up to several hundred hectares) have been described for northern Vancouver Island (e.g., Keenan 1993) and for the north coast of BC (Mitchell 1995). Additional areas of Haida Gwaii have also been considered susceptible (e.g., Pearson 2010). In contrast, Mitchell (1995) found no evidence of a relationship between topographic exposure and large-scale blowdown in BC. However, local studies show that a combination of hydroriparian subregions and site-level ecosystems best defined units that experienced similar disturbance frequencies on the north and central coasts of BC. Pojar *et al.* (1999) noted that within the valleys and inlets of the BC mainland coast, localized outflow winds can be the predominant wind disturbance, in contrast to larger-scale storm systems. Geomorphic events and, even more rarely, fire are the more prevalent stand-replacing disturbances in BC (Banner *et al.* 1983) with return intervals of greater than 4,000 years (Pearson 2010).

To understand how forest structure influences habitats for plants, animals, and microbes, it is important to characterize the salient features of the "old-growth" age class or structural class. Its features are specific to the forest type, but include the branch and canopy structure of large dominant trees, vertical canopy stratification, and patchiness (horizontal heterogeneity) in overall structure (Franklin *et al.* 2002; MacKinnon 2003). A diversity of sizes and decay classes of coarse woody debris and snags (which provides structure and stores and recycles nutrients) is a key component of this structure. In southeast Alaska, the interaction between average tree size and tree density is a useful indicator of old-growth forests on the landscape (Caouette and DeGayner 2005).

It may take two centuries or more to reach the old-growth developmental stage, depending on the feature or process of interest (Banner and LePage

A) Wind Protected

B) Wind Exposed

FIGURE 4.02. Comparison of idealized overall stand structure of northern rainforests that are protected from or subject to periodic high-intensity windstorms.

2008; Gerzon *et al.* 2011). This characteristic old-growth structure can develop in temperate coastal rainforests after centuries of canopy gap disturbances alone or in concert with infrequent larger-scale disturbances (Spies 2004; Gutierrez *et al.* 2009; Nowacki and Kramer 1998). Although "classic" old growth is more prevalent in wind-protected terrains (Kramer *et al.* 2001; DeGayner *et al.* 2005), old-growth forests can develop on nutrient-rich sites on wind-exposed terrains if storms are absent for more than two centuries. In coastal temperate rainforests, old-growth forests can also be defined on the basis of a structure that develops after centuries of gap-phase disturbance processes alone, or in concert with infrequent larger-scale disturbances (Spies 2004; Gutierrez *et al.* 2009). In general, forests that have developed from small-scale gap processes tend to have complex, more open, multicanopy structures and a broader range of tree sizes than those originating from larger-scale disturbances (fig. 4.02; Kramer *et al.* 2001). However, some of the most commercially valuable forest occurs on windthrow-exposed areas and old debris slides, especially when stands are able to develop two centuries or more following disturbance (Kramer *et al.* 2001; DeGayner *et al.* 2005).

In some sites, such as windthrow-prone Pacific silver fir (*Abies amabilis*) and hemlock-dominated sites in northern coastal BC, as well as western hemlock and Sitka spruce (*Picea sitchensis*) ecosystems in coastal

Alaska, large-scale windthrow may promote nutrient release and help maintain forest productivity (Bormann *et al.* 1995; Kimmins 2004). Forests that develop after large-scale windthrows may achieve exceptional density and biomass not only because these stands typically have higher nutrient availability but also because single-cohort stands of moderate density typically retain higher densities of large trees with old-growth characteristics than all-aged stands (Caouette and DeGayner 2005; Kramer *et al.* 2001). Examples of these areas in southeast Alaska include the high-volume old-growth forests on the west coast of Admiralty Island. Historically stands with similar structure also occurred in many areas on Prince of Wales, such as the central western coast. Since most of these stands have now been harvested, it is difficult to reconstruct their dynamics. There are many pathways to old-growth characteristics in northern coastal rainforests, including large-scale stand replacing, multicohort-generating disturbances and small-scale gap-dynamics processes (Alaback 1982; Alaback and Juday 1989; Hanley and Brady 1997; Spies 2004; Nowacki and Kramer 1998).

A key question for conservation and management is the extent to which larger-scale windthrow disturbances are equivalent to human-generated disturbances such as clear-cut logging. Comparing human disturbances such as logging with natural types of disturbances in forests has a long history and a strong intuitive appeal. Pickett and White (1985), for example, conceptualized disturbance in terms of a pattern of intensity and frequency of disturbance, or a disturbance regime. This framework would seem to apply equally to anthropogenic as well as natural disturbances such as windthrow or fire. However, understanding the differences in management practices relative to these natural disturbance regimes is critical; these regimes may differ at the stand scale (e.g., in terms of residual stand structure after the disturbance) or landscape level (e.g., total amount of forest remaining and spatial arrangement of residual patches) (Perera *et al.* 2004).

There is much evidence that although stand-replacing windstorms do occur, they affect a relatively small percentage of the landscape as compared with clear-cut logging (table 4.1). For example, one study using aerial photographs from Prince of Wales Island documented that about 1.6% of the forest area (or 1% of timber volume) had detectable canopy openings; most of this was due to a single windstorm event (Harris 1989). These larger windthrow-caused openings ranged from 0.4 to 400 ha with a median of 2 to 8 ha (Nowacki and Kramer 1998). The largest of these openings were the result of serial multiple windthrow events (Harcombe *et al.* 2004; Lertzman

TABLE 4.1. Comparison of landscape patterns of windthrow disturbance to clear-cutting over the past century in the Tongass National Forest in southeast Alaska.[1]

	WINDTHROW	CLEAR-CUT
Median Size: (exposed slopes)	8 ha	20 ha
(protected areas)	<0.01 ha	20 ha
Median Retention:[2]	5%-15%	~0%[3]
Location: (exposed slopes)	1%-10%	5%
(protected slopes)	<1%	20%

1 Data sources: Nowacki and Kramer 1998; Kramer *et al.* 2001.
2 Proportion of original dominant and codominant trees that remain after disturbance. This represents "legacy" from the previous stand (Lindenmayer and Franklin 2002).
3 Recent changes in the Tongass land use plan (USDA Forest Service 1997b) include proposed experimental variable stand retention in the range of 5%–50%, but the vast majority of clear-cuts on the landscape today continue to have minimal retention of dominant or codominant trees.

et al. 1996; Ott and Juday 2002). Analysis of three additional subregions within southeast Alaska (on northeast Chichagof, southeast Chichagof, and Kuiu Island) also showed that windthrow disturbance only affected 1% to 17% of the land area per century, (Nowacki and Kramer 1998). Timber harvest in these same study areas across the Tongass from the 1950s to the 1990s show that rates of clear-cut logging were 4 to 10 times the natural rates of stand-replacing windthrow events (fig. 4.03; Nowacki and Kramer 1998).

Strong contrasts between landscape patterns of logging and natural disturbances have also been documented in the coastal forests of BC. For the central coast of BC, openings from logging comprised approximately twice the forested area of openings from natural disturbances over the last 140 years. Further, the average size of patch openings by logging was larger than those for other events (excepting geomorphic disturbances) (Pearson 2010). Infrequent high-intensity fires have long been assumed to play a key role in defining overall structure of old-growth rainforests in coastal BC. Recent work, however, has shown that, in fact, small-scale gap disturbances, not fires, were the dominant influence in these forests (Gavin *et al.* 2003a; Lertzman et al. 2002). Large-scale clear-cut logging has therefore created a structure that contrasts strongly with the historical structure of these landscapes, just as it has in southeast Alaska (Daniels and Gray 2006).

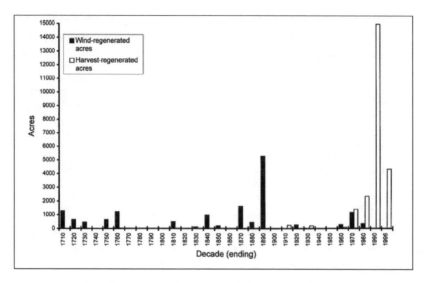

FIGURE 4.03. Overall pattern of windthrow and clear-cutting disturbances over four study areas in southeast Alaska. Adapted from Nowacki and Kramer (1998).

Another contrast between natural patterns of stand-replacing disturbances and clear-cut logging is the location of disturbances on the landscape and the size of the patches (table 4.1). Since wind-disturbed sites generally have smaller and less economically valuable trees, timber harvesting is concentrated on protected or mixed-disturbance regime patches. In BC's central coast, high-productivity stands (e.g., river valley Sitka spruce at lower elevations, <200 m) are preferentially harvested. On Kuiu Island in southeast Alaska, 0%–7% of timber harvest occurred on forests with high wind exposure whereas 15% to more than 20% was logged on wind-protected landscapes (Kramer *et al.* 2001). This suggests that if logging continues in the locations and at the rates of the recent past that the overall landscape structure will increasingly diverge from historical patterns. The ecological effects of changes in landscape patterns are even more striking because silvicultural prescriptions for cutover lands generally call for reharvest within 100 years after the first harvest. This management practice has the potential to permanently change the disturbance regime of these forests from long-term gap dynamics (with dominant trees persisting an average of 300 to 500 years or more) to more frequent stand-replacing disturbance. A key ecological consequence of these short-duration disturbance cycles is the elimination of late-successional habitats.

Because large trees never regrow, the legacy of coarse woody debris from previous stands is greatly reduced, degrading habitat for many species associated with these structures. Work by Price *et al.* (1998) demonstrated lower levels of structural heterogeneity in maturing stands initiated by clear-cutting than in stands of the same age regenerated following natural blowdown. Management activities that minimize the earliest stages of succession by accelerating tree establishment can further diminish wildlife habitat as well (Swanson *et al.* 2011).

DISTURBANCE AND UNDERSTORY PLANTS

One of the great challenges to conservation in southeast Alaska and northern BC is to retain a diverse and productive layer of understory vegetation under young to middle-aged, productive, well-drained forests. It is more difficult to retain understory forage plants for species such as Sitka black-tailed deer in this region than in other areas due to the climatic and ecological setting which fosters dense forest regrowth (Wallmo and Schoen 1980; Person and Brinkman, this volume, chapter 6). North Pacific coastal rainforests are dominated by western hemlock or multiple layers of hemlock and Sitka spruce that have dense canopies that may intercept as much as 99% of incoming sunlight (Alaback 1982; Tappeiner and Alaback 1989). The consequences of low light levels are magnified by low nutrient availability and a persistently cloudy, cool climate, so that little energy is available for understory plants to grow, reproduce, and chemically defend themselves from herbivores (Bryant *et al.* 1983). On well-drained sites where most clear-cut timber harvest and windthrow is concentrated, understory plants generally are shaded out within 25 years of disturbance.

In the central and north coasts of BC, patterns of long-term reductions in understory vegetation and associated wildlife habitat in logged second-growth forests are similar to those in old-growth forests. Although most plant species found in the young forests are present in old forests, old growth has higher species richness because of the presence of additional cryptogam species and herbaceous species of low cover and constancy (Banner and LePage 2008). A significantly higher cover of shrub, herb, and bryophyte species differentiated old forests from second-growth (40–100 year old) forests (particularly in productive, nutrient-rich forests); western redcedar, a preferred harvest species, was scarce in second growth. With commercial rotation lengths of between 80 and 120 years, these forests will not maintain, at either stand or landscape scale, the full complement of species characteristic of their old-growth (>250 years) seral and structural stage (Banner and LePage 2008).

Thinning of second-growth forests can temporarily improve some aspects of vegetation structure, but it is unlikely that such interventions can restore the full complexity or functioning of old-growth forests (Cole *et al.* 2010; DellaSala *et al.* 1996; Hanley 2005). Patterns of snow deposition and wind exposure also should be considered in prioritizing areas for restoration, since these strongly influence wildlife habitat quality (Doerr *et al.* 2005). More dramatic changes to forest structure, such as promoting mixed canopies of alder and conifers, may also be helpful in creating more diverse understory vegetation on cutover lands (Deal 2007; Hanley 2005).

Preliminary studies on the effects of partial harvesting suggest that understory vegetation and its associated wildlife habitat can often persist throughout the logging cycle (Deal 2007; Deal 2001; Beese, this volume, chapter 9). The creation of artificial canopy gaps in younger forests may also increase plant biodiversity and increase deer carrying capacity up to the age when these stands can be commercially thinned or partially harvested (Alaback and Ausman, unpublished data).

RECONCILING NATURAL AND ANTHROPOGENIC DISTURBANCES

One of the greatest challenges in developing a scientific approach to conservation for North Pacific coastal temperate rainforests is reconciling the profound changes in temporal scale and pattern of timber harvesting with the long-term patterns of forest dynamics that have previously dominated these regions (Daniels and Gray 2006; Nowacki and Kramer 1998). A further complication is accounting for the likely effects of climate change on future patterns of forest dynamics (Alaback and McClellan 1993; McGuire *et al.* 2002).

Ultimately, it would be ideal to be able to develop and maintain a landscape structure highly resilient to the stresses created by a changing climate, while at the same time providing for the greatest degree of native biodiversity and ecosystem services that were associated with historical conditions. Given the uncertainties of the effects of climate change on the complex range of microenvironments and the equally complex range of potential ecological responses to these changes, conservation goals are most likely to be met by returning the region to a structure and disturbance process more similar to its historical condition than the pattern we are now generating. Caution suggests that we recommend this stance until we understand more about the specific challenges of climate change to this region.

Climate change will clearly have direct implications for stand and landscape dynamics and wildlife habitat relationships in these high-latitude forests (Alaback and McClellan 1993; Daniels and Gray 2006; McGuire *et al.* 2002). Climatic variation has had clear consequences to forest dynamics in the past, in particular on windthrow patterns, flooding events, and fire disturbances, and should become even more important as the climate rapidly changes (Dale *et al.* 2001). Given that most forest species are near the northern limit of their geographical distribution, we would also expect that climate change will affect the persistence of individual species in the region. Modelling of rates of change in bioclimate envelopes for tree species suggests that some species will not be able to migrate quickly enough to remain within preferred climatic conditions and persist over time (Aitken *et al.* 2008). A well-known example of a species response to climatic changes in the region is Alaskan yellow cedar (*Callitropsis* [=*Chamaecyparis*] *nootkatensis*) decline (D'Amore *et al.* 2009). Alaskan yellow cedar or yellow cypress occurs from the Cascade Mountains in Oregon north through southeast Alaska, but it is most common and ecologically important in northern rainforests. It is a key component of peatland bogs and other poorly drained ecosystems, along with its close relative, western redcedar (*Thuja plicata*). Yellow cedar has been in notable decline on over 200,000 ha in northern southeast Alaska and shows a similar decline in northern British Columbia. Extensive work over many decades by P. E. Hennon and his colleagues suggests that the rapid recent decline is ultimately caused by a subtle change in climate (e.g., lack of persistent snowpack) that has led to freezing of fine roots; that in turn has led to a change in nutrient balance and associated biological factors. This has also resulted in a loss of competitive advantage relative to western redcedar (D'Amore *et al.* 2009).

Another key uncertainty for ecosystem responses to climate change is whether coarse-scale fire disturbances will become a more important factor in the disturbance ecology of the southern portion of the region, and how this may influence species interactions. If changes in storm patterns and frequencies occur as predicted, this could affect overall stand dynamics (Solomon *et al.* 2007). Of key concern will be the frequency of low-rainfall summer periods and their associated risks with fire and other stresses on rainforest-adapted species, as well as increases in fall storms, which affect the frequencies of both flooding and wind disturbances. Such events have occurred rarely as far north as southern southeast Alaska. Even a small change in their occurrence could have profound implications for landscape structure in these regions.

The overall pattern of forest development in northern coastal rainforests has always been influenced by both short-term and long-term climatic patterns (Gavin *et al.* 2003a; Gavin and Hu 2006; Lertzman *et al.* 1996; Veblen and Alaback 1996). Long lag times characterized previous responses of these forests to climatic variation, suggesting that historical landscape structures may have contributed to their relative resiliency. Historical landscapes were complex mosaics of mostly older multicanopied forests, but recent anthropogenic disturbances have created coarse-scale patchworks with dense secondary forests that appear to be particularly susceptible to windstorms and other disturbances, as has been found in other rainforest regions. Maintenance of stand and landscape legacies and moving these landscapes towards a finer-grained structure should therefore be useful interim strategies in helping promote resiliency of this forest under future climatic and direct human-caused stresses—until we can develop more specific knowledge on the localized effects of climate change (Franklin *et al.* 2007).

The scientific evidence on natural disturbance regimes indicates that ecologically sustainable forest practices should better approximate the structures and functioning of forests maintained by natural disturbance events such as windthrows. Knowledge generated by studying natural disturbance regimes in temperate rainforests over the past several decades suggests that one of the guiding principles for this region should be developing heterogeneous structures at stand and landscape scales that promote connectivity. Complex patchy structure has always characterized the temperate rainforests of southeast Alaska and adjacent coastal BC, and that pattern appears to be key to its ecological functioning as well. Clearcut logging creates a more homogenous and a more pronounced and persistent early successional stage than what results from gap dynamics in old-growth forests (Alaback 1982; Lindenmayer and Franklin 2002). Recent work on intense windthrow disturbances shows that the landscape pattern which results from clear-cut logging is more fragmented than what results from natural patterns of disturbance as well.

A sustainable forest conservation strategy that better maintains ecosystem services, such as wildlife habitat productivity and overall biodiversity, will require a high degree of structural legacies following logging, similar to what follows natural disturbances. This could involve careful design of reserves within and around timber harvest areas to promote connectivity of mid- and late-seral conditions for specific wildlife species, or in some cases it could involve a switch from clear-cut logging to increased reliance on variable retention strategies (Beese, this volume, chapter 9). Kimmins (2004) suggests that a mixture of harvest approaches, including clear-cutting, reserve retention, shelterwood, and group selection, may more closely reproduce landscape-level effects of natural disturbance on structure and pattern. Partial-cutting silvicultural strategies will need to be tailored more closely to the specifics of each site than is required with clear-cutting, including using precise models of windscapes, integrated with spatial data on soils, hydrology, and forest structure. Since the largest patches of highly productive forests were logged in the past century, restoration of these habitats will be of key importance to returning the landscape to a more productive structure and function as well. In the north and central coasts of BC, implementation of legislated ecosystem-based management requires ecosystem-level representation outside of harvested areas based on historical range of variability for that system, and additional stand-level retention of at least 15% of area. Both scales of retention will have to be evaluated over time for their utility in retaining landscape- and stand-level biodiversity and features characteristic of old growth for these forests.

In general, restoration strategies at the stand level will need to promote heterogeneity by creating or retaining a range of stand density and structures, using techniques such as thinning, gap creation, and the retention of unthinned thickets (Carey 2001). Since legacies of standing dead and downed woody material and the plant communities associated with them are key elements of the differences between clear-cut logging and windthrow disturbance, it will also be essential that these structures be retained or enhanced with restoration activities. This could be achieved with partial-retention strategies and transitioning these stands to a more complex multicanopy structure.

In contrast to most other forest regions in the world, the coastal North Pacific temperate rainforest still has many outstanding examples of relatively intact undisturbed forest, including whole watersheds (DellaSala 2011; Schoen and Dovichin 2007). These watersheds could play an increasingly important role in promoting forest conservation in this region, not only as reservoirs of biological diversity and as stepping stones or buffers between more intensively managed watersheds, but also as baseline areas from which we can continue to learn more about how these ecosystems respond to climate change and other environmental stressors. These watersheds can also play a critical role as baseline areas for restoration.

Conservation strategies that focus on legacy and landscape connectivity may appear to be similar to what has been called for in many forest regions, but the special challenge for southeast Alaska and the northern coast of BC will continue to be its geography. As an island archipelago with many isolated populations and habitats (Cook and MacDonald, this volume, chapter 2), many species at the northern limit of their range, and the vast majority of land area having unsuitable habitat for many species of interest (not to mention rugged topography, energy limitations, low nutrient availability, low solar radiation, and occasional deep snowpack), it will be particularly challenging to promote functional connectivity in the face of climate change. Thus, land managers and local residents will have to be even more skillful in developing landscape strategies than what would be required for regions that are inherently more connected and more productive. Despite the significant impacts from resource development activities during the past century, southeast Alaska and north coastal BC still retain globally significant conservation values and awe-inspiring landscapes. A scientifically based landscape-level strategy for conservation that better approximates natural disturbance regimes, retains key undisturbed watersheds, and considers social, economic, and ecological values should have great potential to improve the effectiveness of conservation in this special place, and serve as a model for conservation planning elsewhere.

ACKNOWLEDGMENTS

The USDA Forest Service's Tongass National Forest and Pacific Northwest Research Station provided support for some of the research reported here. The authors also thank the editors and reviewers for helpful comments and Audubon Alaska and the Nature Conservancy for supporting this synthesis effort.

5

Indigenous and Commercial Uses of the Natural Resources in the North Pacific Rainforest with a Focus on Southeast Alaska and Haida Gwaii

Lisa K. Crone and Joe R. Mehrkens

INTRODUCTION

In this chapter, we first examine historic indigenous uses of the natural resources of the region. Although other indigenous groups lived in the region, our focus is on the primary occupants of southeast Alaska and Haida Gwaii—the Tlingit and the Haida. We describe the arrival of the Tlingit and Haida and the territories they occupied, their socioeconomic structure, their use and trade of resources, and finally the changes to their land rights and resource use after Russian-European contact. Then we examine the past, present, and potential future commercial uses of the Tongass National Forest (hereinafter, Tongass) since its establishment in 1902 through 1907. The commercial uses addressed here include logging and wood products, mining, commercial fishing, tourism, and hydropower. We include comparisons with coastal British Columbia (BC) for the logging and wood products industries. The commercial uses affect noncommercial uses of the forest, such as subsistence, noncommercial ecosystem services, research, and nonuse values. These uses are harder to measure but no less important in attracting and keeping businesses and residents, drawing visitors to the region, or in other ways affecting the quality of life for current or future residents of the region.

ARRIVALS AND TERRITORIES

Archeological evidence reveals human presence in the region as far back as 13,000 years ago with continuous occupation during approximately the past 5,000 years (Erlandson *et al.* 2008; Pritzker 2000; Fedje and Mackie 2005). The timing, migration route, and place of origin of the first people to arrive in southeast Alaska are unknown (Kemp *et al.* 2007). Radiocarbon dating of sites used as Tlingit villages and fish camps on Admiralty Island reveal that these sites were used at least as long as the past 1,600 years (Moss *et al.* 1989). Additionally, weir stakes at one site on the island were radiocarbon-dated as more than 3,200 years old. Moss *et al.* (1989, 541) state, "While there is no way to directly link the 3,200 year old Favorite Bay Weir with Tlingit groups, we believe the hypothesis that Tlingit culture evolved in situ over a period of several thousand years should be considered." Remnants of a spruce root utility basket found near Thorne River was radiocarbon-dated at 5,450 ± 50 BP. The technique used on this basket is similar to twentieth-century basketry techniques used by the Tlingit and Haida (Carrlee 2009).

According to Tlingit belief and oral history, they have been in southeast Alaska since time immemorial. Their stories about how they migrated to this region usually have them originate at the source of a big river (such as the Alsek, Taku, Copper, Stikine, Unuk, Chikamin, Skeena, or Nass) from which they migrated down to the coast (Garfield 1947; De Laguna 1972; Keithahn 1973; Peck 1986; Langdon 1993; Hope and Thornton 2000). Some tribal leaders claim that the Tlingit were once part of the Tsimshian, and many authors believe that the oldest clans migrated north from Tsimshian territory in the Nass and Skeena river valleys of British Columbia (Swanton 1909; Paul 1979; Peck 1986; Emmons 1991; Langdon 1993; Pritzker 2000).

Haida occupation of Haida Gwaii, on the northern BC coast, dates to at least 10,600 years BP (Fedje *et al.* 2004); they arrived in southeast Alaska more recently. In the early to mid-1700s, a group of Haida emigrated to the southern end of Prince of Wales Island and became known as the Kaigani (Emmons 1991; Goldsmidt and Haas 1998). It is not clear whether this move to the north was peaceful. Some writers (Emmons 1991; Drucker 1955; Langdon 1993; Campbell 1989) suggest that the Tlingit were driven from south Prince of Wales, while Olson (1967) offers a contrary view. Contemporary Haida and Tlingit Natives claim that their oral histories indicate that the Tlingit welcomed the Haida ashore.

In 1887, about 800 Tsimshians followed William Duncan (their evangelical religious leader) from their village (Metlakatla) near Prince Rupert in British Columbia to Annette Island in southeast Alaska. Here they established a new village they called New Metlakatla (Dauenhauer and Dauenhauer 1994; Arctander 1909). Because the Tsimshian did not arrive in the region until after Russian-European contact, our focus here will be on the Tlingit and Haida.

The territory occupied by the Tlingit extended from the Nass River, BC, north to the coast just southeast of the Copper River delta, Alaska. This included almost all of the Alexander Archipelago, except the southernmost end of Prince of Wales Island. Tlingit also occupied the interior portions of British Columbia and the Yukon Territory. The Tlingit territory covered four major areas that represent ecological, linguistic, and cultural divisions. The southern Tlingit occupied the region from the Nass River north to Frederick Sound. North of Frederick Sound to Cape Spencer, including Glacier Bay and the Lynn Canal, were the northern Tlingit. North of Cape Spencer, along the coast of the Gulf of Alaska to Controller Bay and Kayak Island, were the gulf coast Tlingit. The inland Tlingit lived along the large interior lakes and the drainage of the Taku River as well as in the southern Yukon Territory and subsisted in a manner similar to their Athabascan neighbors, although both the Teslin and Taku Tlingit had access to abundant salmon. Inland, the Tlingit occupied major river corridors that flow into the Pacific Ocean, including the Alsek, Tatshenshini, Chilkat, Taku, and Stikine rivers (Pritzker 2000).

The extent of territory occupied by the Kaigana Haidas is not clear (Moss 2008). Norton (1981, 436) wrote, "The Haida had established villages at Kasaan on the eastern shore of Prince of Wales Island and on Sukkwan, Dall, and Long Islands. These islands and waterways, along with the rocky offshore islands, Forester, Lowrie, Petrel and Wolf . . . were their primary fishing and gathering grounds."

SOCIOECONOMIC STRUCTURE

The Tlingit and Haida shared similar customs and habits. Both groups had cooperative socioeconomic systems with well-established property rights—especially for names, oral histories, and cultural items (Krause 1956). Tribal/clan territory, winter villages, summer camps, salmon streams, trade routes, food gathering areas, as well as sacred sites associated with cultural events were considered property. Goldschmidt and Hass (1998, 7) wrote, "the customs of the Tlingit and Haida with respect to property ownership are more closely akin to those of industrial society than are nearly any other aboriginal people in the territory now included in the United States."

The Tlingit and Haida were nations in the sense that the people belonging to each group had a common language, a common name, and a common set of customs, traditions, and religious beliefs (Goldschmidt and Hass 1998). In British Columbia, in fact, the Tlingit and Haida (and other aboriginal groups) are referred to as First Nations, and recent land-use planning exercises between these First Nations and BC's provincial government have proceeded on a government-to-government basis (Price *et al.* 2009). In southeast Alaska, the tribe was a geographical grouping rather than a political organization (Rogers 1960). Each tribe had at least one permanent village and some had as many as eight villages. The Tlingit referred to themselves as being from a particular *kwaan*, which means they are occupants of a particular area (Dauenhauer and Dauenhauer 1994). Thornton (2008, 44) wrote that the term *kwaan* "marks Tlingit individuals as inhabitants of a certain living space consisting of the total lands and waters used and controlled by clans residing in a particular winter village." Over time, many Tlingit villages consolidated into larger and more complex communities. In Haida Gwaii, many villages were abandoned in the nineteenth century owing to population decline because of disease; survivors relocated to Skidegate and Massett (Gough 1989).

The Tlingit and Haida had matrilineal societies, with a person's identity established through their mother's lineage. Both the Tlingit and Haida clans organized into two moieties. The Tlingit moieties were Raven and Eagle/Wolf. The Haida moieties were Raven and Eagle. The moieties were composed of clans, and clans were composed of houses or house groups. Each clan had a name, which usually denoted its place of origin, a story of its genesis, and a history of its migration (Oberg 1973). A Tlingit or Haida child is born into their mother's moiety, clan, and house group. The socioeconomic function of moieties transcended the entire culture and was the main mechanism in reciprocity of wealth distribution and redistribution, enforcing laws, settling disputes, and the rearing of children (Goldschmidt and Hass 1998). In a single Tlingit or Haida village, there were often members of the two moieties, local divisions of two or more clans, various numbers of house groups associated with each local clan division, and various numbers of families associated with each house group (Oberg 1973). A principal purpose of moieties was to prevent inter-marriages within a moiety.

The house group was the basic unit of Tlingit society. Dauenhauer and Dauenhauer (1994) suggested it is best to think of house groups as a kinship term, realizing that not all members of a house group physically resided in the ancestral house and that not all residents of a clan house are members of that house group. They also note that as house groups grew in popula-tion and stature they sometimes became independent clans: "Thus, many now-independent clans began as house groups of an older clan" (Dauen-hauer and Dauenhauer 1994, 9). A house group had two to three social classes: nobles, commoners, and slaves. However, each house was also home to more loosely related relatives, including other females belonging to other named houses, clans, and moieties. Clans or house groups owned use rights to physical property, such as salmon streams, halibut banks, hunting grounds, sealing rocks, berry areas, shellfish beds, canoe-landing beaches, and physical landmarks. They also had rights to symbolic prop-erty, including names, stories, songs, regalia, crests, and other cultural icons such as clan ancestors (Thornton 2008). Some oral histories describe regional resource use (e.g., fishing, berry picking, or hunting) by a particu-lar clan or house group in particular locales for more than two thousand years. Each house group acted much like a modern corporation with spe-cialized trade-goods, tribal crests, and wealth redistribution ceremonies (similar to a product line, trademark, and charitable giving) (Miller, n.d.).

Intermarriage between clans, tribes, or even trading partners formed an elaborate kinship network. Clan relations extending beyond the bound-aries of any one community or tribe were recognized, so that a clan mem-ber with a relative in a distant village could use that clan's property, after asking permission from the local clan head in that village (Goldschmidt and Hass 1998). This socioeconomic structure facilitated trade.

INDIGENOUS USES OF NATURAL RESOURCES
Trees

Tlingits (and Haidas) south of Fredrick Sound used western redcedar (*Thuja plicata*) for nearly all of their industrial and domestic needs. They used the wood for houses, canoes, utensils such as bowls and spoons, bentwood boxes, drums, chests, body armor, totem poles, mortuary col-umns, bows, quivers, and carvings (Drucker 1955; Holm 1984; Stewart 1984;

Emmons 1991; Turner 2004). Redcedar bark was used to make baskets, mats, clothing, shrouds, fishing lines, cordage, and as splints for broken bones (Emmons 1991). Cedar bark mats were used for bedding, floor covering, room dividers, insulation, tablecloths, and canoe covers (Oberg 1973; Holm 1984; Stewart 1984; Langdon 1993).

Redcedar is rare north of Fredrick Sound; consequently, the Tlingits living there primarily used Sitka spruce (*Picea sitchensis*) roots for basketry. Spruce root baskets were used for gathering and preparing food (picking and cleaning berries, boiling fish or meat, etc.), storage, packing, drinking cups, feast dishes, bailers, and baby carriers (De Laguna 1972; Norton 1981; Emmons 1991; Turner 2004). Natives from Yakutat, Hoonah, and Sitka were considered the best basket makers (Newton and Moss 2005). Yakutat baskets were traded from Vancouver Island, BC, to Kodiak Island, Alaska. Both rain hats for everyday use and ceremonial hats were made from spruce roots. Spruce roots were also used for lashings, cords, ropes, and fishnets (De Laguna 1960, Emmons 1991, Thornton 1998). The Haida used a molded spruce-root hook for catching black cod (*Anoplopoma fimbria*) (Drucker 1965).

Spruce wood was used for houses, poles, retaining planks, canoes, oil crates, fish traps, bows, arrows, body armor, spearing and gaffing shafts, herring rakes, cooking tongs, firewood, and for smoking foods (Gorman 1896; De Laguna 1972, 1990; Norton 1981; Holm 1984; Emmons 1991; Thornton 1998). Straight young trees were used to make spits for roasting salmon (Norton 1981). The pitch was used as a fire starter; as a glue, filler, and sealer for watercraft and food storage containers; for both external and internal medicine; and as a chewing gum (Alaska Department of Natural Resources 1977; Norton 1981; Kuhnlein and Turner 1991; Thornton 1998). Fresh young spruce tips were used for making jams, syrups, and teas (Thornton 1998). The cambium was eaten (De Laguna 1972; Alaska Department of Natural Resources 1977). Spruce branches were used to slap boys on the back to toughen them up (Kayaani Commission 2006).

Alaskan yellow cedar (*Callitropsis* [=*Chamaecyparis*] *nootkatensis*) wood was used for plank houses, memorial poles, canoes, canoe paddles, bentwood boxes, drums, chests, bowls, dishes, bailers, masks, household utensils of various kinds, halibut hooks, and arrows (Gorman 1896; Holm 1984; De Laguna 1990; Turner 2004; Newton and Moss 2005; Kayaani Commission 2006). Yellow cedar was also preferred for carving; many ceremonial objects, such as hats, masks, staffs, dance wands, rattles, shaman's figures, and feast dishes were carved from this wood (Gorman 1896; Holm 1984; Stewart 1984). Bark was used for baskets, oil crates, oil skimmers, clothing, and both external and internal medicine (Stewart 1984; Newton and Moss 2005; Kayaani Commission 2006). The ashes of small pieces of yellow cedar bark were combined with locally cultivated tobacco to make snuff (Peck 1986; De Laguna 1990). Roots were used for the framework in baskets and hats (Gorman 1896).

Western hemlock (*Tsuga heterophylla*) wood was used for firewood, fish traps, bows, arrows, bailers, spear and harpoon shafts, wedges, hammers, cooking tongs, and smoking fish (driftwood hemlock preferred) (De Laguna 1972, 1990; Keithahn 1973; Emmons 1991; Newton and Moss 2005). Hemlock needles were used for both internal and external medicine and for preserving and seasoning food (Newton and Moss 2005; Alaska Department of Natural Resources 1977). The cambium was processed and eaten. The boughs were used for collecting herring roe and for removing worms from cod (Schroeder and Kookesh 1990a; Thornton 1998; Newton and Moss 2005). The bark was used for shelters and houses, for drying racks for berries, as medicine, for tanning hides, and to make dyes (De Laguna 1972; Emmons 1991).

Red alder (*Alnus rubra*) wood was used to make paddles, masks, war helmets and armor, ceremonial hats, rattles, bowls, dishes, spoons, halibut hooks, harpoon and spear shafts, for smoking fish, and for dyes (Emmons 1991; Drucker 1955; Holm 1984; Thornton 1998; Gorman 1896; Newton and Moss 2005; Turner 2004). The bark was used to make a medicinal tonic and dyes (Schroeder and Kookesh 1990b). The Haida may have used alder charcoal for tattooing (Curtis 1916). Additional trees and shrubs that provided important resources included Sitka alder (*Alnus viridis*), Pacific yew (*Taxus brevifolia*), and western crabapple (*Malus fusca*) (Gorman 1896; Keithahn 1973; Oberg 1973; Alaska Department of Natural Resources 1977; Holm 1984; Turner 1995; Kayaani Commission 2006).

Food

Food was a central part of Tlingit and Haida culture; the land and ocean provided abundant resources, many of which were available year round. No other food resource received as much emphasis as salmon; all five Pacific salmon species (chinook [*Oncorhynchus tshwawytscha*], sockeye [*O. nerka*], pink [*O. goruscha*], coho [*O. kisutch*], and chum [*O. keta*]) were harvested (De Laguna 1990; Thornton 1998). Other fish species, either eaten or used for oil, including Pacific halibut (*Hippoglossus stenolepis*), Pacific herring (*Clupea pallasi*), and eulachon (*Thaleichthys pacficus*), are detailed in Oberg (1973), De Laguna (1990), Schroeder and Kookesh (1990b), Emmons (1991), Thornton (1998), and Newton and Moss (2005). Marine invertebrates eaten included a variety of clams and cockles, crabs, chitons, limpets, mussels, octopus, sea cucumbers, squid, sea urchins, and shrimp (De Laguna 1972; Schroeder and Kookesh 1990b; Goldschmidt and Haas 1998; Thornton 1998; Newton and Moss 2005).

Land animals eaten included brown bear (*Ursus arctos*) and black bear (*Ursus americanus*), moose (*Alces alces*), Sitka black-tailed deer (*Odocoileus hemionus sitkensis*), mountain goat (*Oreamnos americanus*), Dall sheep (*Ovis dalli*), hoary marmot (*Marmota caligata*), porcupine (*Erethizon dorsatum*), beaver (*Castor canadensis*), snowshoe hare (*Lepus americanus*), and red squirrel (*Tamiasciurus hudsonicus*) (Oberg 1973; Alaska Department of Natural Resources 1977; Dhe Laguna 1990; Schroeder and Kookesh 1990b; Emmons 1991). In an excavation in northern Haida Gwaii, terrestrial animals recovered from food residues included caribou (*Rangifer tarandus*), black bear, dog (*Canis familiaris*), and river otter (*Lutra canadensis*) (Christensen and Stafford 2005). Marine mammals eaten included fur seals (*Callorhinus ursinus*), harbor seals (*Phoca vitulina*), sea lions (*Eumetopias jubatus*), sea otters (*Enhydra lutris*), and porpoise and whales when they washed up on shore (De Laguna 1972; Oberg 1973; Emmons 1991). Birds eaten (flesh or eggs) included a variety of waterfowl, ptarmigan (*Lagopus lagopus*), grouse (*Falcipennis canadensis* and *Dendragapus obscurus*), gulls (*Larus* spp.), loons (*Gavia* spp.), sandhill crane (*Grus canadensis*), great blue heron (*Ardea herodias*), tufted puffin (*Fratercula cirrhata*), and murrelets (*Brachyramphus* spp.) (De Laguna 1972; Oberg 1973; Schroeder and Kookesh 1990b; Emmons 1991; Newton and Moss 2005; Kaayani Commission 2006).

Marine plants eaten included seaweed, kelp, and hair grass (Schroeder and Kookesh 1990b; Newton and Moss 2005; Kaayani Commission 2006). Various berry species used for food or medicine are described in Norton (1981), Schroeder and Kookesh (1990b), Turner (2004), Newton and Moss (2005), and Kaayani Commission (2006). Many other plants were used as food, for teas, for cooking other foods, or for medicinal purposes, with specific plants and their uses detailed in De Laguna (1972), Norton (1981),

Schroeder and Kookesh (1990b), Thornton (1998), Turner (2004), Newton and Moss (2005), and Kaayani Commission (2006).

The Tlingit hunted or trapped black bear, fox, mountain goat, wolf (*Canis lupis*), wolverine (*Gulo gulo*), mink (*Neovison vison*), river otter, beaver, lynx (*Lynx canadensis*), muskrat (*Ondatra zibethicus*), ermine (*Mustela erminea)*, seal, sea otter, and sea lion for their pelts (Krause 1956, Oberg 1973, Schroeder and Kookesh 1990b, Emmons 1991).

Oberg (1973), De Laguna (1972, 1990), and others have detailed the annual cycle of production of the Tlingit.

> *In the aboriginal Tlingit economy, food was the dominant project in terms not only of time allocation, but also ideology. . . . Specific foods are harvested and processed at specific times of the year depending on abundance, distribution, accessibility, and need. . . . However, it is important to note that each village's seasonal round—indeed that of every house group— varied to a degree as a result of micro-ecological differences affecting the factors listed above. (Thornton 2008, 119–120)*

Minerals

Pure native copper was obtained through trade from Natives in the Copper River region. Copper was made into arrowheads, lance points, awls, scrapers, tiny nails, jewelry (bracelets, necklaces, pendants, and nose rings), breastplates, and ornaments (De Laguna 1972: Emmons 1991). It was scarce, highly prized, and expensive to obtain. The most valuable copper object was the hammer shield–shaped "copper." Only clan or house group heads owned coppers, but they really belonged to the lineage or family. They were displayed, bought, sold, given away, or even destroyed to humiliate rivals at potlatches (Emmons 1991). Copper lost some of its value when Russian and European traders made ordinary copper, silver, and gold readily available (Krause 1956).

Iron was not smelted along the North Pacific coast, but early Russian and European explorers noted that Natives possessed knives and bracelets made of iron. Most of this iron came from shipwrecked debris brought to the Alaska coast by the Japanese current. In 1741 Steller observed Aleuts from the Shumagin Islands with iron knives (Emmons 1991). Moreover, Holmberg (1985) and Jochelson (1933) cite Kodiak oral histories indicating that Native use of drift iron predated initial Russian contact. They also speculate that the westernmost Aleuts may have even traded with the Chinese, Japanese, or early Russian adventurers. The Tlingit also used iron from meteorites that landed in the area (Holm 1984).

Indigenous Trade

With regular travel up the coastal mainland rivers, the Tlingit developed extensive trade networks with Athabascan tribes of the interior and commonly intermarried with them. Certain clans and villages had monopolies on the trade routes into the interior (Oberg 1973). De Laguna (1972), Oberg (1973), Emmons (1991), and Thornton (1998) provide details on specific items exchanged between the Tlingit and Athabascan tribes, the Tlingit and the Haida, the Tlingit and the Tsimshian, the island and the mainland Tlingit, and the southern and northern Tlingit. The Tlingit and other tribes used dentalia shell as a unit of currency; the Haida used slaves as a unit of value (Krause 1956).

Native cultures in southeast Alaska and northern British Columbia flourished and were sophisticated long before contact with Russians and Europeans. These people thrived over many generations by understanding and adapting to the environment. This in turn allowed for a broad array of natural resource uses and a strong cultural identity with natural resources. Equally important was their ability to specialize in and take full advantage of any comparative advantage their clan, house group, or family territory provided. The Tlingit and Haida had to be very industrious to accumulate sufficient surpluses to subsist and manage extensive trade. A good deal of the Tlingit/Haida success was due to (1) their highly developed sense of property rights, (2) their sense of fair value, and (3) a belief in duality (the moiety system).

PERIOD OF TRANSITION

Alexie Chirikov made the initial Russian contact with the Tlingits in 1741. He was followed by the Spanish (Bruno de Hezeta [1775] and Alejandro Malispina [1791]), the French (Jean Francois Galaup, Comte de La Pérouse [1786]), and the English (George Vancouver [1793]) (Krause 1956). Initial European contact with the Haida on Haida Gwaii was contemporaneous: the Spaniards Juan Pérez (1774) and Juan Francisco de la Bodega y Quadra

(1775) were followed by a series of British, French, and American explorers, including George Vancouver in 1793.

In 1799, the Russian America fur company built a fort at Sitka, but the Tlingit defeated them in 1802. The Russians rebuilt the fort in 1804 and stayed until 1867, when Russia sold Alaska to the United States (Drucker 1965). There was no Native consent or involvement in the US purchase. The issue of Native land claims was not directly addressed until 1971.

From 1867 to 1968, the Tlingit and Haida became more and more disenfranchised from their traditional territories and resources. This was especially true after industrial fisheries and timber operations began in the late 1800s and mid-1900s. In addition to losing places, traditional and customary uses came under attack as well. Missionary efforts and government policies were designed to assimilate, not accommodate, Natives' customary and traditional uses. Potlatches and the speaking of Native languages in schools were prohibited in both Canada and the United States in the late nineteenth century (Rogers 1960; Langdon 1993); discrimination was common (Silverman *et al.* 2009). Perhaps the most disastrous impact was the introduction of Caucasian diseases, which killed more than half of the Tlingit and Haida people (Goldin and Matsen 1996). The estimated Alaska Native population in southeast Alaska was 11,800 from 1740 to 1780, but it fell to only 5,685 by 1909 (Rogers 1960). The population of Haida on Haida Gwaii was reduced from at least 10,000 precontact to no more than 600 by 1900.

In 1947, the Alaska Territorial Legislature urged Congress to settle fairly Alaska Native land claims (Mackovjak 2008). The *Tongass Timber Act of 1947* was passed to allow large timber sales on the Tongass to proceed despite the uncertainty of future Native land claims. Federal stumpage receipts were to be put into a special fund and were to remain in escrow until the land claims were settled (Rakestraw 1981). Seeking compensation for the loss of hunting and fishing rights and the value of the more than 20 million acres of land appropriated by the US, the Tlingit and Haida filed a suit against the US government in the US Court of Claims on October 1, 1947 (*New York Times* 1959). In 1959, the five-judge court unanimously agreed with the Tlingit and Haida, and in 1969, the Central Council of Tlingit and Haida Indian Tribes of Alaska (as the representative of the approximately 7,000 Tlingits and Haidas included in the suit) was awarded $7.5 million from the Tongass National Forest Timber Fund. The court also ruled that the Indians had title to 2,634,744 acres in Alaska (*New York Times* 1959; Naske and Slotnick 1979; Haycox 2007).

The court found that, by virtue of unextinguished Aboriginal title, the
Tlingit and Haida Indians of Alaska had owned all of the land in the
Alexander Archipelago in 1867. . . . The court found further that between
1905 and 1907 the United States had extinguished much of this title, all
but 2.6 million acres of nearly 18 million acres, in the creation of the
Tongass National Forest. (Haycox 2007, 93)

In 1966 Secretary of the Interior Stewart L. Udall imposed a land freeze until Native land claims could be settled, and in 1971, the Alaska Native Claims Settlement Act (1971; hereinafter ANCSA) was passed. This act was designed to permanently extinguish aboriginal land claims (with minor exceptions such as the Annette Indian Reservation). As compensation, Alaska Natives received $962.5 million in a cash settlement and rights to select 44 million acres of federal land. The cash settlement was on a per capita basis so southeast Alaska Natives received $250 million. Ironically, the primary motivation to pass ANCSA was to clear the way for the Trans-Alaska pipeline. Although the ANCSA legislation passed, Native lands claims were far from over.

Under ANCSA approximately 571,000 acres of the Tongass National Forest have been conveyed to the Alaska Natives. However, ANSCA did not create village or urban corporations for about 4,300 (landless) Natives in five southeast Alaska communities (Haines, Tenakee Springs, Petersburg, Wrangell, and Ketchikan). These groups are now seeking urban corporation status, the entitlement of 23,040 acres, and $650,000 for each new corporation (Golden 2009b).

Sealaska Corporation, from southeast Alaska, is one of thirteen regional corporations created under ANCSA. Sealaska is currently seeking to finalize their ANCSA land entitlement from Tongass lands that are outside the original selection areas set aside under ANCSA. They are seeking legislation to obtain (1) up to 85,000 acres of timberlands to continue their log export business, (2) 5,000 acres in various future sites for tourism and renewable energy development (hydro, tidal, geothermal), and (3) up to 3,600 acres of sacred and cultural sites (US Congress 2009).

In BC, treaties have not been established with the Haida and Tlingit and most other First Nations. In the 1990s, BC committed to negotiating treaties with its First Nations, and the BC Treaty Commission Process was established. The Haida are in "Stage 3" treaty negotiations (following statements of intent and procedural agreements; the goal of Stage 3 is to negotiate a framework agreement). Land-use agreements have been established for central and north coast BC (the "Great Bear Rainforest") and for Haida Gwaii. These government-to-government (Provincial Government to First Nations governments) agreements establish broad land-use zones (including protected areas) over millions of acres (Price *et al.* 2009). Land-use planning processes are parallel to, and "without prejudice" to, ongoing treaty negotiations.

COMMERCIAL USES OF THE TONGASS: 1900 TO PRESENT

Unlike the indigenous uses of the region's natural resources, which largely took place within the region, commercial uses of the Tongass resources largely involved exporting them from the region or, in the case of tourism, attracting visitors to the region.

Timber and Forest Products

The prospects for a large-scale timber and wood products industry in southeast Alaska have always faced a number of obstacles. Among them are high operating costs due to a relatively severe climate, difficult terrain, the physical characteristics of the resource, the need to set up and supply logging camps at remote locations, the need to transport logs long distances to mills and products long distances to markets, the absence of integrated road and rail networks, and high labor and other factor costs (Crone 2007). Owing to the lack of previous large-scale harvest or other major stand replacing disturbances such as fire, almost all of the Tongass commercial forest land was in old-growth stands. These stands contained both high-value sawtimber trees and low-quality trees suitable only for fiber production. As one economist stated, Alaska has the most valuable and some of the least valuable softwood trees in the world (Flora 2003). Most early industry proponents concurred that to establish a viable large-scale industry in the region, uses and markets for both the high- and low-value components of the timber resource were required.

Pulp production was the US Forest Service's solution for utilizing the low-value components. Mackovjak (2008) suggests that the "wood pulp agenda for the Tongass" probably had its roots in Bernard Fernow's report on Alaska's forests following the 1899 Harriman expedition, but he credits

Royal Kellogg with tying the production of pulp to stewardship of the forest. Mackovjak (2008, 75) cited the following from a 1910 Kellogg publication: "The annual growth of the coast forests is far in excess of the local needs, and unless methods of utilization are developed which will result in the export of forest products, these forests cannot be handled rightly. . . . Utilization for other purposes than for lumber should be encouraged. The most promising of these is for pulp. Both spruce and hemlock are undoubtedly good pulp woods, and taken together, they comprise almost the entire forest." Proponents both within and external to the Forest Service also believed that clear-cutting was the best way to convert the "all aged overmature and defective" old-growth stands to "thrifty managed" second-growth stands.

Despite vigorous attempts by many parties to promote the industry, it took more than 40 years for this pulp dream to materialize. Earlier attempts and failures are documented in Mackovjack (2008), Rakestraw (1981), and Haycox (1990). The first roll of pulp was produced in May of 1954 at the Ketchikan Pulp Company's (KPC) mill in Ward Cove; production at Alaska Pulp Company's (APC) mill near Sitka began in late 1959. The start up of these pulp companies with their associated sawmill operations and their 50–year cutting rights marked a dramatic increase in the scale of harvesting on the Tongass (fig. 5.01). The pulp companies were granted subsidies in the form of a guaranteed 50–year supply of cheap timber. They were also exempted from state and local taxes under the Alaska Industrial Incentive Act of 1957 (Crone 2004; Tussing *et al.* 1968).

Also important were the social engineering and regional economic development promises promulgated by the Forest Service and others in their promotion of the industry. In 1926, Congress prohibited the export of round logs from the Tongass (Exportation of Timber Act of 1926). In 1957, the Forest Service defended this primary manufacturing rule, which was designed to allow the region to capture more of the economic benefits associated with the timber resource.

> *It has been the policy of the Department to refuse to authorize export in the unmanufactured form of logs cut from the national forests of Alaska for these reasons:*
>
> 1. *Increased development of Alaska will have to come largely through more industry, which in turn must be based on the resources as are present there.*

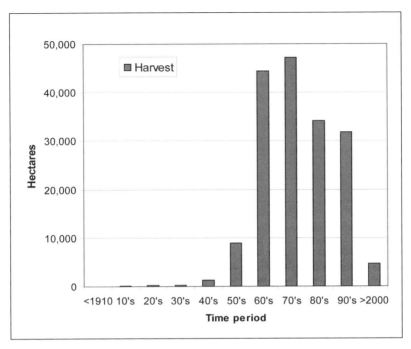

FIGURE 5.01. Hectares of timber harvested on the Tongass National Forest. From USDA Forest Service (2008d, exhibit 6).

2. *Especially in southeastern Alaska, one of the natural resources which can make a substantial contribution to more industrial development is the forest resource.*

3. *The purpose of industrial development is to expand the economic base, to provide jobs, and to increase population.*

4. *Stable development of Alaska requires that such development be based on year-round activity rather than seasonal activity.*

5. *The harvesting of logs only would result in a limited contribution to the Territorial economy because of a relatively small number of jobs and the seasonal character of the work.*

6. *The processing of logs into lumber or pulp in the Territory would contribute a significant number of jobs and would provide work that can be on a year-round basis or a near year-round basis.*

7. *From the above, the Department has concluded that because it is in the public interest to foster the development of Alaska it is proper for the Department to insist on use of national forest timber*

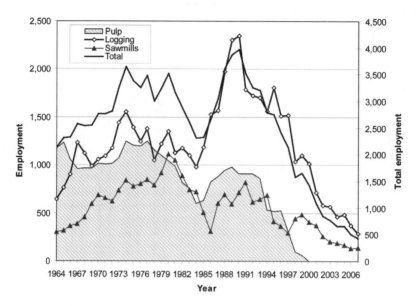

FIGURE 5.02. Employment in Alaska's pulp, logging, and sawmill industries, 1964–2007. Figure adapted from Crone (2004) and updated with data from Alaska Department of Labor and Workforce Development (2009).

> resources in such a way that they will make the greatest feasible
> contribution to the Territory's economy. Such a course is also in
> the interest of national defense. (Rogers 1960, 296)

In Ketchikan, Sitka, and other southeast Alaska areas with sawmills or logging operations, employment opportunities and populations did increase significantly following the opening of the pulp mills. In 1957, KPC had approximately 407 hourly employees and 100 salaried positions at the plant itself. During the logging season it employed about 200 men in the woods, not including those employed as independent logging contractors (Rogers 1960). In 1960, APC was reported to employ 440 workers in its plant, 75 people for its own logging operations and about 150 people who worked for independent logging contractors (Mackovjack 2008). Figure 5.02 shows employment in Alaska's pulp, logging, and sawmill sectors from 1964 to 2007.

The dramatic increase in logging employment beginning in 1984 is largely attributable to harvests from Native corporation lands that began in 1979 (fig. 5.03). With the exception of 1988, Native harvests have exceeded

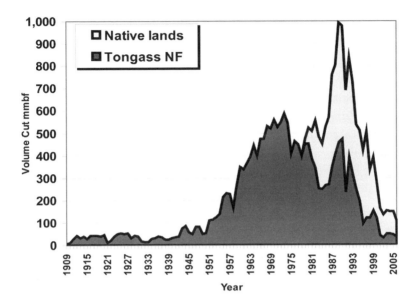

FIGURE 5.03. Timber harvests in million board feet (mmbf) from the Tongass National Forest and Native lands in southeast Alaska, 1909–2007. Figure by Crone with data from Knapp (1992), USDA Forest Service, Alaska Region, "Cut and Sold Reports," various years; and USDA Forest Service (2000, 2006).

Tongass harvests in every year since 1986. Native harvests are not subject to the primary manufacture rule, so most of their logs are exported in the round rather than processed locally. As of 2007, about 827,000 acres had been cut in southeast Alaska from all ownerships. At least 28% of the original large-tree forests in the region had been cut, but the actual percentage may be more than 50% (Albert and Schoen 2007a). The amount of Native corporation timber harvest is about 320,000 acres or 39% of the total harvest from all ownerships.

The APC mill shut down in September of 1993, and the KPC mill closed in March of 1997. Reasons for their closure include (1) reduced harvests from both the Tongass and Native lands, (2) decreased world demand for their product (dissolving pulp), (3) the *Tongass Timber Reform Act of 1990* (TTRA), which removed many of the direct and indirect subsidies the pulp companies had been granted in their 50–year contracts and in the *Alaska National Interest Lands Conservation Act of 1981* (ANILCA), (4) increased harvest costs because most of the accessible timber had already been harvested, and (5) their inability to compete in the global market place with newer, less polluting and more efficient mills (Crone 2004, 2005). Regarding TTRA and ANILCA, Crone wrote the following:

> The Tongass Timber Reform Act of 1990 *(TTRA) passed in response to concerns about the environment and below-cost timber sales, revised the long-term contracts to make timber sales authorized under these contracts more consistent with independent timber sales in terms of planning, management requirements, and environmental assessment procedures.* The Alaska National Interest Lands Conservation Act of 1980 *(ANILCA) had set aside 5.4 million acres of the Tongass for wilderness. To offset the potential decrease in timber harvest associated with the wilderness designation and the selection of land by Native corporations and the state, the act included a section that set the target timber supply from the Tongass National Forest at 4.5 billion board feet (BBF) per decade, and included an annual appropriation of at least $40 million to fund the road preparations, cultural treatments, and logging systems to maintain this offer level (Morse 2000).* The TTRA removed the 4.5 BBF per decade requirement, *decreased the annual appropriation to $4 million, and directed the Forest Service to set the harvest level each year to meet "market demand" and sell timber at a profitable price. (2004, 50)*

Today, proponents of a large-scale timber and wood products industry in southeast Alaska find themselves in much the same position as before the pulp mills opened—searching for a use and market for the low-value material.

> When the pulp mills closed, the marginal position of the Alaska wood products manufacturers in the cyclical and global wood products industry became more evident and acute. As high-cost producers, Alaska manufacturers feel the effects of market downturns first. With the pulp mills no longer ready markets for their mill residues and chips, Alaska firms must now compete with more efficient and lower-cost suppliers from other regions in the global marketplace. (Crone 2004, 52)

Due to the lack of markets for low-value timber, in 1998 the Forest Service instituted an optional removal clause, whereby timber purchasers would no longer have to remove the low-value logs from the woods, thereby reducing logging and hauling costs. Section 318 of the Consolidated Appropriations Resolution of 2003 mandated that timber on the Tongass could be offered for sale only if it appraised positively; each subsequent annual appropriations act has included this requirement. In an attempt to get more sales to appraise positively, the Tongass adopted a new policy called the Limited Interstate Shipments Policy in 2007. This policy represents a partial retraction of the primary manufacture rule. Under the policy, the regional forester authorized the shipment of certain sizes and grades of Sitka spruce and western hemlock sawlogs to the continental US. The total amount of logs that can be shipped from a single sale is limited to 50% of the total sawlog contract harvested of all species in that particular sale (Bschor 2007). Despite these attempts to improve the economics of timber sales and the continued $4 million annual appropriation from Congress, many sales on the Tongass continue to receive no bids. Forest Service information from fiscal years 1998 to 2007 shows that 45% of the Tongass timber volume offered for sale never received a single bid. Moreover, much of this volume was repackaged, offered, and sold, but nearly half of it ended up in defaulted or cancelled sales (Mehrkens 2009).

Currently the sawmilling industry in southeast Alaska is a small industry producing limited amounts of valuable products. Decreased supplies of old-growth timber from other regions have resulted in a scarcity of some traditional solid wood products in domestic markets; the majority of southeast Alaska wood products are flowing to these markets. Although some cants are still being produced and shipped to export markets, in the past two years 80% of the wood products have been sold in domestic markets. Small amounts (8%–10%) of the products remain in Alaska, but the majority (70% in 2006) is being shipped to the lower 48 states (Brackley and Crone 2009).

Most of the wood products that are staying in Alaska are coming from smaller mills. Petersen and Bruns (2005, 70) wrote, "Mill owners in southeast Alaska are no longer satisfied with shipping their raw material out of state, only to see others capitalize on the 'value-added' portion of the commodity. Dry kilns have been installed at various mill sites, planers and pattern machines have been put in place, and sawmill owners are looking at an altogether different market than they did 10 years ago." One company, for example, sells directly to a variety of end users, including a custom hot tub manufacturer from Haines, a furniture maker from Juneau, and other custom woodworkers who rely on consistent quality of wood.

The manufacture of pellets or other wood-based heating products in southeast Alaska is being considered as an option to reduce local communities' dependence on petroleum products for heating. The city of Craig recently installed a wood-fired boiler system to supplement propane and oil heating systems for their municipal pool water, pool building, and elementary and middle school buildings. They expect this system to reduce their heating costs by $40,000 to $60,000 a year (Alaska Department of Natural Resources 2008). This facility uses residues from local sawmills. One of the larger mills in southeast Alaska is currently selling firewood in Ketchikan and on a trial basis in other southeast Alaska communities (*Juneau Empire* 2008).

In the past few years, some parties have promoted the idea of moving the Tongass timber program away from the harvest of old growth into harvesting second growth. This may be politically desirable, but the current age and composition of second-growth stands and the fact that so many potential old-growth sales fail makes it difficult to believe that such harvests would be profitable now or in the foreseeable future. Southeast Alaska's comparative advantage has always been the uniqueness (scarcity elsewhere) of the high-quality component of its old growth. The second-growth resource as it exists today is more of a commodity product. Its value cannot overcome the higher costs associated with operating in southeast Alaska and transporting products to markets. On average, second growth is composed of lower quality timber than old growth. In addition, many roads that access second growth have not been maintained; reconstructing them will be expensive. The Tongass has some of the highest road construction costs in the national forest system, and roads are the biggest contributor to uneconomic timber sales. In the mid-1980s, a new planning tool called a Logging System Transportation Analyses (LSTA) became available. The tool allowed for a better design of the total sale layout—that is the first, second, and third harvest entries. By paying more attention to the second and third harvest entries, total costs could be reduced up to 28% (USDA Forest Service 1985). LSTA was also used to evaluate first-entry roads as a long-term investment. Most of the best and most accessible timber was harvested from first-entry roads. However, this practice impacted economics for the second harvest entry, which was uneconomic or barely a break-even situation. The most significant factor in this result was the amount of new road construction and reconstruction of the initial roads. The third harvest entry was even more uneconomic.

Simply stated, the problems were high road costs and the lower quality and value of the remaining old growth.

The implication for future harvest of second-growth forests is that high road reconstruction costs will persist. If old-growth harvests are uneconomic and require subsidies, second-growth harvests are likely to require even larger subsidies because second growth, unlike the high value component of the old-growth resource, is a commodity product that must compete with lower-cost products from many other regions. For more on this issue, see Beck Group (2009) and Alexander *et al.* (2010).

Forest management on the Tongass continues to be a controversial issue on a national scale. For a more detailed discussion of national forest management conflict and political decision making on the Tongass, see Nie (2006).

Crone (2007) discussed the similarities between the southeast Alaska and coastal BC timber resources and wood products industries and much of the following comparison comes directly from that paper. The forested lands in these two areas have similar landforms, climatic conditions, and timber type characteristics. Temperate rainforest, intact watersheds, islands, fjords, rugged shorelines, and steep mountainous terrain characterize much of north coastal BC and southeast Alaska. Many areas in both regions are unroaded and sparsely populated. Given their biogeoclimatic similarities, it is not surprising that most of the commercial timber species in southeast Alaska also occur in north coastal BC. These include Alaska yellow cedar, western redcedar, Sitka spruce, and both western and mountain hemlock (*Tsuga mertensiana*). Both areas also have a small amount of lodgepole pine (*Pinus contorta*). Coastal BC also has Douglas-fir (*Pseudotsuga menziesii*) in its southern region, and a much larger amount of Pacific silver fir (*Abies amabilis*) than southeast Alaska. Western hemlock and Pacific silver fir have very similar appearance and physical properties and are therefore processed and marketed as a species group designated *hem-fir*. Although there are differences in species composition (table 5.1), both areas have high value species such as cedar and spruce, but also large proportions in the lower- value hem-fir category.

Most of the timberland in southeast Alaska is only slightly more productive than the minimum needed to qualify as timberland. On the Tongass, 88% of the timberland has sawtimber stands and 90% of them are more than 150 years old (Campbell *et al.* 2004). Roughly 77% of the volume on forested land in coastal BC is estimated to be greater than 160 years old

TABLE 5.1. Comparison of timber species (in percent) in southeast Alaska and coastal British Columbia.

SPECIES	SOUTHEAST ALASKA (TONGASS)	COASTAL BC
Hem-fir	63	61
Spruce	30	5
Cedars	7	27
Douglas-fir	0	6
Lodgepole	<1	1

Sources: Southeast Regional Timber Industry Task Force (1997); Council of Forest Industries (2000).

(BC Ministry of Forests and Range 2006b). In recent times, 75% of the wood processed in coastal BC has been old growth (All Forest Solutions, Inc. 2006); in southeast Alaska, almost all of the wood processed has also been old growth.

The modus operandi in coastal BC has been to harvest the highest quality and most accessible timber first (Constantino and Haley 1987; Sedjo 1997; Wood Products Industry Advisory Committee [WPIAC] 2006). WPIAC (2006, 14) notes the "evolution in the Crown timber resource to less economic, lower quality trees and lesser valued species." This modus operandi also existed in southeast Alaska (Helmers 1960; The Wilderness Society 1986; Sisk 2007).

Crone (2007) provided a detailed examination of the many competitive disadvantages faced by the southeast Alaska and coastal BC (especially northern coastal BC) wood products industries in comparison to the wood products industries in the US Pacific Northwest (Oregon and Washington) and interior BC. She summarized these as (1) higher harvesting cost because of isolated and remote locations, rugged terrain, and old-growth timber stands, (2) poor infrastructure and industries characterized by smaller, outdated, and less efficient mills operating at lower capacity rates, (3) high transportation costs to markets (3) limited product mix and markets, due largely to the characteristics of the timber resource (4) lack of local markets for mill residues or the low value species and grades of timber, and (5) lower levels of capital reinvestment. "Given the similarity of their competitive disadvantages (as outlined above) it is no surprise that the southeast Alaska and coastal BC industries are on the same downward trajectory" (Crone 2007, 38).

Mining

Many early mines in southeast Alaska were near Juneau. These mines, the Alaska Juneau (AJ), Treadwell, and Alaska Gastineau mining complexes, were the driver behind white settlement and development of the Juneau-Douglas area (table 5.2). At their peaks, the Treadwell and AJ complexes employed 2,000 and 1,000 workers, respectively.

With the exception of the reworking of mine tailings, uranium pentoxide production (1957 through 1971), and barite production (1966 through 1970), all early mining operations in the region ended by 1944. In 1974, the Quartz Hill molybdenum deposit (considered one of the largest in the world) was discovered in Misty Fords National Monument, but, for economic reasons, this deposit has not yet been developed (USDA Forest Service 1997b).

In 1973, a large silver deposit was discovered on Admiralty Island near Greens Creek. Development of Greens Creek Mine began in 1987, with full production starting in 1989. By the end of 2007 the mine had produced around 150 million ounces of silver, more than 1 million ounces of gold, over 970,000 tons of zinc, more than 75,000 tons of lead, and 8,400 tons of copper. Greens Creek is currently the largest silver mine in the world; in 2007 the mine had an estimated 116 million ounces of silver reserves and resources, with an expected mine life to 2019 (Szumigala *et al.* 2008). This mine is the largest private employer in the city and borough of Juneau and also its largest taxpayer.

Coeur Alaska began looking into reopening mining operations at the Kensington and Julian gold mine properties located about 72 km north-northwest of Juneau in the late 1980s. The method the company proposed to handle tailings from the operation (to discharge them into Lower Slate Lake) was the subject of a lawsuit filed by several conservation groups. The company appealed to the Supreme Court after the 9th Circuit Court of Appeals ruled the Army Corps of Engineers violated the Clean Water Act when it issued a "fill material permit" to Coeur Alaska (Golden 2009a). The Supreme Court overturned the lower court's decision in a 6 to 3 ruling. The company estimated it will produce around 150,000 ounces of gold during the early years of production, have a mine life of 10 years, employ

TABLE 5.2. Mineral production in southeast Alaska, 1880–1994.

MINING DISTRICT	PRODUCTION
Juneau	Gold: 6.75 million ounces
	Silver: 3.3 million ounces
	Copper: 3.3 million pounds
	Lead: 48.3 million pounds
	Zinc: 111 thousand pounds
	Platinum group metals: 14 thousand ounces
	Nickel, molybdenum, and iron: unrecorded quantities
Ketchikan	Gold: 2,569 kilograms
	Silver: 13 metric tons
	Copper: more than 18,200 metric tons
	Lead: 1,040 metric tons
	Zinc: 41 metric tons
	Tungston trioxide: 32 metric tons
	Paladium: 639 kilograms
	Uranium petoxide: 79,392 metric tons
	Marble: 2.3 million short tons
Chichagof	Gold: 810,257 ounces
	Silver: 235,400 ounces
	Gypsum: 500,000 short tons
Petersburg & Kupreanof	Gold: 15,000 ounces
	Silver: unrecorded quantities
	Barite: 786,888 short tons

Sources: Kaufman (1958); Redman (1986); Mass *et al.* (1995, 1996); Still *et al.* (2002); and Szumigala *et al.* (2008).

200 people with an annual payroll of $14 million, and generate $2 million in tax revenues for the city and borough of Juneau (Coeur d'Alene Mines Corporation 2008). Gold production at the mine began in June of 2010. At the end of 2011, the mine was estimated to contain 1.3 million ounces of proven and probable gold reserves, with an additional 587,320 ounces indi-

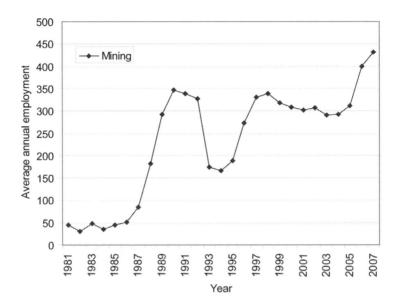

FIGURE 5.04. Mining employment in southeast Alaska, 1981–2007. Figure by Crone with data from Alaska Department of Labor and Workforce Development (2002, 2009).

cated and 169,680 ounces inferred gold mineral resources (Coeur d'Alene Mines Corporation 2012).

Figure 5.04 displays mining employment (includes rock, sand, and gravel) in southeast Alaska from 1981 to 2007.

In 2007, exploration activities took place at Greens Creek Mine on Admiralty Island; Kensington and Julian properties north of Juneau; Niblack, Bokan Mountain, Cracker Jack, and Mount Andrew properties on Prince of Wales Island; Duke Island property south of Ketchikan; Woewodski Island property in Duncan Canal; and Palmer property near Haines (Szumigala *et al.* 2008). The driver of this exploration activity was most likely an increase in mineral prices. Exploration activities at Bokan Mountain were driven by the rare earth elements found there. "The global mining industry has ramped up exploration for mineral deposits containing rare earth elements to meet the perceived future demand. High prices for rare earth elements continue to drive exploration" (Szumigala and Werdon 2010).

Commercial Salmon Fishing

Forested land plays a primary role in the commercial salmon fishing industry of southeast Alaska by providing spawning, rearing, and wintering habitat for salmon. After the purchase of Alaska from Russia, American interests (many from outside Alaska) recognized the value of salmon in the region and began building canneries in southeast Alaska. Between 1900 and 1920, technological changes, including automated butchering machines, floating fish traps, the sanitary can, and the introduction of gasoline-powered fishing boats, led to rapid expansion of the industry. The number of canneries increased from 30 to 82 during this period. The floating traps were very efficient in harvesting fish, but in some areas they caused entire runs to be wiped out. In 1924, 65 canneries were operating in southeast Alaska; 350 traps were being used (Thorsteinson 1950).

As noted previously, salmon have always been extremely important in the economic, social, and cultural systems of Natives in the region. Natives suffered greatly as they witnessed packing companies destroy the runs in their traditional fishing areas one after another. The commercial salmon industry depleted the highest value species first, before moving on to the other lower value species. Sockeye salmon catch peaked in 1904, chum in 1919, chinook in 1937, pink in 1941, and coho in 1950 (Rogers 1960). Salmon harvests reached a historic low in 1960 (fig. 5.05). Many, including the Alaska Native Brotherhood (ANB), blamed the continued decimation of the salmon fishery on the powerful lobby of the Alaska Packers Association, which was successful in thwarting the "federal brigade" from enforcing measures to conserve and rehabilitate the fisheries (Goldin and Matsen 1996).

Testifying before a House subcommittee about the situation in 1955, Cyrus Peck, Sr., a spokesman for the ANB, stated the following:

> *Beginning with our convention of 1920, every year this body has proposed fishing regulations that would conserve the fisheries of Alaska, but in no case except one has the Secretary of the Interior adopted any of them. . . . In 1928, we informed the commissioner of fisheries that the annual pack should be limited to 4,500,000 cases, and we suggested that 4 million cases would be safer. His answer was that we could produce fully 8 million cases each year, and so the regulations were adjusted to that figure with the results that are known. . . . When the white people came to Alaska, they were amazed, and the quantity of fish was so huge that they claimed it*

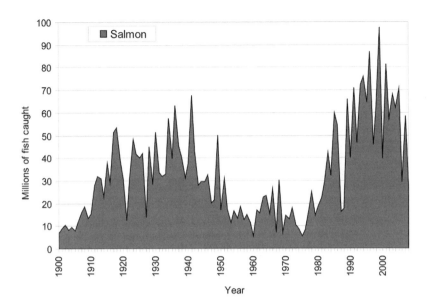

FIGURE 5.05. Commercial salmon catch in southeast Alaska, 1900–2008. Figure by Crone with data from Rigby *et al.* (1991) and Tingley and Davidson (2008).

could not be exhausted and acted accordingly, at first utilizing only the
red salmon. After destroying that species, all parties joined in a refrain
composed by the Bureau of Fisheries; namely, that southeast Alaska was
a pink salmon area and that all regulations should be made to conform
to that fact. But the destruction continued. Within the last two years, we
proposed a sure method, and cheap, to restock our salmon streams and
the present commissioner of fisheries said he could find nothing wrong
with it, but he has done nothing to activate it. (US Congress 1956, 108)

Similarly, Haycox (2000,166) wrote, "residents believed that the industry continued to rape the territory through government collusion with the packers, manifested in limited enforcement budgets and fish agents who were willing to do favors for their corporate clients."

The federal government finally moved to ban the use of fish traps in 1959. When the state of Alaska took control of all submerged lands in 1960, they refused to issue licenses for traps and banned them on all state lands (Rogers 1960). The Alaska Department of Fish and Game began research and conservation efforts, but because of the large increase in the size of the seine and driftnet industries, salmon runs did not recover. In 1972, a constitu-

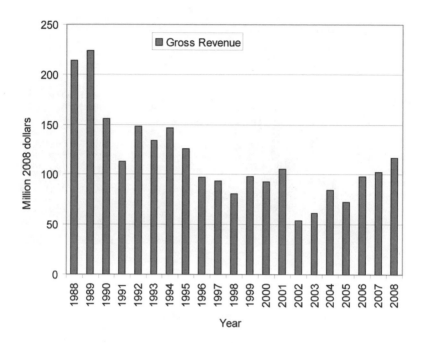

FIGURE 5.06. Estimated salmon harvest gross earnings in southeast Alaska, 1988–2008. Figure by Crone with data from Tingley and Davidson (2008).

tional amendment was passed that limited entry into fisheries through the issuance of a fixed number of tradable permits. This limited entry policy, along with research, conservation, and enhancement efforts, led to the steady increase in southeast Alaska commercial salmon harvests (fig. 5.05).

Baker *et al.* (1996) and Halupka *et al.* (2000) found that most salmon populations in southeast Alaska were stable in the mid- to late 1990s. Woodby *et al.* (2005, 8) wrote,

"In Alaska, with few exceptions, our runs are in excellent shape, supporting sustainable, record harvest levels over the past 20 years. The ocean environment was extremely favorable in the 1980s and early 1990s. Good fisheries management and a pristine environment have allowed Alaska's salmon populations to make the most of favorable ocean conditions and to allow users the opportunity to achieve record level harvests."

Salmon harvests in the region have generally increased since the mid-1970s, but competition from farmed salmon began putting downward pressure on Alaskan salmon's market share, prices, and operator profitability in the early 1990s. The estimated gross revenue from salmon harvesting in

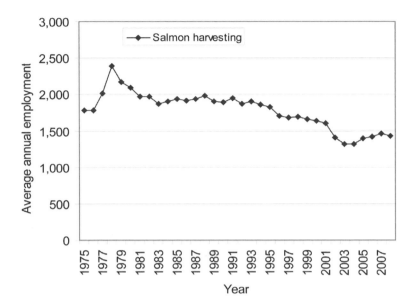

FIGURE 5.07. Estimated southeast Alaska direct salmon harvesting employment, 1975–2008. Figure by Crone with data from Tingley and Davidson (2008) and McDowell Group (1989).

southeast Alaska reached a low in 2002 (fig. 5.06). Marketing campaigns to promote the health benefits of eating wild Alaska salmon have resulted in an increase in salmon prices, and gross revenues since that time. Estimated employment in the salmon fishing industry in southeast Alaska was still lower in 2008 than in 2000 but has rebounded slightly from its low in 2004 (fig. 5.07).

Unless the level of other commercial activities (logging, mining, tourism, and others) in the region increases significantly or the regulations currently in place to protect salmon habitat when these activities occur are relaxed, it is unlikely that management of the forest will lead to significant changes in the southeast Alaskan commercial salmon fishing industry.

Tourism

Tourism began in the 1880s, when steamships began carrying tourists up the Inside Passage to view glaciers, fiords, Native villages, canneries, and the gold rush towns. In 1884, 1,650 tourists took the Inside Passage tour; by 1890, this figure increased to 5,007. Steamship travel continued to be

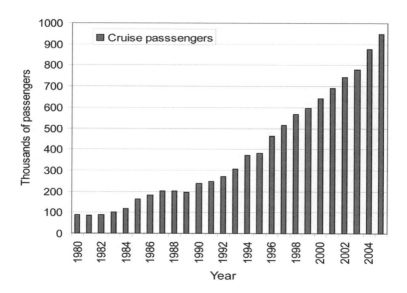

FIGURE 5.08. Cruise ship visitors to Juneau, 1980–2005. Figure by Crone with data from USDA Forest Service (1997b, 2008b).

the primary method of reaching the area through the 1930s. Improvements in transportation infrastructure during World War II resulted in increased tourism following the war. The Alaska Marine Highway system began operations in 1963, again increasing visits to the region. The 1970s marked the beginning of cruising to southeast Alaska. In 1973, 36,556 visitors traveled to Alaska on cruise ships; by 1980 almost 87,000 cruise passengers visited Juneau (fig. 5.08). Most cruise ships stop in Juneau, providing a relatively good measure of cruise passenger volume growth in the region. Between 1990 and 2005 the volume of cruise passengers visiting Juneau more than tripled (fig. 5.08).

Another segment of the tourist industry is independent travelers, both pure independent or indie-package (McDowell Group 1991). Pure independent travelers are tourists who make all their own arrangements and do not participate in package tours. Indie-package visitors, on the other hand, may or may not make their own arrangements, but participate in tour packages, such as an all inclusive stay at a fishing lodge. Anecdotal reports suggest that the number of independent travelers to the region remained fairly stable between 1990 and 2002, but good data for this segment is unavailable (Schroeder *et al.* 2005). McDowell Group (2002) estimated that independent travelers accounted for around 25% of the total number of visitors to southeast Alaska in 2001.

Due to its sheer volume, the cruise sector has the greatest influence on tourism-based economic activity in its ports of call. However, on a per visitor basis, independent travelers probably spend more in the region, since they use local accommodations for eating and lodging and local transportation within the region. Many tourism businesses have emerged or expanded in or near cruise ship ports of call to serve the multitude of cruise passengers engaging in land or sea excursions while the ships are docked. These tours range from historic and cultural tours to a full range of nature-based activities. Many of the tours or activities take place on public lands for which the tour operators must obtain permits from the land management agencies. Between 1993 and 2007 the number of permits issued to commercial tour operators on the Tongass increased from 73 to 274 (Cerveny 2005; Jones 2009).

These are three of the key findings from a recent study of nature-based tourism in southeast Alaska (Dugan *et al.* 2007, 1–2):

* Tourism in southeast Alaska is primarily focused on nature-based activities, since people are attracted to the region for its beautiful scenery, fisheries, wildlife, marine mammals, glaciers, and other natural attributes.

* Nature-based tourism creates a significant economic ripple effect that keeps money circulating through many sectors of the economy. The money supports jobs in marketing, support services, food and beverages, accommodations, fuel sales, government, and other sectors.

* A large and growing portion of southeast Alaska's visitors are cruise ship passengers. Both cruise passengers and independent travelers are similarly interested in nature-based tourism services. The majority of cruise ship shore excursions offer nature activities, from hikes and glacier viewing to flight seeing and forest canopy zip lines.

Guided sport fishing is one of the most popular tourism activities for both cruise passengers and independent travelers in some areas of southeast Alaska (figs. 5.09 and 5.10). Charter fishing is a subset of guided sport fishing.

The increase in registered charter vessels and the associated increase

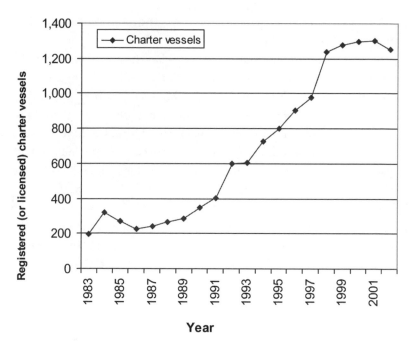

FIGURE 5.09. Number of registered (or licensed) charter vessels in southeast Alaska, 1983–2002. Figure by Crone with data from Holmes *et al.* (2003).

in sport fish harvests has been the source of much controversy and in some cases outright hostility in many southeast Alaska communities (Cerveny 2005). Southwick Associates *et al.* (2008) estimated that nonresident anglers generated almost $51 million in direct income and 1,662 direct jobs in southeast Alaska in 2007.

Employment in the leisure and hospitality sector of southeast Alaska for 2007 was 4,082 average annual equivalents (Alaska Department of Labor and Workforce Development 2009). (Not all employment in this sector is due to tourism and not all tourism employment is captured by this sector.) Tourism generates revenues for local governments through moorage and passenger fees, sales tax, property taxes, and bed taxes. McDowell Group (1998) estimated that in 1997 cruise-related revenues to local governments exceeded cruise-related costs to local governments by more than 6.8 million in southeast Alaska ports of call. Cerveny (2005) provides an excellent discussion of both the positive and negative economic, sociocultural, and resource effects of tourism on three representative southeast Alaska communities.

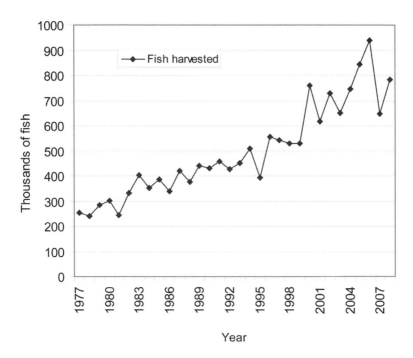

FIGURE 5.10. Southeast Alaska sport fish harvest, 1977–2008. Data from Alaska Department of Fish and Game, Division of Sport Fish (2009a, 2009b).

Tourism in southeast Alaska will probably not increase as rapidly as it has in the past two decades. Cruise visitation to Alaska (including southeast Alaska visitation) actually decreased by 0.6% between 2008 and 2009 and 14.5% between 2009 and 2010 (McDowell Group 2011). McDowell Group (2011) also noted that total visitor volume to the state decreased in 2008, 2009, and 2010 after fairly consistent growth in the first part of the decade. Managing tourist versus local conflicts and resource impacts on the Tongass will be increasingly important as the types of activities engaged in and places visited continue to develop and expand.

Hydropower

Early hydropower in the region was developed primarily to support industry. The Treadwell Mines in Douglas constructed their first hydro project in 1882. In 1909, The New England Fish Company built a hydro plant at Herring Bay to operate a cold storage plant. In 1915, the first pulp mill in southeast Alaska was built as part of a hydro project to serve anticipated mining near Port Snettisham (Mackovjack 2008). The Forest Service and the Federal Power Commission worked together for decades to establish pulp mills with hydropower facilities. By 1924, 49 undeveloped sites were identified with the capability to produce 335,520 horsepower (Dort 1924). By the mid-1950s, about half of the region's electricity was generated by hydropower.

In 2007, 47 hydroelectric plants operated statewide and provided about 24% of the state's electrical energy (Alaska Energy Authority and Renewable Energy Alaska Project 2007). Southeast Alaska has more than 3,000 megawatts of power available, but only around 200 megawatts have been developed (Forgey 2009). Ketchikan, Petersburg, Wrangell, Juneau, Sitka, and Haines use hydropower for nearly all their electric needs. Moreover, low-cost, in-stream hydrosystems may offer significant additional savings. Small hydropower is being aggressively developed in BC, where 50% of new electric generation must be from renewable sources. One of the primary environmental concerns regarding hydropower is possible impacts to anadromous salmon streams.

The high cost of power is often mentioned as an impediment to attracting business to many of the smaller communities in southeast Alaska (Southeast Conference and Central Council of Tlingit and Haida Indian Tribes of Alaska 2006; Information Insights 2010). The proposed Southeast Alaska Intertie Project is intended to connect all the major towns of southeast Alaska to common power grids. The objective is to minimize the consumption of fossil fuels; the estimated cost is more than $300 million (Bradner 2007).

The potential to reduce the consumption of fossil fuels in southeast Alaska and northern coastal BC through greater use of hydroelectric power is substantial. Yanity (2009) suggests that increased hydroelectric power in southeast Alaska could be used for heating homes and buildings, charging electric vehicles, and future hydrogen production. There are also opportunities for large-scale projects that could generate energy for export (Forgey 2009). Such projects would require a future transmission line to British Columbia and the continental power grid. Major issues will be environmental protection and the high costs of construction and transmission.

SUMMARY

The indigenous people of southeast Alaska and Haida Gwaii used a multitude of the region's natural resources to sustain themselves. This use was strongly influenced by their highly developed sense of place and use rights to specific resources, such as salmon streams and berry patches. Most of the resources were harvested and used locally, but local surpluses were used to trade with other indigenous groups within or near the region for items not available locally. In contrast, as the region became settled by Russians and Europeans, the acquisition of natural resources focused largely on their export from the region.

The natural resources of the North Pacific coastal rainforest region were the drawing card for the region's economic development and population growth by nonindigenous peoples. Mining was the first resource-based industry to develop, followed by commercial fishing, timber and wood products, and tourism. Economic development was driven by the desire to establish more and larger settlements in the region and the belief that this would only occur if year-round job opportunities were available. Each of the industries discussed above have been only partially successful in this endeavor. Many of the smallest communities that developed around mining, cannery, or logging activities either no longer exist or are struggling to survive. Many of the employment opportunities in the fishing and tourism industries are seasonal and are filled by workers coming from outside the region. In southeast Alaska, employment is no longer dominated by direct employment in the natural resource–related industries (fig. 5.11).

Because the Tongass accounts for around 80% of the land area in southeast Alaska, people continue to focus on its resources and management as a limiting factor in economic growth. For many reasons, the probability of a large expansion in year-round jobs in any of the resource extraction industries is not high. It may be possible to create more or better-paying jobs for locals in the tourism industry by developing recreation infrastructure that results in more or higher-quality experiences and draws more independent travelers to the region. This could also improve opportunities for local recreational users. In Civilian Conservation Corps days, people were employed in the building of recreation infrastructure such as the Admiralty Canoe Route, trails, cabins, and recreational areas (Otis *et al.* 1986; USDA Forest Service 2009).

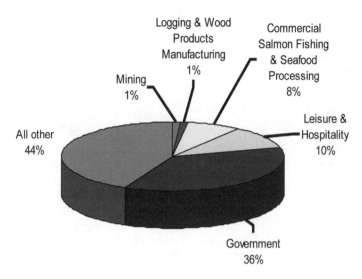

Logging & Wood
Products
Manufacturing
1%

Mining
1%

Commercial
Salmon Fishing
& Seafood
Processing
8%

All other
44%

Leisure &
Hospitality
10%

Government
36%

FIGURE 5.11. Shares of employment by sector for southeast Alaska, 2007. Figure by Crone with data from Alaska Department of Labor and Workforce Development (2009), Tingley and Davidson (2008), and McDowell Group (1989).

One comparative advantage of the region that has not been fully tapped is the opportunity for education and research. Because of its distinctive ecosystems and the absence of fire or other large disturbances, the coastal North Pacific temperate rainforest provides opportunities for research on the consequences of climate change and dynamics of relatively pristine ecosystems that do not exist anywhere else in the world. This research could employ many students or technicians in the field, lab, and office. In addition, the region would make a remarkable classroom for many disciplines. If educational institutions are established to take advantage of these opportunities, year-round jobs could be created.

Southeast Alaska has a long history of hydroelectric power development, but the region's potential is largely untapped. Future investments can potentially meet nearly all the local demand for electricity and possibly create a surplus for export. However, it is important that these projects occur where impacts to salmon habitat are minimized.

Restoration projects are another source of economic opportunities. Recent projects on the Tongass have used logs, harvested as part of thinning projects, to improve riparian and wildlife habitat and to build public recreational cabins. These cabins were built by students participating in log home construction courses. Another benefit to local communities was the provision of firewood from thinning projects. Other types of restoration activities include decommissioning, storing, and storm-proofing roads; removing, replacing, or repairing culverts; stream restoration; and eradication of invasive species.

Restoration has both political and economic components. Since forest and watershed restoration projects provide both market and nonmarket goods, the level of implementation may be best left to political process—not unlike how federal wilderness allocations are made. Within the political context, forest restoration has been a good organizing tool for some environmental groups, in part to blunt the criticism that they negatively impacted the timber industry and local economies. Many groups have suggested that restoration can provide long-term, local green jobs. However, the economic component of restoration may be problematic.

If it were clear that restoration projects could pay for themselves or that we could clearly identify who benefits from these projects, the merits of restoration would be relatively straightforward. However because restoration projects usually provide multiple benefits over varying time periods, the issue of how and when to allocate joint costs to the beneficiaries is unclear. Further, restoration projects may be expensive, require repeated efforts, and extend over long periods. These types of projects usually work against private investments. Paraphrasing Hurd (2009), the problem isn't that forest and watershed restoration activities do not produce valuable goods and services, it's that there are few traditional markets in which these products can be bought and sold. For example, if fishers (commercial, charter, recreational, and subsistence) or consumers believe larger salmon runs will result from restoration projects, will they be willing pay for these projects? Perhaps, but the most likely scenario is that funding for forest restoration will come from government, with some joint ventures with nongovernmental organizations. These types of joint-venture restoration projects are already taking place on the Tongass and on many other national forests in the western United States (Pemberton 2009).

Similar to timber sales on the Tongass, whether restoration projects are well placed or not, they are likely to involve subsidies (McDowell Group 2008; Hjerpe 2011). If functioning markets for things such as clean air and water, healthy aquatic and terrestrial wildlife habitat, and carbon sequestration existed and if incremental improvements in these services could be quantitatively and accurately tied to specific restoration projects, this might not be the case.

The local natural resources (which sustained indigenous peoples for millennia) continue to contribute to the socioeconomic well-being and quality of life of residents in southeast Alaska and northern BC. Today these resources must be managed in the context of a global economy and global environmental changes. Underlying questions persist as to the proper balance between market and nonmarket goods and to what degree to participate in or insulate forest users from the global economy.

Past management has primarily focused on sustainability and providing multiple uses. It is time to factor in global implications, whether or not they are beyond local control. Such information will allow us to better plan and react. Forest management must go beyond the current interdisciplinary planning approach, which leads to a solution that is deemed a compromise between diverse and conflicting user groups. Forest planners and managers are highly skilled in evaluating causes and effects, tradeoffs, and long-term cumulative impacts. However, a major shortcoming of this approach is that it tries to impose a highly technical, scientific solution on a truly political problem—what is the right balance between market and nonmarket goods and services? This has always been much more than an economics question.

ACKNOWLEDGMENTS

Our thanks go to Andy MacKinnon for his valuable contributions to this chapter regarding Haida Gwaii and her indigenous people. We thank John Schoen and Gordon Orians for their reviews, editorial contributions, and guidance. Finally, we thank two anonymous reviewers for their useful comments and suggestions.

1   Northern Chichagof Island in the Tongass National Forest, looking across Icy Strait at Mount Fairweather, between Glacier Bay National Park in southeast Alaska and northwestern British Columbia. This primary watershed encompasses a mosaic of old-growth forest, muskeg bogs, and surrounding alpine ridges, draining into a productive estuary with abundant salmon runs, brown bears, bald eagles, and a variety of other fish and wildlife species characteristic of the North Pacific temperate rainforest. Photo by John Schoen.

2   Aerial view of the old-growth forest canopy of a mixed hemlock–spruce forest in southeast Alaska. Unlike many portions of the world, the North Pacific temperate rainforest is still dominated by old growth. This view shows the ragged, broken canopy and standing dead trees characteristic of old growth. The gaps in the canopy allow penetration of sunlight that supports an abundant and diverse understory plant community. The multilayered canopy and large limb structure increases habitat diversity and also intercepts snow during winter months. Photo by John Schoen.

3   Banks Island, looking northwest over the top end of the island towards the BC mainland, in the vicinity of the mouth of the Skeena River. Typical exposed, hypermaritime,
outer coastal lowland, with "coastal muskeg" (bog–forest complex), is covering the subdued
terrain in the foreground. Trees of the bog woodland are primarily yellow cedar, redcedar,
western hemlock, mountain hemlock, and shore pine. Soils are mostly organic Histosols
and Folisols. More productive forest, with Sitka spruce and Pacific silver fir joining western
hemlock and redcedar, is confined to steep hillslopes and along streams and beaches. At
about 8,600 km2, Banks is one of the largest nearshore islands in the province. In 2006,
19,120 ha of the island—including all that is shown in the bottom half of the photo—was
established as the Nii Luutiksm/Banks Conservancy. Photo by Jim Pojar.

4   John Hopkins Glacier in Glacier Bay National Park, southeast Alaska. The biological
and physiographic history of the North Pacific rainforest was significantly influenced by
thousands of years of active glaciation. Today, glaciers are still a dynamic force in the ecology of southeast Alaska, which encompasses the most southerly tidewater glaciers in North
America. Photo by John Schoen.

5   Islands, like these adjacent to southwestern Prince of Wales Island in southeast Alaska, are a defining feature of the North Pacific temperate rainforest. More than 6,000 islands, ranging in size from less than 1 ha to more than 6,000 km2, occur along this highly dissected coast from Cape Caution on the central coast of British Columbia to Alaska's Yakutat Bay. The recent glacial history and island biogeography of the region contribute substantially to the high degree of endemism along this coast. Photo by John Schoen.

6   Newcombe's Butterweed (*Sinose-necio newcombei*) is a beautiful sunflower family plant found only on Haida Gwaii, generally at subalpine to alpine elevations on rocky slopes, boggy spots, or in heath. Photo by Hans Roemer.

7 The Kermode bear (*Ursus americanus kermodei*), the unique white phase of the black bear, is often called the "spirit bear." It is concentrated on Gribbel, Princess Royal, and surrounding islands of the Great Bear Rainforest, off the northern coast of British Columbia. Photo by Kevin J. Smith/Maple Leaf Adventures.

8 Estuaries—like Kadashan on Chichagof Island—are highly productive areas and provide a key interface between terrestrial, aquatic, and marine environments. Thousands of streams and rivers—many providing spawning habitat for millions of anadromous fish—drain the mountain slopes and valleys of North Pacific temperate rainforest and distribute huge amounts of nutrients that enrich the marine ecosystem. Photo by John Schoen.

9 This riparian floodplain forest borders the King Salmon River on Admiralty Island, running from the forest on the left and draining into the estuary in the center right of the photo. Note the band of tall Sitka spruce bordering the river along the well-drained, alluvial floodplain. At the top left and bottom of the photo are sparsely forested (predominately western hemlock and shore pine) and poorly-drained muskeg bog wetlands. This complex forest mosaic is characteristic of many of the lowlands of the North Pacific temperate rainforest. Photo by John Schoen.

10 Each year, a pulse of marine-derived nutrients flows upstream into coastal watersheds in the form of millions of Pacific salmon and other anadromous fish that spawn in the thousands of streams and rivers flowing into the North Pacific. Bears, like this Alaskan brown bear, wolves, river otters, mink, marten, and a variety of other mammals, birds, and invertebrates feast on this annual bounty and help distribute these important nutrients throughout the rainforest's terrestrial and aquatic ecosystems. Photo by John Schoen.

11   The North Pacific temperate rainforest encompasses a fine-grained mosaic of cover
types, as depicted in this photo of a small primary watershed on southeastern Admiralty
Island. This watershed rises from sea level to over 800 m elevation. The main stream flows
down the watershed and enters a small estuary (*a*) at tidewater just outside the beach fringe
forest (*b*). The riparian floodplain forest (*c*), dominated by Sitka spruce with a devil's club
and salmonberry understory, occurs on well-drained alluvial soils. On poorly drained soils,
at lower to mid elevations, are muskeg bogs (*d*) with sparse forest cover of stunted hemlock
and shore pine. These peatland bogs are dominated by ericaceous shrubs. Mixed hemlock–
spruce forests (*e*), with an understory of blueberry shrubs, trailing bramble, bunchberry,
and a variety of other herbs, shrubs, and ferns, occur on moderately drained soils at low
to mid elevations. Avalanche slopes (*f*) occur on steep slopes prone to snow slides. These
areas are dominated by alder, devil's club, salmonberry, and current shrubs. Alpine tundra
(*g*), dominated by heath communities, are found on ridge tops above tree line. This fine-
grained forest mosaic shows distinctive changes in vegetation at a scale of tens of meters
and is influenced by soil drainage and a variety of natural disturbances, including small-
scale wind events. Photo by John Schoen.

12   Old-growth forests are characterized by uneven-aged stands that include seedlings, saplings, pole-size trees, and large-diameter trees. Dominant trees are generally more than 300 years old, and some stands may have individual trees nearly 1,000 years old. These stands have broken, multilayered canopies that allow light to penetrate to the forest floor, enabling the growth of diverse and abundant understories of shrubs, herbs, ferns, mosses, and fungi. Standing dead and down trees are common in such stands and add structural diversity and habitats for a variety of plants and animals. Arboreal lichens are abundant in old growth. Old growth has much more structural diversity than younger second-growth stands. Much of the old growth in this region is the product of relatively small-scale natural disturbances. Following complete removal of the overstory, it may take 300 years or more for a stand to develop the ecological characteristics of old growth. Photo by John Schoen.

13   Haida village of Ninstints on Anthony Island in Haida Gwaii, now a World Heritage Site. For thousands of years, the Native people of the North Pacific rainforest have depended on the abundance of natural resources to meet their subsistence and cultural needs. Photo by John Schoen circa 1975.

14   Logging on private corporation lands on Dall Island, southwest of Prince of Wales Island. The young forests that replace old growth have a substantially different ecological structure, which affects the habitat values for many species of plants and animals that have adapted to the natural disturbance regime of the North Pacific temperate rainforest. Photo by John Schoen.

15　Purse seiners fishing for pink salmon in southeast Alaska. The North Pacific rainforest supports one of the most productive salmon fisheries in the Pacific Rim. For centuries fish have sustained the indigenous people living along this coast, and today a substantial commercial, sport, and subsistence fishery employs or sustains many of the people living in the region. Photo by John Schoen.

16　Tourism has been a significant growth industry within the North Pacific temperate rainforest over the last three decades, although it has recently declined or stabilized within the last few years with the global recession. This aerial view of downtown Juneau (Alaska's state capitol and the largest city in the North Pacific rainforest) shows five tour ships in the harbor on a busy summer day. Photo by John Schoen.

17   A various-aged patchwork of clear-cut logging (from recent clear-cuts to several-decades-old second growth) and the associated road network on Prince of Wales Island on the Tongass National Forest in southeast Alaska. The ragged canopy of fragmented old-growth patches is visible in the foreground and middle potion of the photo. Clear-cutting fragments old growth, reduces patch size, increases the distance between old-growth patches, and significantly changes forest structure. Road networks further fragment forests and introduce a variety of ecological effects. Photo by John Schoen.

18   The stem-exclusion stage in this 60-year-old second-growth stand in southeast Alaska has relatively low habitat values for many species of plants and animals. The low light levels in such even-aged, closed-canopy stands significantly reduce the abundance of understory plants. These stands have low structural diversity compared to more heterogeneous, uneven-aged old growth. Once canopy closure occurs (generally from 25 to 35 years after harvest), it can take several centuries before the ecological characteristics and structure of old growth develop. Photo by John Schoen.

19   The Taku River in northern southeast Alaska, south of Juneau, is a large transboundary river with high salmon values for all five species of Pacific salmon, plus steelhead.
This is one of the most significant salmon watersheds in northern southeast Alaska and
interior British Columbia and an important international fishery. The international border
is approximately 20 km from tidewater and it drains a major area of northern interior BC.
Photo by John Schoen.

20   Chaik Bay is an example of a small- to moderate-sized (9,300 ha) primary watershed flowing directly to tidewater. This intact watershed located on southwest Admiralty Island in northern southeast Alaska still maintains the natural range of variability of all its vegetation communities, from beach-fringe forest to alpine tundra. It has good runs of coho, chum, and pink salmon, and abundant black-tailed deer and brown bear populations. The prospect of maintaining the ecological integrity of this intact watershed is high, particularly since most of Admiralty Island is protected as a national monument, including the watersheds adjacent to Chaik Bay. Photo by John Schoen.

21   Lower Skeena River, looking upriver in late March. During early spring, eulachon (oolichan, candlefish) come up the river to spawn along its lower, tidal reaches. The pulse of biomass is tracked by gyres of gulls, hundreds of eagles, seals, sea lions, and First Nations people, who harvest the oily, smelt-like fish. British Columbia spans 11 degrees of latitude and 25 degrees of longitude and covers 948,600 km2. In the middle of all that is the Skeena River, draining 54,430 km2 in west central BC. It's a big river basin, the second largest in the province. The Skeena watershed provides spawning and rearing habitat for all five species of Pacific salmon, plus steelhead and at least 30 other fish species. The Skeena between the cities of Terrace and Prince Rupert cuts through BC's Coast Mountains, and the resulting valley is spectacular. Bold massive mountains of monolithic granite, laced with avalanche tracks and waterfalls, rise up from near sea level. The temperate rainforest here is dominated by western hemlock, Pacific silver fir, and western redcedar, with lots of Sitka spruce and black cottonwood on the river's floodplain. Photo by Jim Pojar.

22   Port Houghton, on the central mainland coast of southeast Alaska in the Tongass
National Forest, is an example of a conservation priority watershed identified by Albert
and Schoen (2007a) in the Audubon Alaska–TNC conservation design for southeast
Alaska. This watershed is an intact primary watershed in a remarkable setting. Port
Houghton lies south of Juneau and extends 15 miles from its mouth along Stephens Passage
to the entrance of a salt chuck, or tidal basin, nestled into steep forested slopes adjacent to
ice fields and precipitous 2,600 m mountains along the Canadian border. This watershed
supports good runs of sockeye, coho, pink, and chum salmon, plus steelhead. It provides
important habitat for brown and black bears and marbled murrelets, and it also has high
values for large-tree forests and estuaries. Photo by John Schoen.

23 Kitlope, looking east over the compound estuary of the Kitlope and Tsaytis rivers, and up the Tsaytis River valley. The Kitlope River enters from the right. This location is at the head of the long twisting fiord of Gardner Canal, in the plutonic heart of the Kitimat Ranges. The entire Kitlope/Tsaytis watershed is protected as the 320,000 ha Huchs-duwachsdu Nuyem Jees/Kitlope Heritage Conservancy. This remarkable Conservancy connects Tweedsmuir Park and Conservancy in the east with Fjordland Conservancy in the west, and it contains within its boundaries Earth's largest intact coastal temperate rainforest watershed. The valley was known as "Hushuwashsdu" or "source of the milky blue water" to the Haisla First Nation. The Kitlope is traditional territory of the Haisla, who comanage the Conservancy with BC Parks. Sizeable runs of salmon and oolichan spawn here, and the area is important habitat for black and grizzly bears, moose, mountain goats, and marbled murrelets. Photo by Jim Pojar.

6

Succession Debt and Roads

SHORT- AND LONG-TERM EFFECTS OF TIMBER
HARVEST ON A LARGE-MAMMAL PREDATOR-PREY
COMMUNITY IN SOUTHEAST ALASKA

David K. Person and Todd J. Brinkman

INTRODUCTION

Unlike most regions of North America, the rainforests of southeast Alaska and northern coastal British Columbia retain most of their postglacial legacy of wildlife (MacDonald and Cook 2007). Along with fish and other marine foods, those wildlife resources helped to sustain human populations for at least 9,000 years before the arrival of Europeans, despite dramatic postglacial geological and ecological changes to the landscape (Baichtal and Swanston 1996; Larsen *et al.* 2005; Carstensen 2007). Beginning in the 1950s, industrial-scale harvesting of timber occurred throughout much of the region. In coastal British Columbia, 67% of watersheds greater than 5,000 ha were developed by 1991, mostly for logging (Lertzman and MacKinnon, this volume, chapter 8). From 1954 to 2008, greater than 325,000 ha of rainforest were clear-cut logged and greater than 6,000 km of road were built in southeast Alaska (Albert and Schoen 2007a). Prior to logging, the coastal forest landscape was a product of edaphic factors, long-term abiotic forces, and short-term agents of disturbance such as wind and disease (Alaback *et al.*, this volume, chapter 4). Industrial-scale clear-cut logging does not mimic the natural agents and patterns of disturbance, and it initiates a chain of events that have complex ecological and social implications (Hanley 1993; Kramer *et al.* 2001; DellaSala *et al.* 2011;

Alaback *et al.*, this volume, chapter 4). In addition, roads built to facilitate logging provide new pathways of access, enabling the footprint of human activity to extend into previously remote inland areas. Roads alter ecosystems in ways that affect ecological processes, populations of plants and animals, and human interactions with landscapes (Forman and Alexander 1998; Trombulak and Frissell 2000; Forman *et al.* 2003; Brinkman *et al.* 2007; Brinkman *et al.* 2009). In southeast Alaska and coastal British Columbia, those changes have profound and long-term effects on many wildlife species and the ecological communities with which they are linked.

The inexorable process of forest succession following clear-cut logging in North Pacific rainforests transitions through several distinct stages with varying effects on wildlife, but it ultimately reaches a condition (corresponding to the *stem exclusion* stage) that is largely unproductive for many species (Alaback 1982; Schoen *et al.* 1988; Alaback *et al.*, this volume, chapter 4). We refer to circumstances affecting wildlife populations resulting from that chain of events as *succession debt* (Person 2001). Short-term economic and social benefits of industrial harvesting of timber will be paid for by long-term ecological consequences resulting from patterns and processes of forest succession and roads. There may be short-term benefits for some wildlife species, but succession debt implies that those benefits are ephemeral and do not reflect conditions for those species over the long term. Although succession debt will affect many species of forest-dependent wildlife within coastal British Columbia and southeast Alaska, we chose to illustrate this concept by focusing on the realized and potential effects of timber harvest and roads on a predator-prey ecological community located on Prince of Wales Island in southeast Alaska. The system is a complex network of marine and terrestrial influences and includes several predators, fish and ungulate prey, human hunters, and the land and seascapes upon which they all depend. Although our case study focuses on predator-prey dynamics within North Pacific temperate rainforests, it highlights the general difficulties of conserving large mammalian carnivores within rapidly changing landscapes and is relevant to other forest ecosystems exposed to large-scale anthropogenic disturbance. Moreover, by discussing changes at a community level, we encourage a systems approach to thinking about effects of those disturbances rather than focusing on individual species (Dörner 1996).

THE PREDATOR-PREY COMMUNITY
ON PRINCE OF WALES ISLAND

Prince of Wales Island is located within the southern portion of the Alexander Archipelago in southeast Alaska (fig. 6.01). It is 6,700 km^2 and is the third largest island in the United States. The landscape is dominated by rugged mountains less than 1,200 m high, the slopes of which are covered mostly by a mosaic of coniferous forests and muskeg heaths. Most of the land is encompassed by the Tongass National Forest, however, more than 178,000 ha (8%) are owned by the state of Alaska and private landowners, which include Alaska Native corporations. Under provisions of the Alaska Native Claims Settlement Act (1971), more than 30,000 ha of additional forest land may be conveyed to Native corporations within the next decade. Approximately 130,000 ha of productive timberland (about 29% of the productive old growth) were clear-cut logged on private, state, and federal lands from 1955 to 2005 (Albert and Schoen 2007a). Most nonfederal lands were logged from 1980 through 2009. In addition, more than 4,000 km of road were built, mostly to facilitate logging. About 20% of the land area was logged and is in various stages of forest succession; 39% of the area is old-growth forest containing a volume of timber more than 45 m^3/ha, and the rest is alpine, muskeg heath, or scrub forest. Sitka black-tailed deer (*Odocoileus hemionus sitkensis*), wolves (*Canis lupus ligoni*), black bears (*Ursus americanus*), and beaver (*Castor canadensis*) are the principal components of a complex large-mammal predator-prey system. Numerous lakes and streams sustain large populations of anadromous and resident fish. Salmon (*Oncorhynchus* spp.) are important prey for both wolves and bears and serve as key agents in cycling nutrients between aquatic and terrestrial ecosystems (Willson and Halupka 1995; Hocking and Reimchen 2002; Gende *et al.* 2004; Darimont and Reimchen 2002). Hunting deer for subsistence is an important activity. For many local residents, venison constitutes their only supply of red meat (Brinkman *et al.* 2009). In addition, bear, wolves, beavers, and salmon are harvested by hunters, trappers, and fishers. Consequently, humans also play a critical role in the predator-prey community as predators on all component species and agents of habitat change.

The US Forest Service's Tongass Land and Resource Management Plan (TLMP) established a series of old-growth forest reserves as part of

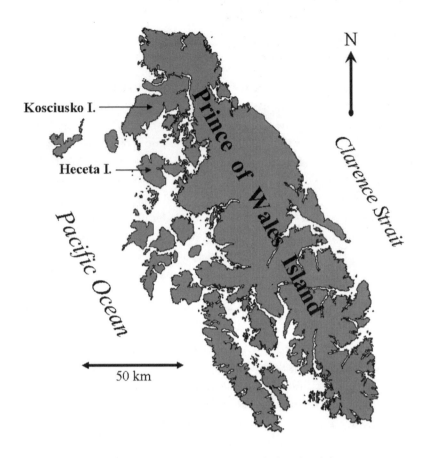

FIGURE 6.01. Prince of Wales Island in southeast Alaska. Also shown are Heceta and Kosciusko islands. Game management unit 2 designated by the Alaska Department of Fish and Game encompasses Prince of Wales and all of the smaller adjacent islands.

a comprehensive strategy for the conservation of biodiversity (USDA Forest Service 1997a, 2008a). In theory, the reserves are expected to preserve sufficient high-quality habitat to sustain ecological communities, such as the wolf-bear-deer predator-prey system on Prince of Wales Island, in the absence of suitable habitats within the intervening matrix of managed lands. In addition, TLMP-specified guidelines for managed lands are intended to reduce the risk of wildlife populations becoming extirpated or ecological functions becoming impaired (USDA Forest Service 2008a).

Prey

Suitable habitats for deer, beavers, and salmon are essential for the viability of the predator-prey ecological community on Prince of Wales Island. Humans have altered habitats and landscapes that affect each of those prey.

DEER. Prince of Wales Island supports 60,000 to 70,000 Sitka black-tailed deer, a small subspecies of mule deer adapted to northern Pacific old-growth rainforests (Person *et al.* 2009). Deer are the principal prey of wolves and an important prey for black bears (Person *et al.* 1996, Kohira and Rexstad 1997). Old-growth forest stands contain a mix of young, subdominant, and older dominant trees that create a canopy of multiple layers (see Alaback *et al.*, this volume, chapter 4). The dense forest canopy intercepts snow and rain, but numerous gaps allow sunlight to penetrate to the forest floor, enabling understory plants that provide important food for deer to flourish. Within five years after the forest canopy is removed by logging, vegetative growth responds to unrestricted sunlight by producing an abundance of forage, although much is of lower quality compared with the same species of plants grown in shade (Hanley and McKendrick 1983). Forage biomass reaches maximum abundance on productive sites 12 to 19 years after logging (table 6.1; Alaback 1982; Farmer and Kirchhoff 2007). Consequently, over the short-term (0–19 years after logging), clear-cutting enhances the quantity (but not the quality) of forage available to deer during summer and mild winters. Nonetheless, naturally regenerating conifers begin to form a dense canopy 20 to 30 years after logging that shades out understory plants (Alaback 1982). Eventually, young seral stands enter a *stem exclusion* stage in which the dense canopy of even-aged young trees almost completely eliminates forage plants, creating unproductive year-round habitat conditions that may last more than 150 years. Although during summer and mild winter conditions, deer may benefit from young clear-cuts, the long-term prognosis is permanent loss of suitable foraging habitat.

Deer populations in southeast Alaska and coastal British Columbia contain resident and migratory deer (Schoen and Kirchhoff 1985; McNay and Voller 1995). During summer, migratory deer move up in elevation as snowline recedes and eventually occupy lush alpine meadows composed of highly nutritious deciduous forbs situated above 600 m elevation. Migratory deer remain there until snowfall or senescence of deciduous plants in autumn forces them to move down to forested hillsides at lower

TABLE 6.1. Forage biomass (kg/ha) available to deer during summer in different habitats on Heceta Island in southeast Alaska (Farmer 2002; Farmer and Kirchhoff 2007). Data represent averages of oven-dried weights of evergreen and deciduous herbaceous forbs and *Vaccinium* spp. shrubs (current annual growth) sampled within 0.2-ha circular plots (*n* = 394).

HABITAT CLASS (N)	EVERGREEN FORBS	SE	DECIDUOUS FORBS	SE	SHRUBS	SE
Clearcuts <20 years old (73)	290.8	23.0	7.6	1.3	67.0	4.5
Clearcuts 20–39 years old (47)	168.5	47.0	8.6	2.2	71.7	10.3
Open-canopy old growth[a] (77)	165.1	16.9	19.9	2.8	38.8	3.7
Productive old growth[b] (118)	105.3	11.9	9.0	1.3	46.8	3.1
Nonforest[c] (29)	94.6	16.9	32.0	8.3	14.5	3.3
Riparian spruce old growth[d] (5)	57.1	49.7	12.1	7.7	29.2	17.8
Stem-exclusion seral forest[e] (45)	10.6	7.8	1.3	1.2	2.4	1.0

a   Old-growth forest with timber volume <58.3 m^3/ha.
b   Old-growth forest with timber volume ≥58.3 m^3/ha.
c   Sparsely forested and nonforested lands, mostly muskeg heaths and alpine habitats.
d   Closed-canopy old-growth forest with timber volume ≥290 m^3/ha situated on productive alluvial soils.
e   Clear-cuts >39 years old.

elevations. Migratory deer tend to overwinter in forested habitat at higher elevations than resident (nonmigratory) deer, although severe winter weather may force them to move down into valley bottoms where they compete with resident deer for winter forage. Resident deer do not move to alpine habitat during summer and remain within the same home ranges throughout the year. On Prince of Wales Island, resident deer generally select young clear-cuts (<20 years post-logging) and open-canopy forest stands during summer and mild winters (Yeo and Peek 1992; Farmer 2002; Doerr *et al.* 2005; Person 2009). When snow depths exceed 10 cm, most of the herbaceous plants in open habitats are buried, making important forage unavailable to deer. Cost of locomotion increases dramatically as depth of snow approaches chest height (50 cm) (Parker *et al.* 1984), and deer (resident and migratory) select old-growth forest stands with basal areas greater than 45 m^3/ha where snow depth is less and evergreen forbs and shrubs are still available. During severe winters when snow depth exceeds brisket height, most deer select productive old-growth stands with a volume of timber greater than 175 m³/ha at elevations below 240 m and avoid northerly exposures (Kirchhoff and Schoen 1987; Schoen and Kirchhoff 1990). Some deer may escape deep snow by moving to beaches and feeding on kelp and other seaweed. Mortality of deer from malnutrition, disease, and predation often is high during those winters (Schoen *et al.* 1988; Farmer *et al.* 2006; Person *et al.* 2009; Brinkman *et al.* 2011). Climate change may bring milder winter conditions on average, and it is tempting to speculate that winter habitat will become less important in the future (Scenarios Network for Alaska Planning 2009). Nonetheless, precipitation and probability of extreme storms may increase, and with it, risks of deep snow. Indeed, despite almost 30 consecutive years of relatively mild conditions, extreme snowfall occurred during the winter of 2006–2007 that substantially reduced deer numbers throughout southeast Alaska. Predation during and shortly after those winters can drive ungulate populations to very low levels, from which it may take years to recover. Consequently, it is not average conditions that really matter, but the probability of extreme events.

Clear-cut logging fragments forest patches, increasing edges; roads built to facilitate logging also contribute to forest fragmentation. Deer are attracted to forest edges and roadsides presumably because penetration of sunlight supports abundant forage production (Doerr *et al.* 2005). Nonetheless, deer that use edges and areas adjacent to roads frequently are at increased risk of predation by wolves, harvesting by hunters, and vehicular collisions (Person 2001; Farmer *et al.* 2006). Fragmented landscapes composed of small patches of old-growth timber may trap deer in those patches during winters in which snow hinders movement between patches (McNay 1995). Indeed, habitat suitability models for black-tailed deer in coastal British Columbia include distances between forest patches as a critical parameter (BC Ministry of Forests 1996). Mortality from predation and malnutrition may be high in logged and fragmented watersheds during snowy winters (Farmer *et al.* 2006), and deer populations may decline rapidly as a result (Brinkman *et al.* 2011).

OTHER PREY. Although deer are the principal prey of wolves, other species are important, particularly when deer abundance is low. Beaver frequently are consumed by wolves, but very little is known about their ecology in the region (Person *et al.* 1996; Kohira and Rexstad 1997). In coniferous forests of the Pacific Northwest, hardwoods such as alder (*Alnus* spp.) established along streams and on disturbed sites are important sources of food for beavers (Leidholt *et al.* 1989). In southeast Alaska, anecdotal evidence from trappers suggests beavers may benefit from alder regeneration on roadbeds and sites disturbed by logging; however, there are no data useful for evaluating population effects of logging or roads. Certainly, beavers take advantage of roadbeds adjacent to stream crossings by blocking culverts and allowing the road to dam the watercourse. Nonetheless, roads also provide trappers with convenient access to beaver habitat. Dams created by beavers may have negative effects on some anadromous fish such as sockeye (*Onchorhynchus nerka*)and chum (*O. keta*) salmon by blocking spawning migrations (McCurdy 2008) and a positive effect, particularly for coho salmon (*O. kisutch*), by creating pools (Bryant and Everest 1998).

Salmon are very important seasonal prey for wolves and bears (Person *et al.* 1996; Kohira and Rexstad 1997; Darimont and Reimchen 2002; Peacock 2004). Indeed, wolves often locate rendezvous sites near spawning streams and estuaries where they have easy access to salmon during August through October (Person and Russell 2009). In coastal British Columbia, Darimont *et al.* (2008) concluded that the availability of salmon seasonally decoupled wolves from their reliance on ungulate prey. Salmon are a critical resource for bears prior to hibernation and are likely a principle factor in sustaining high densities of black bears on Prince of Wales Island and elsewhere in the northern rainforests of Alaska and British Columbia. Fish, particularly salmon, are a vital food source for human subsistence. In addition, commercial and recreational fishing industries are the largest and most stable contributors to the island economy (Everest 2005; Crone and Mehrkens, this volume, chapter 5), but this is not necessarily the case on much of the north coast of British Columbia.

Clear-cuts and roads can change patterns of runoff and water flow and remove trees that are the sources of large woody debris in streams (Heifetz *et al.* 1986; Murphy and Koski 1989). In logged areas, streams may become channelized, banks destabilized, and pools for rearing fish lost, although unlogged forest buffers along streams and rivers can provide a source of woody debris and stabilize banks if they are wind firm (Murphy *et al.* 1986). Logged hillsides and roads increase the frequency of landslides, leading to soil erosion and sedimentation (Montgomery 1994; Swanston 1997). More immediately, roads may impair movement of fish throughout watersheds when culverts and other stream crossing structures are improperly designed or installed, or become blocked because of inadequate maintenance (Flanders and Cariello 2000; USDA Forest Service 2002). Many species of anadromous and resident fish must be able to migrate seasonally within watersheds to reach spawning and rearing habitats (Armstrong 1974; Bryant and Lukey 2004).

Abundant rainfall in the region creates high densities of streams and rivers that must be crossed when roads are built. In the Tongass National Forest, permanent roads cross anadromous fish streams more than 920 times and resident (nonanadromous) fish streams more than 1700 times (Flanders and Cariello 2000). Those numbers do not include temporary roads designed for short-term use, roads built on state and private lands, or roads crossing streams in which fish populations have not been documented. A survey of road conditions on national forest lands, including Prince of Wales Island, indicated that only 34% of culverts and bridges intersecting anadromous fish-bearing streams were adequate for adult and juvenile fish passage, and only 15% were adequate for passage of resident fish (Flanders and Cariello 2000). Surveys of forest roads on private lands on Prince of Wales Island showed similar results (Nichols and Frenette 2003). Most culverts were perched above the water level of the stream or the slope gradient was too steep to accommodate fish. Structures that did not block fish generally were recent installations, indicating that current standards may be adequate. Nonetheless, the legacy of older bridges and culverts is a persistent problem that affects the functioning of riparian ecosystems and may influence fish populations over the long term.

Predators

Wolves, bears, and humans all consume or exploit deer, beavers, and salmon on Prince of Wales Island, and therefore, they may compete for those resources during periods of scarcity. In addition, anthropogenic changes to landscapes and habitats influence the availability of prey to wolves and bears, and roads increase the risk of wolves and bears being killed by humans.

WOLVES. Wolves on Prince of Wales Island are an insular population (about 250–300 animals) probably derived from a few founders that reached the island before it was isolated from other islands and the main-

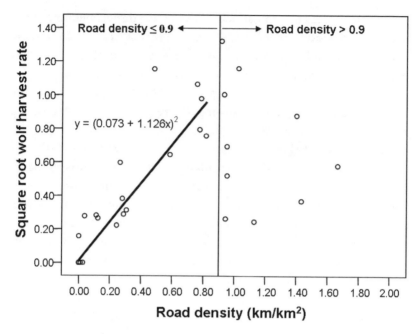

FIGURE 6.02. Relationship between road density (km/km^2) and average annual harvest rate of wolves (wolves/100 km^2) within all 32 wildlife analysis areas in game management unit 2 (Prince of Wales and adjacent islands), 1990–1999. Harvest rate is square root transformed to stabilize variance for analysis by linear regression. Data and figure are from Person and Russell (2008).

land by postglacial rise in sea level (Weckworth *et al.* 2005). Wolf populations are composed of resident pack members and nonresident wolves that are dispersing or are floating between several packs prior to or shortly after terminating dispersal (Person 2001; Person and Russell 2008). Wolves primarily prey on deer, annually consuming an estimated 18 to 32 deer per wolf (Person *et al.* 1996). In addition, salmon and beavers may constitute as much as 25% of the volume of their diet (Kohira and Rexstad 1997; Person *et al.* 1996; Szepanski *et al.* 1999).

Wolves strongly avoid young seedling and shrub-sapling stage clearcuts but may move through older stem exclusion stands (Person 2001). Wolves avoid clear-cuts and seral forest stands when selecting den sites, however, they tend to be tolerant of logging and other human activity near dens if the disturbances are of short duration (Person and Russell 2009). Roads offer convenient pathways for wolves through logged watersheds, but they also provide access to humans, increasing risk of death of wolves from

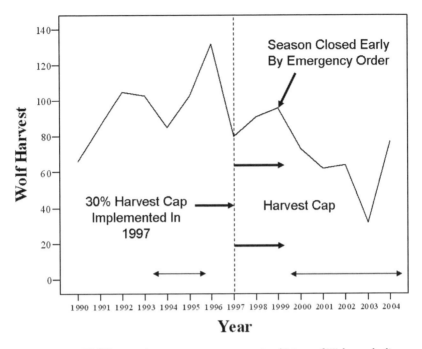

FIGURE 6.03. Wolf harvest in game management unit 2 (Prince of Wales and adjacent islands), 1990–2004. Harvest reached unsustainable limits in the mid-1990s, and the Alaska Board of Game implemented a harvest cap in 1997. The harvest quota was set at 30% of the estimated autumn wolf population in the unit. In 1999, the wolf-trapping season was closed by emergency order to prevent overharvest. Double-headed arrows indicate periods in which reliable population estimates of wolves were available. Figure and data are from Person and Russell (2008).

hunting and trapping (Person and Russell 2008). Even roads that are closed to vehicular travel provide convenient trails that facilitate harvest by humans. Person and Russell (2008) demonstrated a strong positive linear relation ($r = 0.89$) between road density less than or equal to 0.9 km/km^2 and harvest rates (fig. 6.02). They reported that densities greater than 0.9 km/km^2 likely resulted in unsustainable harvest. They also reported that 87% of mortality of wolves on Prince of Wales Island was from hunting and trapping. Annual survival rate of dispersing wolves (17%) was very low, with most shot or trapped before settling. Wolves are harvested legally during hunting and trapping seasons. Annually, about 50 to 95 wolves are killed and reported, but illegal take may at times equal the legal harvest (Person and Russell 2008). From 1990 through 1999, wolf harvest reached unsustainable levels, particularly within roaded watersheds, resulting in early closure of the trapping season in 1999 (fig. 6.03; Person and Russell 2008).

BLACK BEARS. There are few data concerning the ecology and demography of black bears in northern temperate rainforests; only harvest data are available for bears on Prince of Wales Island. Nonetheless, in southeast Alaska the densities of black bears were reported as high as 1.5 bears/km^2 within watersheds containing productive salmon streams and clear-cuts less than 25 years old (Peacock 2004). Bears are inactive in dens from November through April; dens are often located in hollow logs, dead standing trees, rock crevices, and ground nests on northern aspects (Erickson *et al.* 1982). When bears emerge in late March and early April, they forage on emergent vegetation and marine foods found along beaches. They feed on carcasses of deer that died during winter; however, they also may kill adult deer when the opportunity arises (Person 2009). The most important predation is on neonate fawns during late May and early June. For example, during a 3-year study of mortality of deer fawns on a portion of Prince of Wales Island, bears killed 60 (39%) of 154 radiocollared neonate fawns within 1 month of birth.(Alaska Department of Fish and Game 2010, 2011, 2012). During midsummer, bears consume large quantities of berries and appear to be attracted to young clear-cuts because of the abundance of blueberry shrubs (*Vaccinium* spp). Indeed, Schwarz and Franzmann (1991) reported black bear density to be higher in watersheds dominated by early successional forests compared with landscapes composed of older-seral forests. When salmon spawning begins in August, bears congregate in estuaries and along streams and rivers where low tide or shallow pools enable them to catch fish. Bears play an important role in transferring nutrients from anadromous fish to terrestrial ecosystems via their feces (Hildebrand *et al.* 1999). Spawning ebbs in late September, and thereafter bears consume deer, vegetation, and late-season berries as they make their way to winter dens.

Black bears are harvested year round except June 15 through August 31. From the years 2000 to 2009, 300 to 500 bears were harvested annually on Prince of Wales Island by mostly nonresident recreational hunters (Porter 2008). Providing logistic support to those hunters is a significant source of revenue for many local people, particularly during spring before popular summer fishing seasons open. Many hunters prefer to hunt for bears along logging roads that give them access to young clear-cuts, muskegs, and stream crossings where bears are visible. Roads and young clear-cuts may facilitate unsustainable harvesting of bears. Indeed, in 2009 the Alaska Department of Fish and Game restricted hunters from using road vehicles to access bear habitat on Prince of Wales Island in an attempt to reduce harvest to a sustainable level (Boyd Porter, pers. comm.).

HUMANS. Human occupants on Prince of Wales Island historically focused on marine food resources such as fish and shellfish. They also used boats to hunt deer and trap furbearers along beaches, particularly during winter. Thus, island interiors served as refugia for deer, wolves, bears, and furbearers. As logging proceeded in southeast Alaska and roads were built, subsistence hunters and trappers began changing their harvesting practices from using boats to using vehicles on roads to hunt inland areas (Ellanna and Sherrod 1987; Brinkman *et al.* 2009). Young clear-cuts, dominated by seedling conifers, became important habitat for hunters because deer were visible from roads. Roads increased the desirability of deer as a stable food resource because they were available during times of the year when marine resources were less abundant, and bad weather conditions had less effect on vehicle use than on boats. Hunting deer from roads required less time and effort than traditional strategies (Brinkman *et al.* 2009), causing most hunters to focus more on deer and less on marine resources (Ellanna and Sherrod 1987). Further, the timber industry attracted workers to southeast Alaska from the contiguous United States who were already accustomed to road-based hunting and trapping (Mazza 2003). Within one generation from the beginning of industrial-scale logging, hunting and trapping from roads largely replaced the traditional shoreline harvesting patterns of many local people (Brinkman *et al.* 2007). Hunters legally harvest 2,500 to 3,000 deer annually on Prince of Wales and adjacent islands; however, many more deer are killed illegally (Porter 2007). The area supports about 60,000 to 70,000 deer (Person *et al.* 2009), therefore, harvest removes 4%– 8% (mostly adult and yearling males) of the deer population each year.

SUCCESSION DEBT: SHORT-TERM BENEFITS VERSUS LONG-TERM CONSEQUENCES

Predator-prey dynamics frequently are described as *top-down* (predator mediated) or *bottom-up* (habitat mediated), divisions that cannot be applied as discrete explanations of the dynamics of complex predator-prey systems, particularly those involving long-lived mammals within rapidly changing environments (Ballard *et al.* 2001; Bowyer *et al.* 2005; Jedrzejewska and Jedrzejewski 2005). Bottom-up systems generally are regulated by the productivity of habitats and intrinsic rates of growth of prey, whereas top-down systems are governed by the density of predators and rates of kill. In reality, the dynamics of predator-prey systems shift along a continuum of integrated processes that are mostly bottom-up at one extreme or mostly top-down at the other (Bowyer *et al.* 2005; Jedrzejewska and Jedrzejewski 2005), and they may change over time. In temperate rainforest ecosystems such as that on Prince of Wales Island, industrial-scale timber harvest reduces carrying capacity for deer, shifting predator-prey dynamics from a largely bottom-up driven system to one in which top-down forcing (predator limitation) exerts greater control (Person 2001). Clear-cuts younger than 30 years and open-canopy forest provide deer with abundant forage during snow-free months. Those habitats also offer deer some protection from predation by wolves. Mortality of deer in extensively logged watersheds is high during severe winters, but their numbers rebound quickly during mild years despite effects of predation and hunting, indicating that population regulation is strongly influenced by bottom-up processes. Therefore, deer thrive in watersheds dominated by early successional forest stands, provided winters are mild.

Between 1955 and 2005, about 22% of deer summer range was clear-cut logged on state, federal, and private lands on Prince of Wales Island. Of the subset of those lands below 240 m elevation and on southerly aspects (90°–270°) that constitute important winter range for deer, 38% was clear-cut by 2005. It is likely that an additional 5%–10% of deer winter range will be logged in the next 20 years, depending on the implementation of TLMP and transfers of lands to private timber corporations. Currently, the median age of a hectare of second-growth forest on federal lands is 34 years. About 75% of all second growth on federal lands is greater than 20 years old. On state and private lands the median age likely is about 5 to 10 years less. Deer are abundant and may remain so during part of the next decade (Brinkman *et al.* 2011). Nonetheless, as clear-cuts continue to age, carrying capacity for deer within logged watersheds (that have transitioned into sterile second-growth habitat) will decline, and the resilience of deer to winter weather, predation, and hunting will diminish. Net annual recruitment of deer also will decline, but in a disproportionate and nonlinear fashion (fig. 6.04). Net annual recruitment represents the portion of a deer population that can be removed additively by predation and hunting

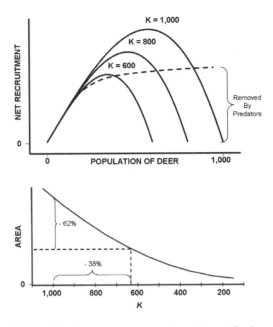

FIGURE 6.04. Relationships between net annual recruitment for deer and population density (*top graph*), and area under recruitment curve and changes in carrying capacity (K) (*bottom graph*). Area under the recruitment curves is reduced in a negative exponential fashion as K is reduced. That area represents the pool of recruits available for removal by predators and hunters without causing a decline in deer population. A 38% decline from historical levels in deer habitat capability (carrying capacity) would reduce the area under the curve by 68%. Time lags in the numerical response of predators to declining deer abundance will mean that they will remove a larger portion of net annual recruitment as K declines. That will increase competition between predators and hunters for deer and will shift the predator-prey systems more strongly toward top-down limitation.

without causing a decline in population. Wolves and bears will remove an increasing proportion of that recruitment until deer populations decline in heavily logged watersheds dominated by stem exclusion seral forest (Person 2001). Future harvesting of seral forest may return those stands to states that are productive for deer but will still leave them vulnerable to severe winter weather with deep snow packs. Moreover, harvesting second growth depends on future demand for Alaska timber, which may be weak owing to the high costs of production, transportation, and competition from producers located where wood is cheaper to grow, harvest, and transport (Crone 2005; Crone and Mehrkens, this volume, chapter 5).

Wolf packs will respond to a decline in deer density in logged watersheds by focusing on areas where deer abundance is higher (unlogged watersheds) or by expanding home ranges into neighboring pack territories, causing strife between packs. Wolves may also focus on alternative prey, but it is unlikely that salmon, which are only seasonally available, and beavers will sustain them indefinitely if deer abundance becomes very low (Person *et al.* 1996; Person 2001). Nonetheless, predation on salmon may temporarily decouple synchrony between deer and wolf population trends by subsidizing summer survival of wolves, particularly pups (Person 2001; Darimont *et al.* 2008). Thus, the time delay between a decline in deer population and similar trend in wolves would be lengthened, causing a stronger and more rapid shift toward top-down forcing.

Black bears are not obligate predators of deer; thus in the short term, a decline in deer will not precipitate a simultaneous decline in bears, a circumstance that likely will exacerbate the effects of bear predation on deer. Eventually, the predator-prey system will shift strongly toward top-down forcing, resulting in a more rapid decline in deer population than would be predicted from simply loss of carrying capacity, as well as periods in which deer populations within logged watersheds are suppressed well below carrying capacity by predation (fig. 6.05; Person 2001).

Migratory deer tend to be at lower risk of predation and benefit from abundant forage in alpine areas during snow-free months (McNay and Voller 1995). They will be less affected by loss of carrying capacity within logged stands, which tend to be concentrated at low elevations. However, during severe winters when they are pushed down into the valley bottoms, migratory deer will be exposed to the same habitat conditions and risks of predation endured by resident deer. Populations of migratory deer should rebound more quickly than resident deer during mild years because they have access to high-quality range in summer and have lower risk of predation. Consequently, the ratio of migratory deer to resident deer within logged watersheds adjacent to alpine terrain should increase over time.

As deer numbers decline and predator-prey dynamics shift more strongly toward predator limitation, subsistence and recreational hunters increasingly will be alarmed at what they perceive as competition by wolves and bears for deer. Strong proprietary attitudes concerning deer exist within many communities on the island and many resident hunters resent sharing "their deer" with off-island hunters. Protective attitudes will precede actual changes in deer population because clear-cuts greater than

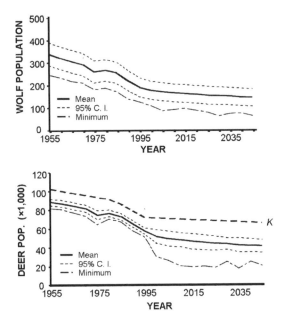

FIGURE 6.05. Results averaged for 2,000 Monte Carlo simulations of a predator-prey model described by Person (2001) that represents past and future conditions on Prince of Wales and Kosciusko islands in southeast Alaska. Simulations account for timber harvest and road construction on federal, state, and private lands; harvest of wolves and deer; and periodic severe winters in which all recruitment to the deer population is lost. Changes in carrying capacity (K) represent loss of deer habitat capability predicted in the Tongass Land Management Plan. Results indicate that wolf and deer populations will decline substantially by 2045. Decline in the deer population will be disproportionately greater than the proportional loss of K. Simulations do not account for bear predation on deer.

10 years old usually are unsuitable for hunting (as a result of increasing cover) despite supporting abundant deer (Brinkman 2007; Brinkman *et al.* 2009). Therefore, unless new cuts are created at the rate existing ones become too old to hunt, there will be a net loss of land preferred for hunting, even along roads that remain open to vehicle use. As a result, as clear-cuts age, hunters will perceive fewer deer in popular hunting areas; feelings of competition with wolves, bears, and other hunters will increase demands for liberal harvests of predators and restrictions on hunting by off-island hunters. Indeed, a perception of competition led to federal regulations implemented in 2003 that restricted hunting opportunities for most off-island hunters (Brinkman *et al.* 2007). Legal and illegal take of

deer, wolves, and bears likely will increase particularly in watersheds accessible by roads or from boats (Person *et al.* 1996; Person 2001), and they may be overharvested despite regulations designed to sustainably manage their populations (Person and Russell 2008). In time, subsistence harvesters may return to a diet that focuses more on seafood. However, salmon spawning and survival of young may be impaired if the long-term effects of logging and roads on stream habitat are not properly addressed. In that event, fewer fish would be available to sustain populations of black bears, provide alternative prey for wolves, and satisfy subsistence needs. Eventually, populations of deer, bears, and wolves in logged landscapes dominated by stem-exclusion forest may only be a fraction of what they were historically (Person 2001).

Succession debt refers to the fact that a healthy predator-prey ecological community during the early stages of forest succession after logging is not a reliable indicator of future conditions. As the capacities of logged landscapes to support deer diminish, nonlinear predator-prey dynamics will dramatically alter those conditions such that populations of wolves, black bears, and deer likely will decline substantially. Moreover, social factors will complicate the situation and could result in further depletion of some species, particularly if harvest (both legal and illegal) is facilitated by roads that leave few inaccessible refugia. In particular, the viability of the wolf population on Prince of Wales and adjacent islands could be at risk (Person 2001).

A similar process involving black-tailed deer, wolves, black bears, and cougars (*Felis concolor*) developed on Vancouver Island in British Columbia (Hatter 1982; Atkinson and Janz 1994; BC Ministry of Forests 1996). Beginning in the 1960s, extensive logging eliminated important winter range for deer, compromising their resilience to predation, hunting, and winter weather (BC Ministry of Forests 1996). Deer numbers declined, hunting opportunities for deer were restricted, and predator control was implemented as an emergency measure to restore deer (Hatter 1982; Atkinson and Janz 1994). Despite reducing predators, deer population density remains much lower than historical levels, and wildlife managers chronically are concerned about the effects of predators on deer. In a further twist, because of low deer population and isolation of habitat, wolves were suspected of being significant predators of Vancouver Island marmots, an endangered species (Bryant and Page 2005).

DISCUSSION AND MANAGEMENT IMPLICATIONS

Globally, the conservation of large-mammal predator-prey systems disturbed by extensive environmental changes and subject to competing human interests is a daunting challenge, because the objective must be to sustain the entire ecological community rather than focusing on individual species. In many places, including southeast Alaska, planning for and implementing actions to conserve ecological communities is more difficult because multiple management agencies are responsible for different components and often have priorities and mandates that are contradictory. Treating individual discrete components of a complex system without regard to interactions between those components is a recipe for failure (Dörner 1996). For example, on Prince of Wales Island, simply closing roads or changing harvest regulations to protect wolves will not guarantee the population remains viable if landscapes can no longer sustain abundant and resilient deer populations (Person 2001). Indeed, it is likely that as the predator-prey system shifts more strongly towards top-down limitation, wolves will need to be harvested to some extent to prevent depletion of deer (fig. 6.06). The challenge will be how to manage that harvest to boost deer population without risking the viability of wolves. It is not enough to maintain deer abundance sufficient for wolves because subsistence hunters rely on those deer as well, and they will kill wolves legally or illegally to protect that resource. The situation is compounded by the extensive road network that greatly facilitates human access and eliminates many refugia for wolves. An additional complication is that the wolf population is genetically distinct and isolated. If wolves are extirpated or reduced to a small population, rescue or recolonization by dispersing wolves from the mainland is unlikely. Deer populations must also be resilient to bear predation, which can have a substantial effect on annual recruitment. Underlying everything are the social and economic pressures to continue logging and sustain a timber industry. As more old-growth forest is logged and additional roads constructed, fewer options remain to conserve intact ecological systems, yet human interests and needs cannot be dismissed easily.

The Tongass Land Management Plan incorporates a conservation strategy that attempts to protect the integrity and functioning of ecological systems on national forest lands in southeast Alaska while allowing

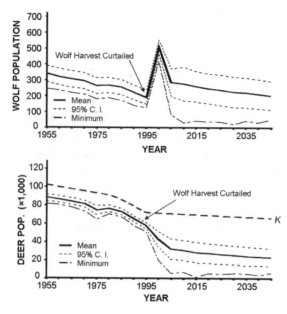

FIGURE 6.06. Results averaged for 2,000 Monte Carlo simulations of a predator-prey model described by Person (2001) that represents past and future conditions on Prince of Wales and Kosciusko islands in southeast Alaska. Simulations account for timber harvest and road construction on federal, state, and private lands; harvest of wolves and deer; and periodic severe winters in which all recruitment to the deer population is lost. Wolf harvest is hypothetically curtailed in 1996, representing changes in regulations if wolves had been listed as threatened under the Endangered Species Act by the US Fish and Wildlife Service (see Person et al. 1996). Changes in carrying capacity (K) represent loss of deer habitat capability predicted in the Tongass Land Management Plan. Results indicate that if wolf harvest were curtailed, the wolf population would still decline in the long term as deer are reduced to very low levels. Deer hunters would be alarmed at competition by wolves for deer and likely would demand harvests of wolves or kill them illegally. Simulations do not account for bear predation on deer.

industrial-scale harvesting of timber. The plan specifies guidelines for densities of roads to reduce risk of mortality of wolves from hunting and trapping. It also sets minimum limits for habitat capability (carrying capacity) for deer; it is presumed that these limits will sustain deer abundance capable of supporting viable wolf populations and meeting the needs of subsistence hunters. Thus, it attempts to address wolves and deer at a community level while also trying to satisfy human desires. The heart of the plan is the establishment of a system of forest reserves and other lands on which logging is deferred; these lands encompass a portion of the productive old-growth forest left on national forest lands (see Lertzmann and MacKinnon, this volume, chapter 8, for a discussion of reserves and a case study in coastal British Columbia). Unlike other areas in the Pacific Northwest, southeast Alaska still has many intact and ecologically functioning watersheds distributed throughout the region. Some of those watersheds are part of the old-growth forest reserve system established by the Tongass Land Management Plan (USDA Forest Service 1997a, 2008a). They are critical to ensuring the long-term sustainability of populations of fish and wildlife (Bryant and Everest 1998; USDA Forest Service 1997a; Albert and Schoen 2007a). Protected and roadless lands at a watershed or larger scale can safeguard important salmon streams from headwaters to their outlets. They maintain the natural composition and connectivity of landscapes, minimize forest fragmentation from roads and other human activities, and limit accessibility of wildlife to human exploitation.

On Prince of Wales Island, about 62% of the habitat capability (surrogate for carrying capacity of winter range) for deer remains after 50 years of industrial-scale logging (Albert and Schoen 2007a). About 58% of that capability is located on lands currently deferred from logging. A key assumption in the TLMP is that deferred lands are sufficient to conserve viable populations of all wildlife species currently inhabiting the island with little additional contribution from managed lands. That untested expectation requires evaluation, using monitoring programs and research focusing on its implicit assumptions (see Smith and Zollner 2005; Smith and Person 2007; Smith et al. 2011). For example, with respect to wolves, no single reserve or aggregate patch of deferred lands is sufficiently large to encompass an entire wolf pack home range. Therefore, very few wolf packs will be immune from logging, road access, hunting, and trapping; managed lands should be considered an integral part of the conservation strategy. Indeed, conservation strategies that focus primarily on systems of habitat reserves and roadless patches frequently fail to meet their objectives because they ignore the importance and function of the intervening matrix of unprotected lands (Noon and Blakesly 2006; Franklin and Lindenmayer 2009). That is particularly true for the conservation of large vagile mammals such as wolves and bears. Moreover, selection of reserve lands must be based on thorough ecological evaluation (Murphy and Noon 1992; Lertzmann and MacKinnon, this volume, chapter 8), rather than simply selecting lands that have not yet been developed or that are not economically valuable. Indeed, a conservation area design proposed for Prince of Wales Island included the protection of intact watersheds with the highest biological values (including winter deer habitat) and restoration for high-value watersheds that had previously been logged and roaded (Schoen and Albert 2007). In the conservation strategy in the TLMP, old-growth forest reserves comprise existing congressionally protected lands and a selection from some of the largest remaining roadless patches of unmanaged forest within the Tongass National Forest (USDA Forest Service 1997a). In extensively logged areas such as Prince of Wales Island, timber harvest targeted the most productive forested watersheds first; therefore, less productive forest often predominates in the unlogged and unroaded watersheds aggregated into forest reserves (Albert and Schoen 2007a). Any strategy to conserve large-mammal predator-prey communities must be able to accommodate their nonlinear dynamics; therefore, they should have large margins for error. In the case of Prince of Wales Island, that includes maintaining as much functionality within the matrix of managed lands as possible, while also maintaining current reserves and adding new high-quality landscapes within reserves. The objective should be to maximize the amount of suitable summer and winter range available to deer, providing habitat capability well in excess of the minimums established by the TLMP so that resilience of deer to predation, hunting, and winter snow conditions is maintained.

The matrix of managed lands surrounding reserves contains the most productive forest lands in southeast Alaska and likely will play a critical role, along with reserve lands, in sustaining wildlife and meeting human subsistence needs. Timber harvest on managed lands on Prince of Wales Island will need to shift away from old growth to seral forest. Indeed, we suggest that all old-growth forest left on federal lands on Prince of Wales and immediately adjacent islands be protected permanently to assure future conservation options and provide a hedge against the transfers of many parcels of productive forested lands to private ownership under provisions in the Alaska Native Claims Settlement Act of 1971. Conveyed lands almost certainly will be logged with little consideration for ecological values and wildlife. If harvest of old growth on federal lands is inevitable, then logging should be done in ways that approximate natural disturbances spatially and temporally (see Alaback *et al.*, this volume, chapter 4 and Beese, this volume, chapter 9). Because highly productive old-growth forest is underrepresented within reserves, it is important that the structure and heterogeneous character of old-growth forest be restored in as many logged watersheds as possible. For example, within stem exclusion seral forest, habitat for deer may be enhanced by thinning and small patch cuts that create gaps in the forest canopy sufficient to reestablish understory plants preferred as forage (Hanley *et al.* 2005; Alaback *et al.*, this volume, chapter 4). Silvicultural treatments to enhance deer habitat (as well as other species) need to be widespread; however, concentrating much of the effort in areas accessible to subsistence hunters by road may help sustain hunters' needs while reducing their motivation to kill wolves and bears illegally. It would also be helpful if timber harvest of seral forest targeted hunter-accessible areas whenever possible.

Most logging roads built in southeast Alaska, and particularly those within the Tongass National Forest, were conceived as long-term capital improvements. Their status as permanent additions to the landscape mandates a commitment by land managers to maintain them and monitor their ecological effects over many years. Weather, climate, topography, and remoteness of the region make maintaining and monitoring roads very expensive and difficult. In addition, managing road access on national forest lands is a difficult process because local residents usually demand use of forest roads, which were paid for by public funds, often making road closures for conservation purposes contentious. Budgets used to maintain, monitor, and close roads, particularly on national forest lands, usually are linked to timber harvesting activities. Timber harvesting, which may entail the construction of new roads, is necessary to pay for the maintenance, monitoring, and decommissioning of old ones. Fluctuations in the amount of timber put up for sale have a direct influence on funds available for roads. Consequently, funding for long-term maintenance and monitoring may not be stable or adequate for the task. That problem is particularly acute on Prince of Wales Island because it has the highest density of logging roads in southeast Alaska.

New roads construction should be avoided or kept to a minimum by careful planning to reduce fragmentation of remaining productive forest stands and wetlands. Where roads are necessary, construction should employ best management practices with respect to methods of construction and placement of drainage and stream-crossing structures. Existing roads that penetrate old-growth reserves should be decommissioned by removing culverts, pipes, and bridges to restore the natural flow of water and limit human access. Culverts and bridges that are inadequate for fish passage should be replaced. Long-term monitoring of the condition of roads within a diverse array of landscapes and research examining the hydrological and ecological effects of roads should be supported. This is particularly critical given the unknown impacts of climate change on the hydrology of this rainforest ecoregion. Alternative sources of funding independent of timber harvesting likely will be needed to sustain those long-term monitoring and research programs.

Rates of harvest and population trends of wolves, bears, deer, and fur-bearers should be closely monitored to prevent unsustainable harvesting and enable informed decisions concerning seasons and bag limits. Harvest reporting is mandatory for wolves, bears, and deer; however law enforce-ment efforts to insure compliance need to be stepped up. We urge fish and wildlife managers to take an ecological perspective when setting harvest objectives, to avoid overemphasizing human desires and neglecting the requirements of other species and their interactions within the system. Long-term programs for adequately monitoring deer, wolf, and bear popu-lations (and other forest-dependent species) need to be implemented. They should take advantage of new developments in estimating populations using noninvasive techniques (Peacock 2004; Brinkman *et al.* 2011) when-ever possible and cost effective. Finally, the responsible management agen-cies need to agree on a common set of goals to conserve the predator-prey community, and results from monitoring and research should be used to set population, harvest, and ecological thresholds that trigger appropriate management actions in a timely fashion.

We focused on a subset of wildlife species inhabiting North Pacific rainforests and ignored other forest-dependent species. For example, brown bears (*U. arctos*), northern flying squirrels (*Glaucomys sabrinus*), marten (*Martes caurina*), goshawks (*Accipiter gentilis*), and spruce grouse (*Falcipennis canadensis*) also are affected by timber harvesting and roads in southeast Alaska and coastal British Columbia (Schoen 1990; Iverson *et al.* 1996; Small *et al.* 2003; Smith *et al.* 2005). Nonetheless, our case study illustrates the overarching importance, regardless of species involved or geographic location, of addressing conservation at the level of ecological communities rather than individual species. We demonstrate that forest management practices or developments in North Pacific temperate rain-forests that deviate from natural patterns of disturbance likely will have long-term and possibly intractable consequences for wildlife, humans, and ecosystems. We also emphasize the need to consider social factors, hunting and trapping in our case, when designing and implementing plans to conserve biodiversity. Indeed, ignorance or denial of those factors could easily derail an otherwise scientifically sound conservation strategy.

ACKNOWLEDGMENTS

The authors thank the senior leadership of the Alaska Department of Fish and Game, particularly Dale Rabe, Doug Larsen, and Rod Flynn for their support of the conference that spawned this chapter. We also thank the sponsors and organizers of that conference. Finally, we appreciate the thorough comments provided by anonymous reviewers of our manuscript.

7

Concepts of Conservation Biology Applied to Wildlife in Old-Forest Ecosystems, with Special Reference to Southeast Alaska and Northern Coastal British Columbia

Bruce G. Marcot

INTRODUCTION

Southeast Alaska and northern coastal British Columbia constitute a contiguous ecosystem of temperate rainforests, fragmented by thousands of islands big and small, and by mountain ranges, glaciers, and ice fields. This largely undisturbed natural laboratory affords spectacular opportunities for understanding how climate, time, ecological interactions, and evolution have influenced the development of the biota and ecosystems we see today.

This laboratory is also home to human settlements dating back millennia, and more recently to resource extraction industries, especially timber harvesting and commercial fishing. Knowing how such activities have affected the region's natural resources and biodiversity is of central importance to resource managers and local communities of the region as the area experiences increased stress from human activities and continued climate change.

The complex topography of the region—its thousands of islands, inlets, snow-covered peaks, glaciers, muskeg bogs, and other features—renders a great challenge for conservation. Many opportunities exist in southeast Alaska and northern coastal BC to study effects of geographic isolation on local adaptation, variations in island size and distances, historical ebbs and flows of terrestrial dispersal routes, local colonization and extinction dynamics, and effects of intensive and long-term forest management activities on the biota.

The region is especially diverse, encompassing beach fringes, riparian vegetation, productive and unproductive old-growth forest, muskeg, alpine, snowfields, and glaciers. The region's biodiversity is influenced also by the ecological linkages among forest, riparian, wetland, and marine environments (Edwards *et al.*, this volume, chapter 3) and by its complex biogeographic history (Cook and MacDonald, this volume, chapter 2). This rich array of environments generates a corresponding richness of ecosystem services (Costanza *et al.* 1997).

The biota and ecosystems of southeast Alaska and northern coastal BC have not been extensively studied. Most investigations have been funded and guided by state and federal natural resource management agencies, favoring a focus on economically and socially important species and issues. Basic inventories of most taxa are still wanting.

Much of the region is little disturbed by human activities; human-caused disturbances are concentrated in several urban centers such as Juneau, Ketchikan, Sitka, Petersburg, and Wrangell in southeast Alaska; on a few islands with intensive timber harvest activity such as Prince of Wales, Zarembo, and northeast Chichagof; and in a few other high timber volume old-growth forests, especially on Native corporation lands. Many of the extensive areas of low timber volume forest are likely to remain economically unprofitable for commercial timber harvest. For this reason, de facto reserves of low-volume old-growth temperate rainforest will likely continue to exist.

In this chapter, I review and suggest concepts of conservation biology that may be, or have proven to be, pertinent to managing old, temperate rainforest ecosystems in southeast Alaska and northern coastal BC. I also describe lessons learned from years of research in the region that have provided new insights into concepts and application of conservation biology more generally. I then evaluate some developing and potential new avenues for conservation biology in southeast Alaska and northern coastal BC and end with conclusions and recommendations on challenges and promises of conservation of the region's temperate rainforests, as well as conservation biology concepts and tools of greatest pertinence and promise for further development.

CONSERVATION BIOLOGY CONCEPTS APPLIED IN SOUTHEAST ALASKA AND NORTHERN COASTAL BRITISH COLUMBIA

Applications of conservation biology concepts to forested landscapes have been well summarized (e.g., Voller and Harrison 1998; Lindenmayer and Franklin 2002). During the past four decades, scientists working in southeast Alaska and coastal BC have made major strides in four main areas of conservation biology: understanding and modeling species-habitat relationships; mapping species distributions; studying and providing conservation guidelines for rare, little-known, endemic, and peripheral species; and better understanding the ecological dynamics of oceanic and land bridge islands and habitat isolates.

Understanding and Modeling Species-Habitat Relationships

Information on species-habitat relationships is necessary to inform forest management options. Traditionally this information, called *wildlife-habitat relationships* or WHR, is presented in tables that denote the association of each wildlife species with each habitat type and structural or successional state. This approach has been usefully extended to include other selected taxa and groups of species, such as those developed for the Interior Columbia River Basin (Marcot 1997).

An approach to modeling species-habitat relationships entails development of *resource selection functions* (RSFs), which quantify the degree to which various habitat conditions are selected and used by organisms. For example, RSFs have been developed for gray wolf (*Canis lupus*) and grizzly bear (*Ursus arctos*) populations in the Arctic (Johnson *et al.* 2004), to determine cumulative effects of forestry on gray wolf habitat use in eastern Canada (Houle *et al.* 2010), to identify conservation corridors (Chetkiewicz and Boyce 2009), and to improve estimates of elk (*Cervus canadensis*) population size in Canada (Allen *et al.* 2008). Belant *et al.* (2010) used RSFs to compare resource selection by sympatric brown bears (*Ursus arctos)* and American black bears (*U. americanus*) in Alaska.

Mapping Species Distributions

Species distribution maps can be based on known occurrences and expert knowledge, inferred from species-habitat relationships, inferred from RSFs, compiled from existing range maps typically varying in quality and resolution, or some combination of these approaches. In the North Pacific temperate rainforests, distributions have been mapped for some mammal (MacDonald and Cook 2007) and bird species (Piatt and Ford 1993; Mendenhall 1992; Kuletz and Piatt 1992). Superimposing species distribution maps can help identify hot spots of species (and subspecies) endemism, rarity, and richness; Cook *et al.* (2006) identified centers of species endemism in the Alexander Archipelago of southeast Alaska and suggested that they be managed for "lineage diversity" (Cook and MacDonald 2001).

Mapping hot spots of species endemism and especially species richness is one component of GAP analysis (Scott *et al.* 1993), which entails overlaying selected distribution maps of taxa or hot spots with boundaries of existing protected areas and determining where protection may be lacking. GAP analyses should specify the habitats of each species, where such environments occur within and outside protected areas, and what each type of protected area is designed to protect. Potential problems of the GAP analysis approach may arise from map inaccuracies (e.g., Johnson and Gillingham 2008), but the general approach has much merit and utility for delineating portions of the landscape that might deserve special conservation attention.

Conserving Rare, Little-Known, Endemic, and Peripheral Species

Rare species are often of special concern (Raphael and Molina 2007). Species can be rare in several ways: (1) being scarce everywhere even if total population size of the species is relatively high, (2) having a small total population size, and (3) occurring as a disjunct or peripheral population (Marcot and Molina 2007). A species can be locally rare if it is a newly colonizing population (founders) or the residual remnants of a shrinking distribution (paleoendemics). Also, rare endemics may include recently evolved populations that develop along range peripheries or in recently colonized isolated locations (neoendemics).

Species can be little-known for several reasons: (1) incomplete knowledge of their taxonomy, (2) an incomplete inventory, and (3) poor understanding of their ecology and environmental factors that determine their distribution and abundance (Marcot and Molina 2007). Soil and forest canopy invertebrates (e.g., springtails, microspiders, flightless terrestrial carabid beetles and other arthropods) and soil and wood fungi are generally poorly known in temperate rainforests. Thus, the ecological roles these species play are likely to be unrecognized and unappreciated.

Conservation of species on the periphery of their ranges may improve their long-term evolutionary potential (Lesica and Allendorf 1995; Bunnell et al. 2004). Peripheral populations may have phenotypes or genotypes not found elsewhere in a species range. Peripheral populations can become important centers of dispersal under changing environmental conditions. They may also be especially vulnerable by having lower genetic diversity than in the core of the species' range, as has been reported for Canada lynx (*Lynx canadensis*) (Schwartz et al. 2003).

Understanding Ecological Dynamics of Oceanic and Land Bridge Islands and Habitat Isolates

Much of the above-mentioned information—understanding and modeling species-habitat relationships; mapping species distributions; and conserving rare, little-known, endemic, and peripheral species—is crucial to understanding the ecological dynamics of species in this region. For example, evaluating viability of populations in southeast Alaska and coastal BC is complicated by dynamics of island biogeography, including the roles of habitat isolates within and among islands and the mainland; the role of mainland species' pools; how ocean currents and wind and storm patterns can facilitate or impede interisland dispersal of terrestrial and airborne organisms; and the roles of refugia as strongholds or sources of species dispersal. It is important also to evaluate natural and anthropogenic changes to environmental and habitat conditions, including effects of climate change, storms (especially windthrow of forest stands), timber harvesting, forest restoration, human habitation and people-wildlife interactions, hunting, and a number of other potential stressors.

As a starting point, researchers can use basic island biogeography theory (Shafer 1990) to evaluate species-area relationships (number of species of a taxonomic group, given island sizes) and incidence functions (probabilities of species presence or population size of a species, given habitat extent on particular islands) based on relationships developed for the region or elsewhere. Such relationships could be further refined with information on resource and habitat selection of individual species (e.g., Allan *et al.* 2008; Chetkiewicz and Boyce 2009; Johnson and Gillingham 2008) and seasonal and geographic variation in resource availability. Collectively, this approach could be used in a GAP analysis—overlaying results of an enhanced island biogeography analysis onto existing or potential habitat designs of reserves and connections—in a threats assessment to determine which species, subspecies, or geographic locations might warrant additional conservation consideration in context of island dynamics and habitat fragmentation (e.g., Perault and Lomolino 2000). To some degree, such assessments have already been conducted, at least in part (Albert and Schoen 2007a; Suring *et al.* 1993). A further consideration would be the influence of island dynamics on genetic isolation and structure of populations (e.g., Schwartz *et al.* 2003), as discussed below.

FUTURE APPLICATIONS OF CONSERVATION BIOLOGY IN TEMPERATE RAINFORESTS

Preserving the biological diversity of northern temperate rainforests while human populations expand, industrial activities increase, and climates change poses challenges for conservation biologists and resource managers. Fortunately, recent developments in conservation biology provide practitioners with some valuable conceptual and technical tools.

Providing for Connectivity

Improved understanding of the dynamic consequences of spatial connections is an important potential contribution of conservation biology. Providing some degree of spatial connectivity may help maintain effective population sizes large enough to avoid deleterious effects of inbreeding depression and local extirpations from random demographic fluctuations and from occasional catastrophic environmental events.

Major swaths of coastal forest have already been designated as protected areas, the largest of which is British Columbia's Great Bear Rainforest, a massive area of 8.5 million ha. About a fourth of this area is off limits to timber harvest; the rest is to be managed under ecosystem-based guidelines. A recent land-use agreement between the British Columbia government and local First Nations increased protection of forests from all industrial development in the Great Bear Rainforest portion of the coast from about 9% to 28% (2.1 million ha). An additional 5% of the land base (370,000 ha) is off limits to logging, but is not strictly protected from mining, road building, and other development.

On the Tongass National Forest, a network of far smaller old forest reserves has been established using the Alexander Archipelago wolf, goshawk (*Accipiter gentilis*), and other species as indicators to guide reserve size and spacing. The intervening matrix lands are to be managed more intensively for timber, roads, or other uses. Whether large reserves or networks of small reserves will best serve a variety of conservation objectives is analyzed in greater detail in chapter 8 of this volume.

To determine the best spatial distribution of protected areas that might be established in the region, information will be needed about individual species' life histories, ecologies, past and current distributions, relationships to insular and patchy environments, and the biotic roles of organisms and abiotic ecosystem processes.

Evaluating Key Ecological Functions

Key ecological functions (KEFs) are activities performed by organisms that influence environmental conditions for other species (Marcot and Vander Heyden 2001). KEFs can be presented as an extensive hierarchical classification system of categories (Morrison *et al.* 2006). KEFs include (1) primary burrow-digging activities of large or small organisms (e.g., badger, mountain beaver, ground squirrel) that provide burrows for a host of secondary-using species, (2) phoretic transportation of one organism by another (e.g., dispersal of plant vegetative parts, seeds, and spores by migrating birds; seed-caching by birds and mammals; dispersal of fungal spores in excrement of rodents and ungulates), (3) physical disintegration of standing and down wood (e.g., by bears and woodpeckers), (4) uploading of marine-derived nutrients to riparian uplands by spawning salmon, and many others. KEF databases have been developed for wildlife species in Washington, Oregon, British Columbia, and the entire Columbia River Basin as part of integrated WHR information systems and models (O'Neil, Johnson, *et al.* 2001). Such databases could be extended and used in southeast Alaska and northern coastal BC.

KEF databases can be used to evaluate a variety of functional patterns in species assemblages. They can identify unique ecological roles of selected (e.g., rare, endemic, threatened, or introduced) species; reveal patterns of functional richness, functional redundancy, and functional diversity at the ecological community or species assemblage levels; identify functional webs of ecological interactions among species within communities; and other interactions among communities or within communities (see Marcot and Vander Heyden 2001). In this way, the manager could determine the degree to which interactions may be weak or declining. Such analyses have been conducted for mammalian carnivores in forests of western North America (Marcot and Aubry 2003), the role of decaying wood in providing for functional webs of associated species (Marcot 2002), and the influence of salmon on the presence and ecological roles of a suite of associated terrestrial wildlife species (Cederholm *et al.* 2001). Forest ecosystems are also subject to a suite of abiotic processes that can be denoted in WHR databases as part of the set of key environmental correlates.

Determining the Distributions of Taxa

A basic understanding of the occurrence and distribution of all taxa is essential for determining the occurrence of subspecies and species of the region, including endemics. Such an inventory should sample major mainland watersheds and at least the larger and midsize islands of southeast Alaska and coastal BC. More intensive sampling of vegetation and habitat conditions at selected locations would provide a starting point for developing predictive models of current and future taxa distribution by using presence data of the taxa and current modeling tools such as Maxent (Phillips and Dudik 2008).

Preparing for Climates in Flux

Predicting the effects of climate change is one of the major conservation issues of the early twenty-first century. Among other things, changing climates can affect the timing and length of growing seasons; hydrologic and nutrient cycles; seasonality of fruiting and flowering plants; emergence and availability of insects as wildlife prey; and migration, survival, and reproductive success of organisms (Slocombe 2001; McGuire *et al.* 2004). Understanding how individual species might respond to changes in vegetation and environmental conditions as affected by climate change would provide an improved basis for planning habitat connections to ensure population persistence.

Bryant (2009) studied potential effects on freshwater ecosystems and Pacific salmonids from increasing temperature and changes in phenology of precipitation caused by projected increases in carbon dioxide levels over the next hundred years. He reported that floodplains and wetlands will flood with melting ice sheets and sea level increases and different stocks of anadromous salmonids will respond differently to changing conditions as a function of their individual life histories. For example, pink and chum salmon (*Oncorhynchus gorbuscha, O. keta*) might migrate to the ocean earlier with increased temperature and lower food availability, and growth and survival of juvenile sockeye and coho salmon (*O. nerka, O. kisutch*) may suffer. Sea level rise might flood spawning and rearing areas of pink and coho salmon. Avoiding loss of salmonid stocks will depend on their genetic diversity and appropriate guidelines for harvest and habitat conservation. And providing for healthy future anadromous runs of salmonids may be key to providing for a number of aquatic and terrestrial wildlife species depending on fish, directly or indirectly, for food and nutrients (Cederholm *et al.* 2001).

Gayton (2008) concluded that (terrestrial) species would respond differently by adapting in place, migrating, or going extinct. He noted that reducing nonclimate related stressors, providing migration corridors along altitudinal and latitudinal dimensions, and conducting long-term monitoring of biotic responses would reduce undesirable effects of climate changes.

Invasive species, air quality, and habitat connections to other areas influence local processes and are, in turn, affected by climate change. Effects on wildlife population viability from fragmentation and isolation of old forests and management of the young forest matrix during climate change influences might be studied using methods of landscape genetics (Holderegger and Wagner 2006; Manel *et al.* 2003). Such studies can help identify local population isolates and can guide optimal planning of habitat corridors for dispersing animals (Epps *et al.* 2007). Cumulative effects of multiple stressors, both within and beyond the focal area, can combine to surpass thresholds of tolerance by some species (e.g., see Shifley *et al.* 2008).

In general, identifying and projecting the influence of climate change on biota, ecosystem conditions and functioning, and sustainability of natural resources and ecosystem services often entails understanding three dimensions of effects: *exposure, sensitivity,* and *adaptation capacity.* Exposure refers to the intensity and duration by which organisms and ecosystems are subject to changes in hydrological, geochemical, biological, and meteorological regimes. Sensitivity refers to the degree to which the distribution and abundance of organisms and the rates and types of ecological processes are susceptible to climate change, that is, their lack of resistance or resilience. Adaptation capacity refers to the extent to which human social, economic, and ecological systems can anticipate and adjust to climate change, such as with effects on soil fertility, forest condition, species distributions, and production of renewable resources.

Studies in southeast Alaska and northern coastal BC have provided a basis for evaluating some aspects of exposure and sensitivity of organisms and ecosystems to climate change effects. However, more work remains on developing adaptation strategies, building on work to date evaluating species viability and approaches to conservation of old forest and other ecosystems. For example, adaptation strategies could be further developed to model and project potential changes in the distribution of habitats and wildlife species assemblages in both mainland and island situations, under climate envelopes resulting from a variety of potential future climate change scenarios. Results then could be used to determine potential movement or migration pathways of vegetation and biota, to conserve key land areas to accommodate such expected spatial shifts (e.g., Beier and Brost 2010) or to identify and conserve today immobile habitats that may become far more isolated and rare in the future. Modeling approaches such as use of circuit theory (Schwartz 2011) may prove useful to identifying potential pathways and habitat isolates and outliers.

Understanding effects of climate change also might help direct what to monitor to ascertain negative trends among habitats, species, and KEF patterns. For example, climate change might have more immediate and recognizable negative effects on local island endemic taxa, on species that rely on subnivian (below the snow) conditions for predator escape or winter resources, on species at the periphery of their overall distribution, or on rare species occupying and constrained by immobile habitats such as lithic environments (Everett and Robson 1991).

Contact zones between ecological communities, such as ecotones and altitudinal transitions among life zones, may be especially sensitive to climate change (Neilson 1993, but see contrary modeling results from Noble 1993). Monitoring species composition and structure along such contact zones might serve as early warning signals of more extensive, impending changes. The capacity of soils and standing vegetation to sequester or release atmospheric carbon may also be affected by climate change (Millar *et al.* 2007; Woodall and Liknes 2008) and could be monitored for early signs of climatic effects. Conversely, some invasive, nonnative species are likely to benefit from climate change.

Clarifying What to Conserve, Reserve, or Protect

Whether a management strategy based on conservation biology research is to address short-term protection of selected species, habitats, or locations, or provide for long-term resilience to changing climate, the specific purpose of the strategy should be quite clear. That is, the goals and objectives for which protected areas are established vary greatly.

For example, a given forest stand or area may to some degree be protected but different types of protection afford different benefits. Logging may be forbidden or permitted with constraints. For example, the Northwest Forest Plan of the Pacific Northwest, US, includes designations of "managed late-successional reserves" in which thinning and other silvicultural activities are permitted if they are deemed to increase growth rates of trees so that they achieve large diameters faster than without such activities.

Addressing Transboundary Issues

Many organisms move over large distances, and they do not carry passports (fig. 7.01). Dealing with these movements and the conservation challenges they pose is difficult. For example, some protected areas in the St. Elias region of Yukon, Alaska, and British Columbia help in cross-border conservation but others are not geographically located to provide consistent connectivity (Danby and Slocombe 2005). They call for interagency and international cooperation to integrate existing protected areas with each other and surrounding landscapes. Similar approaches were suggested by Zbicz (2003) and Brosius and Russell (2003). Marcot *et al.* (2006) further suggested methods for evaluating and managing transboundary wildlife habitats to provide for the suite of native biotic ecological functions between the interior US and Canada.

International agreements between Canada and the United States—

FIGURE 7.01. Where northern coastal British Columbia and southeast Alaska meet. This is Pearse Island, Canada, looking northeast. The channel to the left (north) is Pearse Canal, and the land mass to its left is Misty Fjords National Monument. Here, the coastal temperate rainforests and their wildlife straddle this most imaginary international boundary. Photo by Bruce G. Marcot.

principally the North American Agreement on Environmental Cooperation and the Memorandum of Understanding Establishing the Canada,
Mexico, United States Trilateral Committee for Wildlife and Ecosystem
Conservation and Management—have failed to conserve forest wildlife
across their joint boundary (Jernigan 2006). Reasons for failure include the
fact that different species are listed under the US Endangered Species Act
and Canada's Species at Risk Act, and that the agreements do not address
some of the key anthropogenic stressors to forest wildlife, particularly
forestry activities that fragment and eliminate habitats.

Interchanges are also important across boundaries of terrestrial
upland, freshwater aquatic, and marine environments (Allan 2004). Nutrient linkages between rivers and adjacent riparian zones are especially
important in North Pacific coastal temperate rainforests (Cederholm *et al.*
1999, 2001; Hildebrand *et al.* 1999), and those linkages are affected by timber harvest (Tiegs *et al.* 2008; Sedell and Maser 1994). Conservation biology concepts can also help identify and establish management plans for
biologically rich marine reserves in the region (Ngoc 2010; Levin *et al.* 2009).

Conducting Adaptive Management

Most, if not all, of the above new avenues of conservation biology study
and biodiversity protection could be greatly aided by embracing adaptive
management. In general, the two forms of adaptive management—*passive*,
or learning from experience, and *active*, that is designing management
interventions to reduce decision-critical uncertainty—have their place, but
active adaptive management is especially effective when existing knowledge is sufficient to identify critical information gaps. For example, active
adaptive management, by focusing on the most important data gaps, would
improve the basis for managing resources and biodiversity under stress of
climate change (Lawler *et al.* 2010).

A formal adaptive research and management approach is the most
effective way to test, adjust, and reevaluate models and tools that project
climate change effects on organisms and ecosystems. The adaptive
research part can begin by studying and monitoring what are initially
deemed to be the major forcing functions and parameters of the temperate
rainforest ecosystem that could signal shifts in the composition, occurrence, and functionality of ecological communities. Then, research and
associated monitoring activities would be adjusted to the best temporal

and spatial scales, and perhaps to a more appropriate set of functions and parameters, using what was learned from the initial study results. Ultimately, management guidelines would be adjusted based on overall research results so as to better accommodate adaptation capacity.

Adaptive management focuses attention on predicted ecosystem changes and management standards that would be most effectively employed as the climate changes. Given the current and projected fast pace of climate change, such learning is best accomplished through active adaptive management, where management activities themselves are crafted as scientific experiments with statistically appropriate numbers and allocations of treatments and controls.

Adaptive research, coupled with active adaptive management, could provide critical information on the following key decision-relevant knowledge gaps in southeast Alaska and northern coastal BC that may be time- and disturbance-sensitive. One key knowledge gap is the degree to which locally endemic, island-constrained biota—elements of biodiversity to be conserved—are sensitive to anthropogenic disturbances (e.g., roads, habitations) and climate change effects (e.g., shifts in vegetation communities) on their habitats and resources. For instance, several locally endemic subspecies of birds occur on BC's Queen Charlotte Island (Haida Gwaii), including the northern saw-whet owl (*Aegolius acadicus brooksi*), hairy woodpecker (*Picoides villosus picoideus*), Steller's jay (*Cyanocitta stelleri carlottae*), and pine grosbeak (*Pinicola enucleator carlottae*), and endemic species of small mammals occur elsewhere in the Alexander Archipelago of southeast Alaska, especially on the outer islands (Cook and MacDonald, this volume, chapter 2). How likely are each of these endemic taxa to persist through, and perhaps be able to adapt to, novel disturbances and changing climate? Or would managers need to provide facilitated migration (e.g., Aitken *et al.* 2008, but see Minteer and Collins 2010 for an ethical discussion) across island or mainland sites to ensure their persistence? Other key knowledge gaps are identified throughout the chapters of this volume.

CONCLUSIONS AND RECOMMENDATIONS

Several poignant lessons have been learned from applying principles and methods of conservation biology to southeast Alaska and northern coastal BC, in the form of future challenges for the science and development of new concepts and tools for conservation.

Challenges in Southeast Alaska
and North Coastal British Columbia

The complex geography and climates of southeast Alaska and northern coastal BC pose a constellation of challenges for conservation of temperate old-forest ecosystems and associated biota. Such challenges include dealing with the following:

- an archipelago of islands varying in size, spacing, forest conditions, and disturbance levels;
- a mainland geography of a relatively narrow low-elevation coastal terrestrial area and high mountains with alpine ecosystems;
- an international boundary with different protection and management policies and listed species on each side;
- First Nation peoples who require continued use of forests and their resources for subsistence;
- a set of transboundary protected areas only partially matched to provide linkages for large terrestrial mammals;
- natural fragmentation of old forests by edaphic conditions such as avalanche chutes and muskeg and sphagnum bogs; and
- a history of forest resource use that has created extensive road networks and varying patterns of old-forest fragmentation.

Other stressors and disturbances in the island system of the Alexander Archipelago include industrial logging (Hanley *et al.* 2005), mining (Rudis 2001), human encroachment (Johnson 1990), commercial tourism (Johnson 2002; Kruger 2005), wildlife consumption for subsistence and sport (Snepenger and Bowyer 1990), and invasive species (Cook *et al.* 2006; Heutte *et al.* 2006). Forests of southeast Alaska and coastal BC also have had various phases of historic land and resource use, including late nineteenth-century logging and trapping by Russians, and twentieth-century logging and roading by Americans, especially during the 1970s and 1980s (MacDonald and Cook 2007).

Successful conservation of temperate forest resources of the region might entail changes of focus and reexamination of established paradigms and management approaches (e.g., Schoen *et al.* 1981). Concepts of conservation biology—particularly, island biogeography, protected area networks, habitat fragmentation, movement corridors, metapopulation dynamics,

A WATCH LIST FOR DOGMAS

A number of terms and concepts of conservation biology have developed into mainstay assumptions and postulates which, true to scientific inquiry, require clearer definition and empirical testing than they normally acquire. It might behoove researchers and managers alike if the following lexicon were to be given clarity and quantification for use in southeastern Alaska and northern coastal BC conservation strategies.

CORRIDOR. This term is often used with the untested assumption that individual animals will traverse some assumed linkage between locations, such as protected areas. Actually, corridors can consist of three types. *Dispersal corridors* can facilitate the actual movement, dispersal, or migration of individual organisms from one geographic location to another (e.g., Haas 1995). *Genetic corridors* can facilitate the distribution of genes along an area in which organisms might interbreed, especially if the organisms do not traverse the length of the corridor per se (e.g., Mech and Hallett 2001). *Biodiversity corridors* can help maintain the overall biodiversity (usually measured as species richness) in a broad regional area (e.g., Perault and Lomolino 2000). Analyses of corridors in North Pacific temperate rainforests should clearly specify their type and intended utility (for instance, see Epps *et al.* 2007).

FRAGMENTATION. This term, used on its own without reference to environmental conditions pertinent to specific species, is essentially

(continued)

population viability analysis, and risk analysis—have formed the basis for the current land management plan of Tongass National Forest (Suring *et al.* 1993), but some of these concepts may require some clarification (see sidebar, "A Watch List for Dogmas") or revision in light of new findings and techniques.

For example, techniques in the new field of landscape genetics (Holderegger and Wagner 2006) could be used to determine the recent history meaningless. The term also has come to automatically connote conditions contributing to low viability and high extirpation likelihood of populations. To be useful, the term should be specific to species and their habitat and empirically quantified in terms of the degree to which habitat conditions for a species are discontinuously distributed across a landscape (e.g., Cook *et al.* 2006).

HABITAT. This is one of the most misused words in conservation biology. The term should pertain to the physical space in which an organism lives and the abiotic and biotic conditions occurring there, particularly as resources used and selected in that space (Hall *et al.* 1997). However, the term is often used without reference to organisms or species; in such a context, the more appropriate term should be *environment* or *environmental conditions*. For example, *old-forest (or old-growth) habitat* means nothing if not specific to a given species; various species occupying an old forest will use and select for different sets of resources, structures, and conditions, and habitat for one species may not at all suffice for another species. In this case, an appropriate term would be *old-forest environment*. Pertinent to species, one can indeed refer to old-forest habitat for northern flying squirrels, northern goshawk, etc.

NETWORK. This term is often used in reference to a set of protected areas in a given region, whether or not they are connected in some way with corridors (see above). In the true sense, however, a network implies some degree of connectivity among elements. Whether a set of protected areas truly serves as a network should pertain to specified species. A network (and set of environments and corridors) for one species may not serve at all for another species.

RISK. This term is typically used in place of the more value-neutral *probability*. In risk analysis, *risk* is the probability of *not* achieving a specified objective. More formally, risk combines the probability of an event occurring with the consequences of its occurrence.

of demographic isolation or interaction between populations of some species scattered among island and mainland occurrences. Results of landscape genetics studies could be used to evaluate and readjust guidelines for habitat linkages and metapopulation conservation of some species. Also, techniques in species distribution modeling are constantly being developed and refined, such as use of maximum entropy modeling for identifying habitat patches and corridors (e.g., Doko *et al.* 2011). The availability of new concepts and tools of conservation biology might prompt revisiting precepts and guidelines for management and conservation of temperate rainforests of the region.

The Promise of Conservation of Temperate Rainforest Ecosystems

In southeast Alaska and northern coastal BC, all recently occurring native species are still present, although some persist only in greatly reduced numbers (Duffy *et al.* 1999). This means that we are starting from a point of great advantage from which to suggest alternative conservation strategies, but delays in implementing them will inevitably restriction options, particularly for some relatively rare habitats such as large-tree forest types that have been the focus of timber harvest. Large-tree old growth, characteristic of alluvial fans, floodplain forests, and karst forests (Caouette and DeGayner 2005), likely has always been rare in southeast Alaska and has been the target of most logging (Albert and Schoen 2007a; USDA Forest Service 2008a).

Both ecological and human factors must be understood and incorporated into development of management plans. Planners need to know how people value resources and the ecosystem goods and services they provide and how those values change (Kruger 2005), the distribution of costs and benefits (Dixon and Sherman 1991; Colt 2001), and differences in management approaches across the international border (Beier 2008).

Development of New Concepts and Tools for Conservation Biology

The main issues and information needs for conserving old-forest systems in southeast Alaska and coastal BC include the following:

- developing species-habitat relationships databases, including denoting species' key environmental correlates and key ecological functions;

- assessing patterns of biotic key ecological functions and abiotic processes, as well as effects of natural and anthropogenic disturbances;
- continuing taxonomic work to further identify and map rare, little-known, peripheral, disjunct, and endemic species and subspecies, including consideration of landscape genetics methods;
- mapping hot spots of endemism, rarity, migration routes, and biotic ecological functional patterns;
- delineating key connectivity corridors and landscapes in light of projected climate change;
- performing GAP analyses of existing reserves in light of projected climate change;
- continuing basic field ecology and life history research on selected species and populations;
- continuing assessment and modeling of island biogeographic patterns using recent advancements in island theory and modeling approaches; and
- continuing the monitoring of selected at-risk species and indicators of climate change.

Evaluations of the efficacy of conditions across protected forest areas and across the international border might provide further useful information for conservation management.

Integrating old-forest conservation approaches with the marine environment is important, as the two are strongly interlinked (Edwards *et al.*, this volume, chapter 3). Large trees fall down, get swept to the sea, and settle on the ocean floor to provide unique habitat conditions there for a variety of marine species (Sedell and Maser 1994). Nutrients from upstream-migrating anadromous salmonids are consumed by bears, bald eagles, and many other species, and they end up fertilizing riparian and upslope plants (Cederholm *et al.* 1999, 2001).

A broader ecological framework for old-forest conservation in southeast Alaska and coastal BC also can address cumulative effects of multiple stressors on forest biodiversity. Conservation approaches may be more successful if they also address multiple scales of time, geographic extent, spatial resolution, and multiple levels of biological organization.

A major conservation challenge in the near future is monitoring and accounting for effects of climate change on old-forest continuity. One approach is modeling of potential cumulative effects of land use and climate change on demography, dispersal, and occupancy of old-forest patches (McRae *et al.* 2008).

Recently, much attention has been directed toward identifying and evaluating the suite of ecosystem services provided by old forests (Ruhl *et al.* 2007), such as reliable sources and amounts of clean water; habitat for assemblages of old-forest plant and wildlife species (Marcot and Molina 2006); scenic beauty and areas of recreational, cultural, and spiritual value; gene pools for potential future restoration or reintroduction programs; sequestration and long-term storage of carbon by old trees; and other benefits to people and ecosystems. Assessing the economic and environmental values of such services can be part of a broader, integrated approach to old-forest conservation (Martín-López *et al.* 2009; Verburg *et al.* 2009; Egoh *et al.* 2008). Old forests also can serve as irreplaceable benchmarks for long-term monitoring and research (Trofymow *et al.* 2003).

Incorporating ecosystem services provided by old forests into a broader conservation assessment could be done within a risk analysis and risk management structure. Risk analysis delineates possible outcomes, their probabilities under management alternatives, and their consequence. Risk management, using the analysis results, articulates decision criteria and risk attitudes from which best decision pathways can be discerned that meet explicit management objectives.

Use of risk assessment and decision-support modeling has become popular and includes geographic analysis of optimal land allocations and reserve designs using such tools as MARXAN (www.uq.edu.au/marxan) and Zonation (www.helsinki.fi/bioscience/consplan/software/Zonation). The Nature Conservancy and Audubon Alaska's conservation assessment, resource synthesis, and conservation area design used MARXAN models to identify optimal aggregation of protected areas to achieve conservation objectives in the North Pacific temperate rainforest region (Albert and Schoen 2007a). For example, it has identified Prince of Wales Island as one of the most biologically productive areas of the region and a center of species endemism, but it has also shown that it has the highest level of road development and logging. Also, a GAP analysis of the region might prove useful to help identify geographic locations possibly needing further assessment for conservation of old-forest biota.

New tools and methods for projecting climate change and its effects on wildlife and ecosystems are being developed for parts of western North

America. These could be applied to the southeast Alaska and coastal BC region. Examples include data on downscaled climate projections in coastal British Columbia (Ainslie and Jackson 2010) and in southeast Alaska, provided in the Scenarios Network for Alaska Planning (SNAP) program by University of Alaska, Fairbanks (www.snap.uaf.edu/home), and decision support systems being developed to advise on potential sensitivity of wildlife species to climate change effects in western North America (M. Case, pers. comm.; courses.washington.edu/ccdb/drupal/).

Ultimately, the field and findings of conservation biology as applied to this region will need to continue to intersect with climatology, sociology, environmental economics, and other fields, if objectives are to be achieved for long-term sustainability and conservation of old temperate ecosystems of the region.

ACKNOWLEDGMENTS

My thanks to John Schoen and Gordon Orians for their most helpful reviews and guidance on the manuscript, and to John for initially inviting me into this project. The manuscript benefitted from discussions and presentations by other authors in this compendium, and from helpful comments by two anonymous reviewers.

8

Why Watersheds

EVALUATING THE PROTECTION OF UNDEVELOPED
WATERSHEDS AS A CONSERVATION STRATEGY IN
NORTHWESTERN NORTH AMERICA

Ken Lertzman and Andy MacKinnon

INTRODUCTION

Coastal temperate rainforests are restricted in their global distribution: most of the remaining primary old-growth forest is in northwestern North America, from the central coast of British Columbia north through southeast Alaska. Watersheds with no significant history of development are also globally rare, concentrated in the same area, and pose a significant conservation opportunity. In British Columbia, a protected-areas strategy in the 1990s more than doubled the protected area in the province, with a significant investment in the protection of large, undeveloped watersheds. Subsequent land use plans for BC's Great Bear Rainforest (central and north coasts) and Haida Gwaii increased protected areas to 33% and 50% respectively, again with a focus on protecting undeveloped watersheds. In southeast Alaska, the Tongass National Forest presents an opportunity for watershed-based conservation with many undeveloped watersheds from 1,000 to 10,000 ha in size.

Adjacent watersheds are separated by topographic divides that determine into which stream or river system water flows. Watersheds with their terminus in salt water are termed primary watersheds (Moore 1991). In steeper terrain, watershed boundaries are more pronounced, often are expressed over a smaller spatial scale, and are more likely to have distinct ecological consequences. In coastal British Columbia and southeast Alaska, this topographic structure of watersheds exerts a profound effect on virtually all aspects of forest landscape pattern, structure, and dynamics. For instance, on the south coast of British Columbia a substantial portion of the spatial variation in various indices of forest pattern could be explained by variation in the digital elevation models for those areas (Dorner *et al.* 2002; Dorner 2002).

There is an enormous literature on watershed processes and watershed management. Indeed, the idea of watersheds has even become a rallying concept and organizing principle for public planning processes and citizen's groups across western North America concerned with everything from old growth, forest management, and fish and wildlife habitat to drinking water and rural lifestyles (see, for instance, the CD titled *We All Live Downstream* by the California-based Banana Slug String Band). It has become clear over the past decade that the central issue when thinking about watershed ecosystems ecologically in northwestern North America is their role in connecting ecological processes that otherwise would be disconnected in space and time. Small headwater watersheds integrate ecological processes in terrestrial and aquatic systems via inputs of woody debris and leaf litter from nearby forests (Gomi *et al.* 2002; Keller and Swanson 2007). Research on larger river systems over the last several decades has emphasized functional continuity both longitudinally along river systems (Minshall *et al.* 1983, 1985; Malard *et al.* 2006; Vannote *et al.* 1980; Wipfli 2005) and between river systems and adjacent ecosystems (e.g., Milner *et al.* 2007). Marine systems are linked to freshwater and terrestrial systems by migration, mortality, and consumption of anadromous fish (e.g., Hicks *et al.* 2005; Hocking and Reynolds 2011), and these linkages are increasingly recognized as keystone processes in riparian ecosystems (e.g., Helfield and Naiman 2006; Scheuerell *et al.* 2007). Such studies have firmly established watersheds as functional systems with characteristics predictable from their size, geology, climate, biota, and history. Watersheds have been shown to be logical, functional units of landscapes that integrate ecosystem processes over time and space (O'Neill *et al.* 1986).

Planning reserve boundaries to conform to watershed boundaries has for decades been considered almost a first principle of reserve design (Soulé and Simberloff 1986; Theberge 1989). More recent writers coming from a perspective of watershed processes have strongly reinforced this principle (Pringle 2001; Baron *et al.* 2002). However, the question of for what purposes a watershed does or does not make a better reserve than an area of equivalent size that does not follow watershed boundaries has not been addressed rigorously. Furthermore, the particular opportunities provided by protecting whole undeveloped watersheds are essentially unaddressed.

If society is going to make a significant investment in conserved forest land, under what conditions would reserves based on protecting whole watersheds be better than an equivalent investment in reserves based on other boundaries? We use a framework for evaluating watersheds as reserves based on *reserve content, reserve context,* and *emergent criteria.* Reserve content criteria include how regional pools of species and ecosystems are reflected in a reserve and how a reserve reflects and is influenced by internal ecosystem processes, such as natural disturbances and fluvial processes. Reserve context criteria reflect the regional landscapes and gradients in which reserves sit and the overall goals of the protected areas system of which they are a part. Emergent criteria address issues arising from the interaction between reserve content and context. Examples include population viability and ecosystem integrity, concepts that are often the intuitive and stated goals of reserve design, but are difficult to define operationally. Watersheds score variably over most of the content and context criteria and positively for the emergent criteria (table 8.1).

Many years ago, we wrote a report (with coauthors Fred Bunnell and Laurie Kremsater) in which we discussed the protection of British Columbia watersheds that had no history of industrial development (Lertzman *et al.* 1993). In it we summarized relevant ideas about geomorphology and watershed processes, about organism distributions and landscape ecology, and about the global rarity of undeveloped watersheds. We focused on coastal temperate rainforest watersheds in particular. Reactions from participants in the government advisory process for whom we wrote the report were mixed: those representing the environmental community liked the report, those representing industry did not. The response of one eminent forester was "everything you say here is just a consequence of water flowing downhill under the influence of gravity." Our initial reaction was consternation that all our big ideas could be trivialized in that way, but we came to rethink that response. The rationale for undeveloped watersheds as elements of a conservation strategy really does go back to first principles, such as water flowing downhill under the influence of gravity. We now have a much better understanding of the dynamic interconnectedness of stream reaches across a watershed, of the functional linkages between upland landscape elements and the processes in the drainage network, and, espe-

TABLE 8.1. Summary of the performance of watersheds as reserves. Watersheds are scored positively (+), neutrally (o), or negatively (-) with respect to each assessment criterion.

CRITERIA	SCORE
Reserve Content Criteria	
1. Species Diversity and Representation	+/0/-
2. Ecosystem Diversity and Representation	+/0/-
3. Ecosystem Processes	+
4. Size	+/0/-
Reserve Context Criteria	
5. Location	0
6. Shape	0
7. Ecological Isolation/Connectivity	+/0
8. Transboundary Physical Processes	+
9. Criteria Specific to the System	+/0/-
Emergent Criteria	
10. Population Viability	+/0
11. Ecological Integrity	+

cially in temperate rainforests, the degree to which the entire drainage basin, not just the formal stream channel network, contributes to watershed functioning. Our goal in this paper is not to catalogue the miscellany of watershed processes or justify the interconnectedness of watershed systems—those well-established concepts do not require debate. Instead our goal, given our understanding of the importance of watersheds as units of process in ecological landscapes, is to evaluate the role of "intact," undeveloped watersheds as elements of a regional conservation strategy.

RESERVE SYSTEM DESIGN AND THE WATERSHED CONSERVATION PROBLEM

The field of reserve design encompasses several different approaches. Reserve design has often been conceptualized as an *ecological problem*, usually focused on the ecological character of individual reserves, their distinct or unique biota or geological features, and their configuration and management. Many of the large parks in North America fall into this category—they were selected as reserves not really as part of an a priori, designed system, but because of their own distinct internal character (Scott *et al.* 2001). More recently, there has been significant effort to analyze the design of systems of reserves as an *allocation problem* (Margules and Pressey 2000; Ferrier *et al.* 2000; Margules *et al.* 1988; Pressey *et al.* 1993; Nel *et al.* 2007; Linke *et al.* 2008). In these exercises, a large number of potential reserves are evaluated systematically by algorithms that select subsets based on criteria such as efficiency of representation, complementarity of membership, or irreplaceability of individual reserve elements. These approaches focus on the system of reserves and the relative contributions of reserves to the system as a whole. In parallel with these discussions, a third approach has focused on issues related to *ecological processes* linking individual reserves in a larger reserve system. The "SLOSS" debate, about whether a single large reserve or several small reserves is better, was a manifestation of this discussion. In reality, in many parts of the world, such choices are extremely constrained: reserve options are few and we often need to just take what we can get, if and when we can get it. In some places, however, there remain enough significant conservation options that we confront the very kinds of issues posed by the allocation problem and the SLOSS debate.

Coastal British Columbia and southeast Alaska contain the majority of the world's undeveloped coastal temperate rainforest (Ecotrust *et al.* 1995; DellaSalla 2011). Many areas have experienced extensive logging (fig. 8.01), but significant conservation opportunities remain. Some of the most significant and controversial of those opportunities are the watersheds in which there has been no history of logging or other industrial development, largely distributed from the central coast of BC north through southeast Alaska. These "intact" or undeveloped watersheds have globally significant conservation value. Few places in the world have large river systems that still interact with their associated floodplains and upland ecosystems with minimal impact from human activities (see, for instance, the discussion of South Africa in Nel *et al.* 2007).

As of 1995 only 11 of North America's 46 coastal temperate rainforest watersheds greater than 100,000 ha remained undeveloped—6 in British Columbia and 5 in Alaska (Ecotrust *et al.* 1995). Of primary watersheds—

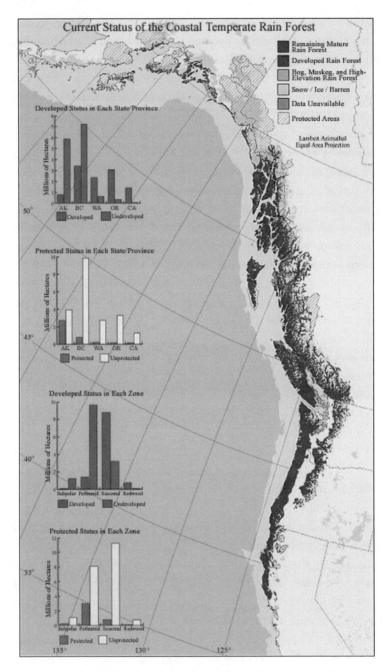

FIGURE 8.01. Development status of coastal temperate rainforest in northwestern North America. From Schoonmaker *et al.* (1997).

those with their terminus in salt water—larger than 5,000 hectares and south of the BC–Washington border, only three (the Elwha River in Washington, Taylor Creek in Oregon, and the Big Sur River in California) were less than 50% developed (Ecotrust *et al.* 1995). In BC, 67% of the watersheds over 5,000 ha on the British Columbia coast had experienced substantial resource development activity by 1991 (Moore 1991) and many of the remaining 33% have experienced development since then. In some parts of the BC coast almost all large watersheds have been extensively modified by forest management (Moore 1991; Hall and McLellan 1990). There are few analyses of the status of temperate rainforest watersheds at regional, continental or global scales. Notable exceptions are Albert and Schoen (2007a) and Schoen and Albert (2007). Largely based on a rationale similar to that discussed here, they proposed that watershed-based planning, and protecting intact watersheds in particular, should be a central organizing idea for the conservation strategy in the Tongass National Forest. They went on to do an inventory and analysis of options for watershed-based protection in the Tongass, conducting a spatial optimization of timber and conservation options.

Currently, most of the remaining undeveloped, unprotected watersheds of significant size in coastal British Columbia are in the central and north coast, the area often referred to as the Great Bear Rainforest. In this area a significant planning process is underway to develop ecosystem-based systems of management, which include protection of a number of intact watersheds (Price *et al.* 2009). If undeveloped watersheds offer distinctive conservation opportunities that are not met in other kinds of reserves within a protected areas system, then there is some urgency to identifying candidates for protected status. Our goal is to discuss the benefits and tradeoffs of protecting whole watersheds, especially undeveloped watersheds, as part of a protected areas system.

Figure 8.02 illustrates the decision tradeoffs. We can allocate a fixed amount of investment in protected area to a traditional mountaintop park representing the higher elevations of multiple watersheds (fig. 8.02a), to focused protection of aquatic systems across several watersheds (fig. 8.02b), to a series of protected areas representing patches of different types of communities distributed across elevational gradients in several watersheds (fig. 8.02c), or we can allocate the area to protecting the entirety of one watershed (fig. 8.02d). In practice, since we are unlikely to completely withdraw protection from streams and other special areas, the protection of whole watersheds is more likely to result in a scenario like that in figure

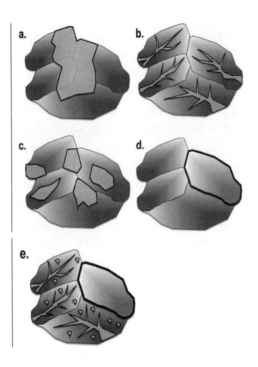

FIGURE 8.02. Illustrations of decision tradeoffs to be considered in allocating protected area among watersheds. In principle, a constant total area is allocated in each case: (*a*) a traditional mountaintop park representing the higher elevations of multiple watersheds, (*b*) focused protection of aquatic systems across several watersheds, (*c*) a series of protected areas representing patches of different types of communities distributed across elevation gradients in several watersheds, or (*d*) the entire protection of one watershed. In practice, since we are unlikely to completely withdraw protection from streams and other special areas in any watershed, the protection of whole watersheds is more likely to result in a scenario like (*e*), where there is some level of protection across all watersheds. This is especially true for areas to be managed under a regime of ecosystem-based management, such as much of the central and northern BC coast (e.g., Price *et al.* 2009).

8.02e, where there is some level of incremental cost from protecting a whole watershed plus core elements of other watersheds.

BRITISH COLUMBIA'S PROTECTED AREAS STRATEGY— A CASE STUDY IN CONSERVATION PLANNING

In 1993, British Columbia established a "Protected Areas Strategy" (Province of British Columbia 1993) that committed the government to protecting 12% of BC's land base by the year 2000. This was a commitment to add approximately 6 million ha of protected areas over 7 years. Since 1993 an additional 534 new protected areas and/or park additions totaling more than 6.9 million ha have been established, bringing the total protected areas representation to 14% of the province. Existing and proposed protected areas were analyzed within an ecological framework (e.g., BC Ministry of Environment 2007; BC Ministry of Forests and Range 2006) to ensure representation of all of the province's diverse ecosystems.

The goals of BC's Protected Areas Strategy, which covers the entire province, were twofold: to protect viable representative examples of the natural diversity of the province and to protect the special natural, cultural heritage, and recreational features of the province. These dual criteria of ecological representation and "specialness" became the foundation of the system. Prior to this process, almost all of BC's protected areas followed administrative boundaries and protected *portions* of watersheds. As a part of the Protected Area Strategy and subsequent land use planning processes, many new unlogged watersheds were added to the protected areas system. In several cases, the boundaries of existing protected areas were modified, with new boundaries drawn along heights of land to incorporate entire watersheds. In developing this strategy, we learned a lot about the tradeoffs of protecting large watersheds through that process—especially when faced, as we were, with a fixed cap on how much total land area could be allocated to protected areas.

In general, areas designed to protect "special natural, cultural heritage, and recreational features" are smaller than those established to protect "viable representative examples of the natural diversity" of the province. The result is a system with many small parks and few large ones (fig. 8.03). In BC, for example, there are currently 1,025 protected areas under Provincial jurisdiction (i.e., exclusive of national parks, municipal parks, and private conservancies), totaling 8.68 million ha in area. These parks would generally fall into International Union for Conservation of Nature (IUCN) protected area categories *Ib (Wilderness Area)* for the larger and more remote units and *II (National Park)* for less remote areas. A few smaller protected areas established to protect a specific species or geological feature would fall under IUCN categories *III (National Monument or Feature)* or *IV (Habitat/Species Management Area)*. For the 1,023 protected areas for which we have data, the mean size is 13,200 ha; but the median size is only 363 ha—that is, half the protected areas are less than 363 ha. As one

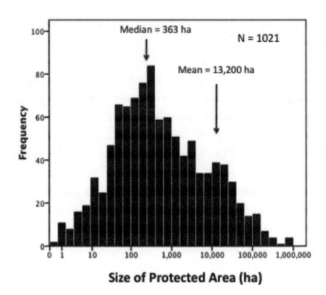

FIGURE 8.03. Size distribution of provincially designated protected areas in British Columbia.

would expect, the area in the protected areas system is dominated by the largest of the parks: the 539 parks less than 1,000 ha in size collectively represent much less than 1% of the total area in the protected areas system (fig. 8.04). In contrast, the 31 protected areas in the largest size class (the 1,000,000 ha class) represent only 3% of the parks but 71% of the area in the system. The 5 largest (Tweedsmuir Park, Tatshenshini-Alsek Park, Spatsizi Plateau Wilderness Park, Northern Rocky Mountains Park, and Wells Gray Park) cover 2.8 million ha, or approximately 20% of the total protected area.

This trend towards a disproportionate amount of area in a few very large parks is not a consequence of recent concerns about watershed-based planning: some of the larger parks are among the earliest in the system. However, many of the largest of the parks (e.g., Tatshenshini-Alsek, Kitlope, Stein) were protected very explicitly in the context of their watershed boundaries, and others were enlarged to reflect watershed boundaries. Concerns about watershed-based planning and intact watersheds thus reinforced the existing size distribution.

One example of a large, watershed-based park from BC's north coast is the Kitlope watershed in the Kitlope Heritage Conservancy, established in 1994. This 321,000 ha coastal temperate rainforest watershed is comanaged

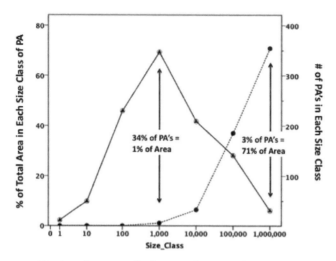

FIGURE 8.04. Number of provincially designated protected areas in British Columbia by size class (ha) and total area in each size class. The number of protected areas (PAs) in each size class (right vertical axis) is represented by a solid line with triangles for data points; the percent of total area in each size class (left vertical axis) is represented by a dotted line with circles for data points.

by BC Parks and the Haisla First Nation. It links the older Tweedsmuir Provincial Park (established in 1938) with the Entiako Provincial Park and Fiordland Conservancy to create a park complex of more than 1.5 million ha. Another is the Tatshenshini-Alsek Park (947,026 ha), which is contiguous with the Yukon's Kluane National Park Reserve and Alaska's Glacier Bay and Wrangell–St. Elias national parks to form a total protected area of 4.4 million ha.

Another goal of the additional protected areas was to expand upon, and in some cases connect, existing protected areas. For example, the older Strathcona Provincial Park (established in 1911, one of BC's first protected areas) contained the upper reaches (about 3,000 ha) of the Megin River watershed. The 1995 Clayoquot Sound land-use decision added the rest of the undeveloped Megin drainage (27,390 ha) and connected Strathcona with the Megin River Ecological Reserve (50 ha) and the Sulphur Passage Provincial Park to create a park complex of more than 250,000 ha.

In many ways this size distribution of protected areas might be interpreted as a great result: we exceeded our 12% target with a very large system of protected areas, with very many small parks and a fair number of very large ones. However it is a system enormously skewed to an investment in very large parks, partly as a consequence of protecting entire watersheds, and we need to consider what the tradeoffs were in creating this system. In particular, to what extent did the allocation of these large protected areas significantly constrain the protection of other areas in their region?

WHAT MAKES A GOOD RESERVE?

Considerable debate has focused on appropriate criteria for evaluating reserves (e.g., Bonn and Gaston 2005). Many studies have examined criteria used to actually establish reserves on the ground (e.g., Moffett and Sarkar 2006; Nilsson and Götmark 1992), but few general principles have emerged. We classify reserve design criteria into three broad categories: those related to reserve *content*, those related to reserve *context*, and those that are *emergent* from combining content and context.

Reserve content addresses issues arising from the species, ecosystems, and processes internal to a given reserve. This includes the distribution and abundance of different ecosystems, species, and physical processes (e.g., geological, geomorphic, and hydrological) within the reserve. Because of species-area relationships and contributions of beta diversity, *reserve size*, which is broadly discussed as an influential criterion for many aspects of reserve functionality (e.g., Margules and Pressey 2000; Williams *et al.* 2005), can be considered a summary statistic for reserve content. Reserve content issues can be positive or negative, since introduced species are usually judged to be undesirable.

Reserve context refers to interactions between a reserve and its surrounding landscape (transboundary processes) and to the reserve in relation to the system of reserves of which it is a part. For instance, ecological or physical isolation of a reserve from other similar areas can affect whether it achieves its intended conservation objectives. Context also refers to constraints imposed by regional and geographic setting. For example, latitude, productivity, or maritime influence affect biota and processes expected within reserves. The allocation issues referred to above—the efficiency and complementarity criteria—are issues of reserve context.

Emergent properties result from interactions among different components of a system and are not present in any individual components; they arise from the interaction between content and context. For instance, population viability may be a consequence of the interaction between reserve content (size, landscape and species diversity, population size) and reserve context (disturbance to the surrounding landscape, distance to nearest other habitat, presence of movement corridors among landscape elements, metapopulation dynamics). Ecosystem integrity is another example of criteria that usually depend on interactions of reserve content and context (see below for more discussion of this criterion). Although these concepts are often the intuitive goals of reserve design and are increasingly specified as formal goals in policy statements or legislation (e.g., Gaudet *et al.* 1997; Balmford *et al.* 2005), they can be difficult to define operationally (and even more difficult to assess in the real world; see, e.g., Stem *et al.* 2005 and Hanley *et al.* 2005).

Reserve Content Criteria

1. SPECIES DIVERSITY AND REPRESENTATION. Reserves are often established to protect particular communities or species of interest. Diversity itself is not as important as the identity of the species contributing to the diversity: rare native or endemic species are typically more highly valued as "content" than common or introduced species. In some cases, the presence of such focal taxa alone can be the primary criterion for reserve evaluation (a purely fine-filter approach, e.g., Rodrigues, Andelman, *et al.* 2004). The presence of a species or community, however, is no guarantee of persistence. Successional processes, natural disturbances, emigration, random population fluctuations, invasions by exotic species, and changes in critical physical variables by processes external to the reserve can all cause local extinctions. One goal of reserve design should be to ensure that populations persist, which may require reference to criteria other than purely reserve content (e.g., metapopulation dynamics involving areas external to a given reserve or reserve system; see Cabeza and Moilanen 2001).

We can imagine three distinct goals for representation which might be considered for species and communities: (1) maintaining a sample within the reserve that is *representative*, in that it matches the relative abundance and distribution of taxa or communities in the surrounding landscape as a whole, (2) maximizing the sample of regional diversity that is represented within a reserve, or (3) overrepresenting taxa or communities that are rarest or under the greatest threat outside the reserves.

2. ECOSYSTEM DIVERSITY AND REPRESENTATION. Planning for protection at the scale of ecosystems and communities is a coarse-filter conservation strategy that has been adopted by many jurisdictions, including British Columbia. We lack reliable information about distributions and habitat requirements for the majority of species in BC's coastal forests, especially among the arthropods, lichens, fungi, and microbes. Without such information, fine-filter (species by species) conservation is impossible. The coarse-filter approach asserts that a majority of species in a region can be protected more efficiently by conserving the ecosystems in which they live than by strategies that use a species-by-species approach (Franklin 1993; Scott *et al.* 1991); Brooks *et al.* (2004) discuss some problems with this assumption. This was a cornerstone of achieving "Goal 1" in BC's Protected Areas Strategy, with ecosystem diversity represented by the Biogeoclimatic Ecosystem Classification (BEC) system stratified by regional landscape units (Pojar *et al.* 1987; Meidinger and Pojar 1991). Thus, effectiveness as a coarse-filter is one criterion for assessing reserves.

How well a reserve or set of reserves represents the range of ecosystem types present in the regional landscape is another criterion for evaluating the reserves (e.g., Gonzales *et al.* 2003; Hockings *et al.* 2000). As with species, there are three options for representation goals: (1) maximize the degree to which the representation (relative proportions) of ecosystem types within a reserve(s) reflects the abundance of those types in the landscape as a whole, (2) maximize the range of regional ecosystem types represented within a reserve, or (3) emphasize the representation of ecosystem types that are rarest or under the greatest threat outside the reserves. This third option is essentially a fine-filter approach applied to ecosystems.

3. ECOSYSTEM PROCESSES. A focus on maintaining ecosystem processes within their historic ranges of variability is a key element of conservation and management discussions (e.g., Landres *et al.* 1999), and the role of disturbance processes in reserve functionality and reserve design is challenging (e.g., Sprugel 1991; Leroux *et al.* 2007). Intuitively, how well a reserve is able to incorporate ongoing processes of disturbance, recovery, and adaptation bears strongly on the notion of ecological integrity.

The significance of many ecological processes varies with reserve size, so we can treat size as a reserve content issue. Especially at smaller reserve sizes, buffering from external processes is a benefit of increasing size. Microclimatic edge effects can penetrate several tree heights or more into the edge of a stand (Harper *et al.* 2005; Chen *et al.* 1992, 1993) and may affect reserve design (e.g., Murcia 1995). Biotic edge effects, such as nest parasites, predators, exotic species, or human hunters can penetrate substantially farther (e.g., Harris 1988; Woodroffe and Ginsberg 1998).

At larger reserve sizes, the ability to incorporate natural disturbance processes into a reserve becomes relevant, and reserve design can consider long-term disturbance dynamics and spatial mechanisms of resilience (Bengtsson *et al.* 2003). Forest ecosystems are shaped by idiosyncratic regimes of natural disturbances. Some disturbances (e.g., extreme fires) can overwhelm an entire reserve of even large size (Bengtsson *et al.* 2003). Attempts to exclude natural disturbances are often costly and frequently result in unanticipated and unwanted changes in the community composition and trajectory (e.g., Bissonette and Storch 2002). In this context, larger reserves or reserve systems may encompass enough area to incorporate the range of natural disturbances without being unduly influenced by any one event, and allow for internal recolonization sources for disturbed patches (e.g., Baker 1992). The size required to achieve this has been termed a *minimum dynamic area* (Pickett and Thompson 1978). The minimum dynamic area will vary with forest type and disturbance regime. Although this area can be extraordinarily large in systems driven by large-scale fires (e.g., Leroux *et al.* 2007), in the wetter types of coastal rainforests of BC and southeast Alaska, where disturbances tend to be smaller in scale (Lertzman *et al.* 1996; Alaback, this volume, chapter 4), we expect the minimum dynamic area to be very substantially smaller—potentially smaller than many watersheds.

Expressing this idea of minimum dynamic area across a system of reserves addresses the idea of *redundancy*—of ensuring that even if a large disturbance overwhelms a reserve within the system, there is enough redundancy in a protected areas network to ensure persistence of the ecosystem across the reserve network. As noted above, given the small and infrequent disturbances characteristic of coastal temperate rainforest today, this is not currently a large concern for the coastal rainforest. However, under scenarios of changing climate, disturbances may become more frequent, extreme, or widespread, and redundancy in a protected areas network may become critical.

4. A FURTHER NOTE ON RESERVE SIZE. Reserve size is not important in and of itself: it becomes important because size influences other criteria

or processes, so it can be used as a proxy for them. Species-area relationships mean that, all other things being equal, larger reserves will capture more species (or more types of ecosystems) and contain larger populations of focal species. Lack of sufficient size may account for extinctions in parks: for instance, in a classic paper, Newmark (1987) hypothesized that all but the largest western North American parks are too small to retain an intact mammalian fauna. However, some smaller areas can represent local high points of species richness, or capture an unusually good representation of local endemism. Further, in all but very large parks, population persistence for many species likely depends more on how a reserve interacts with its surrounding regional landscape (reserve *context*) than its own size (reserve *content*).

When there is a fixed cap on the total amount (of area or money) to be invested in establishing reserves, decisions about reserve size imply necessary tradeoffs among reserve options. Selecting a very large reserve (for instance to encompass watershed boundaries) may require forgoing options to protect many smaller reserves. This was the case in some areas of British Columbia where decisions to protect significant intact watersheds meant that other areas in the same regional accounting of protected area could not be protected. Despite a significant amount of early discussion (e.g., Simberloff 1988; Soulé and Simberloff 1986), the SLOSS debate provides little guidance for making such decisions beyond (1) the best option is "as many as possible, as large as possible," and (2) the specifics will depend on the autecology of the species involved and the goals and objectives for conservation and management.

Reserve Context Criteria

5. LOCATION. A reserve's location on broad environmental gradients (e.g., gradients of altitude, latitude, or marine influence) sets bounds on expectations of reserve content. For northern coastal BC and southeast Alaska, for example, interior areas will have a more continental climate than coastal areas, and forests at sea level differ from forests at subalpine elevations (or nonforested areas above). A protected areas system design should incorporate representation from all of these different ecosystems.

Location along environmental gradients that will become more dynamic in the context of changing climate is an important "context" criterion. In some parts of coastal BC and southeast Alaska, for example, climates could become considerably warmer and drier over the next three to five decades (e.g., Hamann and Wang 2006). Individual species will extend or contract their ranges across these gradients in response to the changes in climate. Managing protected areas and matrix habitat to facilitate species migration is an important component of climate change adaptation.

6. SHAPE OF THE RESERVE. The best shape for a reserve has been hypothesized as circular because a circle has the smallest edge to area ratio of any shape. Blouin and Connor (1985) evaluated shapes of nature reserves, however, and concluded that after accounting for effects of area, shape did not consistently explain a significant amount of the residual variation in species numbers. In a similar vein, Kunin (1997) suggests advantages for non-circular reserves. In practice, the influence of shape on edge to area ratio is of greatest concern in small reserves. In most cases, reserve boundaries should follow natural features of the landscape, biotic and geomorphic, rather than adhere to a priori generalizations. Shape is thus best thought of as an output of the reserve planning process than an input. Very long, thin reserves of even large size—for example, some riparian reserves—may suffer from a poor edge to area ratio, but are a special case. When such reserved areas connect two or more other reserves they are termed corridors and may play strategic roles in a conservation strategy.

7. ECOLOGICAL ISOLATION VERSUS CONNECTIVITY IN THE SURROUNDING LANDSCAPE. The functional integration of a local breeding population into a larger metapopulation is a key issue in population dynamics and viability issues for many taxa (e.g., Hanski and Ovaskainen 2000; Nicholson et al. 2006). This reinforces the critical role of landscape structure in the area surrounding a reserve (Lindenmayer and Franklin 2002). A very large reserve may contain enough habitat to provide for metapopulations of some species, but for large, mobile species (such as grizzly bears) it is unlikely that this could ever be so.

8. TRANSBOUNDARY PHYSICAL PROCESSES. Reserves should be designed to maintain existing strong internal interactions, protect positive external connections (as above), and minimize deleterious interactions across their boundaries. Some ecological problems, both within

and outside reserved areas, have resulted from boundaries following administrative rather than ecological lines, leading to the propagation of strong negative processes across boundaries (Janzen 1986; for Yellowstone fire management examples see the special issue of BioScience 1989, vol. 39 [10]). Indeed, shifting from administrative to ecological or geomorphic boundaries is one cornerstone of ecosystem-based management (Grumbine 1994).

9. CRITERIA SPECIFIC TO THE SYSTEM OF RESERVES. A reserve can be evaluated in terms of its distinct contribution to the reserve system as a whole. Does a given reserve candidate add distinct elements of diversity or ecological processes to a regional system of reserves? Does it enhance functional or representation redundancy? Gap analysis is a good example of this kind of approach to considering the needs of the reserve system (Rodrigues, Andelman, *et al.* 2004; Rodrigues, Akcakaya, *et al.* 2004). Similarly, the approaches discussed above focusing on efficiency of representation, redundancy, complementarity, etc., provide methods for formal analysis (e.g., Margules and Sarkar 2007; Linke *et al.* 2008).

Emergent Criteria

Population viability could be properly treated as a component of ecological integrity, but, since it is so often explicitly addressed as a goal of management in itself, we consider it separately here.

10. POPULATION VIABILITY. What characteristics of a reserve or reserve network lead to the long-term viability of populations within them? An enormous literature relates to this topic, focusing on subjects as diverse as minimum viable population size, the quality of matrix in fragmented landscapes, and the nature of metapopulation dynamics. Inevitably, this mix of factors, including the life history of individual species, their local autecology, as well as the spatial and temporal dynamics of local habitat, are deeply intertwined in addressing this question (e.g., Fahrig 2001). Population viability arises as a consequence of different factors involving both context and content. Ultimately, if this is an issue in assessing a reserve, both the autecology of the species of concern and the nature of the specific reserves must be addressed. The importance of reserve size relative to

population and metapopulation dynamics of species at risk is perhaps the only generalization that can be made.

The reserve sizes that are necessary to maintain viable populations of vertebrate species internal to a reserve are daunting. For instance, Bunnell and Kremsater (1991) discussed minimum viable population sizes and summarized the work of Soulé (1987), World Wildlife Fund Canada (1990), and others. They noted the vast areas needed to maintain minimum population sizes of 50 individuals for top carnivores. The areas estimated as necessary to maintain grizzly bears, wolverines, and wolves are about 49,000 km^2, 42,000 km^2, and 20,250 km^2, respectively (World Wildlife Fund Canada 1990). Carroll *et al.* (2003) found similarly large numbers in their analysis of large carnivore habitat in the Rocky Mountains. Herbivores also require large areas for maintaining minimum viable populations. Belovsky (1987) estimated a minimum land area of 10,000 ha to ensure a 95% probability of persistence for one century of herbivores between 50 and 500 kg body weight; de Vries (1995) suggests using habitat requirements of large herbivores in the design of European nature reserves. However, minimum viable population sizes are much more likely to be measured in the thousands than from fifty to a few hundred as in these earlier papers (Brook *et al.* 2006; Traill *et al.* 2007), suggesting that maintaining viable populations of large mobile species requires truly enormous reserves—or a very functional integration of reserved and nonreserved areas. The areas required to sustain viable populations of the vast majority of species—especially among invertebrates, nonvascular plants, fungi, lichens, and microbes—are largely unknown, though these species will likely require smaller areas.

11. ECOLOGICAL INTEGRITY. The term *ecological integrity* is a central tenet of ecosystem-based management (e.g. Grumbine 1994; Pimentel *et al.* 2000) that has become a frequently stated objective of reserve systems (Gaudet *et al.* 1997; Balmford *et al.* 2005). Unfortunately, it is often vaguely defined and can be difficult to implement and evaluate operationally. By ecological integrity we mean those properties of an ecological system that allow it to (1) persist over the long term with undiminished ecological functionality in the presence of natural disturbances, and (2) adapt to disturbance regimes that may be novel in the history of the system. By *ecological system* we refer to a population, community, ecosystem, or landscape.

In many ways, ecological integrity is the intuitive equivalent to population viability for higher levels of organization (e.g., communities, ecosystems, landscapes).

Several points are critical to our definition:

a. The abilities of any ecological system to persist or adapt are bounded and those bounds (*thresholds*) can be exceeded. For most ecological systems we do not know with any degree of certainty where the boundaries lie, and it is likely to be prohibitively time consuming and expensive to identify them.

b. The properties or processes that confer an ability to persist or adapt differ for populations, communities, or ecosystems, i.e., they vary for the levels of the ecological hierarchy. For most ecological systems we do not know exactly what these properties or processes are, but we generally recognize key processes such as keystone predation or structural characteristics facilitating recovery from disturbance, such as biological legacies (e.g., Lindenmayer and Franklin 2002).

c. The three levels (population, community, ecosystem) really do constitute a hierarchy: there are feedbacks among them, and integrity at one level can be contingent on integrity at the others. For instance, if an exotic plant species invades a community and displaces a substantial component of the native flora, the system as a whole can be considered to have suffered a loss of integrity even though summary measures at a higher order, such as primary productivity, may not decline.

d. It is probably more cost effective to safeguard the mechanisms that maintain ecological integrity than to subsidize systems with compromised ecological integrity. For instance, we should "save" species by protecting the functioning of the broader systems in which they participate—we should keep species from becoming endangered rather than undertaking heroic efforts once they become endangered. We should "save" stands of trees that are highly valued socially by protecting the processes maintaining the surrounding ecosystems.

e. Not understanding the exact nature of the properties that result in ecological integrity does not mean we should ignore it as a goal of policy or specific conservation efforts. Rather it means we should combine our best scientific understanding with a commitment to be conservative regarding the ability of ecological systems to persist and adapt.

It also means we must have a commitment to stating our assumptions clearly, to viewing our management actions as experiments, and to learning from our mistakes.

ARE INTACT WATERSHEDS GOOD RESERVES?

Having summarized criteria for evaluating reserves, we now examine the extent to which reserves that follow watershed boundaries—and "intact" watersheds in particular—meet those criteria.

Reserve Content Criteria

1. SPECIES DIVERSITY AND REPRESENTATION. Watershed-scale reserves are an appropriate coarse filter for representing regional species diversity. We see this as being a critically important point in this discussion. Many species—particularly species of vertebrates and vascular plants—have a fairly well-known autecology in North Pacific coastal ecosystems and species-habitat relationships are fairly well understood. But the majority of species in these coastal forests probably fall into the categories of *rare* or *little known*—where species-habitat relationships are understood poorly, if at all. For these species, including most invertebrates, nonvascular plants, fungi, lichens, and microbes, the best approach to conservation is probably a systems approach (Marcot and Flather 2007; Marcot and Sieg 2007; Possingham *et al.* 2007), where conservation actions focus on ecosystem structure, composition, or functioning (or combinations of these). That is, the best way to conserve the majority of species may be by conserving the diversity of ecosystems on the landscape. And to the extent that protecting watersheds protects ecosystem diversity (see next section), this may represent an effective strategy for conserving the broad array of lesser-known organisms.

Watershed-based reserves should also be an effective component of a fine-filter approach for species that benefit from the particular mix of attributes a watershed-scale reserve provides. This includes species that are intolerant of human activity, that require large areas, and/or that utilize naturally diverse habitats. However, an entire watershed will include both high- and low-priority habitat for any given species. Protecting entire watersheds would be a less effective strategy for species that occur naturally in scattered, disjunct locations and do not require large areas of habitat. If those species are key targets, it would be more efficient to focus conservation efforts on the equivalent area of more scattered suitable habitat patches. Protected watersheds could be a component of a conservation strategy for these species, but would not necessarily be sufficient for them. From a fine-filter perspective, a watershed needs to be judged in the context of the species of concern. Protecting whole watersheds may also be an inefficient strategy for conserving endemic species, depending on the way that endemism is distributed across landscapes.

Reserving entire watersheds will contribute to maintaining spatial patterns of genetic variability over the landscape. Although breeding programs and other *ex situ* practices can maintain a store of genetic variation, they do not typically maintain the spatial pattern of genetic variation— either how it is organized within and between genetic neighborhoods, or how it is distributed along environmental gradients (Rudolph 1990). For example, conifers are genetically diverse, both within and among populations, and differentiation can occur on a surprisingly local scale (Ledig 1988; Rehfeldt 1989; Gapare *et al.* 2005). In some cases, this differentiation can be as fine-scaled as on slopes of different aspect in the same watershed. Maintaining population and genetic variability within a species may be important in maintaining ecosystem resilience and stabilizing production of ecosystem services (Hilborn *et al.* 2003; Schindler *et al.* 2010).

We conclude that watershed-based reserves, because of their utility in protecting a representative sample of ecosystems, are also useful for protecting little-known species. For the better-known species, watersheds can be good for protecting some groups of species, but represent an inefficient approach for others. As with ecosystems (next section), watershed-based reserves should capture species and communities in proportion to their natural variability on the landscape. Unless a watershed is unusual in its species complement, it will not generally allow overrepresentation of species of special concern. Being able to protect the existing spatial structure of subspecies-level genetic variation is important, but for many species this doesn't require that a whole watershed be protected. Indeed, if there is a limit on the total area to be protected for a species, then for species such as anadromous salmonids, where genetic structure varies significantly among watersheds, there is value to distributing conservation effort across watersheds. The utility of watershed-based reserves for conserving genetic diversity will depend upon whether most of a species' genetic diversity is within populations or among populations, and on how those populations are distributed in space.

2. ECOSYSTEM DIVERSITY AND REPRESENTATION. Watersheds characteristically encompass a variety of ecosystem types, from valley bottom to ridge top. By definition they include both riparian and upland areas. In coastal British Columbia and southeast Alaska, even small primary watersheds can contain habitats ranging from low-elevation coastal forests to alpine meadows. Larger watersheds such as the Skeena, Stikine, and Taku span the transition from a dry continental climate at their eastern end to wet, maritime-dominated coastal zones in the west, and from low elevations to subalpine and alpine areas. If climate becomes warmer and drier over much of north coastal BC and southeast Alaska, species are expected to move to higher latitudes and elevations and to moister sites (e.g., Hamann and Wang 2006). Reserves that incorporate a range of climates, site types, and elevations will allow for such movement internally.

Consistent with these differences in ecosystem types is variability in natural disturbance regimes, and thus variability in distributions of seral (successional) stages and the incidence of late-seral refugia. An area that captures a range of ecosystem types distributed across environmental gradients may thus also capture a range of ecosystem dynamics and its correlated suite of habitats and species. Consider, for example, the difference between plant communities in active floodplain systems and nearby upland forests on either deep soils or rocky ridges. In coastal temperate rainforests, these are very different plant communities driven by fundamentally different disturbance processes acting on different time scales (see Gavin *et al.* 2003a, 2003b for an analysis of how fire regimes are partitioned across such a landscape).

Watersheds, by definition, capture variation in ecosystem types in direct proportion to their natural distribution on that particular landscape. They represent natural variation directly, without reference to concerns about overrepresenting rare or threatened types of ecosystems. However, if watersheds in a region vary substantially in their character (orientation, geology, physiography), a single watershed may not capture the range of regional variation in ecosystems. In such cases it would be possible to design a system of protected areas of equal size to a given watershed that did a better job of representing regional ecosystem variation—but this requires good databases and careful planning. In evaluating proposed new protected watersheds in BC's central and north coasts, for example, representation of various biogeoclimatic subzones and variants (areas of distinct climate as reflected by vegetation) was analyzed. Subzone and variant representation was one criterion used in selecting watersheds for protection.

Tautologically, watershed-based protected areas represent ecosystem variation across the landscape in direct proportion to its variation on that landscape. This can be a good thing, but it is not necessarily good. In British Columbia, as in most other jurisdictions globally, we have done an exceptional job in representing alpine ecosystems in protected areas and a much poorer job of capturing higher-productivity, lower-elevation ecosystems, such as forests with high economic value. One approach to correcting this imbalance might be to *under*represent alpine areas in new protected areas. Since protecting whole watersheds protects ecosystems proportional to their occurrence, such deliberate underrepresentation is not possible in this approach. Furthermore, these higher elevation areas may increase in conservation significance as climatic refugia under changing climates, or as threats to them increase with climate warming.

We conclude that protecting whole watersheds usually protects variation in ecosystem characteristics and thus provides a good coarse-filter approach to conservation. Watersheds contain the structured environmental variation inherent within a region. However there are some cases where a nonwatershed-based approach might be better, notably if one has as a goal overrepresenting rare or threatened ecosystems, or if a limited area can be protected and there is substantial variation among watersheds. All other things being equal, with good data and planning, a system of reserves in partially developed watersheds could capture the same range of variation in ecosystems as a reserve in an undeveloped watershed.

3. ECOSYSTEM PROCESSES. Because watershed structure influences the spread of biological and physical disturbance agents across forest landscapes, watersheds are logical units of analysis, management, and conservation from the perspective of natural disturbance regimes. Unless they are very large though, or the disturbances are very small (e.g., gap-phase processes; Lertzman *et al.* 1996), watersheds cannot be presumed to capture a minimum dynamic area. We know of no analysis that has estimated a minimum dynamic area for the regions of concern here. Such analyses generally focus on systems dominated by large disturbances, which require

very large reserves (Leroux *et al.* 2007). In many coastal rainforest watersheds, however, fires are rare and not large: forest dynamics are dominated by gap-phase replacement processes, floodplain dynamics, and occasional slides or windthrow patches of modest size (e.g., Lertzman *et al.* 1996; Gavin *et al.* 2003a, 2003b; DellaSala 2011). In other areas larger windthrow patches are more frequent (Kramer *et al.* 2001). In either case, however, many watersheds are likely to be of sufficient size that they exceed a minimum dynamic area. Reserves of equivalent size that did *not* follow watershed boundaries could be planned to achieve this, but they would be less likely to capture the idiosyncratic variation in disturbance regimes that maps onto watershed-scale gradients such as slope position and aspect (e.g., Gavin *et al.* 2003b; Heyerdahl *et al.* 2007).

Thus from this perspective, watersheds are logical candidates for reserves, and are probably better than nonwatershed-based equivalent areas. However, there should be an analysis of local disturbance regimes before presuming any reserve represents either a minimum dynamic area or captures the range of regional disturbance dynamics. Furthermore, where disturbance regimes are changing in response to regional environmental gradients, the spatial and temporal variability of disturbance types and frequency over complex landscapes challenges the application of these concepts (Baker 1992).

Watersheds are clearly functional units of landscape for hydrological processes and the terrestrial ecosystems with which they are strongly coupled. Stream character is intimately related to the climate, geology, and morphology of the surrounding drainage basin (Lotspeich 1980; Benda *et al.* 2004) as well as local physical factors. Although stream segments are sometimes examined as individual entities, each reach is connected longitudinally to others. A major conceptual thrust in stream ecology, the River Continuum Concept, argues for the longitudinal integration of ecosystem processes over the length of stream systems (Vannote *et al.* 1980; Gomi *et al.* 2002). In very large river systems, however, community structure and production dynamics may be relatively decoupled between headwaters areas and floodplains lower in the watershed, though flood pulses still serve to link the two (Junk *et al.* 1989; Sedell *et al.* 1989; Power and Dietrich 2002). The scale of fluvial ecosystems that dominate those watersheds considered for reserves are generally seen as being strongly coupled throughout their drainage network (Vannote *et al.* 1980; Gomi *et al.* 2002; Lowe *et al.* 2006).

In the section on transboundary physical processes, we focus on issues related to weak external connections among watersheds. The complement to this is strong internal connections within watersheds—especially in relation to hydrological and colluvial processes. These connections are obvious in terms of the formal mapped stream network and the organisms dependent on it. However, in coastal temperate rainforest watersheds, the significance of these strong internal interactions is magnified, because essentially the entire watershed is functionally a part of the drainage network (Scientific Panel for Sustainable Forest Practices in Clayoquot Sound 1995). In these forests, nominally upland areas are permeated by seasonal or ephemeral surface and subsurface drainage channels that are the smallest initial links in the chain of hydrologic processes that define a watershed. These small elements represent the greatest contribution to the overall length of stream network in the watershed and occupy the greatest area of any components of the stream network in the watershed.

The importance and distinct contributions of small headwaters stream segments to watershed hydrology and ecology has been emphasized many times over the past decade (e.g., Gomi *et al.* 2002). They can also pose significant challenges to management because they are so ubiquitous on the landscape—typically there is insufficient area between these first-order drainages to place cutblocks (management units) for logging. Thus management plans must usually incorporate protection for first-order drainages within them, which has had variable success. Thus, in coastal British Columbia and southeast Alaska, undeveloped watersheds pose a distinct kind of opportunity for conservation of an integrated system of physical and ecological processes that is meaningful beyond the individual taxa, communities, or structures that are our normal focus.

4. RESERVE SIZE. Watersheds come in a range of sizes, from very small headwaters catchments to those draining a large portion of the continent. The sizes of watersheds typically considered as reserves in the context of our discussion range from a few thousands to hundreds of thousands of hectares. The biggest of these are big enough that questions of viable populations and metapopulations may be meaningful for most species—though probably not the largest of mobile vertebrates. For such species, large watersheds might be evaluated for their potential as core reserve areas in the context of their surrounding areas.

If the choice is between reserving one large watershed or several other reserves forming parts of more than one watershed, then the decisions should be based on ecosystem- and species-focused conservation needs, isolation, transboundary processes, and ecological integrity: ecologically, size itself is important only because of things with which it may be correlated.

Size in itself becomes a critical part of decisionmaking if the total area allocated for conservation is limited. For example, if there is a limited areal budget for protected areas, protecting a few large watersheds may preclude other options. In British Columbia, concerns about protecting undeveloped watersheds have contributed to the very skewed size distribution of the protected areas system (fig. 8.04). This distribution can be viewed not only in terms of its arguably enormous successes in having created very large protected areas in remote, pristine wilderness environments, but also in terms of the challenges those decisions imposed on meeting conservation needs elsewhere from a significantly diminished budget.

Reserve Context Criteria

5. LOCATION. Watersheds occur everywhere, but is their location relevant to considering watersheds for protection? In some cases it is. If a conservation strategy has a goal of representing regional biogeographic gradients, then the location of undeveloped watersheds relative to other conservation options should be considered. Because undeveloped watersheds often tend to remain in more remote locations (harder or more expensive to access for resource development), they may be clustered in certain areas of regional biodiversity and thus collectively will not represent the range of diversity. Location is also often correlated with climate and processes related to climate. For instance, on the west coast of BC and southeast Alaska, an obvious example is areas of high rainfall, organic soils, and low-productivity forests. As with nonforested areas, these and other such areas with low value for industrial forestry tend to be predominantly undeveloped watersheds—and also to be overrepresented in existing protected areas. Such concerns need be dealt with in relation to the criteria specific to the system of reserves.

6. SHAPE. Shapes of watersheds are highly variable and no generalizations can be made with respect to putative principles of reserve design. Most

watersheds of concern here, however, are large enough that shape should not critically influence a watershed's susceptibility to outside influences. Furthermore, watershed boundaries, irrespective of their shape, will be more effective than arbitrary administrative boundaries at minimizing negative transboundary effects, since heights of land (watershed boundaries) represent barriers for many species and processes.

7. ECOLOGICAL ISOLATION VERSUS CONNECTIVITY IN THE SURROUNDING LANDSCAPE. One reason that an undeveloped watershed—or even better, a cluster of undeveloped watersheds—is very appealing as a reserve is that, for many processes, its degree of connection to surrounding areas is determined largely by the same physical factors in the environment that did so historically. Movement between a watershed and its surrounding areas may be restricted by very steep topography, but larger animals generally can easily move across watershed boundaries (e.g., Post *et al.* 2007; Darimont *et al.* 2005). If a watershed is isolated by steep high-elevation terrain, loss of movement options should be a lesser concern than isolation by urban development or transportation corridors. If the terrain is a barrier to movement among the elements of a metapopulation, at least it always has been so; the barriers thus imposed are not ecologically novel. Further, because water does flow downhill and for some organisms heights of land are effective barriers, this physiographic isolation should protect the interior of the watershed from some external threats (e.g., some introduced species). If the watersheds are unroaded, then they will be protected from some other external threats for which humans are vectors (e.g., weeds, or poachers dispersed along roads; see Gelbard and Harrison 2005).

However, if a watershed reserve is isolated by development that creates a hostile surrounding matrix, it seems likely that the issues of metapopulation dynamics that will arise will be similar to those for other reserves *of similar size in a similar landscape context*. The watershed boundaries may protect the internal dynamics of the reserve, but they won't alleviate potential problems arising from challenges to ecological connectivity outside the reserve. To the extent that watershed-based reserves are likely to be larger, their size may address this issue, but that choice of size reflects a policy decision, not anything inherent about watersheds.

8. TRANSBOUNDARY PHYSICAL PROCESSES. For most land- or water-based physical processes, watersheds have stronger internal interactions

than transboundary interactions. Further, most of these transboundary interactions are asymmetrical—the movement of waterborne material and energy is directed downstream and out of the watershed rather than into it. Quite often disturbance events such as fires can be contained within watershed or subdrainage boundaries (e.g., Swanson *et al.* 1988; Hemstrom and Franklin 1982), so that such boundaries may provide a measure of protection from disturbances originating outside the protected area. Ridgetops and wet pockets may act as firebreaks, creating boundaries in forest age classes that follow topographic lines (Hemstrom and Franklin 1982). Although some of the general relationships are well understood (Swanson *et al.* 1988; Dorner *et al.* 2002; Heyerdahl *et al.* 2007; Jordan *et al.* 2008), the role of landscape structure in influencing the generation, spread, frequency, and type of disturbances is poorly documented.

As with transboundary ecological processes, watershed boundaries may minimize human transboundary processes, such as poaching, if heights of land separate roaded from unroaded areas. Thus we conclude that if transboundary physical processes are a critical issue in reserve planning, watershed-based reserves are a good strategy.

9. CRITERIA SPECIFIC TO THE SYSTEM OF RESERVES. This evaluation is based on the contribution of a particular reserve to the reserve system as a whole. Whether whole watersheds are useful contributions to a protected areas system depends on the goals of that system and the components still required to complete that system. This suggests that whole watersheds will be useful contributions to some reserve systems, and not to others.

Emergent Criteria

10. POPULATION VIABILITY. We address population viability of three broad categories: terrestrial animals, aquatic organisms, and plants.

Terrestrial Animals. Some watersheds encompass enough area to maintain viable populations of many species. This is especially true for smaller and less mobile species. One watershed in isolation, however, even a large one of hundreds of thousands of hectares, is unlikely to sustain in abundance a broad enough distribution of seasonal habitats to supply the needs of all species in a regional pool. Few watersheds likely to be considered for protected status are even within an order of magnitude of the size specified by the World Wildlife Fund Canada (1990) estimates for viable populations of large carnivores. Population viability of species with large home ranges or long migrations depends on favorable conditions in many different places and freedom for individuals to move throughout an area of very large size. For such species, most individual watersheds can be only a component of a network of protected areas linked by a matrix dominated by carefully planned management activities (e.g., Weaver *et al.* 2002).

To maintain systems that support large carnivores, some large, inaccessible areas must be maintained. Roading a watershed to allow even the most environmentally sensitive forest harvesting allows human access that can precipitate a rapid decline in wildlife populations through legal and illegal hunting and other disturbances, such as firewood cutting of snags (see Person and Brinkman, this volume, chapter 6). Large intact watersheds that provide for large carnivore reserve areas that are relatively free of human disturbance could provide core reserves of healthy populations to support metapopulation dynamics more broadly and allow for recolonization of disturbed areas.

We know of no studies that explicitly evaluate the importance of intact, unlogged watersheds to wildlife populations. Several studies report correlations between reserve size and viability of wildlife populations (e.g., McCarthy *et al.* 2005), but none consider whether it is important that reserves follow watershed boundaries. We know of no wildlife species that require absolutely intact watersheds.

Also, the degree of disturbance or habitat alteration that would impact wildlife communities is often poorly understood. Impacts of development are cumulative and initially incremental, but will probably exhibit threshold phenomena; there is a large literature developing around identifying general conclusions about the location of such habitat thresholds (e.g., Dykstra 2004; Poulin *et al.* 2008).

Although intact watersheds may not be necessary to maintain many wildlife populations, watershed structure plays important roles in wildlife ecology. Many species undergo seasonal movements to different parts of watersheds (e.g., Nyberg and Janz 1990; Schoen and Kirchhoff 2007; Maier *et al.* 2005). The physiographic structure of watersheds creates seasonally important habitats and maintains their spatial distribution. The distribution of habitat types over the altitudinal and productivity gradients produced by watershed structure may provide important mixes of critical seasonal habitats for a variety of vertebrate species.

Aquatic Organisms. Watersheds are logical units for conservation of many aquatic organisms—both from the perspective of the physical processes structuring their environments and from a genetic perspective. For many of these species, a single watershed of significant size may contain the entire effective breeding population or metapopulation. Anadromous fish return to traditional spawning areas and headwater creeks, and are typically genetically distinct from watershed to watershed. Nonanadromous fish are often genetically distinct among watersheds (Allendorf and Leary 1988; Ford *et al.* 2004). Even separate low-order streams of the same drainage basin may have distinct genetic populations. Habitat reduction has caused serious losses of genetic variants, especially from small stocks, and caused overall declines in regional abundance (e.g., Schindler *et al.* 2003). Conservation in such cases could be achieved without relying on watershed-scale reserves, but there seems to be a clear consensus from the aquatic research community that, from this perspective, watershed reserves are a high priority (Saunders *et al.* 2002).

Our focus in this discussion of emergent criteria is on maintaining the processes that support diversity. As discussed above, however, if populations differ genetically among watersheds, then protecting a single watershed will miss significant elements of variability elsewhere. Thus to effectively capture both the processes supporting diversity within watersheds and the larger-scale distribution of biological variability, watershed-scale and supra-watershed-scale strategies need to be combined.

Plant Populations. Variation of vegetation structure within watersheds arises primarily from three sources: the underlying mosaic of soils, topography, and other physical features (and their interaction with climate, e.g., Lertzman *et al.* 1996; Heyerdahl *et al.* 2007), differences in successional development, and differences in disturbance regimes (e.g., floodplain dynamics versus fire versus wind). We argued above that watershed boundaries effectively sample the alpha and beta diversity imposed by physical landscape mosaic and that watershed characteristics influence the nature and spread of disturbances and thus contribute significantly to the spatial and temporal distribution of successional stages. If so, watershed-based reserves should do a very good job of capturing a meaningful unit of ecological function in terms of landscape-scale vegetation mosaics.

The extent to which watersheds are functional units for plants from a population genetic perspective is less clear. There are some special cases of genetic association with watershed structure that parallel what is seen for fish, but, for the vast majority of species, very little is known about population genetics, let alone patterns of relatedness within and between drainage basins. Most information available focuses on a few commercial species; little of that can be used to examine this issue directly. Sorensen (1983), however, found distinct genetic subpopulations of Douglas-fir on different aspects of the same watershed, suggesting that for some species, genetic variation may in part reflect watershed structure.

Some plant species are clearly associated with older forests that decline in abundance as a watershed is developed (e.g., Smith 2005; MacKinnon 1998) and there are some species that have been clearly shown to be sensitive to isolation (e.g., Tomimatsu and Ohara 2006; Petit *et al.* 2004). Still, at the population level, most plant species do not require whole watersheds for effective conservation—the meaningful functional units of landscape are smaller.

Thus we conclude that watershed-based conservation can address concerns about viable populations for many species (especially aquatic species and smaller, less mobile terrestrial species—and especially if the watersheds are large). However, they will not do so for other vertebrate species that are often of particular conservation concern. Watershed structure, however, is often associated with critical habitats for such species, and watershed-based conservation could be a significant component of conservation planning for them.

11. ECOLOGICAL INTEGRITY. Our definition of ecological integrity centers on the processes and attributes that lead to long-term persistence (which includes resilience, adaptation, and the processes which lead to them). This is an important concept to include in assessing watersheds as conservation units, despite its inherent uncertainty and its operational difficulty. A sense of the ecological integrity of unmanaged—"natural"— systems is close to the core of many discussions in ecosystem-based management and conservation—for instance the use of historical ranges of variability as management models (e.g., Landres *et al.* 1999). It isn't because we believe those particular historical states of the system to be inherently better than an alternative managed state. The only empirically demonstrated distribution of states to achieve the persistence that those systems displayed in the past was in fact those historical states. They constitute a null model for what a system with "integrity" might look like.

Because of the way they represent species, communities, and ecosystem processes as discussed above, undeveloped watersheds are the best examples we have of landscapes that might capture this intuitive sense of ecological integrity.

Other Considerations for Intact Watersheds as Reserves

Smaller, nonwatershed-based reserves are commonly, and often effectively, used to protect spectacular or representative examples of plant communities or other natural features. Maintaining these as natural benchmarks for research or restoration activities is a common objective for such reserves. Such reserves, however, cannot play this role for larger-scale landscape processes such as longitudinal integration of food webs or propagation of large woody debris along river systems, the complex interaction of floodplain dynamics and riparian forest disturbance and development, or disturbance and successional mosaics in upland forest. If ecological benchmarks for these kinds of processes are a goal for protected areas, then larger, undeveloped (or restored) watersheds should be considered as elements of protected areas systems.

Whole-system responses to changing climatic drivers is something of a wild card for both conservation and forest management in these watersheds. We do not know how the responses of populations will be expressed over elevational and edaphic gradients within watersheds. We know even less how changes in river and other disturbance dynamics will play out over landscapes. The argument for undeveloped watersheds as natural benchmarks for such changes is strengthened by these uncertainties. To the extent that climate change causes climatic envelopes, causing ecosystems and species to shift upwards in elevation—as is predicted to for many areas of BC's coast (e.g., Hamann and Wang 2006)—protecting entire watersheds can provide opportunities for vertical movement of species and ecosystems. Unroaded (and otherwise undeveloped) watersheds may also be logical reserves for reasons of the logistics of management. It is rarely cost effective, especially in remote coastal watersheds with steep topography, to establish a road network in a watershed unless a substantial amount of harvesting is planned; initial road-building costs are usually the greatest expense in a harvesting operation. Thus for economic reasons, it may make sense for harvesting to be concentrated in already roaded watersheds rather than initiating the development of road networks in a large number of new watersheds. This strategy would also result in minimal fragmentation of residual forest. If the value of the conservation opportunity in undeveloped watersheds is considered high enough, then this is an option where economic and ecological criteria may be met jointly.

CONCLUSIONS

Watersheds scored variably over most of the content and context criteria and positively for the emergent criteria (table 8.1). Watershed-based conservation can clearly make sense as a choice if coarse-filter approaches in general, or strict proportional representation of ecological communities, is important. Similarly, watershed-based conservation is likely to be more effective than alternatives if maintaining landscape-scale ecosystem processes, aquatic ecosystem dynamics, or minimizing transboundary processes are important objectives of a reserve system. If fine-filter approaches are critical, such as protecting targeted habitat for special or threatened species (especially if the species are terrestrial, uncommon, and not very mobile), then watershed-based conservation is likely to be an inefficient approach. In those cases, the same investment in area, but spread over smaller reserves targeting focal habitats distributed among several watersheds, may be more effective.

One of the strongest conclusions to arise from our analysis is the critical role of clarity in identifying the goals and objectives of a protected areas system as a basis for making decisions about how conservation effort should be allocated (see also Nicholson and Possingham 2006). If investment in a protected areas system is constrained, as it almost always is, there will necessarily be significant tradeoffs between coarse- and fine-filter strategies. As one might expect, coarse-filter strategies align reasonably well with more process-oriented approaches. We suspect that much of the historical disagreement about the validity or necessity of watershed-based conservation planning arises from a lack of clarity about intended goals.

We recommend that the identification of objectives for potential watershed-scale reserves should be derived from the goals of the protected areas system to which those reserves would belong. It is only at the scale of the system as a whole that tradeoffs of conservation investment among areas and objectives can reasonably be made.

The most compelling argument for watersheds as reserves is that, more than any other delineations of equivalent size (or investment), they represent areas of landscape with strong internal connections among ecosystem processes and weaker external connections. Thus, watershed-based reserves have a greater likelihood of maintaining the ecological integrity of the area over the long-term without significant human subsidies.

From our retrospective analysis, we conclude that British Columbia's protected area system has achieved an impressive mix of protected areas of a wide range of sizes, with a very significant investment in protected areas at the largest end of the size spectrum. We cannot assess from the size distribution alone whether this represents an appropriate investment in large protected areas. It would be worthwhile to undertake more formal analysis of other parameters of the system as part of an assessment of protected areas function across the system as a whole.

We are convinced that undeveloped watersheds are important as conservation targets, but we can imagine circumstances where one might forgo those opportunities. We support the recommendation by others (e.g., Scientific Panel for Sustainable Forest Practices in Clayoquot Sound 1995) that there be a moratorium on development of currently undeveloped watersheds to maintain conservation options until the issues of goals, investment, and allocation have been resolved. As part of this process, the remaining undeveloped and minimally developed watersheds in the region should be enumerated and described in terms of their ecological and physical characteristics as a basis for meaningful assessment of their conservation value.

The emerging importance of the functional connection via food webs between riparian zones, anadromous fish (and seabirds), and forests beyond the "normal" riparian designation emphasizes the need for maintaining the diversity of bidirectional watershed processes linking upland and riparian forests with stream/river and marine systems. From a precautionary perspective, maintaining ecosystem processes at the watershed scale—and even linking watersheds to coastal marine ecosystems—is likely to be critical for maintaining diversity in coastal temperate rainforest ecosystems.

There are many situations where undeveloped watersheds of smaller sizes (e.g., hundreds to a few thousand hectares) pose significant opportunities for protection. In such cases, many of the benefits of watershed-based conservation will accrue, with less of the opportunity cost arising from constraints on overall conservation investment. Since smaller reserves are more likely than larger ones to be at risk from externally driven processes, watershed-based reserve boundaries may help these smaller reserves even more than they would larger ones. We suggest that the discussion of watershed-based reserves might be usefully decoupled from the association with reserve size—it need not, as it has in British Columbia, lead to a large investment in very large reserves. Very large reserves do play an important role in protected areas systems, and, while watershed-based conservation makes sense in that context, it doesn't make sense only in that context.

Southeast Alaska exemplifies the situation of opportunities provided by unlogged watersheds of small to moderate size: there are many unlogged watersheds, and most unlogged watersheds are smaller than those we've discussed in BC, and thus are decoupled from the size/opportunity-cost issue. Thus it may be feasible to build a watershed-based conservation network in the region by starting with the physical template (physiographic provinces, geology, topography), considering the population of undeveloped (plus high-priority developed) watersheds, and then adding conservation priorities by selecting subsets of them and adding other nonwatershed-based areas that score high for other ecological values, such as endemic and rare species. The size distribution of watersheds also suggests that a better scale to consider for reserves than individual watersheds may be clusters of contiguous watersheds or all the watersheds on a smaller island.

SLOSS is a real and meaningful problem in protected areas system design in British Columbia and southeast Alaska. However, the discussion needs to be revisited in the context of the particular conservation issues of those areas. It needs to be treated not just, or even primarily, as a problem of population or community processes, but also fundamentally as one of ecosystem- to landscape-scale processes as well.

Primary watersheds—those with their terminus in salt water—are likely to be special in terms of their role in capturing ecological and genetic diversity and energy and nutrient transfers among terrestrial and marine ecosystems. For some taxa, such as many fish species, these watersheds represent distinct elements of genetic variation. They represent, without having to undertake a significant data gathering and planning exercise, a "complete" sample of ecosystems and communities from headwaters to tidewater.

What does the archipelago nature of the region's landscapes mean in the context of watershed-based protection? Many locally and regionally significant watersheds are smaller than the very large mainland watersheds that are an issue in terms of the size/investment tradeoff discussed here. This should create opportunities for watershed-based protection. In addition, a high proportion of watersheds are primary watersheds. Because there is a population of many more smaller watersheds from which to choose, we should be able to capture representation across regional gradients (e.g., outer to inner coast) and across variation in physiography—e.g., rounded mountains, angular mountains, hills, etc., which translates to significant variation in ecological communities in these systems. This all suggests that from the perspective of adaptive management—or adaptive conservation policy—that there are opportunities for extensive replication of reserve treatments. This should significantly enhance the opportunities for learning about conservation effectiveness—especially if the treatments are planned and the data are collected.

Ideally, we should establish a reserve network based on a framework of priority watersheds that represent the best combination of capturing ecological diversity, evolutionary processes, and ecosystem functionality. If investments in ecosystem functionality come at a high cost (in area or opportunity), then we should try to allocate this area in locations with high diversity value—we need to use our investment in ecosystem processes to support the integrity of diversity hotspots. However, given the history of development (many of the best examples of high-productivity landscape elements have been logged) we will not be able to rely exclusively on undeveloped watersheds to capture significant elements of diversity. We also need to identify priority watersheds with a history of development—and recognize that some will be in need of restoration. An effective conservation strategy should combine both species-based and ecosystem-based approaches to provide a reserve network that jointly addresses issues of content, context, and emergent properties.

Three key research gaps remain.

1. We need more formal research on the overall population of watersheds across the region from southeast Alaska through the central coast of British Columbia (e.g., the kind of work begun by Schoen and Albert [2007]). This should describe the population of watersheds by features such as regional gradients of physiographic characteristics and ecological variation, presence of species at risk, and development and protection status. Superimposing the existing system of protected areas on

this variation should lead to a gap analysis by physiographic province for high-value watersheds.

2. Not enough is understood about natural disturbance regimes and their intraregional variation (such as gradients in the role of chronic and episodic wind disturbance, landslides, and fire). We need a better understanding of variation in minimum dynamic area in relation to the size distribution of watersheds. This should feed in to decisionmaking about to what extent and where we should consider single watersheds, clusters of watersheds, or island-based reserve tactics.

3. We need more research on the effectiveness of existing protected areas systems—including watershed-based and nonwatershed-based protected areas. Ideally, we would undertake formal comparisons of the effectiveness in reserve content, context, and emergent criteria of replicate protected areas stratified across regional gradients.

Finally, we need to recognize that while much of the fundamental science of watershed processes is well understood, many of our conclusions about watershed-based reserves and conservation effectiveness are better thought of as hypotheses. This means that watershed-based reserve design should be treated as an experiment with learning as an objective (i.e., conservation planning needs to be considered as a process of adaptive management).

ACKNOWLEDGMENTS

We would first like to acknowledge the contributions to our thinking about watersheds as conservation opportunities made by our earlier collaborators on this topic, Fred Bunnell and Laurie Kremsater. We were pushed to think carefully and critically about this topic by the discussions of the Old Growth Forests Strategy of the Province of British Columbia, and many of the participants in that process also made useful contributions to our thinking. We very much appreciate John Schoen, Gordon Orians, Audubon Alaska, the Nature Conservancy, and the Wilburforce Foundation for organizing and funding the workshop in Juneau, which occasioned our revisiting these issues and prompted this chapter. Gordon Orians, John Schoen, and two anonymous reviewers made great editorial contributions to this work, which we very much appreciate.

9

Variable Retention Harvesting in North Pacific Temperate Rainforests

William J. Beese

INTRODUCTION

Forest ecosystems and species have evolved in response to climate and other biophysical attributes and a range of natural disturbances at various temporal and spatial scales. If we wish to achieve conservation of biological diversity in forests while harvesting wood and other forest products, an important basic theoretical premise is that since species are adapted to historic local conditions, forest management should use natural disturbance patterns and processes as a guide. Throughout the Pacific coast of North America from Vancouver Island through southeast Alaska, windthrow, insects, disease, landslides and infrequent fire create forests with an abundance of dispersed residual structure (e.g., live and dead standing trees) and varying sizes of canopy gaps (Alaback 1984; Lertzman *et al.* 1996; Ott and Juday 2002). In the past decade, information on the nature of natural disturbances and the role of biological legacies in temperate rainforests has continued to increase (Hennon and McClellan 2003; Banner *et al.* 2005; Daniels and Gray 2006; Pearson 2010; also see Alaback *et al.*, chapter 4 of this volume) along with our efforts to apply these new findings (Beese *et al.* 2003; Deal 2007; Franklin *et al.* 2007). Scientific knowledge should help guide our attempts to sustain productive and diverse forest ecosystems.

However, opinions differ about how, when, and where to apply this knowledge. Should we attempt to imitate natural disturbance, or develop approaches based on broad principles? How much of the forest should be reserved on the landscape and how much stand-level retention is enough? How should we balance the tradeoff between yield of commercial products and biodiversity preservation? Or, what is the greatest value of old forests to society: high-value wood products or long-term carbon storage (Smithwick *et al.* 2002)? Where the goals of forest management include both timber production and conservation of biological diversity, as the public increasingly demands, a variable retention approach to forest harvesting can help managers meet multiple objectives (Gustafsson *et al.* 2012).

Coastal British Columbia (BC) and southeast Alaska share a mountainous coastline stretching from roughly 49° N to 60° N latitude, blanketed by temperate rainforests. Other than the Douglas-fir (*Pseudotsuga menziesii*) forests on southern Vancouver Island and the adjacent BC mainland, this forest is dominated by western hemlock (*Tsuga heterophylla*) with varying amounts of western redcedar (*Thuja plicata*), Sitka spruce (*Picea sitchensis*), Nootka or Alaskan yellow cedar (*Callitropsis* [= *Chamaecyparis*] *nootkatensis*), Pacific silver fir (*Abies amabilis*), mountain hemlock (*Tsuga mertensiana*), and a few other conifers and deciduous broadleaved species. Summers are cool and moist, and winters are kept mild by the influence of the Pacific Ocean (Alaback 1982; Klinka *et al.* 1991). This chapter reviews the implementation and monitoring of variable retention harvesting in the temperate rainforests of the North Pacific coast.

TERMINOLOGY

A variety of terms and uses appear in the literature on stand-level retention, so it is important to define the terms I use in this chapter. I use the term *variable retention* (VR) to describe the overall approach to harvesting and silvicultural systems that retains trees and associated habitat for purposes other than timber management and traditional silviculture goals. Variable retention can be implemented with a wide range of harvesting systems (e.g., hoe-forwarding, cable yarding) and can utilize traditional silvicultural systems, such as shelterwood or selection, to meet forest regeneration objectives. I use *retention system* to refer to a specific silvicultural system designed to meet the goals of variable retention that was originally defined in the BC Operational Planning Regulations (1999). It has three requirements: (1) retained trees are distributed over the area of the cutblock; (2) standing trees are left for the long term (at least one rotation); and (3) distribution of retained trees achieves greater than 50%

a

b

c

d

FIGURE 9.01. Examples of variable retention harvesting: (*a*) dispersed retention, (*b*) group (aggregated) retention, (*c*) mixed retention, (*d*) group selection with reserves.

"forest influence" (the area surrounding a tree or forest edge with a radius equal to its height). This new silvicultural system acknowledges that retention of trees and other structural attributes of forests for purposes other than tree regeneration and timber production are legitimate goals of forest management (Mitchell and Beese 2002). The retention system normally uses a one-pass harvesting approach but may also be prescribed with several harvesting entries. The two main variants of the retention system are grouped (or aggregated) and dispersed. For safety, economic, and ecological reasons, group retention is often preferred; however, both variants and mixed approaches have advantages for specific objectives (Franklin *et al.* 1997, 2007; Beese *et al.* 2003). A cutblock is a specific area of land chosen for harvesting and management as a unit. It includes current cutting areas as well as uncut trees that may be designated for future harvesting or left as reserves (fig. 9.01).

Clear-cut with reserves is a modification of traditional clear-cutting where trees are retained within or adjacent to the cutblock. This approach differs from the retention system in two ways: (1) there is no spatial distribution requirement for the reserves; and (2) the reserves need not be left for the long term. In practice, because clear-cut with reserves usually *does* leave long-term retention, it can be an effective tool within a landscape-level biodiversity strategy. Although leaving an uncut patch adjacent to a cut area is not visibly different from a clear-cut, this approach maintains old-forest attributes over the landscape that would not otherwise have been retained. Where at least some long-term reserves are distributed within the cutblock, the approach can be quite similar to the retention system in both appearance and function. Unfortunately, the term *clear-cut with reserves* is awkward and is often misunderstood by the public.

USE OF VARIABLE RETENTION IN COASTAL BC AND SOUTHEAST ALASKA

Use of variable retention has steadily increased in coastal BC since the term was first introduced by the Scientific Panel for Sustainable Forest Practices in Clayoquot Sound (1995) and subsequently described in a broader context by Franklin *et al.* (1997). Prior to this time, partial-cutting silvicultural systems had been rarely employed in the old-growth forests of the North Pacific coast (Arnott and Beese 1997). In 1998, the largest forest company operating on the BC coast (MacMillan Bloedel [MB] Limited) announced that it would use VR for virtually all forest harvesting as part of a forest management strategy designed to achieve a balance of ecological, social, and economic goals (Dunsworth and Beese 2000). Following this lead, other forest companies in coastal BC adopted VR for varying proportions of their harvesting. Pojar *et al.* (1999) recommended the use of variable retention and a variety of silvicultural systems for a large area of BC's central coast. Weyerhaeuser purchased MB in 1999 and continued phase-in of the VR approach throughout its BC coastal operations over a five-year period, completing over 90% of harvesting using VR in 2003. By 2007, more than 50,000 ha of harvesting had been done using the retention system on the company's private land and public tenures. After several changes in ownership and a merger of three companies, this adaptive management program has continued under Western Forest Products Inc. (WFP) as the "Western Forest Strategy" for managing over 1.4 million ha of forest land on the BC coast. Although implementation and monitoring showed that the retention system was not suitable for all sites, the retention system continues to be used for the majority of the company's harvesting.

From 2004 through 2009, 40% of the forest harvesting on public land in coastal BC was done using the retention system; 2%, other partial-cutting systems; 32%, clear-cut with reserves; and 26%, clear-cut (BC Ministry of Forests and Range 2010). Numerous training sessions and workshops have occurred in BC to help operational foresters meet the goals of VR in a safe and cost-effective manner. Extension materials include a decision aid (Zielke *et al.* 2008), summaries of recent findings (Huggard and Bunnell 2007), and individual company guidelines. BC government legislation requires a minimum of 7% of the area harvested annually to be retained at the stand-level as Wildlife Tree Retention Areas (BC Forest Planning and Practices Regulation 2004). Further requirements may be specified in land-use plans. For example, the Vancouver Island land use plan (BC Integrated Land Management Bureau 2000) assigned landscapes to one of three resource management zones with different emphases on biodiversity conservation and guidelines for retention. Special Management Zones restrict clear-cut size to 5 ha or less and allow cutblocks up to 40 ha for retention, shelterwood, or selection systems. The Clayoquot panel recommendations specified minimums of 15% and 70% retention for different situations. On the central and north coast of BC, an *ecosystem-based management* approach was adopted for land use plans covering a 7.5 million ha area (Coast Information Team 2004). Under ecosystem-based management, at least 15% stand-level retention must be left at the time of harvest within the context of a high level of landscape-level reserves and protected areas.

Although the terms *variable retention* and *retention system* have not been used in management plans and prescriptions for the Tongass National Forest (Tongass) in southeast Alaska (USDA Forest Service 2008a), alternatives to clear-cutting and retention of structural attributes are being implemented. The current Land and Resource Management Plan allows even-aged, two-aged, and uneven-aged systems to be used. In 1994, when the Alternatives to Clearcutting (ATC) study began on the Tongass (McClellan *et al.* 2000), all previous harvesting there was done using clear-cutting. By 1997, the Tongass Land and Resource Management Plan called for 20% of harvesting to be done with "two-aged" management. From 2004 through 2008, 17% of the forest harvesting in the Tongass was done using selection systems, excluding sanitation cutting and thinning (USDA Forest Service 2010). Use of non-clear-cut systems has declined on the Tongass in recent years because of economics, logging feasibility, and safety concerns (Christian and Brackley 2007).

GOALS FOR STAND-LEVEL RETENTION
AND LANDSCAPE RESERVES

Several publications present the fundamental principles behind variable retention—how leaving "biological legacies" at the time of harvesting can contribute to biodiversity conservation by helping to maintain connectivity, landscape heterogeneity, stand complexity, and intact aquatic ecosystems (Franklin *et al.* 1997, 2007; Lindenmayer and Franklin 2002). Specific goals of stand-level retention for old forests include "lifeboating" of species and processes during early successional stages, enriching structural attributes of second-growth forests, and providing habitat connectivity between larger reserves on a managed landscape (Franklin *et al.* 1997). It would be redundant to cover this material here; however, a few points are worth emphasizing.

In forests where timber production is a major goal, both stand-level retention and landscape-level reserves facilitate biodiversity conservation across the landscape (Lindenmayer and Franklin 2002). Neither approach alone is likely to be as effective or efficient as the two in combination (Bunnell *et al.* 2003). An essential element of a broad biodiversity conservation strategy is a network of protected areas and other reserves. The primary function of these landscape-level reserves is to represent the full range of ecosystems within the nonharvestable land base to maintain lesser known species and ecological processes (Kremsater *et al.* 2003). Variable retention in the harvested "matrix" between reserves may perform a complementary role for species that do not require forest interior conditions but rely on certain structural attributes. In fact, a fundamental premise of VR is that more species will thrive in the area if mature forest elements are distributed throughout the production-forest landscape rather than adding an equivalent amount of mature forest to the reserve system. For some birds, retaining 15% to 20% of the original forest distributed over a cutblock can maintain half the population abundance of the uncut forest condition; however, populations of other bird species decline proportionally or more rapidly as the percentage of suitable habitat is reduced

(Huggard and Bunnell 2007). In other words, the habitat for some species may be improved significantly over a wider area than the sum of the retention area. For other species, adding a large patch to a reserve would have greater benefit than dispersing the equivalent forest area as retention.

The role of VR is particularly important in landscapes that are unlikely to have enough protected areas and reserves to maintain biodiversity on their own. At the other extreme, if a high proportion of a landscape is reserved, then stand-level retention may not be very important. Consequently, the higher the level of landscape-level reserves, the less important VR or matrix management may be for sustaining viable populations of forest-dwelling species. Furthermore, there are many other factors to consider besides what to reserve from harvesting. Franklin *et al.* (2007) suggest that intermediate stand treatments to enhance heterogeneity, and recovery periods between regeneration harvests are equally important considerations as retention of biological legacies for an ecological forestry approach. Stand treatments may not be as important in landscapes with a lot of natural heterogeneity (e.g., having a mix of forest ages, productivity classes, wetlands, and complex coastline), as is the case in many parts of southeast Alaska and coastal BC.

WHAT PATTERN AND AMOUNT OF RETENTION?

Ecosystems can be both resistant and resilient to changes from natural disturbances or cutting (Keenan and Kimmins 1993). Multiple pathways and patterns can occur within the limits of ecosystem processes and the range of natural variation. Therefore, even though emulating nature has emerged as a forest management strategy for sustaining both products and biodiversity, it may not be necessary to attempt to truly mimic natural disturbances. The very nature of commercial forestry (i.e., removal of wood) makes precise imitation of natural disturbance impossible (Palik *et al.* 2002). Unfortunately, past practices in coastal temperate rainforests have had little regard for natural disturbances. Pearson (2010) estimated that stand-replacing natural disturbances affected 3.1% of the forested area over the past 140 years on BC's central coast. Although logging affected 5.4% of this same area overall, 59% of valley bottom areas were logged, illustrating that both spatial pattern and scale must be considered when assessing the impact of forestry on ecosystems. Observation of the stand structures and patterns of stands across landscapes produced by natural disturbances provides potential models for the desired stand and landscape condition, but it may not be practical or desirable to emulate the full range of the type, scale, and severity of disturbances present. Simplification of natural structures and patterns may be necessary to improve the efficiency of management or to meet other societal objectives (Mitchell and Beese 2002).

The Pacific coast of BC and southeast Alaska has a diversity of forest ecosystems and species. To be effective, forest management practices need to vary in response to that diversity. No single harvesting or silvicultural system is appropriate everywhere. Clear-cut, seed tree, retention, shelterwood, and selection systems are all ecologically, economically, or socially appropriate in the right context. A mixture of systems can help achieve a range of patch sizes and structures within stands and landscapes. Nevertheless, the variable retention approach is intentionally broad enough to encompass a wide range of forest conditions, harvesting systems, and regeneration requirements. Forest practitioners must choose the most appropriate silvicultural system, based on safety, ecological, and operational factors. Perhaps most importantly, foresters must reconcile or balance the often competing goals of silviculture and biodiversity conservation.

There is no single answer to the question posed in this section—except, when faced with uncertainty, "don't do the same thing everywhere" (Bunnell *et al.* 1999). Different species require different habitats, so it is intuitive to keep the retention "variable." The amount and pattern of retention should be planned to suit the nature of the ecosystems, the objectives, and the species involved (see below). In general, research results from early post-logging studies suggest that amount of retention is more important than pattern for many species (Maguire *et al.* 2005; Huggard and Bunnell 2007). A meta-analysis of 117 studies comparing green tree retention levels up to 50% did not demonstrate statistical differences in species richness and abundance for a variety of taxa among four classes of retention level because of high variability (Rosenvald and Lõhmus 2008); however, this review found a positive relationship between persistence of several species groups and tree density in about two-thirds of the studies and retention pattern in half of the studies. Huggard and Bunnell (2007) examined study results for 69 species of birds and concluded that many less-sensitive species decreased substantially below 15% to 20% retention, and some sensitive species declined more abruptly below 35% to 40% retention. While retaining forest that is representative of the original stand is important, exceptions should be made for features of unusual biological significance (e.g., swamps or other wetlands with forested buffers, rare habitat types, snags). For extreme wind-hazard areas, a minimum group size of 1 ha is appropriate. In many stands, the location of riparian habitats, which are typically the most productive in the area, is the primary influence on the final amount and distribution of retention.

IMPLEMENTING STAND-LEVEL RETENTION PRACTICES

Experience with implementing variable retention in coastal British Columbia on a widespread basis has provided valuable lessons on the practical aspects of this novel approach. This section provides suggestions for applying retention practices more broadly in forest ecosystems using adaptive management.

Zoning

Zoning is a useful framework for applying different regional or landscape-level management goals and standards for retention. The basic concept behind zoning is to create different intensities of management in different landscapes under the hypothesis that a variety of conditions will support a greater variety of organisms. The other purpose is to recognize the ecological differences in the type and frequency of natural disturbances that have shaped the seral-stage distribution and stand structural conditions in a landscape. For example, the zoning currently used by Western Forest Products in coastal BC uses broad ecological units (ecosections), landscape objectives under the Vancouver Island land use plan (BC Integrated Land Management Bureau 2000), and biogeoclimatic subzones (Klinka *et al.* 1991) as a basis for assigning different proportions of the retention system and minimum levels of retention by zone. Landscapes with high windthrow hazard and a timber production emphasis have a target of 10% retention with at least 30% of harvesting meeting the retention system definition. In contrast, landscapes with low windthrow hazard, low levels of landscape reserves due to a long history of development, and a high biodiversity emphasis have targets of 20% retention and at least 70% use of the retention system. The WFP zoning scheme combines elements of different approaches implemented by predecessor companies (Deal *et al.* 2005; Bunnell and Dunsworth 2009). Zoning using a "TRIAD" approach (Hunter and Calhoun

1996), whereby a forest management area is divided into three zones with varying emphasis on conservation and intensive management, is growing in popularity within Canada as a means of fulfilling diverse objectives (Côté *et al.* 2010; MacLean *et al.* 2009; Montigny and MacLean 2006).

Harvesting Systems and Cost

Logistical and economic considerations will influence the pattern of retention, such as the choice of ground-based, cable, or helicopter yarding. For slopes under 30%, ground-based harvesting systems can be used with many options for retention pattern. A study comparing the cost of yarding using hoe-forwarding (shovel logging) for different silvicultural systems found that the cost of forwarding to roadside was 10% higher than clear-cutting where either 25 trees per ha were retained with uniform distribution or where patches were retained (Phillips 1996). The same study found that yarding costs increased by 38% when a quarter of the trees were retained using a shelterwood system. Cable-yarding systems on steeper slopes present the greatest challenge for the design of retention systems and the highest potential increases in costs compared to clear-cutting. Group retention is more cost-effective for cable yarding than dispersed retention because fewer line changes are needed to operate around retained trees. Wedge-shaped aggregates help facilitate cable yarding patterns.

Helicopter yarding reduces or eliminates road building on steep terrain and provides access to forests that would be difficult or impossible to log using conventional systems. Yarding with helicopters enables a wide range of approaches to the layout of variable retention, without a significant increase in yarding costs for less than 25% group retention. Other successful approaches include group selection and alternating harvest and leave strips oriented along slope contours. Standing-stem harvesting is an innovative technique for removing individual stems by helicopter without felling the tree to the ground (MacDonald 2000). A highly trained faller climbs the tree, removes the limbs and tops the tree at a diameter that will result in a stem that is within the maximum lift capacity of the helicopter. Just before removal, the stem is prepared by completing horizontal cuts at the base of the tree, leaving sufficient holding wood to keep the stem standing with the aid of wooden wedges. The helicopter removes the tree with a horizontal grapple, and then flies the stem to a nearby landing or water drop site. This method has been used as a tool in BC since 1998 for managing sites severely restricted from harvesting using conventional methods, such as unstable terrain, viewscapes, and sensitive soils. It is also useful for removal of high-value stems to reduce breakage before conventional yarding. Although helicopter yarding has a light impact on the land and reduces the amount of logging roads, the tradeoff is high consumption of fossil fuels and the resulting negative atmospheric impacts. The other concern is the potential for high-grading—taking only the best-quality trees and leaving a lower-quality stand that may no longer be economical to harvest. High-grading must be avoided through proper silviculture prescriptions in sustainable forestry operations.

Standards, Guidelines, and Measurement

What counts and how to count it has a great influence on what happens on the ground. Field personnel live in the details and focus on what is measured. Guidelines should be flexible to encourage innovation and allow field planners the ability to adapt to varying site conditions, yet standards must be consistent. Clear goals and standards need to be set for the amount and distribution of retention to balance biodiversity and silvicultural objectives. It is important to establish what are *rules* and what are *guidelines* and try to anticipate unintended consequences of a particular standard. An effective means for developing implementation policies is through a working group that combines forest practitioners and research specialists. This working group can help track performance towards indicators—an important element of sustainable forest management certification schemes—and can evaluate progress toward overall goals.

For example, to simplify the operational implementation of the retention system, some guidelines state that retained groups of trees should be greater than 0.25 ha in size and no more than four tree lengths apart. Guidelines are meant to be flexible, but they ensure that retention is well distributed within a cutblock and that the forest influence criterion is achieved. A minimum group size ensures that understory structural attributes are retained, such as undisturbed shrubs, forbs, and mosses, and allows retention of dead trees with an unharvested buffer around them for worker safety. When setting standards, it is important to recognize that stand-level retention is not intended to provide forest interior habitat, free of edge influence. Such habitat needs are best provided through larger, landscape-level reserves.

Marking and layout is another important practical consideration for implementation. Having the harvesting crew (fallers) choose the location of retained trees and aggregates saves costs but creates uncertainty over achieving the desired prescription unless standards are clear and operations are well supervised. Pre-marking provides more certainty that the right attributes are being captured in aggregates, the desired percent retention is achieved, silvicultural prescriptions are optimized, and spatial distribution guidelines are met. Marking also frees the faller to concentrate on doing the job safely. Flexibility to substitute trees and to adjust boundaries for safety or logistics is essential. Training field personnel is also critical. For success, operators need to know the *why* as well as the *how* of variable retention. Training can include field sessions, field guides, tailgate posters, and videos.

Adaptive Management

Because the effectiveness of variable retention in maintaining biodiversity is in the early stages of being tested, *adaptive management* is important for successful implementation. Adaptive management is a structured approach to learning from operational practices, monitoring, and experiments to provide feedback to management and continual improvement (Holling 1978). There are two forms of adaptive management (AM): *passive AM* involves monitoring and evaluation of a single chosen "best" practice or policy, and *active AM* tests alternative management interventions using designed experiments (Walters 1986). Both approaches seek to reduce decision-critical uncertainty through learning. The term *passive* does not imply informal trial and error; this form of AM requires systematic monitoring and feedback. Active AM is especially effective when existing knowledge is sufficient to identify critical information gaps. Most applications of AM in North Pacific rainforests have used a combination of passive and active approaches.

Monitoring is an essential part of AM and is composed of three main elements: implementation or performance (have you met the stated targets and standards?), effectiveness (have you achieved the desired outcomes?), and validation (are the assumptions correct?). Validation asks "why" a practice or strategy is or is not working and also can be considered refinement monitoring or research. Linking monitoring back to management action is fundamental for an effective operational AM program.

Adaptive management is part of the Tongass forest plan and includes implementation, effectiveness, and validation monitoring. Annual reporting provides timely results and an overview of current activities, while a five-year report provides a comprehensive evaluation of data with essential feedback to government and the public on progress towards the plan objectives. The Tongass National Forest Web site contains monitoring reports (1997 to the present) and guidebooks with design and sampling protocols (http://www.fs.fed.us/r10/tongass/projects/tlmp/monitoring/monitoring. shtml). AM has been used successfully to evaluate young-growth management in the Tongass (McClellan 2008). Other monitoring initiatives in southeast Alaska forests include the Sealaska native corporation—the largest timber producer in the coastal rainforests of the state. A fish and forestry monitoring program was started in 1992 and includes fish habitat, riparian buffers, windthrow, large woody debris, and landslides (http:// www.sealaska.com/page/effectiveness_monitoring.html).

In British Columbia, the Forest and Range Evaluation Program (FREP) is a monitoring program designed to assess the effectiveness of the *Forest and Range Practices Act* (BC *Forest and Range Practices Act* 2002) in achieving stewardship of eleven resource values (http://www.for.gov.bc.ca/hfp/ frep/values/index.htm). The program seeks to identify issues regarding forest policies, practices, and legislation by evaluating the status or trends of resource and ecosystem values, determining causal factors, and recommending options for change where required.

Other AM and monitoring initiatives in coastal BC include the Clayoquot Sound region, managed under the Clayoquot science panel recommendations (Scientific Panel for Sustainable Forest Practices in Clayoquot Sound 1995), and the central and north coast (Great Bear Rainforest) region managed under ecosystem-based management guidelines (Price *et al.* 2009). Forests in Clayoquot are managed by Iisaak—a First Nations–owned forest company created in 1998. Monitoring activities include windthrow and residual stand damage; and the distribution and abundance of wildlife trees, coarse woody debris, and native plants (http://www.iisaak.com/monitoring .html). Monitoring is in the planning stages for the ecosystem-based management plan area and is being coordinated by a multiple-stakeholder adaptive management steering committee.

Monitoring and evaluation are integral steps in the adaptive management cycle and may lead to "course corrections," such as revised plans, strategies, practices, and standards, if current management appears to be heading off target. Organizational and environmental conditions are con-

ADAPTIVE MANAGEMENT: CLOSING THE LOOP FOR IMPLEMENTING VARIABLE RETENTION HARVESTING ON THE BC COAST

The following is based on the case study in Bunnell and Dunsworth (2009).

BROAD GOAL: maintain stand structure in harvested stands to provide habitat diversity.

STRATEGY: use variable retention (VR) harvesting; vary standards using landscape zoning.

INDICATORS: percent retention, size of groups, type of structural attributes.

KEY QUESTIONS: what is the best way to implement variable retention? (types and amount of retention); what is VR providing as habitat? (for various species groups); are there major edge effects with aggregated (group) retention?

ACTIVE AM COMPARISONS: establish five experimental comparisons testing retention level, type (dispersed versus group), group size, location (proximity to streams), and group removal (short and long cycles); designed to be three replicates of each (fifteen total); nine actually implemented.

MONITORING AND RESEARCH PROJECTS: use active variable retention adaptive management sites (along with passive operational cutblock monitoring) to examine birds, gastropods, carabid beetles, mycorrhizal fungi, windthrow, forest structure, regeneration, and growth.

WHAT WAS LEARNED: group retention is generally better for providing habitat than dispersed retention; big groups are better than small groups; more retention is better than less, except for impacts on growth of regeneration; retention is vulnerable to wind damage on exposed coastal sites; different species have different response curves to retention amount, type, and edge effects.

WHAT WAS CHANGED: guidelines for VR were updated to encourage greater use of larger groups; zoning standards for stand-level retention were changed for windthrow-prone areas.

stantly changing; AM can provide a mechanism for responding to such changes in a structured manner.

Experimental comparisons are an important part of AM, ensuring scientifically valid information. In the case of the Weyerhaeuser (now WFP) AM program described by Bunnell and Dunsworth (2009), variable retention adaptive management (VRAM) experiments were designed by a team of scientists and foresters to address both biodiversity and silvicultural questions (see sidebar). The treatments and associated studies are described in detail by Beese *et al.* (2005). Monitoring is examining the short-term and long-term impacts of VR options on forest growth, structural attributes, and selected forest-dwelling plant and animal species on nine areas. All VRAM sites include comparable unharvested controls and conventional clear-cuts that were randomly allocated along with the VR alternatives. The VRAM sites parallel the Alternatives to Clearcutting (ATC) study sites in the Tongass (McClellan and Hennon 2005). These two studies share six treatments in common: uncut forest, clear-cut, 5% dispersed, 25% to 30% dispersed, 25% to 30% group/aggregated, and 70% to 75% retention with group/gap removal. Both studies also share similar objectives and treatments with the DEMO (Demonstration of Ecosystem Management Options) study in Oregon and Washington (Aubrey *et al.* 2004). Together with other large-scale silvicultural systems experiments in BC (Vyse *et al.* 2005), there will be a considerable body of long-term research to inform stand-level practices in Pacific coastal ecosystems.

Because it is neither practical nor affordable to conduct all monitoring in an "active" experimental setting, an AM framework must include "passive" operational monitoring activities. WFP's operational monitoring examines structure, forest growth, windthrow, and various species' responses in operational VR settings (Bunnell and Dunsworth 2002). Pilot studies were used to establish an appropriate sampling design and methodologies. Studies on several organisms (breeding birds, gastropods, amphibians, bryophytes, squirrels, mycorrhizal fungi, and carabid beetles) have been underway for various lengths of time. Monitoring also included a random sample of 17% of all cutblocks (248 cutblocks; 7,150 ha) to examine achievement of standards and provide immediate feedback to foresters on retention design (Bancroft and Zielke 2004). Initial findings have been used to examine how the results will link to management practices to strengthen areas that most need improvement.

Evaluating the impacts of forest management practices requires more than stand-level experimentation and monitoring. Landscapes are not merely the sum of stand conditions. Larger-scale attributes, such as landscape-level patterns, connectivity, fragmentation, and cumulative effects of natural and human-caused disturbances affect biological processes and diversity at scales that cannot be observed merely at the stand level. Studying landscape-level habitat loss and fragmentation, which usually coincide but need to be evaluated separately (Fahrig 2003), is a complex endeavor due to the many and varied impacts of both reducing and breaking apart habitat on species and ecosystem processes. Organisms differ in their critical habitat requirements and patch size necessary for survival of viable populations (Laurance *et al.* 2002). Even the landscape context of stand-level comparisons can be problematic for interpretation of results. Bunnell and Dunsworth (2009) describe the difficulty of trying to design either passive or active adaptive management comparisons at the landscape level (e.g., adequate replication, confounding ecological factors, and long time frames for evaluating treatment response, to name a few). They conclude that monitoring trends and conditions of major indicators over an entire landscape or region of interest, along with predictive modeling, is a practical alternative for seeking to understand landscape-level spatial and temporal dynamics. Establishing controls in the form of long-term monitoring plots in large reserves should be part of such a strategy.

Public Perception

Social acceptability of harvesting is an important consideration, particularly on public forest lands. Studies of public perceptions of clear-cutting, variable retention, and traditional silvicultural systems impacts on scenic beauty or visual quality in Pacific coastal forests show consistent trends. For a given retention level, treatments that leave dispersed individual trees receive consistently higher ratings than group or aggregated retention (Clausen and Schroeder 2004; Ribe 2005; Sheppard and Meitner 2005). Low levels of retention (under 15%) of any kind are generally perceived only slightly better than clear-cutting. Unfortunately, public acceptance runs counter to the results of biological studies.

EFFECTIVENESS OF RETENTION— RESULTS OF MONITORING

Ultimately, the value of variable retention for maintaining forest species and ecological functions must be evaluated through monitoring and research. Much has been learned over the past decade about the initial impacts of retention on structural attributes and organisms. This section reviews some of the many ongoing studies applicable to North Pacific temperate rainforests.

Forest Structure

In coastal BC, monitoring of VRAM sites and operational cutblocks by WFP and successor companies documented the structural attributes (i.e., biological legacies and specific habitat elements) provided by retention in relation to benchmark natural forests. Long-term retention in cutblocks averaged 20%, primarily designed as group or mixed retention. From 1999 to 2004, transects were established to monitor retained vegetation structure in 193 VR blocks, 98 uncut sites, and 52 other sites. Measured structural elements included live trees; snags and coarse woody debris (species, diameter, height, and decay class); cover layers (canopy, small tree, shrub, herb, moss, litter, and mineral soil); and dominant shrub and herb species. Detailed analysis examined 86 different habitat elements (Huggard 2006). Initial comparisons assessed whether retention patches provide similar levels of attributes to those found in unlogged forests. Overall, retention tended to have lower levels of some important elements, especially large trees and total basal area, than benchmark sites in the same biogeoclimatic unit. Snag density, size, decay class, and basal area were similar for benchmark sites and retention patches. In some areas, however, tall snags were less common in retention patches because of removal of hazard trees during logging operations. Cutblocks were resampled to assess five-year postharvest changes. Standing tree density in retention declined about 20% over five years. Both growth and mortality rates of trees were higher on the edges of retention patches, with some effects up to 20 m into the patch. Other than small trees, tree mortality was similar in dispersed and group retention.

The DEMO study characterized structural differences among variable retention treatments and found that they were highly influenced by initial stand conditions (Maguire *et al.* 2007). Dispersed treatments maintained significantly greater canopy cover than aggregated treatments at the same retention level. A retrospective study of structural attributes retained by partial cutting over the past century in southeast Alaska found that a tree species composition similar to that in uncut old-growth stands was maintained (Deal and Tappeiner 2002). In general, it is easier to maintain a more similar range of stand attributes to preharvest conditions using group retention than with dispersed retention.

Windthrow

Wind damage has the greatest potential to alter stand structure in the initial years following variable retention harvesting. Windthrow monitoring of 172 VR cutblocks has occurred over the past eight years throughout WFP's BC coastal operations (Rollerson *et al.* 2009). The sample represents over 440 km of edges along external setting boundaries, retention patches, and riparian strips. Results showed that wind damage increases with increasing boundary exposure, fetch distance, topographic exposure, and tree height. There were also regional differences in wind damage. Total damage within 25 m of external cutblock boundaries varied from 11% on southeast Vancouver Island to 19% to 25% on Haida Gwaii and northwest Vancouver Island, respectively. Small patches (average 39% damage) and strips (31%) have higher rates of wind damage over three to five years than external edges (16%) and large patch edges (24%), although over half of total windthrow is due to cutblock edges, because of the greater length of edge. Windthrow also varied with boundary and patch geometry (e.g., symmetrical patches tend to have less damage than irregular patches). Edge treatments appear to be effective for reducing windthrow if topping or pruning penetrates 10 to 15 m into an edge. Long-term windthrow monitoring at the Montane Alternative Silvicultural Systems (MASS) project on east-central Vancouver Island found high rates of wind damage for low levels of dispersed retention (29% of stems lost over six years) and lower relative damage for a shelterwood (10%) and for the edges of a clear-cut (8%) and large patches (2%) (Beese 2001). Absolute tree losses, however, were greater for the shelterwood (21 stems per ha) than for other systems (4 to 8 stems per ha). Catastrophic winds at MASS seven years later caused substantial damage to the patches and clear-cut edges, showing that wind damage can continue to occur many years after harvesting. Wind damage to retention patches twelve to sixteen years after harvesting in cedar-hemlock forests in northwestern BC averaged 9%, with strongly reduced windthrow with increasing patch size (Steventon 2011).

The ATC study in the Tongass found comparable wind damage to BC coastal monitoring (M. McLennan, pers. com., 2009). Damage was greatest at low levels of retention. After five years, 25% retention areas had lost 19% to 35% of the retained basal area in aggregated treatments and 18% to 55% in selection treatments. In most areas with high levels of retention (75%), losses to wind damage were 5% to 8% of retained basal area, regardless of the retention pattern (only slightly higher than losses over the same five-year period in uncut old-growth forests). Note that absolute losses (i.e., basal area) would be more similar among treatments than the relative (percent of retained basal area) figures suggest. In addition to monitoring, windthrow hazard prediction models and mapping are useful tools for forest planning (Mitchell *et al.* 2001; Scott and Mitchell 2005).

Growth and Regeneration

The main silvicultural concern about variable retention is the potential impact on future stand growth. Permanent plots were established on VRAM sites and supplemental areas to measure the impact of the amount and spatial distribution of retention on tree growth. An innovative "sector" sampling scheme was developed in order to obtain a proportional sample of retained groups and surrounding cut areas (Iles and Smith 2006). A model is under development that tracks growing season light and moisture to predict growth for western hemlock and Douglas-fir. Findings to date suggest that most of the impact of group retention on tree growth is restricted to 10 m from the edge. The results were highly correlated with surficial moisture. For a given retention level, growth impacts on regeneration are greater for dispersed retention than group retention (N. J. Smith, unpublished data). Douglas-fir basal diameter growth was reduced 5 to 6 years after planting under 30% dispersed retention compared to a clear-cut (Smith and Beese 2012).

Ten-year results from planted regeneration studies at the MASS study in coastal BC found reduced growth compared to clear-cutting for Pacific silver fir and western hemlock in a shelterwood with 25% residual basal area, but little impact on growth for 5% dispersed retention and 1.5 ha patch cut treatments (Mitchell *et al.* 2007). Growth rates of regeneration ten years after single tree and group selection in western hemlock–Pacific silver fir old-growth stand on the west coast of Vancouver Island were greater for group selection than single tree selection; volume removal for both systems was 25% (D'Anjou 2003). The greatest impacts on early growth of residual trees are from mortality due to wind damage and from wounding during harvesting. Impacts from both sources are typically greater for dispersed retention than for aggregated retention or group removal (Phillips 1996; Aubrey *et al.* 2004). Studies in southeast Alaska found that dispersed retention resulted in greater tree wounding during timber harvesting than aggregated retention or group selection (McClellan and Hennon 2005); however, a decay projection model estimated that volume losses at the end of an 80-year rotation would be minimal (Hennon and DeMars 1997). Wind damage has more significant impacts on residual trees in northern temperate rainforests than tree wounding during harvesting.

Species and Biological Diversity

Research and monitoring of indicator species should help assess whether or not strategies for leaving representative unmanaged areas and habitat structures actually result in viable populations of forest-dwelling species. Informative focal species are forest-dwelling, sensitive to forest practices, practical to monitor, and provide information that can guide management (Bunnell and Dunsworth 2002, 2009). A review of the biodiversity aspects of retention from 214 studies concluded that aggregates provided better "lifeboating" than single tree retention for a number of organisms (Rosenvald and Lõhmus 2008). Although the success of retention varied for different organisms, the review showed no negative responses for species richness and abundance of different taxa.

On the BC coast, group retention was found to be beneficial for birds typically found in uncut forests, and bird occurrence was positively correlated with percent retention (Preston and Harestad 2007). Overall results to date from bird studies at WFP VRAM sites show that about one-third of individual bird species and all guilds (groups with similar habitat preference) were affected by retention level (Chan-McLeod 2008). Removal of 31% of the original forest in various group sizes (69% retention) had little impact on forest bird communities. Dispersed retention levels of 5% to 10% showed no significant overall difference in bird abundance from clear-cuts, which favored shrub nesters and "open" habitat species. Retention group size appeared to have an impact on some species, with large groups (1 ha) preferred over small- to medium-size groups (0.25 to 0.5 ha), although results with retention type and level were highly variable.

To examine landscape-level trends in bird populations in forested landscapes, a network of over 50 breeding bird survey (BBS) routes was established on the BC coast (Preston and Campbell 2009). Over 2,200 point-count stations were completed by 2008, representing from seven to nine years of annual monitoring. Mean species richness per BBS route per year was 35 on Vancouver Island and 27 on Haida Gwaii. Variation in annual mean species richness remained relatively constant over all years and all regions. Of 15 frequently detected species on 18 BBS routes on Vancouver Island, 11 showed a significant preference for one or two of five forest classes defined by tree height and diameter. Other significant relationships were found with habitat attributes such as shrub height and cover or forest type (i.e., hardwoods versus conifers).

Preston and Campbell (2009) examined trends for selected species and on routes with sufficient data for at least eight years. Winter wren was the only species that showed consistent significant declines among all Vancouver Island routes and regions. In the southwest and east-central regions of the island, a significant negative decrease in abundance was observed for golden-crowned kinglet and varied thrush. Hammond's flycatcher and Townsend's warbler were the only species among those tested that showed significant increases in abundance for both the southwest and east-central Vancouver Island regions. Increases in species' abundance were most notable on northern Vancouver Island and included Townsend's warbler, Swainson's thrush, warbling vireo and Wilson's warbler. On Haida Gwaii, hermit thrush and Pacific-slope flycatcher showed negative trends while Swainson's thrush had a positive trend. Several species showed trends in portions of the BC coast that differed from province-wide trends from USGS surveys (Sauer *et al.* 2008).

In southeast Alaska, DellaSala *et al.* (1996) studied forest bird response to treatment of young forests (thinning and gap creation) and compared bird abundance in young forests to old growth. They recommended leaving patches of old forest during harvesting to enhance habitat of breeding and wintering birds associated with old growth. Three of sixteen common breeding birds were more abundant in old growth than in treated or untreated young forests: red-breasted sapsucker, Pacific-slope flycatcher, and golden-crowned kinglet. Brown creeper had a low frequency of detection but was found exclusively in old forests. Higher use of old growth by wintering birds, such as the golden-crowned kinglet, was related to winter severity because of snow interception by old growth canopies (Kirchhoff and Schoen 1987). Four species were negatively associated with old growth and others did not differ between young and old forests, which illustrates the fact that not all bird species will benefit from retention.

The impact of forest harvesting on species that are sensitive to microclimatic changes and are less mobile is an important aspect of biodiversity conservation that is being investigated on WFP VRAM sites and operational cutblocks. Studies have examined three groups of organisms: gastropods (slugs and snails), carabid beetles, and amphibians. After two to four years, 10 of 12 species of gastropods showed significant treatment effects (Ovaska and Sopuck 2008). The effects were negative for 6 species, positive for 2 species and mixed for 2 others. Significant negative treatment effects were also found for small snails as a group and for species richness at most sites, but not for the overall species diversity. Three common, ecologically important gastropods benefited from VR at some sites. Large retention groups (0.8 to 1.2 ha) were better than small groups (0.5 ha or less) or clear-cuts for maintaining sensitive gastropods regardless of the overall level of retention. Gastropod abundance and species richness were greater for 30% dispersed retention than lower retention levels (5%, 10%), but all were less than the uncut forest. Results suggest that strategies that conserve moisture and protect riparian zones are beneficial for gastropods, such as locating retention groups on wetlands or moist depressions.

Pearsall (2008) examined the potential use of carabid (ground-dwelling) beetles as indicators of forest conditions and biological diversity under various stand-level retention strategies. Group retention at a moist, western hemlock–Pacific silver fir old-growth site showed few differences in forest-specialist carabids among clear-cut and group retention treatments and the uncut old growth. Previous work on drier group retention sites suggests that there may be some lifeboating benefit for forest-specialist beetles in drier climates, and a positive response to patch size on both old-growth and second-growth sites.

Wind (2008) examined the effects of harvesting and buffers on amphibian use of small wetlands. Four amphibian species were found breeding in small ponds: long-toed salamander, rough-skinned newt, Pacific chorus frog, and red-legged frog. Two and three years after harvesting, all four species have continued breeding at small wetlands at each site and standing water has persisted longer in the season. Frogs utilized more wetlands for breeding after harvesting than before harvesting. Wetlands with no canopy cover appeared to have a greater influx of breeding postharvest than wetlands with retention.

The abundance of ectomycorrhizal (EM) fungi on Douglas-fir tree seedlings was studied in relation to dispersed and group retention and cutblock edges. Transects with group retention showed that the abundance of EM fungi decreased with distance from forest edges (Outerbridge and Trofymow 2004). On sites with dispersed retention, EM diversity increased with increasing retention of live trees. EM fungal diversity was greater next to single isolated trees; however, whether or not dispersed residual trees will maintain viable long-term support for EM fungi is uncertain (Outerbridge and Trofymow 2008). Results from studies of EM fungi on the DEMO sites suggest that a combination of group and dispersed retention may be the most effective approach to maintain fungal communities (Aubrey *et al.* 2004). It is important to note, however, that climate change brings uncertainty regarding the distribution and abundance of many forest species.

SUMMARY AND DISCUSSION

Many factors need to be considered when choosing stand-level practices to meet social, biological, and economic goals. The final choice represents a balance among complementary and competing objectives. As such, it is not possible to determine precise and optimal figures for the proportion of different silvicultural systems, the amount of retention in each cutblock, or the spatial distribution of retained aggregates or single trees. Nevertheless, such standards must be chosen based on the best available information, theoretical concepts, and practical considerations. Experience over the past decade in coastal BC suggests the following conclusions that are relevant for applying stand-level retention in northern temperate rainforests:

1. The landscape context determines what is necessary or appropriate for stand-level retention in relation to biodiversity conservation goals.

2. It is not practical to precisely mimic natural disturbance patterns.

3. Riparian networks are a governing factor for retention patterns.

4. Wind damage is a significant challenge for dispersing stand-level retention, making clear-cutting with reserves the most viable option for some sites and landscapes.

5. Monitoring findings indicate that retention can provide habitat for some organisms to persist after harvesting, with a positive correlation between patch size and species survival.

6. Retention has potential long-term benefits for enhancing structural diversity of future forests.

7. Growth impacts on forest regeneration increase with greater dispersion of single trees or small groups.

8. Public visual preferences conflict with ecological goals and operational needs.

9. Variable retention harvesting can be done safely across a wide range of forest types and terrain using a variety of logging and silvicultural systems.

10. Retention leads to higher logging costs that vary by system, as well as economic impacts from merchantable timber left behind.

An emphasis on group or aggregated retention rather than dispersed retention is supported by safety, cost-efficiency, and habitat values. Although it is possible to apply VR across a full range of sites, the last 20% are the most costly to achieve (e.g., steep, cable- or helicopter-yarding blocks). The cost and logistics of cable- and helicopter-logging systems makes retention difficult for steep slopes; however, it may be important to leave retention on these sites for visual aesthetics or to meet local habitat needs for some species. Highly visible slopes present an opportunity to demonstrate variable retention to the public, particularly on sites within the viewscape of recreation areas and cruise ships. Aside from the biological benefits of VR, marketplace demands and public perceptions are important influences on forestry practices that make retention a cost of doing business in many areas.

Although use of VR is becoming more widespread on the Pacific coast, there is much we need to know about its potential impacts. Among the silvicultural challenges in implementing the retention system to meet biodiversity goals is predicting forest growth and inventory and managing future stand health. Forest managers and the public must seek to balance the benefits and costs as this new approach to silviculture is implemented and tested. Critical to the success of these new approaches is the design of cutblocks and stand entries to minimize impacts from wind damage. Losses from wind are unavoidable; however, the risks and economic impacts can be managed through planned salvage or retention of downed wood when it meets habitat objectives.

Finally, it is popular to recommend adaptive management, but can it really work? Unfortunately, most examples in natural resource management have failed because of three main problems: (1) lack of funding for monitoring; (2) failure of decision makers to embrace the AM concept; and (3) lack of leadership to sustain a complex process (paraphrased from Walters 2007). Details on AM approaches and the challenges for implementation are discussed for a number of cases in natural resource management (Stankey *et al.* 2005; Marmorek *et al.* 2006). In the past 10 years, research and monitoring studies in Pacific coastal ecosystems have obtained useful results to inform variable retention practices; however, many aspects of biological monitoring require longer time frames for assessment of impacts (Bunnell and Dunsworth 2009). Monitoring species and forest structure are expected to provide data that will help us demonstrate sustainability and biodiversity conservation. Future challenges for forestry on the Pacific coast include dealing with the uncertainties of climate change, survival in the world marketplace, long-term funding commitments, and our ability to adapt practices to meet changing goals and expectations.

ACKNOWLEDGMENTS

The author thanks the foresters, forestry engineers and planners, and forest workers on the Pacific coast for successfully taking up the challenge to implement variable retention and to do it safely. I am grateful to the many authors of cited studies for their valuable contributions to this topic and for helpful review comments by Michael McLellan and Jerry Franklin. I also thank Bryce Bancroft, Fred Bunnell, John Deal, Glen Dunsworth, Dave Huggard, Laurie Kremsater, Jeff Sandford, Nick Smith, Ken Zielke, and many others who have worked to bring practical changes to silvicultural practices in temperate rainforests. Funding for many studies cited was provided by the BC Forest Investment Account, LBIP and Forest Science Program.

10

Synthesis

Gordon H. Orians, John W. Schoen,
Jerry F. Franklin, and Andy MacKinnon

OUR FOCUS IN THIS BOOK HAS BEEN THE NORTHERN PORTION OF
the coastal North Pacific temperate rainforest of southeast Alaska and
north coastal British Columbia, an area that has been spared much of the
large-scale logging that the southern portion of this rainforest has experienced. We provided a multidisciplinary overview of the functioning of this
complex ecosystem and analyzed several key issues related to the management and conservation of these rainforests. We also compared them with
more intensively modified forests farther south on the Pacific coast and
elsewhere. Previous chapters explored in detail some of the conservation
challenges and opportunities scientists, managers, and conservationists
have confronted in this region, how they are addressing them, and what
they have learned. They also identified some of the critical remaining gaps
in our knowledge of this rainforest. Here, we synthesize those key findings.
We also explore how a broader understanding of those issues can help
inform future decisions of forest managers who are seeking to achieve
economic sustainability, biodiversity conservation, and ecosystem integrity in this region and elsewhere on Earth (also see Nie [2006] for a review
of forest conflict and political decision making on the Tongass). And we
discuss how effective management of the region's ecosystems can enhance
the well-being of the region's human residents.

We selected the topics for the eight invited papers for this book so
that, in combination, they described and analyzed the fundamental ecological processes that shape these forests and reviewed the indigenous and
commercial uses of them. In so doing, we set the stage for considering how
managers can use this information to make decisions that will maintain

the integrity and vitality of the region's ecosystems and thereby sustain the economies of the local human communities that depend on them.

The first part of the book features chapters that explore the current functioning of the region's ecosystems and how they have been influenced by its recent management. They show how the advance and retreat of continental ice sheets and associated changes in sea levels have influenced the distribution of plants and animals. They highlight the tie between the land and sea, including the importance of the great amounts of nutrients that the region's rivers discharge to adjacent marine waters and, conversely, that spawning salmon (*Oncorhynchus* spp.), eulachon (*Thaleichthys pacificus*), and other anadromous fish carry upriver to nourish a variety of animals and enrich riparian vegetation. They also describe how the intensity and frequency of natural disturbances influence the composition and structure of vegetation in this coastal rainforest. The variety of disturbances— windstorms, floods, rare tsunamis, occasional fires, pest outbreaks, avalanches, and landslides—generate a complex mosaic of plant communities in space and time. The biological diversity in this region depends upon the variety of habitats created by these disturbances.

Indigenous humans have interacted with the region's rainforests for millennia. However, humans have caused major changes to the composition, structure, and functioning of the forests only during the last century. The types and frequencies of disturbances generated by human activity differ significantly from historical patterns. The importance of understanding economic and other drivers that have influenced how and why humans have used and continue to use the region are illustrated in these chapters. A better understanding of the genesis of the policies developed to support those activities can help guide a transition to a different and more sustainable use of the region's natural resources.

Later chapters also explore how managers can use new concepts and tools—some very recently developed—to more effectively manage these rainforests. The rapidly expanding fields of conservation biology and ecosystem and landscape ecology provide a rich array of ecological concepts and spatially explicit tools for managers to creatively address the complex issues that confront them. Watershed ecology, which has been widely used to guide thinking about and management of complex landscapes, is one of these conceptual tools. Circumstances under which watersheds are likely to be truly useful management units are described in chapter 8. Insights generated by new on-the-ground management practices designed to maintain a broader array of forest ecosystem goods and services (in addition to traditional wood products) are described in another chapter.

Here we synthesize these insights to provide an overview of the region and the appropriate scales for thinking about and understanding the key processes that drive its ecological and political dynamics.

THINKING AND MANAGING AT MULTIPLE SCALES

To understand the dynamics of coastal North Pacific rainforests and apply that knowledge to management options and human well-being, we need to think carefully about the spatial scales at which different ecological processes manifest themselves. What management and conservation issues (e.g., populations, species, communities, processes) require focus on individual islands, on small versus large watersheds, across the entire rainforest region, or beyond? The problem of determining the temporal and spatial scales at which key ecological and evolutionary processes function, the rates at which they operate, and how that knowledge should inform management decisions pervades all chapters in this book. Accordingly, synthesizing the implications of that problem as applied to specific conservation and management issues is a major focus of this final chapter.

METAPOPULATIONS

Most natural history field guides display maps that show the geographical area over which species are found, but no species is found everywhere within its mapped range. Populations of most species are divided into separated, discrete subpopulations that live in distinct habitat patches surrounded by other habitats in which they do not live. Each subpopulation has its own probability of "birth" (colonization) and "death" (extinction). Because subpopulations are much smaller than the metapopulation of which they are components, local disturbances and random fluctuations in numbers of individuals are more likely to cause the extinction of a subpopulation than the extinction of an entire metapopulation. However, if individuals move frequently between subpopulations, immigrants may prevent declining subpopulations from becoming extinct, a process called the *rescue effect* (Brown and Kodric-Brown 1977).

Metapopulation dynamics function at many different scales. Amphibians may refuse to cross roads. Nonmigratory forest birds may be reluctant to fly across open fields or rivers. Many terrestrial mammals and most amphibians are intolerant of salt water. Some plant species are restricted to alpine habitats. Populations of migratory species may be influenced by events on the breeding and wintering grounds, and/or in the resting and feeding places individuals use during migration. To understand fluctuations in populations of migratory species, ecologists may need to study events on the wintering grounds or at migratory stopovers. Salmon and many seabirds spend the nonbreeding season at sea.

The metapopulation dynamics of the vertebrates of the North Pacific coastal rainforests is discussed in chapter 2. Cook and MacDonald show that opportunities to colonize and recolonize (rescue effect) are influenced by saltwater barriers of varying widths and by critical connecting corridors on individual islands. Lertzman and MacKinnon (chapter 8) show that watersheds also affect probabilities of local extinction. On the one hand, they facilitate within-watershed connectivity, especially for riparian zone species. On the other hand, they impose barriers to movements between watersheds, especially if the boundaries are at high elevations. Although we understand metapopulation dynamics of many of the region's vertebrates, we know little about population dynamics of the region's microorganisms, invertebrates, fungi, and plants.

SPATIAL AND TEMPORAL SCALES

The processes that determine ecosystem structure and functioning also operate at multiple scales. Earth's major biogeochemical cycles function at global scales. Nutrients carried by winds from Sahara dust storms fertilize Caribbean coral reefs (Garrison *et al.* 2003). Ocean currents transport heat and nutrients over vast distances. Discharges from rivers fertilize nearby oceans and may even cause dead zones. Breeding colonies of seabirds fertilize islands. Salmon assimilate and transport nutrients from distant oceans to their natal spawning streams, a trip that may cover thousands of miles (Gende *et al.* 2002; Naiman *et al.* 2002; Reimchen *et al.* 2003; Hocking and Reynolds 2011). Yet, most ecosystem services are provided at local scales. The recreational and aesthetic value of biodiversity decreases rapidly with distance from people's homes.

One of the tenets of landscape ecology is that ecological systems are hierarchically structured and that their study requires a multiscale approach, specifically a focus on at least three distinct scales: the focal scale (e.g., a riparian forest), one level above (the basin), and one level below (the collection of stream reaches). Understanding the system (the riparian forest), and predicting how it will respond to disturbance and management, requires a consideration of at least all three scales. These issues pervade all the chapters of this book. As demonstrated in chapter 2, understanding today's biota requires information over a broad range of temporal scales, ranging from population dynamics time to evolutionary time, that is, enough time for speciation and extinction to happen. Moreover, we have largely ignored the spatial and temporal scales that govern the most important interactions between the terrestrial and marine realms.

Speciation

Spatial and temporal scales also interact. Speciation, the process that generates one of the primary components of diversity we try to protect, requires that gene flow between two populations be interrupted. Gene flow between populations may be interrupted in two major ways, each of which characterizes a mode of speciation. Sympatric speciation (often via chromosome duplication following interspecific hybridization) is common in plants. It requires no physical barriers. Allopatric speciation, the dominant mode of speciation among most groups of animals, usually requires a physical barrier that divides the range of a species. The barrier may be a water body for terrestrial organisms, dry land for aquatic organisms, or a mountain range. Barriers can form when continents drift, sea levels rise, glaciers advance and retreat, and climates change. Allopatric speciation may also result when some members of a population cross an existing barrier and establish a new, isolated population. Both of these processes have been active in the North Pacific rainforest. In much of this chapter we explore the implications and importance of scale for understanding the dynamic properties of coastal North Pacific rainforest ecosystems and for devising appropriate management strategies. To effectively address a problem, the scale at which its outcomes are most strongly expressed needs to be identified. Choosing an inappropriate scale is likely to lead to selecting an ineffective intervention.

BIOGEOGRAPHY AND ECOSYSTEM MANAGEMENT

The complex recent history of coastal North Pacific rainforests profoundly affects the current composition and distribution of the region's biota. During the Pleistocene, most of the region was covered by ice sheets that extended as far south as southern Oregon. Biogeographic and fossil evidence indicates that some coastal areas in the region remained ice free throughout the glacial advances, allowing species able to survive under harsh periglacial environments to persist. However, most of today's biota colonized the region within the last 10,000 to 12,000 years as the ice melted in the lowlands and became restricted to increasingly higher elevations in the coastal mountains. Owing to its complex topography, species colonized the region from different sources and at different times. Animals able to travel over ice could disperse to areas that became islands after ice cover diminished. Early in the warming period, when large quantities of water were still stored in ice sheets, sea levels were lower, and land bridges connected many of today's islands, just as the Bering Land Bridge connected North America with eastern Asia (Hopkins 1967; MacDonald and Cook 2009; Barrie *et al.* 2005). As coniferous forests became established in the region, animals adapted to those forests colonized them, whereas species adapted to tundra environments either became confined to higher elevations or vanished. These processes continue today and, when coupled with human-induced forest fragmentation and modifications to ecological communities, guarantee continued and accelerated fluxes in the region's biota.

Many North Pacific marine coastal islands were connected to the adjacent mainland during the Pleistocene when the storage of vast quantities of water in terrestrial glaciers at times lowered sea levels more than 100 m. These so-called land bridge islands were then readily accessible to terrestrial organisms. Their biotas are similar to those found on the mainland to which they were attached. Once they became islands, however, colonization rates dropped dramatically and extinction rates rose; their native biotas are gradually decreasing.

Habitat islands, sometimes called virtual islands, are much more varied in their dynamics than real islands. Although the surrounding habitats may not support viable populations, they are generally less hostile for terrestrial organisms than the ocean is; stopping, resting, and refueling during dispersal is often possible. Therefore, virtual islands are typically colonized at rates much greater than real islands. Those rates vary tremendously among organisms; some, such as birds and fungi, can more readily traverse oceanic barriers than others, such as amphibians and mammals.

The infrequency and small scale of natural disturbance over much of the coastal North Pacific rainforest means that old-growth forests often predominate in undeveloped landscapes. Old-growth forest stands in intensively managed landscapes may function as virtual islands that provide key habitats for some species (Harris 1984; Schoen and Albert 2007). Conservation biologists pay particular attention to the habitat matrix in which the virtual islands of concern, which may also be on real islands, are embedded. The quality and management of matrix lands separating virtual forest islands is a major factor to consider for landscape-scale conservation and management (Lindenmayer and Franklin 2002; Prugh *et al.* 2008; Franklin and Lindenmayer 2009).

The archipelagos of the coastal North Pacific rainforest are hybrids between oceanic and virtual islands. Owing to the much lower sea levels then, most if not all of these were connected to the mainland when they first emerged from the ice. Because most of the nearby mainland remained covered by ice, it remains unclear when colonization of the islands occurred. Sea levels in the region continue to change in complex ways as a result of interactions between the contrasting processes of isostatic rebound and sea level rise. Some islands constitute stepping-stones by means of which organisms reach other, more distant islands. One result of these complex processes, as described by Cook and MacDonald in chapter 2 of this volume, is that community composition differs substantially across some of the islands within each of the archipelagos and throughout the region. We are just beginning to understand how the region's complex geologic history has shaped these different patterns of diversity. Some coastal rainforest species are well adapted to dispersal in landscapes characterized by small-scale disturbance and dominated by old-growth forest. These species may be poorly adapted to dispersal in anthropogenic disturbances such as large clear-cuts. For example, Winchester and Ring (1996) found a disproportionate number of flightless arthropods in the canopies of old-growth Sitka spruce trees.

DISTURBANCE: NATURAL AND HUMAN-CAUSED

The physical environment everywhere is constantly changing. Organisms deal with some of those changes by altering their behavior. They may seek shelter during a storm, find shade during the heat of the day, or fluff their feathers or fur to increase insulation. Such changes may be important for the lives of individuals, and the behavioral changes may affect reproductive fitness.

Many disturbances, such as earthquakes, landslides, floods, and avalanches, are changes in the physical environment. Although most of these events are of very short duration, their ecological effects may persist for as long as several centuries. Some disturbances, such as diseases and insect outbreaks that massively defoliate plants, are caused by other organisms. Others, such as fire and windthrow, involve a complex interplay between organisms and the physical environment and, sometimes, human activity.

The ecological effects of a disturbance depend on its type, size, frequency, location, and severity, that is, how much and in what ways it alters the environment and the types and scale of biological legacies that are left behind (Franklin *et al.* 2000). An avalanche may kill all organisms buried under it. A severe fire may kill all above-ground life yet leave important habitat structures. A windstorm may knock down many trees but leave in place a complex legacy of living plants and above ground woody debris. The patchiness and legacy of surviving organisms and structures from the previous ecosystem is what distinguishes most "natural" or historical disturbances from contemporary human disturbances and management activities (Lindenmayer and Franklin 2002; Swanson *et al.* 2011). For example, in coastal temperate rainforests one of the most important and frequent disturbances is not a spectacular landscape-altering event but rather the creation of small gaps in the canopy from the death of one or more canopy trees (gap dynamics) (Alaback 1982; Lertzman *et al.* 1996). Over centuries, these small disturbances in combination with high-intensity storms or geological events have influenced the development of the highly complex and variable forests that characterize the region.

Cumulative Effects of Disturbances

All environments are influenced by interactions among multiple disturbances and different types of disturbances over time. The effects of a single disturbance event may combine with other similar or different events to produce much more profound and long-lasting cumulative effects (Paine *et al.* 1998). A single small group of trees falling over in the forest that creates a small opening in the forest canopy may be insignificant, but if one of these gap-creating disturbances occurs every few years somewhere within a forest, over time the whole forest may be affected by them.

Cumulative effects may result when a subsequent event affects an area before it has fully recovered from a previous one. A second wind storm may topple trees before vegetation succession has progressed to an old-growth forest. The effects of disturbances may also accumulate if they overlap in space. Compounding effects may result from synergistic interactions of multiple sources on a single environmental medium or from interaction between natural and anthropogenic effects. For example, clear-cutting a forest may increase the probability of landslides or blowdown of trees along the edges of adjacent forest stands. And the combination of clear-cutting an old-growth forest—altering habitat values—and constructing a road system in a previously undeveloped watershed—increasing human access—can result in substantial cumulative effects on a variety of species.

Cumulative effects become especially important when they cause a system-changing threshold to be reached. For example, when eutrophication exhausts a lake's oxygen, the lake may change to an ecologically different ecosystem. A forest in which the frequency of major disturbances has greatly increased may at a certain point lose species that depend on the structural and functional characteristics of old-growth stands. Many aspects of ecosystem-based management in BC's central and north coasts are based on avoiding habitat supply thresholds caused by logging of old-growth forests (e.g., Price *et al.* 2009). Successive losses of small pieces of suitable habitat may eventually result in the local extirpation of species that depend on that habitat.

To understand how disturbances have influenced an ecosystem, it is necessary to know the long-term history of the types of disturbances that have affected it. Organisms adapt evolutionarily to disturbance patterns that have been relatively predictable over time (see DeGayner *et al.* 2005). Many plants resprout from buried roots and corms after a fire. Others have evolved seeds that can survive dormant in the soil of an old forest for years, but then germinate following a disturbance such as fire or windthrow. Seed banks are not characteristic of most of the trees that dominate the coastal North Pacific rainforest, but dominant conifers must regenerate from currently produced seed. Shrubs may evolve flexible branches that can withstand avalanches, and trees tend to buttress their roots to better resist windstorms when winds come from a consistent direction.

Disturbance History in Coastal North Temperate Rainforests

The climate and topography of coastal temperate rainforests produce a particular constellation of disturbance types and frequencies. Owing to the wet climate and extremely low rate of occurrence of thunderstorms, fires are rare. But due to the combination of rugged topography, high precipitation, and frequent strong winter storms, landslides, avalanches, flooding, and windthrow are relatively common (Pearson 2010; DellaSala, Alaback, *et al.* 2011). Disturbance patterns are similar in the cool temperate rainforests of Tasmania, New Zealand, and southern Chile (DellaSala, Moola, *et al.* 2011), except that avalanches are more common in northern forests, whereas massive landslides associated with earthquakes are more frequent in southern forests. Many groups of organisms of the North Pacific rainforest region have few adaptations to fire because it is very infrequent (e.g., Winchester 1997).

Climate Change and Disturbance Patterns

Predicting the effects of climate change is one of the major conservation issues of the early twenty-first century. A changing climate is certain to affect the timing and length of growing seasons. It will alter hydrologic and nutrient cycles, seasonality of fruiting and flowering, emergence and availability of insects, and migration, survival, and reproductive success of organisms. Climate change is also certain to alter the nature and frequency of disturbances and the ecological and evolutionary responses of species and organisms (Parmesan 2006). In particular, global circulation models predict an increased frequency of extreme weather events over much of the globe (Hulme 2005). An increase in the frequency of powerful winter storms would cause more frequent flooding, landslides, and windthrow in coastal North Pacific rainforests. Rising sea levels and the associated loss of shoreline habitat are expected to compound the effects of these disturbances. However, as the climate warms, the frequency of avalanches may not increase and may even decline, because more precipitation at mid to upper elevations will fall as rain rather than snow, just as happens now during strong El Niño years. One of the key implications of this change is loss of mid-elevation open, shrubby habitats maintained by avalanches. These highly productive summer habitats for bears and other species will likely revert to conifer forest if the frequency of avalanches declines. These changes are already happening at high elevations where successive years of low snowpacks are resulting in fewer avalanches (Millar *et al.* 2007).

Another consequence of climate change could be an increase in summer dryness, particularly in rain shadow areas, such as the east side of Haida Gwaii, northern Lynn Canal, fiords, and valleys tucked in behind the first outer tiers of mountains (e.g., Dean Channel, Gardner Canal). Such a change could increase drought stress in trees, thereby increasing their vulnerability to diseases and outbreaks of defoliating insects, and lead to an increasing role for fire. Ironically, even though these areas have heavy annual rainfall, their shallow soils and lack of aquifers may make them susceptible to summer droughts with a small change in climate. For example, in recently deglaciated areas with poor soil development, many trees and shrubs currently turn yellow or drop their leaves following a few weeks of unseasonably warm and dry weather. Another change that is already well underway is Alaskan yellow cedar dieback, apparently a result of lower spring snowpack, premature dehardening of the trees, and susceptibility to frost (Hennon *et al.* 2006). Such changes could have profound effects on the region's plant and animal life. The implications for conservation are especially problematic given the many genetically distinct populations of species on different islands.

The structure and functioning of riparian zones will significantly change as the climate warms (Edwards *et al.*, this volume, chapter 3). Climate change may also alter stream flows and temperature as a result of reduced mountain snowpack and earlier peaking of snow melt (Furniss *et al.* 2010). Such changes could negatively affect the productivity of salmon spawning and rearing streams in the North Pacific rainforest (Mote *et al.* 1999; Bryant 2009). This effect could be further exacerbated by increases in stream temperatures due to loss of forest cover from logging activities (Bartholow 2000).

Better understanding of how individual species may respond to changes in vegetation and environmental conditions affected by climate change would provide an improved basis for planning habitat connections to enhance population persistence (Marcot, this volume, chapter 7). Identifying and projecting the influence of climate is assisted by considering three dimensions of effects: *exposure, sensitivity,* and *adaptation capacity.* Exposure refers to the intensity and duration of changes to which organisms and ecosystems are subject. Sensitivity refers to the degree to which the distribution and abundance of organisms, and the rates and types of ecological processes, are susceptible to climate change. Adaptation capacity refers to the extent to which human social, economic, and ecological systems can anticipate and adjust to climate change.

Understanding effects of climate change also might help inform what to monitor to ascertain negative trends among habitats and species. For example, climate change might be expected to have more immediate and recognizable negative effects on local island endemic taxa, on species at the periphery of their overall distribution, or on rare species (Everett and Robson 1991).

Human-Caused Disturbance Patterns

Some resource extraction activities cause disturbances that are similar to natural ones. However, most differ strikingly from natural disturbances in several ways. The most profound and consistent patterns of modern human-caused disturbances are the fragmentation of habitats, creation of monocultures or uniformity of forest cover types, and the greatly reduced structural legacies in harvested old-growth forest stands. Thus, many timber management practices result in large areas dominated by trees of a similar size and age. This transformation has long-term consequences because it may take several centuries for these forests to fully develop old-growth characteristics (Alaback 1982; Spies and Franklin 1988; Gerzon *et al.* 2011), if they are allowed to do so.

The most common harvesting technique in both coastal British Columbia and southeast Alaska has been clear-cut logging, in which all trees are clear-cut and removed at once, usually over areas of 10 ha or more. Clear-cutting old-growth forests significantly change forest ecosystems. For example, on Chichagof Island in southeast Alaska, clear-cutting old growth has reduced the area of old growth, decreased old-growth core areas and core-to-edge ratios, decreased old-growth block size, and increased the distance between blocks (Shephard *et al.* 1999). In marked contrast, a typical natural windthrow event creates a complex mosaic of standing, partially broken, stem-snapped, or tipped over trees and patches of root throw mounds, pits, or piles of branches and organic debris. Flooding, avalanches, and insect or disease outbreaks also tend to generate spatially complex landscape patterns.

In addition, whereas natural disturbances may be distributed randomly except with respect to exposure to wind and the effects of previous disturbances, human disturbances usually have a fundamentally different pattern. In most temperate rainforests, traditional logging progresses in a characteristic pattern across the landscape. The first areas to be logged are the most productive and economically valuable, that is, those with the greatest carbon stores that are easily accessible, whether by water or by road. In BC's central coast, for example, approximately 81% of logging has occurred in valley bottoms (Pearson 2010). In the coastal North Pacific rainforest, sites with great carbon stores occupy the small fraction of the landscape with a combination of well-drained, nutrient-rich soils and protection from regular windstorms (although peatland bogs also have high carbon stores). Thus, significant change in the ecological character of the landscape may occur even if only a small area has been logged.

Forest stands that are frequently disturbed by wind, avalanches, or flooding are usually less economically valuable and less likely to be logged (although some old [150–200 year old] stands that regrow after windthrow are economically valuable). Therefore, human disturbance, even if light, may disproportionately impact key habitats of animals, plants (in particular mosses and liverworts), lichens, and fungi that are of conservation interest. Highly productive habitats tend to have higher levels of biological diversity, as well as the most intense interactions between terrestrial and aquatic ecosystems. However, the coastal North Pacific rainforest region's peatlands probably have higher diversity of vascular plants and bryophytes than does productive old growth.

Recently developed restoration forestry techniques and new developments in landscape management offer many potential ways to reduce the dramatic contrast between the highly diverse forests that result from most natural disturbances and the relatively homogenous and less diverse forests that typically develop in the wake of logging. Variable retention harvesting provides forest managers and conservationists with a rich set of tools to better approximate natural disturbance regimes, such as providing higher levels of biological diversity (Beese, this volume, chapter 9). Patches of forest or particular sizes or age classes of trees can be removed, creating vegetation structures more similar to natural ones. However, it is a great challenge to determine how to maintain spatial patterns or structures such as large branches, complex canopies, and coarse woody debris (logs, snags, mounds on the forest floor) that may be of great conservation importance. Given the long and variable history of natural disturbances in the coastal North Pacific region, ecologically informed ways of managing these forests, even if they do not precisely mimic natural disturbance events, are likely to better approximate ecological processes so that they generate and maintain the range of habitat types necessary to support much of the region's biological diversity. The conservation values of such alternative harvesting systems would be greater if new road construction were minimized. Clearly, more experimentation, monitoring, and documentation will be required to make sure these new approaches to approximating natural disturbance processes are having their desired effects, and also to address additional challenges, such as climate change and changes in human demands for the region's ecosystem goods and services. Moreover, to become widely employed in the future, such practices will need to be economically viable. Although past logging on the Tongass National Forest was highly subsidized, such subsidies are unlikely to support future extraction of timber.

Whatever the form of tree harvest, access to areas to be logged typically requires construction of a network of logging roads that have their own set of ecological impacts (Person and Brinkman, this volume, chapter 6). Roads nearly always have a variety of direct and indirect effects on biotas and ecosystem structure and functioning, many of them adverse (Trombulak and Frissell 2000; USDA Forest Service 2001; Person and Brinkman, this volume, chapter 6). They cover and kill vegetation; displace organisms; impede movement by some species; facilitate dispersal of other, especially nonnative species; change hydrological patterns; and, in cold regions, influence snow accumulation and formation of thermokarst. Roads increase human access to an area. Roads increase the numbers of tourists and hunters—if we build it, they will come. Increased human access and mortality pressure on large carnivores continues to be a significant management problem, as described by Person and Brinkman (chapter 6) for southeast Alaska. Although roads can be decommissioned and removed, doing so is very expensive—often nearly as expensive as constructing them.

WATERSHEDS AND CONSERVATION

Numerous ecological studies suggest that conservation and management activities have improved outcomes when they take place at the scale of entire watersheds (Stanford and Ward 1992; Naiman *et al.* 1997, 2000; Schindler 1998; Pringle 2001; Baron *et al.* 2002; Lertzman and MacKinnon, this volume, chapter 8). But watersheds vary enormously in size; the Columbia and Yukon rivers drain large parts of North America. At the other extreme, some watersheds drain no more than a few square kilometers. Moreover, large watersheds are aggregates of countless smaller watersheds of varying size. The Snake River watershed, a component of the larger Columbia River watershed, drains a large area of the western states. Deciding on the most appropriate scale for thinking about watersheds varies with the problem at issue. Doing so is not a simple matter.

Coastal North Pacific watersheds fall into three main categories. One group is composed of rivers that have cut through the rugged coastal mountains. They drain large interior areas with cold, continental climates. Flows in these rivers peak in spring and summer. They have served as corridors for dispersal of plant and animals from the interior to the coast. Rivers with large interior watersheds are more abundant and important in northern British Columbia than in southeast Alaska.

Another group consists of coastal rivers that have their headwaters in glaciers and ice fields. They carry heavy loads of glacial silt and their flows peak in summer. The third group consists of coastal rivers with low-elevation headwaters. They are primarily rain driven and may have peak flows in spring and fall. The most profound hydrologic events are usually rain-on-snow flood events. Most rivers on islands in the North Pacific fall into this third category. Rivers with headwaters in ice fields and glaciers also have tributaries, many of whose headwaters are at low elevation. The ecological characteristics of these tributaries may differ strikingly from those in the main stem. Watershed managers must think and plan at many different spatial scales.

A compelling argument for using watersheds as the basis for reserve design is that, more than other units of equivalent size, they have strong internal connections among ecosystem processes that are mediated by gravity and the downward flow of water. In addition, intact watersheds are the functional ecosystems with greatest likelihood of maintaining their ecological integrity and resilience over time and through environmental change. Populations of all aquatic species and those that live in riparian habitats are intimately tied to the spatial and temporal characteristics of the watershed in which they live. Many of the species and interactions in North Pacific rainforests (e.g., salmon spawning and rearing and the interactions between wildlife species and salmon) are strongly linked to key ecological processes at a watershed scale (e.g., sedimentation, stream flow, and nutrient cycling). In fact, the productivity of coastal ecosystems is strongly linked to salmon, which, by transporting nutrients between the ocean and fresh water, function as "keystone" species (Willson and Halupka 1995). Many other animals use watersheds—specifically riparian habitats—as movement corridors, although watershed boundaries, many of which are at high elevations, may be barriers to movement (Naiman *et al.* 2000). Better than any other landscape feature, intact watersheds also sustain ecosystem processes and ecological integrity (Lertzman and MacKinnon, this volume, chapter 8).

In addition, field studies suggest that watersheds are the appropriate scale at which to measure and manage many cumulative human impacts. Many biological and physical indicators correlate with human activity data when measured at watershed scales (Karr 1991; Muhar and Jungwirth 1998; Pimentel *et al.* 2000; Carignan *et al.* 2002; Pess *et al.* 2002). Watersheds are also useful units for assessing and understanding ecosystem services. The downward flow of water ensures that costs and benefits of ecosystem services provided by watersheds are geographically separated. Flood and erosion control efforts must be concentrated in the upper parts of watershed, whereas the benefits primarily accrue to people along the lower reaches of the rivers. Assessing appropriate payments to upstream people who provide ecosystem services to downstream communities and designing institutions to accomplish wealth transfers are complex management problems.

Protecting intact watersheds with high ecological values is an effective strategy for maintaining the natural range of variation of forest types (i.e., habitat diversity), minimizing habitat fragmentation, and reducing negative road impacts within the protected watersheds. For these reasons, identifying and conserving a range of intact watersheds should be a part of any credible, systematic, science-based conservation analysis. The panel of fish experts consulted for the Tongass Land and Resource Management Plan recommended that the most effective protection of fish habitat on the Tongass National Forest would be reserves that included entire watersheds rather than only parts of them (Dunlap 1997). "The presence, number, and distribution of intact watersheds across the landscape of the TNF (Tongass National Forest) are critical elements for sustainable salmon populations in the face of habitat loss elsewhere in southeast Alaska and the Pacific Northwest" (Bryant and Everest 1998). A watershed-scale conservation strategy for southeast Alaska has been proposed by Schoen and Albert (2007). Most of the new protected areas on BC's central and north coasts and Haida Gwaii incorporate entire watersheds.

To achieve the benefits of maintaining ecological integrity while also providing for some timber harvesting opportunities, logging activities need to be aggregated rather than being evenly distributed throughout a landscape (Franklin 1989). Aggregating timber harvest in fewer watersheds would enable the protection of an additional sample of intact watersheds with high ecological values and may also enhance efficiency of some timber operations.

Protecting intact watersheds would maintain conservation options under environmental uncertainty. Scientists and managers have incomplete knowledge of many ecological processes and species' habitat requirements in the region. Protecting intact watersheds would also increase the probability of maintaining wide-ranging species like brown bears and wolves that are at risk from expanding road systems and associated increased human access.

Watershed-based reserves will be the best option for some, but not all goals (Lertzman and MacKinnon, this volume, chapter 8). Watershed-based conservation adds a focus on physiography, ecosystems, and ecosystem processes to a strategy dominated historically by concerns for species. For large mobile vertebrates, population viability may depend on maintaining metapopulation dynamics across multiple reserves and the intervening semi-natural matrix. Reserves based on the boundaries of entire watersheds are likely to play a more significant role in maintaining population viability than an equal area of reserves scattered across several watersheds. In many cases, a complex of adjacent watershed reserves will provide additional safeguards, particularly for large wide-ranging species. In coastal temperate rainforest watersheds, ecological integrity will be enhanced if the watershed includes adjacent estuarine and near-shore marine areas with which it interacts strongly. Watershed-based conservation should also increase people's ability to benefit from the many goods and services those ecosystems can provide on a sustainable basis.

RESTORATION OF COASTAL TEMPERATE RAINFORESTS

Visionary thinkers have long recognized that by disregarding the processes that enable ecosystems to provide valuable goods and services, people have unwittingly degraded their environments, in some cases leading to societal collapse (Diamond 2005). But they have also pointed out that natural ecosystems have great restorative potential. The American diplomat George Perkins Marsh, after observing environmental degradation in the United Sates and many other countries he visited, in *Man and Nature* (1864) directed readers' attention to the potential of restoration and proposed that people become coworkers "with nature in the reconstruction of the damaged fabric which the negligence or wantonness of former lodgers has rendered untenable."

Despite Marsh's passionate appeal, recognition, and interest, the potential of ecological restoration languished for many decades. Recently, however, ecologists have been calling for greater emphasis on restoration and urging conservationists to incorporate restoration activities more fully into their overall strategies. The Society for Ecological Restoration International was founded in 1988. A rapidly growing body of literature shows that, although ecosystems have considerable restorative potential, not all damages can be completely reversed, and times to recovery vary enormously, from a few decades to many centuries. If species have been exterminated, complete restoration is, of course, impossible. Thus, the most basic rule of ecological tinkering is to save all the pieces (Leopold 1949). This notion is particularly relevant to archipelagos, which have experienced a disproportionately high percentage of documented species extinctions during the past 400 years (Diamond 2005). But species extirpated within a system may survive elsewhere and, thus, can be reintroduced.

Restoration Ecology

A recent review of the restoration literature (Jones and Schmitz 2009) showed that more than a third of the ecosystems for which adequate data were available recovered at least some of the desired functional attributes. Marine benthic ecosystems fouled by oil spills recovered within five years on average. However, residual oil from the 1989 Exxon Valdez spill still persists in beach sediments in Prince William Sound, Alaska (Short *et al.* 2007). Recovery of ecosystems dominated by long-lived woody plants takes much longer. Except for urbanization, agriculture is the most damaging disturbance to most ecosystems, but many wetlands and streams also respond poorly to restoration efforts (Palmer 2009; Zedler 2007). Some over-exploited marine ecosystems shift to an alternative stable state from which recovery is very difficult (Folke *et al.* 2005; Scheffer *et al.* 1993, 2001).

To be successful, a restoration effort needs to be based on an understanding of the dynamic properties of the system to be restored. Recent restoration efforts have been guided by the concept of *adaptive management*. Adaptive management is needed because management interventions are always initiated with incomplete knowledge, but waiting for more complete knowledge is often worse than taking action despite substantial uncertainty. Under *passive adaptive management*, decisions are based on current understanding of how the system is likely to respond to management. The model of nature that has the greatest current support guides decisions. Passive adaptive management is basically learning by doing. Intervention strategies are designed using the best available information, and a monitoring system is incorporated into the experimental design so that the outcomes of the intervention can be assessed. Based on the outcome, future interventions may be altered.

Sometimes, however, knowledge is insufficient to serve as a guide for actions. For those conditions, *active adaptive management*, in which several possible models of system response to management are simultaneously evaluated, is appropriate. Active adaptive management has a dual objective—economic benefit plus learning about system responses. Before major management interventions are initiated, an assessment of existing knowledge is undertaken to determine which gaps in knowledge are decision-critical. Following that assessment, carefully focused interventions are designed to fill those gaps rather than to attempt to accomplish substantial restoration.

Restoration to What State?

An important and often underappreciated first step in designing a restoration program is to determine the restoration goal. To what state do we wish to restore the system? This apparently simple question is actually hard to answer. Many possible reference states may exist and little information may be available to characterize past states. Two major issues surround the choice of baselines. First, what date or state should be chosen as an appropriate baseline? Second, should a specific baseline be established and used thereafter, or should the baseline be updated in response to new information?

The characteristics of an ecological system and its vital processes some time in the past can serve as an appropriate reference state. But at what time in the past? Rarely are data available to characterize environmental states in even the recent past, much less the remote past. Many ecosystems and habitats are so poorly known that even current natural states and processes can be characterized only within broad ranges. Species typical of an environment in even the recent past may have become extinct. At high latitudes, climates and land elevations are still adjusting from the most recent glacial period. Rates of some of these changes are too slow to affect choices of reference states, but some are not.

The most appropriate time that could serve as a useful reference for restoration activities in coastal North Pacific rainforests is relatively recent. Ten thousand years ago most of the region was buried under ice. When people first settled in the region, climate and geography were dramatically different from today. The climate continues to change, and sea levels are still rising, but restoring vegetation to what existed when humans had not yet substantially modified terrestrial habitats is probably realistic; that is, conditions when Russian fur traders arrived may serve as an appropriate basis for establishing restoration goals. An alternative restoration goal is to attempt to restore and maintain the processes that generate the array of environments that have characterized the region. Maintaining processes rather than reference conditions may be the best way to enable organisms to adapt to changes so that ecosystems can continue to provide goods and services for humans (Edwards *et al.*, this volume, chapter 3) and provide future services not currently demanded or even imagined.

Probable future climate change needs to be considered when planning restoration projects because climate is expected to change rapidly in the region and because some critical ecosystem processes respond slowly to interventions. Most animals are short lived, so their populations generally respond rapidly to environmental changes. Trees, on the other hand, grow slowly and may live many centuries. Individuals established today may live under a significantly different climate when they are mature.

Incremental Adaptive Restoration (IAR), a concept developed for hydrological restoration of the Everglades (National Research Council 2007), may be useful in North Pacific rainforests. Recovery of degraded ecosystems can occur in many different ways (fig. 10.01). The simplest is a linear relationship between ecological improvements (investment) and ecological recovery or restoration (curve A). Alternatively, investments may at first cause further degradation; only later do the benefits of recovery accrue (curve B). In another scenario, recovery may not occur until significant investment in ecological improvement has been made (curve C),

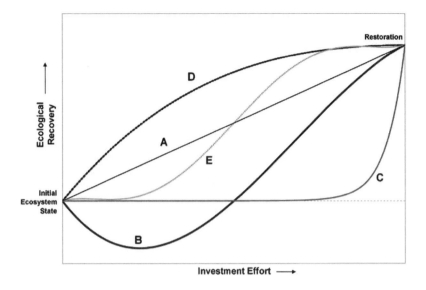

FIGURE 10.01. Potential relationships between investments in ecological improvements and benefits of ecological recovery to full restoration. Adapted from the National Research Council (2007).

or recovery may occur rapidly with small investments (curve D). Finally, ecosystem response may initially be slow but thereafter recovery may accrue rapidly with additional investment (curve E).

Assessing the likely form of the response curve is important as a guide for intervention actions. When is it best to let nature take its course? When and how should we attempt to approximate nature's disturbance patterns to accelerate recovery rates? When should we attempt to produce new patterns that may yield desired results even if the short-term result is further degradation? Which current knowledge gaps are decision-critical? In the next section we describe the data gaps that appear to be the most important to address restoration and management activities in coastal North Pacific rainforests. However, we already know enough to clearly identify three major issues that need to be addressed throughout North Pacific rainforests:

1. restoration of degraded salmon spawning streams and riparian areas;

2. elimination of unnecessary and damaging roads; and

3. long-term restoration of the diversity and patch size of productive old-growth forest types.

DATA GAPS AND RESEARCH NEEDS

The coastal North Pacific rainforest, a complex mixture of islands and mainland that has undergone dramatic climate changes during the past several thousand years, presents many challenges to anyone trying to understand its current structure and functional dynamics. It is easy to develop an extensive list of interesting research projects that would enhance our understanding of this fascinating region. Here, however, we focus on data gaps, which if filled, should materially affect the decisions that managers will be called upon to make, as they act to conserve and sustain the rich natural and cultural heritage of the region.

Current Biogeographic Patterns

Few species survived in the region during recent glacial episodes. Because species have arrived in the region at different times and via different routes, individual islands have distinctive biotas. The distinctiveness of the biotas is poorly known, owing to a paucity of surveys of species for most taxa, particularly invertebrates, mosses, lichens, parasites, and microorganisms. Integrated floral and faunal surveys that are specimen-based and tied to research initiatives using modern analytical techniques are urgently needed to inform decisions concerning how to preserve the region's biodiversity and how to facilitate the continuing colonization of the region as climate warms.

Current Vegetation Patterns

The current structure of the region's low-elevation, productive rainforest differs substantially from what existed less than a century ago because of industrial-scale forestry that began about 50 years ago (Albert and Schoen 2007a). To plan wisely for the future, a thorough assessment of the existing situation is needed. What are the locations and patch sizes of remaining old-growth forest types (e.g., large-tree riparian forest and karst forest on limestone)? What is their distribution over soils of different drainage and productivity and over watersheds of different sizes? What are the distribution, extent, and condition of riparian forests? What are the locations and current conditions of the most important dispersal corridors for different species? We need a comprehensive, consistent, cross-border inventory of spawning and rearing habitat for all anadromous fish species throughout the region. Finally, we need a comprehensive inventory of the location, sizes, and ages of second-growth stands to support planning and implementing the transition from harvesting old-growth to second-growth forest stands. A new set of tools using remote sensing methods can facilitate gathering such data, avoiding the need for intensive and expensive work on the ground.

Understanding and Managing Disturbance

Future harvesting of the region's forests, whether by means of traditional silvicultural techniques (e.g., clear-cutting) or approaches based on structural and compositional retention guidelines (e.g., variable retention harvesting), will continue to alter the vegetation's spatial patterns, with uncertain effects on the region's biota. Decisions governing the nature and extent of harvest of the region's forests, whatever the management goals may be, need to be better informed by information on how different harvesting methods affect such properties and processes as the species composition of managed forests, nutrient cycling, and erosion. When, where, and why should management attempt to approximate natural disturbance patterns? What would be the consequences of continuing to clear-cut the remaining blocks of old-growth forest versus selective harvesting of individual trees? What interventions, that is, restoration tools, might accelerate the transition of second-growth forests to old-growth conditions? Which old-growth characteristics are most important to different species of concern?

Climate Change and Carbon Dynamics

Understanding how climate change may affect hydrology, anadromous fish, nutrient cycling, forest insect infestations, plant succession, and other ecological processes is a major need. Additionally, gathering information on carbon dynamics—sequestration, sink/source, and how those processes are likely to respond to climate change—is an important research priority for the region.

Identifying Thresholds

The most important changes in ecosystem structure and dynamics often result not from gradual changes but from the crossing of thresholds that nudge the system into an alternative state (Folke *et al.* 2005; Scheffer *et al.* 1993, 2001). From the human perspective, most of those alternative states are likely to be less desirable than current ones. Unfortunately, when, where, and why thresholds will occur is difficult to predict (e.g., Price *et al.* 2007). Most models of the dynamics of complex systems, whether of climate or ecosystems, do not include processes that might yield sudden nonlinear responses, because few long-term data sets exist that provide the information needed to construct those models. Nevertheless, analyses can help identify where and why thresholds are likely to occur and suggest actions that might avert crossing them. Implementation of ecosystem-based management on BC's central and north coasts and Haida Gwaii is largely premised on avoiding crossing habitat supply thresholds (Price *et al.* 2009). However, the thresholds established in legislation are derived almost entirely from research in other ecosystems in other regions of the world; their utility in North Pacific temperate forest regions is unknown.

Transboundary Issues

The dynamic properties of the coastal North Pacific rainforest are influenced by events outside the region, as well as those taking place within it. Rivers with large interior watersheds are corridors for dispersal of animals and plants into the region; they discharge their nutrient loads into coastal waters. Salmon swim upstream to spawn and rear far from the coast. Ocean currents carry nutrients and organisms into and out of the region. Economic activities have been driven primarily by export of the region's natural resources. The nature, extent, and likely future conditions of these extraregional drivers are, for the most part, poorly understood. Continuing ignorance of their roles is certain to be detrimental.

It will doubtless have not escaped the attention of our readers that this book is focused almost entirely on the terrestrial environment. The marine environment has entered our discussions primarily as a source of returning salmon and as a recipient of water and nutrients from the region's rivers. The rich marine environments of the region are poorly known, yet they are an integral part of this coastal rainforest ecosystem. Their potential as sources of varied inputs to the region's future should be investigated while we determine the most appropriate ways to manage the region's terrestrial and freshwater ecosystems.

Historically, there has been little international coordination of inventory, management, and research activities within the coastal North Pacific rainforest. This is regrettable, in that the border is a political rather than ecological line on the map. Recognizing the need to rectify this unfortunate situation, researchers and managers in British Columbia and southeast Alaska (including several authors of this volume) are now engaged in a collaborative transboundary project to compile available data on forest composition and structure and topographic features (e.g., watershed boundaries) for the coastal temperate rainforest biome, extending from Cape Caution on British Columbia's central coast to Yakutat Bay in southeast Alaska. The initial objectives of this project are to standardize data to a common format and scale and calculate preliminary measures of landscape structure and composition. GIS layers and metadata, which will be housed at agencies in both Alaska and British Columbia, will assist land managers, conservation organizations, and industries to better understand the ecological dynamics of the coastal North Pacific temperate rainforest. We hope the availability of these data will encourage future research collaborations.

Watershed Inventory

The North Pacific rainforest provides one of the best opportunities in the word for watershed-scale conservation. A comprehensive inventory of watersheds throughout the region would provide important information on regional gradients in watershed physiographic and ecological characteristics, show their degree of development and protection status, and provide better information about distributions of species and communities at risk (Lertzman and MacKinnon, this volume, chapter 8). Some work on developmental status of watersheds in the coastal temperate rainforest has been conducted (Wolf *et al.* 1995) but is badly in need of updating.

Reserve Design and Effectiveness of Existing Reserve Network

Many important management decisions for the region cannot and will not await the filling of critical data gaps by the research we have just identified. In particular, decisions about the nature, size, and location of protected areas should be made relatively soon, because delays will inevitably decrease the range of available options. Habitat fragmentation will increase and fewer relatively intact watersheds will exist. Rare endemic species may be further endangered or extirpated. Important dispersal corridors may be lost.

The coastal North Pacific rainforest currently encompasses millions of hectares of undeveloped areas having variable degrees of protection. A preliminary analysis in southeast Alaska found that most protected areas were dominated by watersheds with high proportions of rock and ice or scrub forest (Albert and Schoen 2007b). Therefore, an assessment of the effectiveness and ecological representation of the existing protected areas in southeast Alaska, north coastal British Columbia, and Haida Gwaii should be conducted. This analysis should include an evaluation of both watershed-based and nonwatershed-based protected areas, including comparisons of the effectiveness of reserve content, context, and emergent criteria of replicate protected areas stratified across regional gradients (Lertzman and MacKinnon, this volume, chapter 8).

Intraregional Variation of Natural Disturbances

We currently have limited understanding of the region's natural disturbance regimes and their intraregional variation (e.g., gradients in the role of wind disturbance, landslides, etc.). It will be important to increase our understanding of such variation in relation to the size distribution of watersheds (Lertzman and MacKinnon, this volume, chapter 8). These data would enhance decision making regarding where and to what extent protecting single watersheds, clusters of watersheds, or island-based reserves would be most effective in achieving conservation objectives.

Assessment of Past Timber Harvests

A comprehensive analysis of the consequences of the timber harvesting that has already occurred in the region would generate information of great value in deciding where to establish reserves. That is, a retrospective research project that compares sets of watersheds that have been subjected to a wide range of manipulations, ranging from untouched to extensive clear-cutting, would generate data that tell us how the kinds and extent of resource extractions activities have affected different components of those ecosystems. The past may not be a perfect guide to the future, but knowing the consequences of past activities is certain to be of great value in predicting the consequences of future activities.

THE FUTURE OF CONSERVATION, ECOLOGICAL INTEGRITY, FOREST ECONOMICS, AND QUALITY OF HUMAN LIFE

Although tropical forests have been the focus of most recent attention by ecologists, conservation biologists, and climate change scientists, increased attention recently has been directed to high-latitude forests (Lawford *et al.* 1996; Schoonmaker *et al.* 1997; DellaSala 2011). Climate is already warming rapidly at these latitudes and is projected to continue to warm more rapidly there than elsewhere on Earth. Thus, what happens to high-latitude forests is certain to have major implications for global climate change, as well as humanity's efforts to reduce the rate and magnitude of those changes and to mitigate the negative effects of the unavoidable changes that will occur.

Conservation and management options for coastal North Pacific rainforests are strongly influenced by the range of economically viable uses of the landscape. The cool, wet climate makes the region unsuitable for agriculture. Harvesting of timber and marine resources, recreation, and tourism offer the greatest long-term economic potential in the region. However, because trees grow slowly, harvest and transportation costs are high, and long-term sustainable harvest levels are modest, short-term over-exploitation has been and continues to be a temptation and problem.

In southeast Alaska and northern coastal British Columbia, resource managers, scientists, and conservationists have an excellent opportunity to protect the ecological integrity and natural qualities of the northern portion of the coastal North Pacific rainforest while also sustaining local economies and maintaining the quality of life valued by the people who live and work in the region. However, the management paradigm will need to change from the original large-scale clear-cutting programs and export of raw logs, to more sustainable, smaller-scale harvests that approximate natural disturbance patterns and value-added processing of forest products prior to export. For example, under the 2006 land use order (BC Land Use Order 2006) for BC's central and north coast (as amended in 2009), a minimum of 15% of each area (cutblock) scheduled for logging must be retained. The opportunities for conserving intact landscapes (including all their functional parts) have largely disappeared throughout much of the world. In this coastal temperate rainforest, a conservation strategy can be developed with a much cleaner slate than is possible with most other forests. There is more old growth and many more intact watersheds in this region than in coastal regions to the south and elsewhere on Earth. Thus, we have opportunities to manage these forests proactively, which is often less costly than reactive management, which is often the only available option. Also, methods employed to maintain the natural range of cover types and ecological communities and ensure landscape and habitat connectivity in North Pacific rainforests can be applied in other coastal areas with similar conservation opportunities, such as the Kamchatka Peninsula in Russia and the Valdivian region of Chile.

To maintain conservation options in the coastal North Pacific region, scientists and resource managers must evaluate and refine BC's and Alaska's regional conservation strategies through an international, science-based, collaborative, and interdisciplinary process. We have the analytical tools and ecological theory to help us make smart decisions on how to implement land management to conserve biological diversity and ecological integrity while also providing economic opportunities for sustaining local communities. These two goals—often expressed as "healthy ecosystems and healthy communities"—form the basis of the land-use plans developed for BC's central and north coasts and Haida Gwaii over the last decade (Price *et al.* 2009). Balancing these two goals is always challenging, because it involves both long-term values of ecological services (e.g., clean water and salmon production) as well as short-term economic gain. It will also be important to consider and plan for climate change and how it may affect this region. As we discuss next, three major issues—getting the scale right, functional connectivity, and economic connectivity—must be addressed if we are to have success in these efforts.

GETTING THE SCALE RIGHT

As previously described, the physical environment of the coastal North Pacific rainforest has changed dramatically during the past 10,000 years. A thick mantle of ice covered most of the region and glacial climates prevailed. As glaciers retreated and the climate warmed, increasing amounts of land were exposed, sea levels changed, many islands became connected to the mainland, only to become islands again as sea levels rose. The ecological and evolutionary processes that accompanied these dramatic changes in the physical environment have operated at many different temporal and spatial scales. If we are to respond effectively to the many issues of concern to North Pacific rainforest ecosystem managers we must identify the most appropriate scale at which analyses should be focused and management interventions employed for each challenge.

Allopatric speciation, which depends on the existence of physical barriers to gene flow, typically requires thousands of years for the accumulation of sufficient genetic differences to prevent successful hybridization between populations when their ranges subsequently overlap. Some of the endemic animals of the coastal North Pacific region apparently evolved their genetic distinctness during their long-term isolation in unglaciated refugia during the most recent glacial advances. However, we do not know whether those populations are sufficiently genetically different from recent mainland invaders to resist hybridization and competition from them. Moreover, given that the distributions of only a few of the major groups of microorganisms, plants, fungi, and animals are even moderately well known, prohibiting deliberate introductions of species to islands where they do not currently exist and avoiding inadvertent introductions would be a prudent policy.

Colonization of the coastal North Pacific rainforest region following retreat of the glaciers has happened at various times and by various routes. Similar variability is likely to characterize future colonization of the region, especially as climate warms and dispersal corridors become available to species that have not heretofore been able to use them.

Organisms on relatively small islands are more vulnerable to extinction than species on the mainland because of both small population size and geographic isolation. Most species of birds that have become globally extinct during the past 500 years were island species. Species on islands in the coastal North Pacific rainforest region are clearly vulnerable and, in the absence of reliable data on population trends, they might well become critically endangered before their plight is recognized. Some island species may be particularly susceptible to extirpation or extinction due to introduced species. For example, almost all of the 1.5 million seabirds breeding on Haida Gwaii nest in or on the ground; predation from introduced rats and raccoons has greatly reduced some seabird populations (Golumbia 2000).

Vegetation succession unfolds relatively slowly, particularly in the cool climate of the coastal North Pacific rainforest. The carefully studied plant succession in Glacier Bay indicates that several centuries may be required before the full suite of characteristics of old-growth forests are achieved after a major disturbance (Chapin *et al.* 1994). Populations of most animals, which are characterized by relatively high annual mortality rates, may decline long before succession has achieved a more or less steady state. Thus, reductions in remaining stands of old-growth forests may jeopardize persistence of species that depend on those habitats even if substantial areas of secondary forest are managed as restoration reserves.

The unfolding of physical and biological processes since glacial retreat has resulted in rapid and repeated change in the accessibility of different islands for different organisms. One result is substantial endemism and complex biogeographic patterns. In addition, some rare habitats became common while others decreased in size and connectivity. Some habitat types—estuaries, limestone outcrops, and avalanche chutes—are and probably always have been distributed on the landscape as relatively small patches isolated from other similar patches. Great variability in the composition of biological communities in these habitats is likely, much of it currently undetected. Management strategies need to reflect those patterns, if they are to maintain the region's existing biological diversity and allow ecological and evolutionary processes to generate new biodiversity patterns in the future. Getting the scale right is difficult, but it is an essential component of sound management.

FUNCTIONAL CONNECTIVITY

The ecological processes that drive landscape structure and dynamics depend in part on the powerful functional connectivity that exists among landscape components. The most obvious, and probably best understood, connectivity is generated by the downward flow of water, but there are others. Salmon returning to spawn in fresh waters bring large amount of nutrients with them. Although salmon typically die in the water, bears and a variety of scavengers may carry their carcasses hundreds of meters into the riparian zone where they fertilize the forest (Quinn *et al.* 2009).

In contrast, connectivity along the North Pacific rainforest coast is naturally limited by water barriers between islands, natural physiographic pinch points on both islands and mainland, and extensive nonforest habitats. Overlaying this is a network of logging roads and timber harvest units that further fragment forest types and plant and animal habitats relative to historic conditions. Although the surrounding matrix lands provide dispersal opportunities for many organisms, others (e.g., amphibians, flying squirrels) may face a less-connected landscape that isolates them demographically or genetically.

Prior to significant human intervention, the region's ecosystems supported all of the species likely to be of conservation concern. Therefore, maintaining connectivity is likely to help restore and maintain the region's biodiversity. Doing so should enhance survival of species distributed as metapopulations and maintain corridors for dispersal of organisms into and out of the region. At the same time, however, increasing connectivity beyond natural levels may facilitate spread of undesirable exotic species and create conditions that favor rapid dispersal of pathogens. If dispersal corridors are narrow, predators may find it profitable to position themselves along a corridor where dispersing prey are particularly vulnerable. Dispersing individuals may compete with or hybridize with indigenous species. During recent times, humans have deliberately or inadvertently introduced thousands of species around the world. Most of them are adapted to disturbed habitats and readily spread through environments along disturbance corridors. Exotic plants in the North Pacific rainforest region are concentrated in urban and suburban areas and along forest roads. Management needs to proceed with careful consideration of when and when not to enhance connectivity in the landscape.

ECONOMIC CONNECTIVITY

Indigenous people have lived in this region and used its natural resources for thousands of years (Crone and Mehrkens, this volume, chapter 5). The first human inhabitants of coastal North Pacific rainforests lived in relative isolation from people elsewhere. They depended on local resources for all their needs; they exported little other than fish oil from coastal to interior villages (Crone and Mehrkens, this volume, chapter 5). As human cultures developed in the region, a limited amount of trading developed, but people's lives depended almost entirely on local resources. In today's extensively interconnected economic world, however, no region is an economic island. Indeed, during recent decades, economic development in the North Pacific rainforest region has been driven largely by export of natural resources, particularly wood, fish, and minerals, and import of many of the goods and materials on which modern civilization is based (Crone and Mehrkens, this volume, chapter 5).

For this reason, economic developments are vulnerable to economic activities elsewhere in the world—over which the region's inhabitants have little or no control. Also, the current economic situation is probably unsustainable, because it depends on an unsustainable rate of exploitation of one natural resource (high-quality old-growth wood), insufficient attention to within-region exchange of resources, and insufficient reliance on alternative goods and services—carbon sequestration, recreation, ecotourism— that could be provided by the region's ecosystems.

The region's vulnerability to economic perturbations elsewhere could be decreased by increasing internal use of its natural resources. The modest needs of the region's construction industry clearly could be provided on a sustainable basis by harvest of the region's second-growth forests, while maintaining all other ecological values. Gravel and other construction materials can also be supplied locally. The region's electricity needs can be supplemented by a combination of hydropower and biomass generation from wood waste at lumber mills and from thinning and restoration projects. The region's fish and wildlife resources can provide a significant proportion of the diets of local residents, particularly those living in rural communities and Native villages, although the region's limited agricultural potential guarantees that food imports will inevitably be needed.

How much the region can or should depend on income derived from export of its natural resources is a more complex problem. Because the region is far from large markets and labor, transportation, and energy costs are high, it is at a substantial disadvantage in competition with suppliers elsewhere (Crone and Mehrkens, this volume, chapter 5). This issue is of particular concern with respect to timber resources. A small international market exists for the wood of clear-grained, old-growth trees with narrow growth rings. This wood is wanted for specialty uses, such as making guitars, other musical instruments, and furniture. An opportunity exists in the North Pacific rainforest for marketing high-quality specialty wood products. These products could be provided on a sustainable basis, but at a greatly reduced scale than the unsustainable harvest of the past five decades. A more selective harvest of individual trees could also be done in a manner that mimics natural disturbance patterns characteristic of this region, thus maintaining the structure and diversity of the old-growth forest community.

The future market for wood from lower-quality second-growth forests is uncertain. This wood has more knots and wider growth rings and is similar to the quality of wood from more southerly latitudes, where trees grow faster and are closer to large markets. What management strategies would be appropriate in the coastal North Pacific rainforest if a strong market were to develop for export of second-growth timber? In what ways would those strategies differ from what would be viable without such a market?

However, opportunities may exist to provide local economic diversification within the timber industry through watershed restoration projects focused on restoring the highest-quality salmon watersheds that have been degraded. In addition, for second-growth watersheds that are most appropriate for continued timber management, stewardship contracting can enhance the quality and productivity of those stands for the yield of wood products and energy (through utilization of wood waste products, as long as mature trees are not harvested for energy). An opportunity exists in BC for more local employment and revenue through local wood processing: most of the trees cut on BC's north and central coast and Haida Gwaii are milled elsewhere.

The region is currently a major exporter of Pacific salmon (Crone and Mehrkens, this volume, chapter 5). The fishery has been well managed, and it is certified as sustainable by the Marine Stewardship Council. Given that most of the world's fisheries are already over-exploited while demand for marine protein is certain to increase, a major export fishery for "wild Alaska salmon" from the region is likely to be viable in the foreseeable future. According to Alaska Department of Fish and Game 2007 commercial harvest data, 58.6 million salmon were harvested in southeast Alaska for an estimated ex-vessel value of $113,359,000. This activity is less important on the BC side of the border: according to Fisheries and Oceans Canada 2007 commercial harvest data, 7.8 million salmon were harvested on BC's north and central coasts and Haida Gwaii. Clearly, the coastal North Pacific rainforest plays a major role in providing significant spawning and rearing habitat for Pacific salmon.

Currently substantial economic wealth is generated by general tourism, recreation, wildlife viewing, and sport fishing. If the region's natural resources are well managed, the economic yield from these activities should increase. A new economic opportunity created by global markets is payment for carbon sequestration, for which the region has great potential. In combination, the above opportunities and others may provide forest managers and local communities with an integrated forest economy scaled appropriately for long-term economic and environmental sustainability.

The 2009 land-use plan for BC's central and north coasts recognized the need to diversify local economies beyond reliance on extraction of natural resources. Accordingly, two funds were established. The permanent Coast Conservation Endowment Fund received $60 million from private donors (largely environmental NGOs); each year, interest from the fund is used locally to protect and manage ecosystems. The Coast Economic Development Fund, intended to last five to seven years, received $60 million from the Canadian and BC governments; grants from this fund support sustainable First Nations businesses and economic development (Smith and Sterritt 2007).

SUMMARY AND CONCLUSIONS

The North Pacific temperate rainforest of north coastal British Columbia, Haida Gwaii, and southeast Alaska is the largest coastal temperate old-growth rainforest ecosystem in the world. The Tongass National Forest is both the largest US national forest and also the only one that spreads across a large island archipelago, with the endemism and genetic distinctiveness typical of island ecosystems worldwide. This island nature and endemism is also characteristic of north coastal British Columbia and particularly Haida Gwaii.

This coastal rainforest still features intact food webs with nearly all post-Pleistocene trophic levels, including large predators. It is naturally fragmented by a globally significant marine ecosystem, whose fjords produce a large and complex land–sea interface. The ecosystem features an elevation gradient from lowland valley old-growth forest to alpine rock and ice within short distances. The landscape includes a variety of ecosystem types in a complex spatial pattern, including large undeveloped and unroaded areas. Fires are rare.

Despite undeveloped watersheds and roadless areas, substantial change has occurred in this region during the last century. Since the mid-twentieth century, rates of human-related change have been many times greater than rates caused by natural disturbance. Thus the basic ecological character of this rainforest ecosystem has been modified. Age-class distribution has changed, and there has been disproportionate harvest of specific old-growth forest types, especially nonrandom removal of the biggest trees in highly productive, large-tree stands in valley bottoms and lower hillside slopes. Greater than 13,000 km of roads now fragment the landscape (8,000 km in southeast Alaska and 5,700 km on BC's north coast and Haida Gwaii). These changes pose challenges for future management of the region's natural resources.

We close with a list of conclusions and recommendations that emerge from our analyses and deliberations.

1. Indigenous people have lived in this region and used its natural resources for thousands of years (Crone and Mehrkens, this volume, chapter 5). Native communities need to be more fully involved in discussions and decisions regarding the future of the region. For BC's central and north coasts and Haida Gwaii, the recent regional land use plans were established jointly by First Nations and the provincial government in a government-to-government relationship.

2. The conservation vision of achieving and maintaining the ecological integrity of the coastal North Pacific temperate rainforest should be based on clear, measurable, well-defined, multiscale metrics that will enable us to measure progress toward identified goals and objectives.

3. Connectivity in this coastal rainforest is naturally limited by water barriers between islands, natural physiographic pinch points, and extensive nonforest habitats. These barriers to dispersal have resulted in considerable endemism and genetic distinctness of many island populations (Cook and MacDonald, this volume, chapter 2). Overlaying this natural pattern is a network of logging roads and timber harvest units that further fragment the landscape (Person and Brinkman, this volume, chapter 6). Greater attention to issues of connectivity and endemism would strengthen conservation within this temperate rainforest.

4. Without baseline information and archival collections, management interventions designed to preserve a region's biological diversity have the potential to be poorly targeted and, thus, ineffective. A proper taxonomic inventory, using modern genetic techniques, is essential for

developing a comprehensive conservation strategy for the region (Cook and MacDonald, this volume, chapter 2).

5. Deliberate introduction of species to islands and landscapes currently outside their range should be prohibited and steps should be taken to avoid inadvertent introductions.

6. Because clear-cutting fundamentally alters the structure and composition of rare and valuable old-growth forest stands (Alaback *et al.*, this volume, chapter 4; Person and Brinkman, this volume, chapter 6) transition from harvesting old growth to harvesting second-growth stands is desirable. Where old-growth harvest occurs, it should be designed to approximate natural disturbance patterns in terms of frequency, intensity, spatial scale, and location. Evidence from retrospective studies of selective harvest, as well as research and demonstration sites on variable retention harvest, show that significant ecological benefits may be achieved with those techniques (Beese, this volume, chapter 9).

7. Any future harvest of old growth within the region (preferably through selective or variable retention harvest), should be accompanied by a requirement or incentive for local value-added processing. This would increase local opportunities and benefits for small, economically sustainable forestry operations—a better option than exporting valuable old-growth logs for manufacturing outside the region.

8. Intact watersheds are areas of the landscape with strong internal and external connections among ecosystem processes. Therefore, watersheds have a greater likelihood of maintaining long-term ecological integrity and resilience without significant ongoing management investment than do other conservation strategies (Lertzman and Mac-Kinnon, this volume, chapter 8). Because primary watersheds—those with their terminus in salt water—are likely to be a key in capturing ecological and genetic diversity and trophic-level interactions among terrestrial and marine ecosystems, these watersheds represent important conservation and restoration targets for this rainforest ecosystem.

9. The remaining undeveloped and minimally developed watersheds within the coastal North Pacific temperate rainforest region should be inventoried and evaluated in terms of their geographic, geomorphic, and ecological characteristics and their conservation values (Lertzman and MacKinnon, this volume, chapter 8). We recommend a moratorium on future development of such watersheds to maintain future

conservation options pending a comprehensive evaluation of conservation goals and management alternatives.

10. Ecological restoration, an important goal for this temperate rainforest ecosystem, should focus on incorporating riparian and upland restoration projects that help restore the composition, structure, and functioning of the original old-growth forest habitat. A representative sample of previously developed watersheds—historically some of the most productive lands—should be selected for ecological restoration. Riparian and in-stream restoration should receive high priority.

11. Scientific benchmarks should be established for long-term ecological research and monitoring in selected watershed reserves within representative areas of the coastal North Pacific temperate rainforest. Such benchmarks will be important for evaluating ecological effects of climate change, as well as for establishing guidelines for restoration.

12. In addition to conservation reserves, conservation measures should be developed and implemented in the surrounding matrix of developed lands. Particular emphasis should be placed on maintaining riparian buffers and productive salmon spawning and rearing habitat throughout the region.

13. More emphasis should be placed on interdisciplinary and transboundary collaboration and coordination of long-term research and monitoring programs relative to forestry, forest ecology, fish and wildlife management, community economics, and climate change. Interdisciplinary collaboration will be particularly important for integrating knowledge of the marine, aquatic, and terrestrial interfaces, as well as for assessing future effects of climate change (Edwards *et al.*, this volume, chapter 3). Additional data and analyses should address the role of the coastal Pacific Northwest rainforest in terms of carbon storage, its relationship to climate change, and the opportunity for providing local economic benefits from carbon credits. Better understanding of how individual species may respond to changes in vegetation and environmental conditions affected by climate change would provide an improved basis for planning habitat connections to ensure population persistence. Conservation biology and related disciplines provide new conceptual and technical tools for gaining useful knowledge (Marcot, this volume, chapter 7). Understanding effects of climate change will also help us determine what to monitor to predict and understand

potential negative trends affecting habitats, species, and ecosystem functionality.

14. Finally, renewed emphasis on local environmental education (K–12) is essential for generating the informed cadre of future citizens who will care about, understand, and therefore support the broad vision for sustainable development of the region.

Although these comments and suggestions are derived from work in the North Pacific rainforest of north coastal British Columbia and southeast Alaska, the general principles they embody are widely applicable. Archival collections and experts to curate and interpret them are needed everywhere. Unfortunately they are generally in short supply. Everywhere we need to assess what can and cannot be restored and determine the costs of restoration efforts or their absence. Getting the scale right, thinking clearly about connectivity, distribution of reserves, management of matrix lands, and assessing transregional connections need to be components of natural resource management everywhere. The quality of the lives of local people cannot be ignored, and we must not neglect the youth who will be a region's future leaders.

The lack of knowledge about nature and, hence, lack of appreciation of nature that accompanies growing up in a modern technological society bodes ill for efforts to preserve Earth's biodiversity. What can the loss of the passenger pigeon, once the most abundant bird in North America, mean to a child who has never seen a wren? Indirect experiences of nature do not generate the emotional involvement with living organisms that is necessary to motivate people to care about biodiversity and devote their time and money to help preserve it.

On the north coast of British Columbia and in southeast Alaska, we have an unprecedented opportunity to impart to people an understanding and appreciation of the beauty and wonder of the region's ecosystems. The motivation engendered by that knowledge should also increase broad public support to develop and implement conservation and management plans for the region; these plans will restore and maintain vibrant ecosystems that can provide the full array of goods and services upon which local people depend and others value. There are few regions on Earth where this opportunity still exists. This coastal rainforest has many intact watersheds without roads or significant development, and it retains the strong interactions between its terrestrial, aquatic, and marine ecosystems. The North

Pacific temperate rainforest can also become a place where the value of long-term monitoring of the effects of climate change and resource development activities on naturally functioning ecosystems can be demonstrated. In this way, what we do in this region could serve as models that stimulate creative human activities here and elsewhere on Earth.

ACKNOWLEDGMENTS

The authors would like to acknowledge N. Walker for graphics support and D. DellaSala, M. Kirchhoff, B. Noon, M. Smith, and one anonymous reviewer for their valuable review and editorial suggestions.

LITERATURE CITED

Agee, J. K. 1993. *Fire ecology of Pacific Northwest forests*. Washington, DC: Island Press.

Aguilar, A., G. Roemer, S. Debenham, M. Binns, D. Garcelon, and R. K. Wayne. 2004. High MHC diversity maintained by balancing selection in an otherwise genetically monomorphic mammal. *Proceedings of the National Academy of Sciences* 101:3490–3494.

Ainslie, B., and P. L. Jackson. 2010. Downscaling and bias correcting a cold season precipitation climatology over coastal southern British Columbia using the Regional Atmospheric Modeling System (RAMS). *Journal of Applied Meteorology and Climatology* 49:937–953.

Aitken, S. N., S. Yeaman, J. A. Holliday, T. Wang, and S. Curtis-McLane. 2008. Adaptation, migration or extirpation: climate change outcomes for tree populations. *Evolutionary Applications* 1:95–111.

Alaback, P. B. 1982. Dynamics of understory biomass in Sitka spruce–western hemlock forests of southeast Alaska. *Ecology* 63:1932–1948.

———. 1984. A comparison of old-growth forest structure in the western hemlock–Sitka spruce forests of southeast Alaska. In *Fish and wildlife relationships in old-growth forests*, edited by W. R. Meehan, T. R. J. Merrell, and T. A. Hanley, 219–226. Morehead City, NC: American Institute of Fishery Research Biologists.

———. 1991. Comparative ecology of temperate rainforests of the Americas along analogous climatic gradients. *Revista Chilena Historia Natural* 64:399–412.

———. 1996. Biodiversity patterns in relation to climate in the temperate rainforests of North America. In *High-latitude rainforests of the west coast of the Americas: Climate, hydrology, ecology, and conservation*, edited by R. Lawford, P. Alaback, and E. R. Fuentes, 105–133. Ecological Studies, vol. 116. Berlin: Springer-Verlag.

Alaback, P. B., and G. P. Juday. 1989. Structure and composition of low elevation old-growth forests in research natural areas of southeast Alaska. *Natural Areas Journal* 9:27–39.

Alaback, P. B., and M. McClellan. 1993. Effects of global warming on managed coastal ecosystems of western North America. In *Earth system responses to global change: Contrasts between North and South America*, edited by H. A. Mooney, E. Fuentes, and B. I. Kronberg , 299–327. San Diego, CA: Academic Press.

Alaska Department of Fish and Game. 2010. *Survivorship of Sitka black-tailed deer fawns in Southeast Alaska.* Federal Aid Annual Progress Report Grant W-33–8, Project 2.14. Juneau, AK.

———. 2011. *Survivorship of Sitka black-tailed deer fawns in Southeast Alaska.* Federal Aid Annual Progress Report Grant W-33–9, Project 2.14. Juneau, AK.

———. 2012. *Survivorship of Sitka black-tailed deer fawns in Southeast Alaska.* Federal Aid Annual Progress Report Grant W-33–10, Project 2.14. Juneau, AK.

Alaska Department of Fish and Game, Division of Sport Fish. 2009a. *Statewide harvest survey reports, 1977–2004.* http://www.sf.adfg.state.ak.us/statewide/participationandharvest/SWHS_History.cfm.

———. 2009b. *Southeast Alaska sport fish harvest by species, 1996–2007.* http://www.sf.adfg.state.ak.us/statewide/participationandharvest/main.cfm.

Alaska Department of Labor and Workforce Development. 2002. Employment database. Unpublished data, Crone private collection.

———. 2009. Current employment statistics. http://laborstats.alaska.gov.

Alaska Department of Natural Resources. 1977. *General development plan for Totem Bight State Historic Park.* Anchorage, AK: Division of Parks.

———. 2003. *Forest resources and practices act.* Juneau, AK: Division of Forestry.

———. 2008. *Briefing paper: Alaska wood energy development task group.* Anchorage, AK: Office of the Commissioner and Division of Forestry. May 20, 2008.

Alaska Energy Authority and Renewable Energy Alaska Project. 2007. *Renewable energy atlas of Alaska: A guide to Alaska's clean, local, and inexhaustible energy resources.* Anchorage, AK: Alaska Energy Authority and Renewable Energy Alaska Project.

Alaska National Interest Lands Conservation Act of 1980. Public Law 96–487, 94 Stat. 2371–2251.

Alaska Native Claims Settlement Act of 1971. Public Law 92–203, 43 *US Code* 1601 et seq.

Albert, D., and J. Schoen. 2007a. A conservation assessment for the coastal forests and mountains ecoregion of southeastern Alaska and the Tongass National Forest. In *The coastal forests and mountains ecoregion of southeastern Alaska and the Tongass National Forest: A conservation assessment and resource synthesis*, edited by J. Schoen and E. Dovichin, chapter 2. Anchorage, AK: Audubon Alaska and The Nature Conservancy. http://www.conserveonline.org/workspaces/akcfm.

——. 2007b. A comparison of relative biological value, habitat vulnerability, and cumulative ecological risk among biogeographic provinces in southeastern Alaska. In *The coastal forests and mountains ecoregion of southeastern Alaska and the Tongass National Forest: A conservation assessment and resource synthesis*, edited by J. Schoen and E. Dovichin, chapter 3. Anchorage, AK: Audubon Alaska and The Nature Conservancy. http://www.conserveonline.org/workspaces/akcfm.

Albert, D., L. Baker, S. Howell, K. V. Koski, and R. Bosworth. 2008. *A framework for setting watershed-scale priorities for forest and freshwater restoration on Prince of Wales Island*. Juneau, AK: The Nature Conservancy Alaska Field Office.

Alexander, S. J., E. B. Henderson, and R. Coleman. 2010. *Economic analysis of southeast Alaska: Envisioning a sustainable economy with thriving communities*. R10-MB-725. Juneau, AK: USDA Forest Service, Alaska Region.

Allan, J. D. 2004. Landscapes and riverscapes: the influence of land use on stream ecosystems. *Annual Review of Ecology and Systematics* 35:257–284.

Allen, J. R., L. E. Mcinenly, E. H. Merrill, and M. S. Boyce. 2008. Using resource selection functions to improve estimation of elk population numbers. *Journal of Wildlife Management* 72:1798–1804.

Allendorf, F. W., and R. F. Leary. 1988. Conservation and distribution of genetic variation in a polytypic species, the cutthroat trout. *Conservation Biology* 2:170–184.

All Forest Solutions Inc. (AFSI). 2006. *Descriptive overview of the coast forest industry: Report to Port Alberni Port Authority*. On file with Port Alberni Port Authority, 2750 Harbour Rd., Port Alberni, British Columbia, Canada, V9Y 7X2.

Anderson, C. B., G. M. Pastur, M. V. Lencinas, P. K. Wallem, M. C. Moorman, and A. D. Rosemond. 2009. Do introduced North American beavers *Castor canadensis* engineer differently in southern South America? An overview with implications for restoration. *Mammal Review* 39:33–52.

Arctander, J. W. 1909. *The apostle of Alaska: The story of William Duncan of Metlakahtla*. New York: Fleming H. Revell Company.

Armstrong, R. H. 1974. Migration of anadromous Dolly Varden trout (*Salvelinus malma*) in southeastern Alaska. *Journal of Fisheries Research Board of Canada* 31:435–444.

Arnott, J. T., and W. J. Beese. 1997. Alternatives to clearcutting in BC coastal montane forests. *Forestry Chronicle* 73:670–678.

Arroyo, M. T. K., M. Riveros, A. Peñaloza, L. Cavieres, and A. M. Faggi. 1996. Phytogeographic relationships and regional richness patterns of the cool temperate rainforest flora of southern South America. In *High-latitude rainforests of the west coast of the Americas: Climate, hydrology, ecology, and conservation*, edited by R. Lawford, P. Alaback, and E. R. Fuentes. Ecological Studies, vol. 116. Berlin: Springer-Verlag.

Arsenault, A. 1995. Pattern and process in old growth temperate rainforest of southern British Columbia. PhD Dissertation, University of British Columbia, Vancouver.

Atkinson, K. T., and D. W. Janz. 1994. *Effect of wolf control on black-tailed deer in the Nimpkish Valley on Vancouver Island*. Wildlife Bulletin B-73. Nanaimo, BC: British Columbia Ministry of Environment, Lands, and Parks.

Aubrey, K. B., C. B. Halpern, and D. A. Maguire. 2004. Ecological effects of variable-retention harvests in the northwestern United States: the DEMO study. *Forest Snow Landscape Research* 78:119–137.

Baichtal, J. F., and R. J. Carlson. 2010. Development of a model to predict the location of Early-Holocene habitation sites along the western coast of Prince of Wales Island and the Outer Islands, Southeast Alaska. *Current Research in the Pleistocene* 27:64–67.

Baichtal, J. F., R. J. Carlson, and S. J. Crockford. 2008. Paleogeography of the Late Pleistocene and Quaternary coastlines of southeast Alaska and their potential archaeological significance. Abstract, Ninth International Symposium, Sitka, AK, 29 April–2 May, 2008. Accessed March 2011. http://geohab.org/sitka.html.

Baichtal, J. F., and D. N. Swanston. 1996. *Karst landscapes and associated resources: A resource assessment*. General Technical Report PNW-GTR-383. Portland, OR: USDA Forest Service.

Baker T. T., A. C. Wertheimer, R. D. Burkett, R. Dunlap, D. M. Eggers, E. I. Fritts, A. J. Gharrett, R. A. Holmes, and R. L. Wilmot. 1996. Status of Pacific salmon and steelhead escapements in southeastern Alaska. Special issue, *Fisheries* 21:6–18.

Baker, W. L. 1992. The landscape ecology of large disturbances in the design and management of nature reserves. *Landscape Ecology* 7:181–194.

Ballard, W. B., D. Lutz, T. W. Keegan, L. H. Carpenter, and J. C. deVos Jr. 2001. Deer-predator relationships: a review of recent North American studies with emphasis on mule and black-tailed deer. *Wildlife Society Bulletin* 29:99–115.

Balmford, A., L. Bennun, B. ten Brink, D. Cooper, I. M. Côté, P. Crane, A. Dobson, *et al.* 2005. The convention on biological diversity's 2010 target. *Science* 307 (5707): 212 - 213.

Bancroft, B., and K. Zielke. 2004. *Implementation monitoring: five-year summary of variable retention.* Contract report to Weyerhaeuser, BC Coastal Timberlands. West Vancouver, BC: Symmetree Consulting Group.

Banner, A., and P. LePage. 2008. Long-term recovery of vegetation communities after harvesting in the coastal temperate rainforests of northern British Columbia. *Canadian Journal of Forest Research* 38:3098–3111.

Banner, A., P. LePage, J. Moran, and A. de Groot. 2005. *The HyP3 Project: pattern, process, and productivity in hypermaritime forests of coastal British Columbia—a synthesis of 7-year results.* Spec. Rep. 10. Victoria, BC: BC Ministry of Forests Research Branch. Accessed May 20, 2010. http://www.for.gov.bc.ca/hfd/pubs/Docs/Srs/Srs10.htm.

Banner, A., J. Pojar, and G. E. Rouse. 1983. Postglacial paleoecology and successional relationships of a bog woodland near Prince Rupert, BC. *Canadian Journal of Forest Research* 13:938–947.

Baron, J. S., N. L. Poff, P. L. Angermeier, C. N. Dahm, P. H. Gleick, N. G. Hairston Jr., R. B. Jackson, C. A. Johnston, B. D. Richter, and A. D. Steinman. 2002. Meeting ecological and societal needs for freshwater. *Ecological Applications* 12:1247–1260.

Barrie, J. V., K. W. Conway, H. Josenhans, J. J. Clague, R. W. Mathewes, and D.W. Fedje. 2005. Late quaternary geology of Haida Gwaii and surrounding marine areas. In *Haida Gwaii: Human history and environment from the time of the loon to the time of the iron people,* edited by D. W. Fedje and R.W. Mathewes, 7–20.Vancouver: UBC Press.

Barry, P. D., and D. A. Tallmon. 2010. Genetic differentiation of a subspecies of spruce grouse (*Falcipennis canadensis*) in an endemism hotspot. *The Auk* 127:617–625.

Bartholow J. 2000. Estimating cumulative effects of clearcutting on stream temperatures. *Rivers* 7:284–297.

BC Forest Planning and Practices Regulation. 2004. BC Reg. 14/2004. Accessed May 20, 2010. http://www.bclaws.ca/EPLibraries/bclaws_new/document/ID/freeside/12_14_2004.

BC Forest and Range Practices Act. 2002. SBC, chapter 69. Accessed May 20, 2010. http://www.bclaws.ca/EPLibraries/bclaws_new/document/ID/freeside/00_02069_01#part1.

BC Integrated Land Management Bureau. 2000. *Vancouver Island summary land use plan.* Province of British Columbia. Accessed May 20, 2010. http://archive.ilmb.gov.bc.ca/slrp/lrmp/nanaimo/vancouver_island/plan/summary_lup/toc.htm.

———. 2007. *Haida Gwaii strategic land use agreement.* Accessed April 29, 2010. http://www.ilmb.gov.bc.ca/slrp/lrmp/nanaimo/haidagwaii/index.html.

———. 2009. *Central and north coast EBM implementation.* Accessed April 29, 2010. http://archive.ilmb.gov.bc.ca/slrp/lrmp/nanaimo/central_north_coast/index.html.

BC Land Use Order. 2006. BC Land Use Order for the central and north coast. Accessed October 3, 2012. http://archive.ilmb.gov.bc.ca/slrp/lrmp/nanaimo/cencoast/docs/CNC_consolidated_order.pdf.

BC Ministry of Environment. 2007. *Environmental trends in British Columbia: 2007.* Victoria, BC: BC Ministry of Environment. http://www.env.gov.bc.ca/soe/.

BC Ministry of Forests. 1996. *Habitat and predator concerns. Report no. 4: Coastal black-tailed deer study.* Victoria, BC: Ministry of Forests, Forest Science Program.

BC Ministry of Forests and Range. 2006a. *The state of British Columbia's forests, 2006.* Victoria, BC: Ministry of Forests and Range. http:// www.for.gov.bc.ca/hfp/sof/.

———. 2006b. *British Columbia forest resource reporting from the National Forest Inventory Database.* Victoria, BC: Ministry of Forests and Range, Forest Analysis and Inventory Branch.

———. 2010. Annual reports. Accessed April 8, 2011. http://www.for.gov.bc.ca/mof/annualreports.htm.

BC Operational Planning Regulations. 1999. Forest Practices Code of British Columbia Act. SBC, chapter 41.

Beck Group. 2009. *Transitioning to young growth: Prince of Wales Island, south-east Alaska.* Report prepared for The Nature Conservancy. Juneau, AK: Beck Group.

Beese, W. J. 2001. Windthrow monitoring of alternative silvicultural systems in montane coastal forests. In *Windthrow assessment and management in British Columbia: Proceedings of the Windthrow Researchers Workshop, Richmond, BC, January 31–February 1, 2001*, compiled by S. J. Mitchell and J. Rodney, 2–11. Accessed April 2011. http://www.for.gov.bc.ca/HFD/library/documents/windthrow.pdf.

Beese, W. J., B. G. Dunsworth, and N. J. Smith. 2005. Variable retention adaptive management experiments: testing new approaches for managing British Columbia's coastal forests. In *Balancing ecosystems values: innovative experiments for sustainable forestry*, Gen. Tech. Rept. PNW-635, edited by C. E. Peterson and D. A. Maguire, 55–64. Portland, OR: USDA Forest Service PNW Research Station.

Beese, W. J., B. G. Dunsworth, K. Zielke, and B. Bancroft. 2003. Maintaining attributes of old-growth forests in coastal BC through variable retention. *Forestry Chronicle* 79: 570–578.

Beier, C. 2008. Influence of political opposition and compromise on conservation outcomes in the Tongass National Forest, Alaska. *Conservation Biology* 22:1485–1496.

Beier, P., and B. Brost. 2010. Use of land facets to plan for climate change: Conserving the arenas, not the actors. *Conservation Biology* 24:701–710.

Belant, J. L., B. Griffith, Y. Zhang, E. H. Follmann, and L. G. Adams. 2010. Population-level resource selection by sympatric brown and American black bears in Alaska. *Polar Biology* 33:31–40.

Belovsky, G.E. 1987. Extinction models and mammalian persistence. In *Viable populations for conservation*, edited by M. E. Soulé, 35–37. Cambridge: Cambridge University Press. Benda, L., N. L. Poff, D. Miller, T. Dunne, G. Reeves, G. Pess, and M. Pollock. 2004. The network dynamics hypothesis: how channel networks structure riverine habitats. *BioScience* 54:413–427.

Bengtsson, J., P. Angelstam, T. Elmqvist, U. Emanuelsson, C. Folke, M. Ihse, F. Moberg, and M. Nyström. 2003. Reserves, resilience and dynamic landscapes. *Ambio* 32:389–396.

Bickford, D., D. J. Lohman, N. S. Sodhi, *et al.* 2007. Cryptic species as a window on diversity and conservation. *Trends in Ecology and Evolution* 22:148–155.

Bidlack, A. L., and J. A. Cook. 2001. Reduced genetic variation in insular northern flying squirrels (*Glaucomys sabrinus*) along the North Pacific coast. *Animal Conservation* 4:283–290.

———. 2002. A nuclear perspective on endemism in northern flying squirrels (*Glaucomys sabrinus*) of the Alexander Archipelago, Alaska. *Conservation Genetics* 3:247–259.

Bissonette, J. A., and I. Storch, editors. 2002. *Landscape ecology and resource management: linking theory with practice.* Washington, DC: Island Press.

Blouin, M. S., and E. F. Connor. 1985. Is there a best shape for nature reserves? *Biological Conservation* 32:277–288.

Bonn, A., and K. J. Gaston. 2005. Capturing biodiversity: selecting priority areas for conservation using different criteria. *Biodiversity and Conservation* 14:1083–1100.

Bormann, B. T., H. Spaltenstein, M. H. McClellan, F. C. Ugolini, J. K. Cromack, and S. M. Nay. 1995. Rapid soil development after windthrow disturbance in pristine forests. *Journal of Ecology* 83:747–756.

Both, C., S. Bouwhuis, C. M. Lessells, and M. E. Visser. 2006. Climate change and population declines in a long-distance migratory bird. *Nature* 441:81–83.

Bowyer, R. T., D. K. Person, and B. M. Pierce. 2005. Detecting top-down versus bottom-up regulation of ungulates by large carnivores: implications for conservation of biodiversity. In *Large carnivores and the conservation of biodiversity*, edited by J. C. Ray, K. H. Redford, R. S. Steneck, and J. Berger, 342–361. Covelo, CA: Island Press.

Boyd, Philip W., *et al.* 2004. The decline and fate of an iron-induced subarctic phytoplankton bloom. *Nature* 428:549–553.

Brackley, A. M., and L. K. Crone. 2009. *Estimating sawmill processing capacity for Tongass timber: 2005 and 2006 update.* Res. Note. PNW-RN-553. Portland, OR: USDA Forest Service, Pacific Northwest Research Station.

Bradner, T. 2007. Hydro's bad image gets boost in Southeast. *Alaska Journal of Commerce*, September 2, 2007. http://www.alaskajournal.com/stories/090207/hom_20070902010.shtml.

Brinkman, T. J. 2007. *Prince of Wales Island deer hunter survey: summary report.* Ketchikan, AK: Alaska Department of Fish and Game.

———. 2009. Understanding key components in a deer hunting system to enhance resilience. PhD Dissertation, University of Alaska, Fairbanks.

Brinkman, T. J., F. S. Chapin III, G. P. Kofinas, and D. K. Person. 2009. Linking hunter knowledge with forest change to understand changing deer harvest opportunities in intensively logged landscapes. *Ecology and Society* 14:36.

Brinkman, T. J., G. P. Kofinas, F. S. Chapin III, and D. K. Person. 2007. Influence of hunter adaptability on resilience of subsistence hunting systems. *Journal of Ecological Anthropology* 11:58–66.

Brinkman, T. J., D. K. Person, F. S. Chapin III, W. Smith, and K. J. Hundertmark. 2011. Estimating abundance of Sitka black-tailed deer using DNA from fecal pellets. *Journal of Wildlife Management* 74: in press.

Brinson, M. M. 1993. *A hydrogeomorphic classification for wetlands*. Technical Report WRP-DE-4. , Vicksburg, MS: US Army Engineers Waterways Experiment Station.

Brook, B. W., L. W. Traill, and C. J. A. Bradshaw. 2006. Minimum viable population size and global extinction risk are unrelated. *Ecology Letters* 9:375–382.

Brooks, D. R. 2004. Reticulations in historical biogeography: The triumph of time over space in evolution. In *Frontiers of biogeography: New directions in the geography of nature*, edited by M. V. Lomolino and L. R. Heaney, editors. Sunderland, MA: Sinauer Associates.

Brooks, T. M., G. A. B. da Fonseca, and A. S. L. Rodrigues. 2004. Protected areas and species. *Conservation Biology* 18:616–618.

Brosius, J. P., and D. Russell. 2003. Conservation from above: an anthropological perspective on transboundary protected areas and ecoregional planning. *Journal of Sustainable Forestry* 17:39–66.

Brown, J. H. 1971. Mammals on mountaintops: Non-equilibrium insular biogeography. *American Naturalist* 105:467–478.

Brown, J. H., and A. Kodric-Brown. 1977. Turnover rates in insular biogeography: Effects of immigration on extinction. *Ecology* 58:445–449.

Bryant, A. 2002. The Vancouver Island marmot: Year end report for 2002. Accessed January 9, 2009. http//dsp-psd.pwgsc.gc.ca/collection/cw69–14 –109–2002E.pdf.

Bryant, A. A., and R. E. Page. 2005. Timing and causes of mortality in the endangered Vancouver Island marmot (*Marmota vancouverensis*). *Canadian Journal of Zoology* 83:674–682.

Bryant, J. P., F. S. Chapin III, and D. R. Klein. 1983. Carbon/nutrient balance of boreal plants in relation to vertebrate herbivory. *Oikos* 40:357–368.

Bryant, M. D. 2009. Global climate change and potential effects on Pacific salmonids in freshwater ecosystems of southeast Alaska. *Climatic Change* 95:169–193.

Bryant, M. D., and F. H. Everest. 1998. Management and condition of watersheds in southeast Alaska: The persistence of anadromous salmon. *Northwest Science* 72:249–267.

Bryant, M. D., and M. D. Lukey. 2004. Movement of Dolly Varden and cutthroat trout in high gradient headwater streams with implications for fish passage standards. Juneau, AK: USDA Forest Service Progress Report, PNW.

Bryant, M. D., N. D. Zymonas, and B. E. Wright. 2004. Salmonids on the fringe: Abundance, species composition, and habitat use of salmonids in high-gradient headwater streams, southeast Alaska. *Transactions of the American Fisheries Society* 133:1529–1538.

Bschor, D. E. 2007. Limited interstate shipments of unprocessed Sitka spruce and western hemlock timber. Memo to the Forest Supervisor, Tongass National Forest, March 14. http://www.fs.fed.us/r10/ro/policyreports/for _mgmt/ship_timber/FS_correspondence3_13.doc.

Bunnell, F. L. 2005. Refining conservation priorities in British Columbia. Final Technical Report LOI Y051023. Forest Sciences Program. Accessed March 3, 2011. http://www.for.gov.bc.ca/hfd/library/FIA/2005/FIA2005 MR119.pdf.

Bunnell, F. L., R. W. Campbell, and K. A. Squires. 2004. Conservation priorities for peripheral species: The example of British Columbia. *Canadian Journal of Forest Research* 34:2240–2247.

———. 2005. Assessing the need for species conservation action in British Columbia. *BC Journal of Ecosystems and Management* 6:29–37.

Bunnell, F. L. and B. G. Dunsworth. 2002. Making adaptive management for biodiversity work—the example of Weyerhaeuser in coastal British Columbia. *Forestry Chronicle* 80:37–43.

———. 2009. Forestry and biodiversity: Learning how to sustain biodiversity in managed forests. Vancouver: UBC Press.

Bunnell, F. L., B. G. Dunsworth, D. Huggard, and L. L. Kremsater. 2003. Learning to sustain biological diversity on Weyerhaeuser's coastal tenure. Contract report to Weyerhaeuser, BC Coastal Timberlands. Vancouver, BC: UBC Centre for Applied Conservation Research.

Bunnell, F. L., and L. L. Kremsater. 1991. Sustaining wildlife in managed forests. *Northwest Environmental Journal* 6:243–269.

Bunnell, F. L., L. L. Kremsater, and E. Wind. 1999. Managing to sustain vertebrate diversity in forests of the Pacific Northwest: Relationships within stands. *Environmental Review* 7:97–146.

Burles, D. W., A. G. Edie, and P. M. Bartier. 2004. *Native land mammals and amphibian of Haida Gwaii with management implications for Gwaii Haanas National Park Reserve and Haida Heritage Site.* Technical Reports in Ecosystem Science no. 40. Halifax, NS: Parks Canada.

Byun, S. A., B. F. Koop, and T. E. Reimchen. 1999. Coastal refugia and postglacial colonization routes: A reply to Demboski, Stone, and Cook. *Evolution* 53:2013–2015.

Cabeza, M., and A. Moilanen. 2001. Design of reserve networks and the persistence of biodiversity. *Trends in Ecology and Evolution* 16:242–248.

Calder, J. A., and R. L. Taylor. 1968. Flora of the Queen Charlotte Islands. Part 1, Systematics of vascular plants. Research branch, Canada Department of Agriculture Monograph no. 4. Ottawa: Duhamel.

Campbell, C. R. 1989. A study of matrilineal descent from the perspective of the Tlingit NexA'di Eagles. *ARTIC* 42(2): 119–127.

Campbell, S., W. S. van Hees, and B. Mead. 2004. *Southeast Alaska forests: inventory highlights.* Gen. Tech. Rep. PNW-GTR-609. Portland, OR: USDA Forest Service, Pacific Northwest Research Station.

Cannings, R. J. 1994. Endangered terrestrial and freshwater invertebrates in British Columbia. In *Biodiversity in British Columbia: Our changing environment,* edited by L. E. Harding and E. McCullum, 47–51. Ottawa: Canadian Wildlife Service.

———. 1998. The birds of British Columbia—a taxonomic catalogue. Wildlife Bulletin No. B-86. Victoria, BC: British Columbia Ministry of the Environment, Lands and Parks, Wildlife Branch.

Caouette, J., and E. DeGayner. 2005. Predictive mapping for tree size and densities in southeast Alaska. *Landscape and Urban Planning* 72:49–63.

Cardini, A., R. W. Thorington, and P. D. Polley. 2007. Evolutionary acceleration in the most endangered mammal of Canada: Speciation and divergence in the Vancouver Island marmot (Rodentia, Sciuridae). *Journal of Evolutionary Biology* 2007:1833–1846.

Carey, A. B. 2001. Experimental manipulation of spatial heterogeneity in Douglas-fir forests: Effects on squirrels. *Forest Ecology and Management* 152:13–30.

Carignan, R., P. D'Arcy, and S. Lamontagne. 2000. Comparative impacts of fire and forest harvesting on water quality in boreal shield lakes. *Canadian Journal of Fisheries and Aquatic Sciences* 57 (Supplement 2): 105–117.

Carrlee, E. 2009. Archeological basketry and PEG in Alaska. In *Fiber/Perishable Interest Group Newsletter,* Summer 2009:1–2.http://www.saa.org/Portals/O/SAA/FPIG2009SummerNewsletter.

Carrara, P. E., T. A. Ager, and J. F. Baichtal. 2007. Possible refugia on the Alexander Archipelago of southeastern Alaska during the late Wisconsin glaciations. *Canadian Journal of Earth Sciences* 44:229–244.

Carrara, P. E., T. A. Ager, J. F. Baichtal, and D. P. VanSistine. 2003. Map of glacial limits and possible refugia in the southern Alexander Archipelago, Alaska, during the Late Wisconsin Glaciation. Miscellaneous Field Studies Map MF-2424:1–13 (+ map). Denver, CO: USDI, US Geological Survey.

Carroll, C., R. F. Noss, P. C. Paquet, and N. H. Schumaker. 2003. Use of population viability analysis and reserve selection algorithms in regional conservation plans. *Ecological Applications* 13:1773–1789.

Carstensen, R. 2007. Terrestrial habitats of southeast Alaska. In *A conservation assessment and resource synthesis for the coastal forests and mountains ecoregion in southeast Alaska and the Tongass National Forest*, edited by J. W. Schoen and E. Dovichin, chapter 5. Anchorage, AK: Audubon Alaska and The Nature Conservancy. http://www.conserveonline.org/workspaces/akcfm.

Carter, C. G., D. F. Houlihan, and I. D. Mccarthy. 1992. Feed utilization efficiencies of Atlantic salmon (*Salmo salar* L.) parr: Effect of a single supplementary enzyme. *Comparative Biochemistry and Physiology* 101:369–374.

Cederholm, C. J., M. D. Kunze, T. Murota, and A. Sibatani. 1999. Pacific salmon carcasses: essential contributions of nutrients and energy for aquatic and terrestrial ecosystems. *Fisheries* 24:6–15.

Cederholm, C. J., D. H. Johnson, R. E. Bilby, L. G. Dominguez, A. M. Garrett, W. H. Graeber, E. L. Greda, *et al.* 2001. Pacific salmon and wildlife: Ecological contexts, relationships, and implications for management. In *Wildlife-habitat relationships in Oregon and Washington*, edited by D. H. Johnson and T. A. O'Neil, 628–685. Corvallis, OR: Oregon State University Press.

Cerveny, L. 2005. *Tourism and its effects on southeast Alaska communities and resources: Case studies from Haines, Craig, and Hoonah, Alaska*. Res. Pap. PNW-RP-566. Portland, OR: USDA Forest Service, Pacific Northwest Research Station.

Chadwick, D. H. 2007. The truth about the Tongass. *National Geographic* 212: 102–125.

Chan-McLeod, A. 2008. An experimental study of variable-retention harvest methods on forest birds: 2007–08. Contract Report to Western Forest Products. Vancouver, BC: UBC Faculty of Forestry.

Chapin, F. S. III, L. Walker, C. Fastic, and L. Sharman. 1994. Mechanisms of primary succession following deglaciation a Glacier Bay, Alaska. *Ecological Monographs* 64:149–175.

Chapman, A. D. 2005. *Uses of primary species-occurrence data, version 1.0.* Copenhagen: Global Biodiversity Information Facility. http://www.gbif.org/orc/?doc_id=1300.

Chavez, F. P., T. Takahashi, W. J. Cai, G. Friederich, B. Hales, R. Wannuinkhof, and R. A. Feely. 2007. Coastal oceans. In *The first state of the carbon cycle report (SOCCR): The North American carbon budget and implications for the global carbon cycle*. Product 2.2. Washington, DC: US Climate Change Science Program.

Chen, J., J. F. Franklin, and T. A. Spies. 1992. Vegetation responses to edge environments in old-growth Douglas-fir forests. *Ecological Applications* 2:387–396.

———. 1993. Contrasting microclimates among clearcut, edge, and interior of old-growth Douglas-fir forest. *Agricultural and Forest Meteorology* 63:219–237.

Chetkiewicz, C. L., and M. S. Boyce. 2009. Use of resource selection functions to identify conservation corridors. *Journal of Applied Ecology* 46:1036–1047.

Christensen, T., and J. Stafford. 2005. Raised beach archaeology in northern Haida Gwaii: Preliminary results from the Cohoe Creek site. In *Haida Gwaii: Human history and environment from the time of loon to the time of the iron people*, edited by D. W. Fedje and R. Mathewes, 245–273. Vancouver, BC: UBC Press.

Christian, L. E., and A. M. Brackley. 2007. Helicopter logging productivity on harvesting operations in southeast Alaska, using ecologically based silvicultural prescriptions. *Western Journal of Applied Forestry* 22:142–147.

Clague, J. J., R. W. Mathewes, and T. A. Ager. 2004. Environments of northwestern North America before the Last Glacial Maximum. In *Entering America*, edited by D. B. Madsen, 63–94. Salt Lake City, UT: University of Utah Press.

Clarke, T. E., D. B. Levin, D. H. Kavanaugh, and T. E. Reimchen. 2007. Rapid evolution in the *Nebria gregaria* group (Coleoptera: Carabidae) and the paleogeography of the Queen Charlotte Islands. *Evolution* 55:1408–1418.

Clausen, D. L., and R. F. Schroeder. 2004. Social acceptability of alternatives to clearcutting: discussion and literature review with emphasis on southeast Alaska. Gen. Tech. Rep. PNW-GTR-594. Portland, OR: USDA Forest Service, Pacific Northwest Research Station.

Coast Information Team. 2004. *Ecosystem-based management planning handbook*. http://archive.ilmb.gov.bc.ca/citbc/c-ebm-hdbk-fin-22mar04.pdf.

Cody, M. 2006. *Plants on islands*. Berkeley, CA: University of California Press.

Coeur d'Alene Mines Corporation. 2008. Kensington annual meeting PowerPoint presentation. http://dnr.alaska.gov/mlw/mining/largemine/kensington/pdf/coeur2008ppt.pdf.

———. 2012. Kensington-Alaska leading Coeur's growth in gold. http://www.coeur.com/operations/kensington—-alaska.

Cole, E., T. A. Hanley, and M. Newton. 2010. Influence of precommercial thinning on understory vegetation of young-growth Sitka spruce forests in southeastern Alaska. *Canadian Journal of Forest Research* 40:619–628.

Colt, S. 2001. The economic importance of healthy Alaska ecosystems. Anchorage, AK: Institute of Social and Economic Research, University of Alaska.

Conroy, C. J., J. R. Demboski, and J. A. Cook. 1999. Mammalian biogeography of the Alexander Archipelago of southeast Alaska: A north temperate nested fauna. *Journal of Biogeography* 26:343–352.

Conservation International. 2012. The biodiversity hotspots: Japan. http://www.conservation.org/where/priority_areas/hotspots/asia-pacific/Japan/Pages/default.aspx.

Consolidated Appropriations Resolution. 2003. Public Law 108–7, 117 *US Statutes at Large* 11 (2003).

Constantino, L. F., and D. Haley. 1987. Trends in wood quality for the British Columbia coast and the United States, Pacific Northwest, westside. *Forest Science* 34(1): 176–189.

Cook, J. A., A. L. Bidlack, C. J. Conroy, J. R. Demboski, M. A. Fleming, A. M. Runck, K. D. Stone, and S. O. MacDonald. 2001. A phylogeographic perspective on endemism in the Alexander Archipelago of the North Pacific. *Biological Conservation* 97:215–227.

Cook, J. A., N. G. Dawson, and S. O. MacDonald. 2006. Conservation of highly fragmented systems: the north temperate Alexander Archipelago. *Biological Conservation* 133:1–15.

Cook, J. A., and S. O. MacDonald. 2001. Should endemism be a focus of conservation efforts along the North Pacific coast of North America? *Biological Conservation* 97:207–213.

Costanza, R., R. d'Arge, R. de Groot, S. Farber, M. Grasso, B. Hannon, K. Limburg, *et al.* 1997. The value of the world's ecosystem services and natural capital. *Nature* 387:253–259.

Côté, P., R. Tittler, C. Messier, D. D. Kneeshaw, A. Fall, and M. J. Fortin. 2010. Comparing different forest zoning options for landscape-scale management of the boreal forest: Possible benefits of the TRIAD. *Forest Ecology and Management* 259:418–27.

Council of Forest Industries (COFI). 2000. *COFI Factbook 2000.* Accessed August 15, 2006. http://www.cofi.org/reports/factbooks.htm.

Crawford, W. A., P. J. Brickley, and A. C. Thomas. 2007. Mesoscale eddies dominate surface phytoplankton in northern Gulf of Alaska. *Progress in Oceanography* 75: 287–303.

Crone, L. K. 2004. Rural manufacturing and the US wood products industry:

Trends and influences on rural areas. In *Economic growth and change in southeast Alaska*, edited by R. Mazza, 33–71. Gen. Tech. Rep. PNW-GTR-611. Portland, OR: USDA Forest Service, Pacific Northwest Research Station.

———. 2005. Southeast Alaska economics: A resource-abundant region competing in a global marketplace. *Landscape and Urban Planning* 72:215–234.

———. 2007. *Review of "Timber products output and timber harvests in Alaska: Projections for 2005–25."* Report prepared for The Wilderness Society. Crone private collection.

Curtis, E. S. 1916. *The North American Indian. Volume II: Nootka, Haida.* Norwood, NJ: The Plimpton Press.

Dale, V. H., L. A. Joyce, S. McNulty, R. P. Neilson, M. P. Ayres, M. D. Flannigan, P. J. Hanson, *et al.* 2001. Climate change and forest disturbances. *Bioscience* 51(9): 723–734.

Daly, C., R. P. Neilson, and D. L. Phillips. 1994. A statistical-topographic model for mapping climatological precipitation over mountainous terrain. *Journal of Applied Meteorology* 33:140–158.

D'Amore, D. V., N. S. Bonzey, J. Berkowitz, J. Rüegg, and S. Bridgham. 2011. Holocene soil-geomorphic surfaces influence the role of salmon-derived nutrients in the coastal temperate rainforest of southeast Alaska. *Geomorphology* 10:205–209.

D'Amore, D. V., J. B. Fellman, R. T. Edwards, and E. Hood. 2010. Controls on dissolved organic matter concentrations in soils and streams from a forested wetland and sloping bog in southeast Alaska. *Ecohydrology* 3:249–261.

D'Amore, D. V., J. B. Fellman, R. T. Edwards, E. Hood, and C. L. Ping. 2012. Hydropedology of the North American coastal temperate rainforest. In *Hydropedology: Synergistic integration of soil science and hydrology*, edited by H. Lin, 351–380. Amsterdam and Boston: Academic Press.

D'Amore, D. V., P. E. Hennon, P. G. Schaberg, and G. J. Hawley. 2009. Adaptation to exploit nitrate in surface soils predisposes yellow-cedar to climate-induced decline while enhancing the survival of western redcedar: A new hypothesis. *Forest Ecology and Management* 258: 2261–2268.

Damschen, E. I., N. M. Haddad, J. L. Orrock, J. J. Tewksbury, and D. J. Levey. 2006. Corridors increase plant species richness at large scales. *Science* 313:1284–1286.

Danby, R. K., and D. S. Slocombe. 2005. Regional ecology, ecosystem geography, and transboundary protected areas in the St. Elias Mountains. *Ecological Applications* 15:405–422.

Daniels, L. D., and R. W. Gray. 2006. Disturbance regimes in coastal British Columbia. *BC Journal of Ecosystems and Management* 7:44–56.

D'Anjou, B. 2003. *Single-tree and group selection harvesting in an old-growth forest on the west coast of Vancouver Island, British Columbia*. Technical Report TR-024. Nanaimo, BC: BC Ministry of Forests, Vancouver Forest Region.

Darimont, C. T., P. C. Pacquet, and T. E. Reimchen. 2008. Spawning salmon disrupt tight trophic coupling between wolves and ungulate prey in coastal British Columbia. *BMC Ecology* 8:14. doi:10.1186/1472–6785–8–14.

Darimont, C. T., P. C. Paquet, T. E. Reimchen, and V. Crichton. 2005. Range expansion by moose into coastal temperate rainforests of British Columbia, Canada. *Diversity and Distributions* 11:235–239.

Darimont, C. T., and T. E. Reimchen. 2002. Intra-hair stable isotope analysis implies seasonal shift to salmon in gray wolf diet. *Canadian Journal of Zoology* 80:1–5.

Darwin, C. 1859. *On the origin of species by means of natural selection*. London: J. Murray.

Dauenhauer, N. M., and R. Dauenhauer. 1994. *Haa kusteeyi: Our culture*. Seattle, WA: University of Washington Press.

Dawson, N. G. 2008. Vista Norteña: tracking historical diversification and contemporary structure in high latitude mesocarnivores. Unpublished dissertation, University of New Mexico, Albuquerque.

Deal, J. A., S. Haight, and I. McDougall. 2005. *Sustainable resource management plan: Biodiversity chapter for the Upper Nimpkish landscape unit*. BC Ministry of Agriculture and Lands. Accessed 1 September 2012. http://archive.ilmb.gov.bc.ca/slrp/srmp/coast/northisland_centralcoast/reports/Upper_Nimpkish_LUP.pdf.

Deal, R. L. 2001. The effects of partial cutting on forest plant communities of western hemlock - Sitka spruce stands in southeast Alaska. *Canadian Journal of Forest Research* 31: 2067–2079.

Deal, R. L. 2007. Management strategies to increase stand structural diversity and enhance biodiversity in coastal rainforests of Alaska. *Biological Conservation* 137: 520–532.

Deal, R.L., and J.C. Tappeiner. 2002. The effects of partial cutting on stand structure and growth of western hemlock-Sitka spruce stands in southeast Alaska. *Forest Ecology and Management* 159:173–186.

DeGayner, E. J., M. G. Kramer, J. G. Doerr, and M. J. Robertsen. 2005. Windstorm disturbance effects on forest structure and black bear dens in southeast Alaska. *Ecological Applications* 15:1306–1316.

De Laguna, F. 1960. *The story of a Tlingit community: A problem in the relationship between archeological, ethnological and historical methods.* Bureau of American Ethnology Bulletin 172. Washington, DC: Government Printing Office.

———. 1972. *Under Mount Saint Elias: The history and culture of the Yakutat Tlingit.* Smithsonian Contributions to Anthropology 7 (in three parts). Washington, DC: Smithsonian Institution Press.

———. 1990. Tlingit. In *Handbook of North American Indians. Volume 7: Northwest Coast*, edited by W. Suttles and W. C. Sturtevant. Washington, DC: Smithsonian Institution.

DellaSala, D., ed. 2011. *Temperate and boreal rainforests of the world: Ecology and conservation.* Washington DC: Island Press.

DellaSala, D., P. Alaback, T. Speribille, H. von Wehrden, and R. Nauman. 2011. Just what are temperate and boreal rainforests? In *Temperate and boreal rainforests of the world: Ecology and conservation*, edited by D. DellaSala, 1–41. Washington DC: Island Press.

DellaSala, D., F. Moola, P. Alaback, P. Paquet, J. Schoen, and R. Noss. 2011. Temperate and boreal rainforests of the Pacific coast of North America. In *Temperate and boreal rainforests of the world: Ecology and conservation*, edited by D. DellaSala, 42–81. Washington DC: Island Press.

DellaSala, D. A., J. C. Hagar, K. A. Engel, W. C. McComb, R. L. Fairbanks, and E. G. Campbell. 1996. Effects of silvicultural modifications of temperate rainforest on breeding and wintering bird communities, Prince of Wales Island, southeast Alaska. *Condor* 98:706–721.

Demboski, J., and J. Cook. 2001. Phylogeography of the dusky shrew, *Sorex monticolus* (Insectivora, Soricidae): Insight into deep and shallow history in northwestern North America. *Molecular Ecology* 10:1227–1240.

Demboski, J. R., B. K. Jacobsen, and J. A. Cook. 1998. Endemism in the Alexander Archipelago, southeast Alaska: An assessment of genetic variation in flying squirrels (Rodentia: *Glaucomys sabrinus*). *Canadian Journal of Zoology* 76:1–7.

de Vries, M. F. W. 1995. Large herbivores and the design of large-scale nature reserves in western Europe. *Conservation Biology* 9:25–33.

Diamond, J. M. 2005. *Collapse: How societies choose to fail or survive.* London: Allen Lane/Penguin.

Dickerman, R. W., and J. Gustafson. 1996. The Prince of Wales spruce grouse: A new subspecies from southeastern Alaska. *Western Birds* 27:41–47.

Dixon, J. A., and P. B. Sherman. 1991. Economics of protected areas. *Ambio* 20:68–74.

Dixon, J. D., M. K. Oli, M. C. Wooten, T. H. Eason, J. W. McCown, and D. Paetkau. 2006. Effectiveness of a regional corridor in connecting two Florida black bear populations. *Conservation Biology* 20:155–162.

D'Odorico, P., and S. Fagherazzi. 2003. A probabilistic model of rainfall-triggered shallow landslides in hollows: A long-term analysis. *Water Resources Research* 39:1–14.

Doerr, J. G., E. Degayner, and G. Ith. 2005. Winter habitat selection by Sitka black-tailed deer. *Journal of Wildlife Management* 69:322–331.

Doko, T., H. Fukui, A. Koiman, A. B. Toxopeus, T. Ichinose, W. Chen, and A. K. Skidmore. 2011. Identifying habitat patches and potential ecological corridors for remnant Asiatic black bear (*Ursus thibetanus japonicus*) populations in Japan. *Ecological Modeling* 222:748–761.

Dorner, B. 2002. Forest management and natural variability: The dynamics of landscape pattern in mountainous terrain. PhD Dissertation, Simon Fraser University, Burnaby, BC.

Dorner, B., K. P. Lertzman, and J. Fall. 2002. Landscape pattern in topographically complex landscapes: Issues and techniques for analysis. *Landscape Ecology* 17:729–743

Dörner, D. 1996. The logic of failure: Recognizing and avoiding error in complex situations. New York: Metropolitan Books.

Dort, J. C. 1924. Report to the federal power commission on the water powers of southeastern Alaska. Washington, DC: Government Printing Office.

Drucker, P. 1955. *Indians of the Northwest coast.* American Museum of Natural History Anthropological Handbook 10. New York: McGraw Hill.

———. 1965. *Cultures of the North Pacific coast.* San Francisco: Chandler Publishing Co.

Duffy, D. C., K. Boggs, R. H. Hagenstein, R. Lipkin, and J. A. Michaelson. 1999. Landscape assessment of the degree of protection of Alaska's terrestrial biodiversity. *Conservation Biology* 13:1332–1343.

Dugan, D., G. Fay, and S. Colt. 2007. Nature-based tourism in southeast Alaska: Results from a 2005 and 2006 field study. Anchorage, AK: Institute for Social and Economic Research.

Dunlap, R. 1997. Summary of the 1997 fish habitat risk assessment panel. Appendix 1. In *Use of risk assessment panels during revision of the Tongass Land and Resource Management Plan*, edited by C. Shaw III. General Technical Report PNW-GTR-460. Portland, OR: USDA Forest Service, Pacific Northwest Research Station.

Dunsworth, B. G., and W. J. Beese. 2000. British Columbia, Canada: New approaches in managing temperate rainforests. In *Mountains of the world: Mountain forests and sustainable development,* edited by M. Price, T. Kohler, and T. Wachs, 22–23. Berne: Centre for Development and Environment, Inst. of Geography, University of Berne.

Dykstra, P.R. 2004. *Thresholds in habitat supply: A review of the literature.* Wildlife Report no. R-27. Victoria, BC: BC Ministry of Sustainable Resource Management. http://www.env.gov.bc.ca/wld/documents/techpub/r27 _thresholds.pdf.

Ecotrust, Pacific GIS, and Conservation International. 1995. *The rain forests of home: An atlas of people and place.* Portland, OR: Ecotrust.

Edwards, R. T. 1998. The hyporheic zone. In *River ecology and management,* edited by R. J. Naiman and R. E. Bilby. New York: Springer.

Edwards, R., D. D'Amore, E. Hood, and F. Biles. 2007. Regional DOC fluxes for the Tongass National Forest in southeast Alaska. Published abstracts of the Annual Meeting of the American Geophysical Union, December 15–19, San Francisco, CA.

Egoh, B., B. Reyers, M. Rouget, D. M. Richardson, D. C. Le Maitre, and A. S. Van Jaarsveld. 2008. Mapping ecosystem services for planning and management. *Agriculture, Ecosystems and Environment* 127:135–140.

Ellanna, L. J., and G. K. Sherrod. 1987. *Timber management of fish and wildlife use in selected southeastern Alaska communities: Klawock, Prince of Wales Island, Alaska.* Technical Paper Number 126. Juneau, AK: Alaska Department of Fish and Game, Division of Subsistence.

Elmqvist, T., C. Folke, M. Nyström, G. Peterson, J. Bengtsson, B. Walker, and J. Norberg. 2003. Response diversity, ecosystem change, and resilience. *Frontiers in Ecology and the Environment* 1:488–494.

Emili, L., J. Price, and D. Fitzgerald. 2006. Hydrogeological influences on forest community type along forest-peatland complexes in coastal British Columbia. *Canadian Journal of Forest Research* 20:2819–2837.

Emmons, G. T. 1991. *The Tlingit Indians.* Edited by F. De Laguna. Anthropological papers of the American Museum of Natural History, vol. 70. Seattle, WA: University of Washington Press.

Epps, C. W., J. D. Wehausen, V. C. Bleich, S. G. Torres, and J. S. Brashares. 2007. Optimizing dispersal and corridor models using landscape genetics. *Journal of Applied Ecology* 44:714–724.

Erickson, A., B. Hanson, and J. Brueggeman. 1982. *Black bear denning study, Mitkof Island, Alaska.* Final Report. Seattle, WA: University of Washington, School of Fisheries, College of Ocean and Fishery Sciences.

Erlandson, J. M., M. L. Moss, and M. D. Lauriers. 2008. Life on the edge: Early maritime cultures of the Pacific coast of North America. *Quaternary Science Reviews* 27:2232–2245.

Everest, F. H. 2005. Setting the stage for the development of a science-based Tongass land management plan. *Landscape and Urban Planning* 72:13–24.

Everett, R., and K. Robson. 1991. Rare cliff-dwelling plant species as biological monitors of climate change. *Northwest Environmental Journal* 7:352–353.

Exportation of Timber Act of 1926. Public Law 69–100. 16 *US Code* 616, 617.

Fabry, V. J., B. A. Seibel, R. A. Feely, and J. C. Orr. 2008. Impacts of ocean acidification on marine fauna and ecosystem processes. *ICES Journal of Marine Science* 65: 414–432.

Fahrig, L. 2001. How much habitat is enough? *Biological Conservation* 100:65–74.

———. 2003. Effects of habitat fragmentation on biodiversity. *Annual Review of Ecology, Evolution, and Systematics* 34:487–515.

Farmer, C. J. 2002. Survival and habitat selection of Sitka black-tailed deer (*Odocoileus hemionus sitkensis*) in a fragmented coastal temperate rainforest. PhD Dissertation, State University of New York, College of Environmental Science and Forestry, Syracuse.

Farmer, C. J., and M. D. Kirchhoff. 2007. Ecological classification of deer habitat in the Tongass National Forest, Alaska. *Northwestern Naturalist* 88:73–84.

Farmer, C. J., D. K. Person, and R. T. Bowyer. 2006. Risk factors and mortality of black-tailed deer in a managed forest landscape. *Journal of Wildlife Management* 70:1403–1415.

Fedje, D. W., and Q. Mackie. 2005. Overview of cultural history. In *Haida Gwaii: human history and environment from the time of the loon to the time of the iron people*, edited by D. W. Fedje and R. W. Mathewes, 154–162. Vancouver, BC: UBC Press.

Fedje, D. W., and R. W. Mathewes, eds. 2005. *Haida Gwaii: human history and environment from the time of the loon to the time of the iron people*. Vancouver, BC: UBC Press.

Fedje, D. W., R. J. Wigen, D. McLaren, and Q. Mackie. 2004. *Archaeology and environments of karst landscapes in southern Haida Gwaii (Queen Charlotte Islands), West Coast, Canada*. Paper presented at the 2004 Northwest Anthropological Conference, Eugene, OR.

Fellman, J. B., D. V. D'Amore, E. Hood, and R. D. Boone. 2008. Fluorescence characteristics and biodegradability of dissolved organic matter in forest and wetland soils from coastal temperate watersheds in southeast Alaska. *Biogeochemistry* 88:169–184.

Fellman, J. B., E. Hood, D. V. D'Amore, R. T. Edwards, and D. White. 2008. Seasonal changes in the chemical quality and biodegradability of dissolved organic matter exported from soils to streams in coastal temperature watersheds. *Biogeochemistry* 95: 277–293.

Fellman, J. B., E. Hood, R. T. Edwards, and D. V. D'Amore. 2008. Return of salmon-derived nutrients from the riparian zone to the stream during a storm in southeastern Alaska. *Ecosystems* 11:537–544.

———. 2009. Changes in the concentration, biodegradability and fluorescent properties of dissolved organic matter during stormflows in coastal temperate watersheds. *Journal of Geophysical Research* 114: G01021. doi:10.1029/2008JG000790.

Fellman J., E. Hood, R. Edwards, J. Jones. 2009. Uptake of allochthonous dissolved organic matter from soil and salmon in coastal temperate rainforest streams. *Ecosystems* 12:747–759.

Fellman, J. B., R. G. Spencer, P. J. Hernes, R. T. Edwards, D. V. D'Amore, and E. Hood. 2010. The impact of glacier runoff on the biodegradability and biochemical composition of terrigenous dissolved organic matter in near-shore marine ecosystems. *Marine Chemistry* 121:112–122.

Ferrier, S., R. L. Pressey, and T. W. Barrett. 2000. A new predictor of the irreplaceability of areas for achieving a conservation goal, its application to real-world planning, and a research agenda for further refinement. *Biological Conservation* 93:303–325.

Fitzgerald, D. F., J. S. Price, A. de Groot, A. Banner, and P. LePage. 2002. Surface water discharge and groundwater storage patterns in a hypermaritime bog near Prince Rupert, BC. Extension Note. Smithers, BC: Research Station, BC Ministry of Forests.

Fitzgerald, J., D. DellaSala, J. McNeely, and E. Grumbine. 2011. A global strategy for rainforests in the era of climate change. In *Temperate and boreal rainforests of the world: Ecology and conservation*, edited by D. DellaSala, 260–274. Washington DC: Island Press.

Flanders, L. S., and J. Cariello. 2000. *Tongass road condition survey*. Technical Report No. 00–7. Juneau, AK: Alaska Department of Fish and Game.

Fleming, M. A., and J. A. Cook. 2002. Phylogeography of endemic ermine (*Mustela erminea*) in southeast Alaska. *Molecular Ecology* 11:795–808.

Flora, D. F. 2003. Forest economics research at the Pacific Northwest Research Station, to 2000. General Tech. Report PNW-GTR-562. Portland, OR: USDA Forest Service, Pacific Northwest Research Station.

Folke, C., S. Carpenter, B. Walker, M. Scheffer, T. Elmqvist, L. Gunderson, and

C. S. Holling. 2005. Regime shifts, resilience, and biodiversity in ecosystem management. *Annual Review of Ecology, Evolution, and Systematics* 35:557–581.

Ford, M. J., D. Teel, D. M. Van Doornik, D. Kuligowski, and P. W Lawson. 2004. Genetic population structure of central Oregon coast coho salmon (*Oncorhynchus kisutch*). *Conservation Genetics* 5:797–812.

Forgey, P. 2009. Renewable energy report ignores southeast Alaska. *Juneau Empire*, June 25, 2009. http://www.juneauempire.com/stories/062509/loc_454405172.shtml.

Forman, R. T. T., and L. E. Alexander. 1998. Roads and their major ecological effects. *Annual Review of Ecology and Systematics* 29:207–231.

Forman, R. T. T., D. Sperling, J. A. Bissionette, A. P. Clevenger, C. D. Cutshall, V. H. Dale, L. Fahrig, *et al.* 2003. *Road ecology*. Covelo, CA: Island Press.

Forsyth, R. G. 2004. Land snails of British Columbia. Victoria, BC: Royal BC Museum.

Foster, J. B. 1965. The evolution of the mammals of the Queen Charlotte Islands, British Columbia. *British Columbia Provincial Museum Occasional Papers* 14:1–130.

Frances, J. 2008. Differentiation of peripheral populations of wolverine. Unpublished Thesis, University of New Mexico, Albuquerque.

Frankham, R. 1995. Inbreeding and extinction—a threshold effect. *Conservation Biology* 9:792–799.

Franklin, J. F. 1989. The "new forestry." *Journal of Soil and Water Conservation* 44:549.

———. 1993. Preserving biodiversity: Species, ecosystems, or landscapes? *Ecological Applications* 3:202–205.

Franklin, J. F., D. R. Berg, D. A. Thornburgh, and J. C. Tappeiner. 1997. Alternative silvicultural approaches to timber harvesting: variable retention harvest systems. In *Creating a forestry for the 21st century: The science of ecosystem management*, edited by in K. A. Kohn and J. F. Franklin, 111–139. Washington, DC: Island Press.

Franklin, J. F., K. Cromack, Jr., W. Denison, A. McKee, C. Maser, J. Sedell, F. Swanson, and G. Juday. 1981. *Ecological characteristics of old-growth Douglas-fir forests*. General Technical Report PNW-118. Portland, OR: USDA Forest Service, Pacific Northwest Research Station.

Franklin, J. F., and K. Johnson. 2004. Forests face new threat: global market changes. *Issues in Science and Technology* 20(4): 41–48.

Franklin, J. F., and D. B. Lindenmayer. 2009. Importance of matrix habitats in maintaining biodiversity. *Proceedings of the National Academy of Sciences* 106:349–350.

Franklin, J. F., D. Lindenmayer, J. MacMahon, A. McKee, J. Magnuson, D. Perry, R. Waide, and D. Foster. 2000. Threads of continuity: Ecosystem disturbance, recovery, and the theory of biological legacies. *Conservation Biology in Practice* 1:8–16.

Franklin, J. F., R. Mitchell, and B. Palik. 2007. *Natural disturbance and stand development principles for ecological forestry.* General Technical Report NRS-19. Newton Square, PA: USDA Forest Service, Northern Research Station.

Franklin, J. F., T. A. Spies, R. Van Pelt, A. B. Carey, D. A. Thornburgh, D. R. Berg, D. B. Lindenmayer, *et al.* 2002. Disturbances and structural development of natural forest ecosystems with silvicultural implications, using Douglas-fir as an example. *Forest Ecology and Management* 155:399–423.

Furniss, M., B. Staab, S. Hazelhurst, C. Clifton, K. Roby, B. Ilhardt, E. Larry, *et al.* 2010. *Water, climate change, and forests: Watershed stewardship for a changing climate.* General Tech. Report PNW-GTR-812. Portland, OR: USDA Forest Service.

Gapare, W. J., S. N. Aitken, and C. E. Ritland. 2005. Genetic diversity of core and peripheral Sitka spruce (*Picea sitchensis* [Bong.] Carr) populations: Implications for conservation of widespread species. *Biological Conservation* 123: 113–123.

Gardiner, W. R., and P. Geddes. 1980. The influence of body composition on the survival of juvenile salmon. *Hydrobiologia* 69: 67–72.

Garfield, V. E. 1947. Historical aspects of Tlingit clans in Angoon, Alaska. *American Anthropologist* 49:438–452.

Garrison V. H., E. A. Shinn, W. T. Foreman, D. W. Griffin, C. W. Holmes, C. A. Kellogg, M. S. Majewski, L. L. Richardson, K. B. Ritchie, and G. W. Smith. 2003. African and Asian dust: From desert soils to coral reefs. *BioScience* 53:469–480.

Gaston, A. J., T. E. Golumbia, J. L. Martin, and S. T. Sharpe, eds. 2008. *Lessons from the islands: Introduced species and what they tell us about how ecosystems work.* Proceedings from the Research Group on Introduced Species 2002 Symposium, Queen Charlotte City, Queen Charlotte Islands, British Columbia. Ottawa: Canadian Wildlife Service, Environment Canada.

Gaudet, C. L., M. P. Wong, A. Brady, and R. Kent. 1997. How are we managing? The transition from environmental quality to ecosystem health. *Ecosystem Health* 3:3–10.

Gavin, D. G., L. B. Brubaker, and K. P. Lertzman. 2003a. Holocene fire history of a coastal temperate rain forest based on soil charcoal radiocarbon dates. *Ecology* 84:186_201.

———. 2003b. An 1800-year record of the spatial and temporal distribution of fire from the west coast of Vancouver Island, Canada. *Canadian Journal of Forest Research* 33:573–586.

Gavin, D. G., and F. S. Hu. 2006. Spatial variation of climatic and non-climatic controls on species distribution: The range limit of *Tsuga heterophylla*. *Journal of Biogeography* 33:1384–1396.

Gayton, D. V. 2008. Impacts of climate change on British Columbia's biodiversity: A literature review. Kamloops, BC: FORREX Forest Research Extension Society.

Geertsema, M., J. J. Clague, J. W. Schwab, and S. G. Evans. 2006. An overview of recent large catastrophic landslides in northern British Columbia, Canada. *Engineering Geology* 83: 120–143.

Geiger, H. J., and S. McPherson. 2004. Stock status and escapement goals for salmon stocks in southeast Alaska. Special Publication No. 04–02. Anchorage: Alaska Department of Fish and Game.

Gelbard, J. L., and S. Harrison. 2005. Invasibility of roadless grasslands: An experimental study of yellow starthistle. *Ecological Applications* 15:1570–1580.

Gende, S. M., R. T. Edwards, M. F. Willson, and M. S. Wipfli. 2002. Pacific salmon in aquatic and terrestrial ecosystems. *BioScience* 52:917–928.

Gende, S. M., A. E. Miller, and E. Hood. 2007. The effects of salmon carcasses on soil nitrogen pools in a riparian forest of southeastern Alaska. *Canadian Journal of Forest Research* 37: 1194–1202.

Gende, S. M., T. P. Quinn, M. F. Willson, R. Heintz, and T. M. Scott. 2004. Magnitude and fate of salmon-derived nutrients and energy in a coastal stream ecosystem. *Journal of Freshwater Ecology* 19:149–160.

Gerzon, M., B. Seely, and A. MacKinnon. 2011. The temporal development of old-growth structural attributes in second-growth stands: A chronosequence study in the Coastal Western Hemlock zone in British Columbia. *Canadian Journal of Forest Research* 41:1–13.

Gibson, J., J. Price, D. Aravena, D. Fitzgerald, and D. Maloney. 2000. Runoff generation in a hypermaritime bog-forest upland. *Hydrological Processes* 14:2711–2730.

Gimbarzevsky, P. 1988. Mass wasting on the Queen Charlotte Islands: A regional overview. Land Mgmt. Rep. no. 29. Victoria, BC: BC Ministry of Forests and Lands.

Golden, K. 2009a. "Court to hear arguments on mine tailings." *Juneau Empire*, January 12. http://www.juneauempire.com/stories/011209/loc_376499748 .shtml.

Golden, K. 2009b. "'Landless' Natives try for redress." *Juneau Empire*, May 19. http://www.juneauempire.com/stories/051909/sta_441623956.shtml.

Goldin, L. A., and B. C. Matsen. 1996. *The land is ours*. Juneau, AK: Aurora Films. Video recording, 60 min.

Goldschmidt, W. R., and T. H. Haas. 1998. *Haa Aaní, our land*. Seattle, WA: University of Washington Press.

Golumbia, T. E. 2000. Introduced species management in Haida Gwaii (Queen Charlotte Islands). In *Proceedings of a conference on the biology and management of species and habitats at risk, Kamloops, BC, 15–19 February 1999, Vol. 1*, edited by L. M. Darling, 327–332. Victoria: BC Ministry of Environment, Lands, and Parks.

Gomi T., R. C. Sidle, and J. S. Richardson. 2002. Understanding processes and downstream linkages of headwater systems. *BioScience* 52:905–916.

Gonzales, E. K., P. Arcese, R. Schulz, and F. L. Bunnell. 2003. Strategic reserve design in the central coast of British Columbia: Integrating ecological and industrial goals. *Canadian Journal of Forest Research* 33:2129–2140.

Gorman, M. W. 1896. Economic botany of southeastern Alaska. *Pittonia* 3:64–85.

Gough, B. M. 1989. The Haida-European encounter, 1774–1900: The Queen Charlotte Islands in transition. In *The outer shores*, edited by G.G.E. Scudder and N. Gessler, 249–260. Based on the proceedings of the Queen Charlotte Islands First International Symposium. Skidegate, BC: Queen Charlotte Islands Museum Press.

Goward, T. 1994. Rare and endangered lichens in British Columbia. In *Biodiversity in British Columbia: Our changing environment*, edited by L.E. Harding and E. McCullum, 77–80. Ottawa: Canadian Wildlife Service.

Grumbine, R. E. 1994. What is ecosystem management? *Conservation Biology* 8:27–38.

Gustafsson, L., S. C. Baker, J. Bauhus, W. J. Beese, A. Brodie, J. Kouki, D. B. Lindenmayer, *et al.* 2012. Retention forestry to maintain multifunctional forests: a world perspective. *BioScience* 62: 633–645.

Gutierrez, A. G., J. J. Armesto, and J. C. Aravena. 2004. Disturbance and regeneration dynamics of an old-growth North Patagonian rain forest in Chiloe Island, Chile. *Journal of Ecology* 92(4):598–608.

———. 2009. Structural and environmental characterization of old-growth temperate rainforests of northern Chiloe Island, Chile: Regional and global relevance. *Forest Ecology and Management* 258:376–388.

Haas, C. A. 1995. Dispersal and use of corridors by birds in wooded patches on an agricultural landscape. *Conservation Biology* 9:845–854.

Hall, B. M., and J. F. McLellan. 1990. *Alphabetical list of major unlogged watersheds on Vancouver Island*. Victoria, BC: Province of British Columbia, Ministry of Forests, Inventory Branch.

Hall, L. S., P. R. Krausman, and M. L. Morrison. 1997. The habitat concept and a plea for standard terminology. *Wildlife Society Bulletin* 25:173–182.

Hall, T. E., H. Heaton, and L. E. Kruger. 2009. Outdoor recreation in the Pacific Northwest and Alaska: Trends in activity participation. General Tech. Report PNW-GTR-778. Portland, OR: USDA Forest Service, Pacific Northwest Research Station.

Halupka, K. C., M. D. Bryant, M. F. Willson, and F. H. Everest. 2000. *Biological characteristics and population status of anadromous salmon in southeast Alaska*. General Technical Report PNW-GTR-468. Portland, OR: USDA Forest Service, Pacific Northwest Research Station.

Hamann, A., and T. Wang. 2006. Potential effects of climate change on ecosystem and tree species distribution in British Columbia. *Ecology* 87:2773–2786.

Hanley, T. A. 1993. Balancing economic development, biological conservation, and human culture: The Sitka black-tailed deer (*Odocoileus hemionus sitkensis*) as an ecological indicator. *Biological Conservation* 66:61–67.

———. 2005. Potential management of young-growth stands for understory vegetation and wildlife habitat in southeastern Alaska. *Landscape and Urban Planning* 72:95–112.

Hanley, T. A., and W. W. Brady. 1997. Understory species composition and production in old growth western hemlock Sitka spruce forests of southeastern Alaska. *Canadian Journal of Botany* 75:574–580.

Hanley, T. A., and J. D. McKendrick. 1983. Seasonal changes in chemical composition and nutritive value of native forages in a spruce-hemlock forest, southeastern Alaska. Resource Paper PNW-312. Portland, OR: USDA Forest Service.

Hanley, T. A., W. P. Smith, and S. M. Gende. 2005. Maintaining wildlife habitat in southeastern Alaska: Implications of new knowledge for forest management and research. *Landscape and Urban Planning* 72:113–133.

Hanski, I., and O. Ovaskainen. 2000. The metapopulation capacity of a fragmented landscape. *Nature* 404:755–758.

Harcombe, P. A., S. E. Greene, M. G. Kramer, S. A. Acker, T. A. Spies, and
T. Valentine. 2004. The influence of fire and windthrow dynamics on a
coastal spruce-hemlock forest in Oregon, USA, based on aerial photographs spanning 40 years. *Forest Ecology and Management* 194:71–82.

Harper, K. A., S. E. MacDonald, P. J. Burton, J. Chen, K. D. Brosofske, S. C. Saunders, E. S. Euskirchen, D. Roberts, M. S. Jaiteh, and P. A. Esseen. 2005. Edge
influence on forest structure and composition in fragmented landscapes.
Conservation Biology 19:768–782.

Harris, A. S. 1989. *Wind in the forests of southeast Alaska and guides for reducing
damage.* General Tech. Report PNW-GTR-244. Portland, OR: USDA Forest
Service, Pacific Northwest Research Station.

Harris, L. D. 1984. *The fragmented forest, island biogeography theory, and the
preservation of biotic diversity.* Chicago: University of Chicago Press.

———. 1988. Edge effects and conservation of biotic diversity. *Conservation
Biology* 2:330–332.

Hatter, I. W. 1982. Predator-ungulate relationships in second-growth forest
on Vancouver Island: A problem analysis. IWIFR-5. Victoria, BC: Ministries
of Environment and Forests.

Haycox, S. 1990. Economic development and Indian land rights in modern Alaska:
the 1947 Tongass Timber Act. *Western Historical Quarterly* 21(Feb.): 20–46.

Haycox, S. H. 2000. Owning it all in Alaska: The political power of a rhetorical
paradigm. In *Land in the American West: Private claims on the common
good,* edited by W. G. Robbins and J. C. Foster, 164–189. Seattle, WA: University of Washington Press.

———. 2007. "Then fight for it": William Lewis Paul and Alaska Native land
claims. In Let right be done: Aboriginal title, the Calder case, and the future
of indigineous rights, edited by H. Foster, H. Raven, and I. Welber, 85–97.
Vancouver, BC: UBC Press.

Heaton, T. H., and F. Grady. 2003. The Late Wisconsin vertebrate history of
Prince of Wales Island, southeast Alaska. In Ice age cave faunas of North
America, edited by B. W. Schubert, J. I. Mead, and R. W. Graham, 17–53.
Bloomington: Indiana University Press.

Heaton, T. H., S. L. Talbot, and G. F. Shields. 1996. An Ice Age refugium of large
mammals in the Alexander Archipelago, southeastern Alaska. *Quaternary
Research* 46:186–192.

Hebda, R., and C. Whitlock. 1997. Environmental history. In *The rain forests
of home: An atlas of people and place,* edited by E. Wolf, A. Mitchell, and
P. Schoomaker, 227–254. Portland, OR: Ecotrust.

Heifetz, J., M. L. Murphy, and K. V. Koski. 1986. Effects of logging on winter habitat of juvenile salmonids in Alaskan streams. *North American Journal of Fisheries Management* 6:52–58.

Helfield, J. M., and R. J. Naiman. 2001. Effects of salmon-derived nitrogen of riparian forest ecology. *Ecology* 82:2403–2409.

———. 2006. Keystone interactions: Salmon and bear in riparian forests of Alaska. *Ecosystems* 9:167–180.

Helmers, A. E. 1960. Alaska forestry—A research frontier. *Journal of Forestry* 58:465–471.

Hemstrom, M., and J. F. Franklin. 1982. Fire and other disturbances of the forests in Mount Rainier National Park. *Quaternary Research* 18:32–51.

Hennig, W. 1966. Phylogenetic systematics. Urbana: University of Illinois Press.

Hennon, P. E. 1995. Are heart rot fungi major factors of disturbance in gap-dynamic forests? *Northwest Science* 69:284–293.

Hennon, P. E., D. D'Amore, D. Wittwer, A. Johnson, P. Schaberg, G. Hawley, C. Beier, S. Sink, and G. P. Juday. 2006. Climate warming, reduced snow, and freezing injury could explain the demise of yellow-cedar in southeast Alaska, USA. *World Resource Review* 18: 227–250.

Hennon, P.E., and D. DeMars. 1997. Development of wood decay in wounded western hemlock and Sitka spruce in southeast Alaska. *Canadian Journal of Forest Research* 27:1971–1978.

Hennon, P. E., and M. H. McClellan. 2003. Tree mortality and forest structure in the temperate rain forests of southeast Alaska. *Canadian Journal of Forest Research* 33:1621–1634.

Hetherington, R., J. V. Barrie, and R. G. B. Reid. 2004. Paleogeography, glacially induced crustal displacement, and Late Quaternary coastlines on the continental shelf of British Columbia, Canada. *Quaternary Science Reviews* 23:295–318.

Heusser, C. J. 1960. *Late Pleistocene environments of Pacific North America.* Special Publication 35. New York: American Geographical Society.

Heutte, T., and E. Bella. 2003. *Invasive plants and exotic weeds of southeast Alaska.* Anchorage, AK: USDA Forest Service, State and Private Forestry, and Chugach National Forest.

Heutte, T., E. Bella, J. Snyder, and M. Shephard. 2006. Invasive plants and exotic weeds of southeast Alaska. Anchorage, AK: USDA Forest Service.

Heyerdahl, E. K., K. Lertzman, and S. Karpuk. 2007. Local-scale controls of a low-severity fire regime (1750–1950), southern British Columbia, Canada. *Ecoscience* 14:40–47.

Hicks, B. J., M. S. Wipfli, D. W. Lang, and M. E. Lang. 2005. Marine-derived nitrogen and carbon in freshwater-riparian food webs of the Copper River Delta, southcentral Alaska. *Oecologia* 144:558–569.

Hilborn, R., T. P. Quinn, D. E. Schindler, D. E. Rogers. 2003. Biocomplexity and fisheries sustainability. *Proceedings of the National Academy of Sciences* 100:6564–6568

Hildebrand, G., T. Hanley, C. Robbins, and C. Schwartz. 1999. Role of brown bears *(Ursus arctos)* in the flow of marine nitrogen into a terrestrial ecosystem. *Oecologia* 121:546–550.

Hjerpe, E. 2011. Seeing the Tongass for the trees: The economics of transitions to sustainable forest management. Washington, DC: The Wilderness Society.

Hoberg, E. P., L. Polley, E. J. Jenkins, and S. J. Kutz. 2008. Pathogens of domestic and free-ranging ungulates: Global climate change in temperate to boreal latitudes across North America. *Revue Scientifique et Technique Office International des Épizooties* 27:511–528.

Hoberg, E. P., A. V. A. Koehler, and J. A. Cook. In Press. Complex host-parasite systems in *Martes*: Implications for conservation biology of endemic faunas. In *Biology of marten*, edited by S. Buskirk and K. Aubry. Ithaca, NY: Cornell University Press.

Hoberg, E. P., S. J. Kutz, K. E. Galbreath, and J. Cook. 2003. Arctic biodiversity: From discovery to faunal baselines—revealing the history of a dynamic system. *Journal of Parasitology* 89:S84–S95.

Hocking, M. D., and T. E. Reimchen. 2002. Salmon-derived nitrogen in terrestrial invertebrates from coniferous forests of the Pacific Northwest. *BMC Ecology* 2:4–14.

Hocking, M. D., and J. D. Reynolds. 2011. Impacts of salmon on riparian plant diversity. *Science* 331(6024): 1609–1612.

Hockings, M., S. Stolton, and N. Dudley. 2000. *Evaluating effectiveness: A framework for assessing the management of protected areas.* Gland, Switzerland: IUCN.

Holderegger, R., and H. H. Wagner. 2006. A brief guide to landscape genetics. *Landscape Ecology* 21:793–796.

Holling, C. S. 1978. *Adaptive environmental assessment and management.* New York: John Wiley and Sons.

Holm, B. 1984. The box of daylight: Northwest coast Indian art. Seattle, WA: Seattle Art Museum and University of Washington Press.

Holmberg, H. J. 1985. *Holmberg's ethnographic sketches.* Translated by F. Jaensch.

Rasmuson Library Historical Translation Series, Vol. 1. Fairbanks, AK: University of Alaska Press.

Holmes, R. A., T. E. Brookover, M. W. Schwan, S. H. Hoffman, R. E. Chadwick, D. F. Fleming, R. P. Ericksen, *et al.* 2003. *Area management report for the sportfisheries of Southeast Alaska, 2002.* Fishery Management Report No. 03–11. Anchorage: Alaska Department of Fish and Game.

Hood, E., J. Fellman, R. G. M. Spencer, P. J. Hernes, R. Edwards, D. D'Amore, and D. Scott. 2009. Glaciers as a source of ancient and labile organic matter to the marine environment. *Nature* 462:1044–1047.

Hope, A. III, and T. F. Thornton. 2000. *Will the time ever come? A Tlingit source book.* Fairbanks, AK: University of Alaska, Native Knowledge Network, Center for Cross-Cultural Studies.

Hopkins, D. M. 1967. *The Bering land bridge.* Stanford, CA: Stanford University Press.

Houle, M., D. Fortin, C. Dussault, R. Courtois, and J. P. Ouellet. 2010. Cumulative effects of forestry on habitat use by gray wolf (*Canis lupus*) in the boreal forest. *Landscape Ecology* 25:419–433.

Huggard, D. 2006. *Habitat monitoring 1999 to 2006--summary and data report.* Contract report to Western Forest Products, Adaptive Management Program. Vancouver, BC.

Huggard, D. J., and F. L. Bunnell. 2007. *Stand-level retention and forest birds: A synthesis of studies.* Vancouver, BC: University of BC, Centre for Applied Conservation Research, Forest Sciences Centre. Pamphlet.

Hulme, M. 2005. Recent climate trends. In *Climate change and biodiversity,* edited by T. Lovejoy and L. Hannah, 31–40. New Haven, CT: Yale University Press.

Hunter, M. L., Jr., and A. Calhoun. 1996. A TRIAD approach to land-use allocation. In *Biodiversity in managed landscapes,* edited by R. C. Szaro and D. W. Johnstone, 477–491. Oxford: Oxford University Press.

Hurd, J. 2009. *Economic benefits of watershed restoration.* The Political Economy of Watershed Restoration Series. Missoula, MT: Wildlands CPR.

Iles, K., and N. J. Smith. 2006. A new type of sample plot that is particularly useful for sampling small clusters of objects. *Forest Science* 52:148–154.

Information Insights. 2010. *Alaska forums on jobs and economic development.* Final Report prepared for President Barack Obama and Secretary of Agriculture Tom Vilsack. Palmer, AK: USDA Service Center.

IPCC. 2007. Summary for policymakers. In *Climate change 2007: The physical science basis. Contribution of working group I to the fourth assessment report of the intergovernmental panel on climate change,* edited by S. D. Solomon, M. Qin, M. Manning, Z. Chen, M. Marquis, K. B. Averyt, M. Tignor, and H. L. Miller. Cambridge and New York: Cambridge University Press.

Iverson, G. C., G. K. Hayward, K. Titus, E. DeGayner, R. Lowell, D. Crocker-Bedford, P. Schempf, and J. Lindell. 1996. *Conservation assessment for the northern goshawk in southeast Alaska.* General Technical Report PNW-GTR-387. Portland, OR: USDA Forest Service.

Janzen, D. H. 1986. The eternal external threat. In *Conservation biology: The science of scarcity and diversity,* edited by M. E. Soulé, 286–303. Sunderland, MA: Sinauer Associates Inc.

Jedrzejewska, B., and W. Jedrzejewski. 2005. Large carnivores and ungulates in European temperate forest ecosystems: Bottom-up and top-down control. In *Large carnivores and the conservation of biodiversity,* edited by J. C. Ray, K. H. Redford, R. S. Steneck, and J. Berger, 230–245. Covelo, CA: Island Press.

Jenkins, E. J., A. M. Veitch, S. J. Kutz, E. P. Hoberg, and L. Polley. 2006. Climate change and the epidemiology of protostrongylid nematodes in northern ecosystems: *Parelaphostrongylus odocoilei* and *Protostrongylus stilesi* in Dall's sheep (*Ovis dalli dalli*). *Parasitology* 132:387–401.

Jernigan, C. 2006. The howling of lat. forty-nine: Assessing collaborative wildlife management efforts along the western Canada–US border. *Journal of International Wildlife Law and Policy* 9:55–89.

Jochelson, W. 1933. *History, ethnology and anthropology of the Aleut.* Washington, DC: Carnegie Institution of Washington.

Johnson, A. C., and R. T. Edwards. 2002. Physical and chemical processes in headwater channels with red alder. In *Congruent management of multiple resources: Proceedings from the wood compatibility initiative workshop,* General Technical Report PNW-563, edited by A. C. Johnson, R. W. Haynes, and R. A. Monserud, 101–110. Portland, OR: USDA Forest Service, Pacific Northwest Research Station.

Johnson, A. C., D. N. Swanston, and K. E. McGee. 2000. Landslide initiation, runout, and deposition within clearcuts and old-growth forests of Alaska. *Journal of the American Water Resources Association* 36:17–30.

Johnson, C. J., M. S. Boyce, R. Mulders, A. Gunn, R. J. Gau, H. D. Cluff, and R. L. Case. 2004. Quantifying patch distribution at multiple spatial scales: Applications to wildlife-habitat models. *Landscape Ecology* 19:869–882.

Johnson, C. J., and M. P. Gillingham. 2008. Sensitivity of species-distribution models to error, bias, and model design: An application to resource selection functions for woodland caribou. *Ecological Modeling* 213:143–155.

Johnson, D. 2002. Environmentally sustainable cruise tourism: A reality check. *Marine Policy* 26:261–270.

Johnson, N. P. 1990. Nesting bald eagles (*Haliatus leucocephalus*) in urban areas of southeast Alaska: Assessing highway construction and disturbance impacts. *Transportation Research Record* 1279:60–68.

Johnson, W. K., L. A. Miller, N. E. Sutherland, and C. S. Wong. 2005. Iron transport by mesoscale Haida eddies in the Gulf of Alaska. *Deep-Sea Research II* 52:933–953.

Jones, H. P., and O. J. Schmitz. 2009. Rapid recovery of damaged ecosystems. *PLoS ONE* 4:e5653. doi:10.1371/journal.pone.0005653.

Jones, S. 2009. Personal communication. Resource Specialist, Tongass National Forest, 204 Siginaka Way, Sitka, AK 99835.

Jordan, G. J., M. J. Fortin, and K. P. Lertzman. 2008. Spatial pattern and persistence of historical fire boundaries in southern interior British Columbia. *Environmental and Ecological Statistics* 15:523–535.

Josenhans, H., D. Fedje, R. Pienitz, and J. Southon. 1997. Early humans and rapidly changing Holocene sea levels in the Queen Charlotte Islands-Hecate Strait, British Columbia, Canada. *Science* 277:71–74.

Juneau Empire. 2008. "Brisk business." December 22, 2008. http://www.juneau empire.com/stories/122208/loc_370142262.shtml.

Junk, W. J., P. B. Bayley, and R. E. Sparks. 1989. The flood pulse concept in river-floodplain systems. In *Proceedings of the international large river symposium*, edited by D. P. Dodge. *Canadian Special Publication of Fisheries and Aquatic Sciences* 106:110–127.

Karr, J. R. 1991. Biological integrity: A long neglected aspect of water resource management. *Ecological Applications* 1:66–84.

Kaufman, A. 1958. *Southeastern Alaska's mineral industry.* Information Circular 7844. Washington, DC: USDI Bureau of Mines.

Kavanaugh, D. H. 1992. Carabid beetles (Insecta: Coleoptera: Carabidae) of the Queen Charlotte Islands, British Columbia. *Memoir of the California Academy of Sciences* No. 16.

Kayaani Commision. 2006. *Ethnobotany field guide to selected plants found in Sitka, Alaska.* Sitka, AK: The Kayaani Commission, Sitka Tribe of Alaska.

Keenan, R. J. 1993. Structure and function of western redcedar and western hemlock forests on northern Vancouver Island. PhD Dissertation, University of British Columbia, Vancouver.

Keenan, R. J., and J. P. Kimmins. 1993. The ecological effects of clear-cutting. *Environmental Review* 1:121–144.

Keller, E.A., and F.J. Swanson. 2007. Effects of large organic material on channel form and fluvial processes. *Earth Surface Processes and Landforms* 4:361–380.

Kellogg, E. 1992. *Coastal temperate rain forests: Ecological characteristics, status and distribution worldwide.* Occasional paper, series 1. Portland, OR: Ecotrust and Conservation International.

Kellogg, R. S. 1910. *The forests of Alaska.* USDA Forest Service Bull. No. 81. Washington, DC: Government Printing Office.

Kemp, B. M., R. S. Malhi, J. McDonough, *et al.* 2007. Genetic analysis of early Holocene skeletal remains from Alaska and its implications for the settlement of the Americas. *American Journal of Physical Anthropology* 132:605–621.

Kimmins, H. P. 2004. Emulating natural forest disturbance: What does this mean? In *Emulating natural forest landscape disturbances: Concepts and applications,* edited by A. H. Perera, L. J. Buse, and M.G. Weber, 8–28. New York: Columbia University Press.

Kirchhoff, M. D., and J. W. Schoen. 1987. Forest cover and snow: Implications for deer habitat in southeast Alaska. *Journal of Wildlife Management* 51:28–33.

Klein, D. R. 1965. Postglacial distribution patterns of mammals in the southern coastal regions of Alaska. *Journal of the Arctic Institute of North America* 18:7–20.

Klinka, D. R., and T. E. Reimchen. 2009. Adaptive coat colour polymorphism in the Kermode bear of coastal British Columbia. *Biological Journal of the Linnaean Society* 98:479–488.

Klinka, K., J. Pojar, and D. V. Meidinger. 1991. Revision of biogeoclimatic units of coastal British Columbia. *Northwest Science* 65:32–78.

Knapp, G. K. 1992. Native timber harvest in southeast Alaska. General Tech. Report PNW-GTR-284. Portland, OR: USDA Forest Service, Pacific Northwest Research Station.

Koehler, A. V. A. 2006. Systematics, phylogeography, distribution, and lifecycle of *Soboliphyme baturini.* Unpublished Thesis, University of New Mexico, Albuquerque.

Koehler, A. V. A., E. P. Hoberg, N. E. Dokuchaev, N. A. Tranbenkova, J. S. Whitman, D. W. Nagorsen, and J. A. Cook. 2009. Phylogeography of a Holarctic nematode, *Soboliphyme baturini* among mustelids: Climate change, episodic colonization, and diversification in a complex host-parasite system. *Biological Journal of the Linnaean Society* 96:651–663.

Kohira, M., and E. A. Rexstad. 1997. Diets of wolves, *Canis lupus,* in logged and unlogged forests of southeastern Alaska. *Canadian Field-Naturalist* 111:429–435.

Kondzela, C. M., C. M. Guthrie, S. L. Hawkins, C. D. Russell, J. H. Helle, and A. J. Gharrett. 1994. Genetic relationships among chum salmon populations in southeast Alaska and northern British Columbia. *Canadian Journal of Fisheries and Aquatic Sciences* 51:50–64.

Koski, K. V. 2009. The fate of coho salmon nomads: The story of an estuarine-rearing strategy promoting resilience. *Ecology and Society* 14:4.

Kramer, M. G., A. J. Hansen, M. L. Taper, and E. J. Kissinger. 2001. Abiotic controls on long-term windthrow disturbance and temperate rainforest dynamics in southeast Alaska. *Ecology* 82:2749–2768.

Kramer, M. G., P. Sollins, and R. S. Sletten. 2004. Soil carbon dynamics across a windthrow disturbance sequence in southeast Alaska. *Ecology* 85:2230–2244.

Krause, A. 1956. *The Tlingit Indians: Results of a trip to the Northwest coast of America and the Bering Straits.* Translated by E. Gunther. Seattle, WA: University of Washington Press.

Kremsater, L. L., F. L. Bunnell, D. Huggard, and B. G. Dunsworth. 2003. Indicators to assess biological diversity: Weyerhaeuser's coastal British Columbia forest project. *Forestry Chronicle* 79:590–601.

Kruger, L. 2005. Community and landscape change in southeast Alaska. *Landscape and Urban Planning* 72:235–249.

Kuhnlein, H.V., and N. J. Turner. 1991. *Traditional plant foods of Canadian indigenous peoples: Nutrition, botany and use.* Philadelphia, PA: Gordon and Breach Science Publishers.

Kuletz, K., and J. Piatt. 1992. Distribution of marbled and Kittlitz's murrelets in three bays in Alaska. *Pacific Seabird Group Bulletin* 19:50.

Kunin, W. E. 1997. Sample shape, spatial scale and species counts: Implications for reserve design. *Biological Conservation* 82:369–377.

Kutz, S. J., E. P. Hoberg, L. Polley, and E. J. Jenkins. 2005. Global warming is changing the dynamics of Arctic host-parasite systems. *Proceedings of the Royal Society London B* 272:2571–2576.

Landres, P. B., P. Morgan, and F. J. Swanson. 1999. Overview of the use of natural variability concepts in managing ecological systems. *Ecological Applications* 9:1179–1188.

Langdon, S. J. 1993. *The native people of Alaska.* Third edition. Anchorage, AK: Greatland Graphics.

Larsen, C., R. Motyka, J. Freymueller, K. Echelmeyer, and E. Ivins. 2005. Rapid viscoelastic uplift in southeast Alaska caused by post-Little Ice Age glacial retreat. *Earth and Planetary Science Letters* 237:548–560.

Laurance, W. F., T. E. Lovejoy, H. L. Vasconcelos, E. M. Bruna, R. K. Didham, P. C. Stouffer, C. Gascon, R. O. Bierregaard, S. G. Laurance, and E. Sampaio. 2002. Ecosystem decay of Amazonian forest fragments: A 22-year investigation. *Conservation Biology* 16:605–618.

Lawford, R., P. Alaback, and E. R. Fuentes, editors. 1996. *High latitude rain forests of the west coast of the Americas: Climate, hydrology, ecology and conservation.* Ecological Studies 113. Berlin: Springer-Verlag.

Lawler, J. J., T. H. Tear, C. Pyke, M. R. Shaw, P. Gonzalez, P. Kareiva, L. Hansen, et al. 2010. Resource management in a changing and uncertain climate. *Frontiers in Ecology and the Environment* 8:35–43.

Ledig, F. T. 1988. The conservation of diversity in forest trees: Why and how should genes be conserved? *BioScience* 38:471–479.

Leidholt, K. L., W. McComb, and D. E. Hibbs. 1989. The effects of beaver on streams and stream-side characteristics and coho populations in western Oregon. *Northwest Science* 63(2).

Leighty, W. W., S. P. Hamburg, and J. Caouette. 2006. Effects of management on sequestration in forest biomass in southeast Alaska. *Ecosystems* 9:1051–1065.

Leopold, A. 1949. *A Sand County almanac and sketches here and there.* New York: Oxford University Press.

Leroux, S. J., F. K. A. Schmiegelow, R. B. Lessard, and S. G. Cumming. 2007. Minimum dynamic reserves: A framework for determining reserve size in ecosystems structured by large disturbances. *Biological Conservation* 138:464–473.

Lertzman, K. P., D. G. Gavin, D. J. Hallet, L. B. Brubaker, D. Lepofsky, and R. Mathewes. 2002. Long-term fire regime estimated from soil charcoal in coastal temperate rain forests. *Ecology and Society* 6:5. http://www.ecologyandsociety.org/vol6/iss2/art5.

Lertzman, K. P., and C. S. Krebs. 1991. Gap-phase structure of a subalpine old-growth forest. *Canadian Journal of Forest Research* 21:1730–1741.

Lertzman, K., L. Kremsater, A. MacKinnon, and F. Bunnell. 1993. *Why watersheds? Are intact watersheds the best units for conserving forest ecosystems?* Draft prepared for BC's Old Growth Strategy. Victoria, BC.

Lertzman, K. P., G. Sutherland, A. Inselberg, and S. Saunders. 1996. Canopy gaps and the landscape mosaic in a temperate rainforest. *Ecology* 77:1254–1270.

Lesica, P., and F. W. Allendorf. 1995. When are peripheral populations valuable for conservation? *Conservation Biology* 9:753–760.

Lessa, E. P., J. A. Cook, and J. L. Patton. 2003. Genetic footprints of demographic expansion in North America, but not Amazonia, following the Late Pleistocene. *Proceedings of the National Academy of Sciences* 100:10331–10334.

Levin, P. S., I. Kaplan, R. Grober-Dunsmore, P. M. Chittaro, S. Oyamada, K. Andrews, and M. Mangel. 2009. A framework for assessing the biodiversity and fishery aspects of marine reserves. *Journal of Applied Ecology* 46:735–742.

Lindenmayer, D. B., and J. F. Franklin. 2002. *Conserving forest biodiversity*. Washington, DC: Island Press.

Linke, S., R. H. Norris, and R. L. Pressey. 2008. Irreplaceability of river networks: Towards catchment-based conservation planning. *Journal of Applied Ecology* 45:1486–1495.

Lotspeich, F. B. 1980. Watersheds as the basic ecosystem: This conceptual framework provides a basis for a natural classification system. *Water Resources Bulletin* 16:581–586.

Lowe, W. H., G. E. Likens, and M. E. Power. 2006. Linking scales in stream ecology. *BioScience* 56:591–597.

Lucid, M., and J. A. Cook. 2004. Phylogeography of Keen's mouse (*Peromyscus keeni*) in a naturally fragmented landscape. *Journal of Mammalogy* 85:1149–1159.

MacArthur, R. H., and E. O. Wilson. 1967. *The theory of island biogeography*. Princeton Monographs in Population Biology. Princeton, NY: Princeton University Press.

MacDonald, P. 2000. Standing stem logging on the BC coast continues to develop, proving to be a viable harvesting option. *Logging and Sawmilling Journal*. Accessed April 9, 2011. http://www.forestnet.com/archives/June_00/helicopter.htm.

MacDonald, S. O., and J. A. Cook. 1996. The land mammal fauna of southeast Alaska. *Canadian Field-Naturalist* 110:571–598.

———. 2007. Mammals and amphibians of southeast Alaska. Special Publication, *Museum of Southwestern Biology* 8:1–191.

———. 2009. *Recent mammals of Alaska*. Fairbanks, AK: University of Alaska Press.

MacKinnon, A. 1998. Biodiversity and old-growth forests. In *Conservation biology principles for forested landscapes*, edited by J. Voller and S. Harrison, 146–184. Vancouver, BC: UBC Press.

———. 2003. West coast, temperate, old-growth forests. *Forestry Chronicle* 79:475–484.

Mackovjak, J. 2008. *Tongass timber: A history of logging and utilization in southeast Alaska, 1804–1960.* Unpublished draft, author's private collection, Sitka, AK.

MacLean, D. A., R. S. Seymour, M. K. Montigny, and C. Messier. 2009. Allocation of conservation efforts over the landscape: The TRIAD approach. In *Setting conservation targets for managed forest landscapes,* edited by M. A. Villard and B. G. Jonsson. Cambridge: Cambridge University Press.

Maguire, D. A., S. Canavan, C. B. Halpern, and K. B. Aubrey. 2005. Fate of taxa after variable-retention harvesting in Douglas-fir forests of the northwestern United States. In *Balancing ecosystems values: Innovative experiments for sustainable forestry,* edited by C.E. Peterson and D.A. Maguire, 271–279. General Tech. Report PNW-635. Portland, OR: USDA Forest Service, Pacific Northwest Research Station.

Maguire, D. A., C. B. Halpern, and D. L. Phillips. 2007. Changes in forest structure following variable-retention harvests in Douglas-fir dominated forests. *Forest Ecology and Management* 242:708–726.

Maier, J. A. K., J. M. Ver Hoef, A. D. McGuire, R. T. Bowyer, L. Saperstein, and H. A. Maier. 2005. Distribution and density of moose in relation to landscape characteristics: Effects of scale. *Canadian Journal Forest Research* 35:2233–2243.

Malard, F., U. Uehlinger, R. Zah, and K. Tockner. 2006. Flood-pulse and riverscape dynamics in a braided glacial river. *Ecology* 87:704–716.

Mandryk, C. A. S., H. Josenhans, D. W. Fedje, and R. W. Mathewes. 2001. Late Quaternary paleoenvironments of northwestern North America: Implications for inland versus coastal migration routes. *Quaternary Science Reviews* 20:301–314.

Manel, S., M. K. Schwartz, G. Luikart, and P. Taberlet. 2003. Landscape genetics: Combining landscape ecology and population genetics. *Trends in Ecology and Evolution* 18:189–197.

Mann, D., and T. D. Hamilton. 1995. Late Pleistocene and Holocene paleoenvironments of the North Pacific coast. *Quaternary Science Reviews* 14:449–471.

Marcot, B. G. 1997. *Species-environment relations (SER) database.* Portland, OR: USDA Forest Service, Pacific Northwest Research Station. http://www.icbemp.gov/spatial/metadata/databases/dbase.html.

———. 2002. An ecological functional basis for managing decaying wood for wildlife. In *Proceedings of the symposium on the ecology and management of dead wood in western forests, November 2–4, 1999, Reno, Nevada,* edited by W. F. Laudenslayer Jr., P. J. Shea, B. E. Valentine, C. P. Weatherspoon, and T. E. Lisle, 895–910. General Technical Report PSW-GTR-181. Albany, CA: USDA Forest Service, Pacific Southwest Research Station.

Marcot, B. G., and K. B. Aubry. 2003. The functional diversity of mammals in coniferous forests of western North America. In *Mammal community dynamics: Management and conservation in the coniferous forests of western North America*, edited by C. J. Zabel and R. G. Anthony, 631–664. Cambridge: Cambridge University Press.

Marcot, B. G., and C. H. Flather. 2007. Species-level strategies for conserving rare or little-known species. In *Conservation of rare or little-known species: Biological, social, and economic considerations*, edited by M. G. Raphael and R. Molina, 125–164. Washington, DC: Island Press.

Marcot, B. G., and R. Molina. 2006. Conservation of other species associated with older forest conditions. In *Northwest Forest Plan—the first 10 years (1994–2003): Synthesis of monitoring and research results*, edited by R. Haynes, B. T. Bormann, D. C. Lee, and J. R. Martin, 145–179. General Technical Report PNW-GTR-651. Portland OR: USDA Forest Service, Pacific Northwest Research Station.

———. 2007. Special considerations for the science, conservation, and management of rare or little-known species. In *Conservation of rare or little-known species: Biological, social, and economic considerations*, edited by M. G. Raphael and R. Molina, 93–124. Washington, DC: Island Press.

Marcot, B. G., T. A. O'Neil, J. B. Nyberg, A. MacKinnon, P. J. Paquet, and D. H. Johnson. 2006. Analyzing key ecological functions for transboundary subbasin assessments. In *Watersheds across boundaries: Science, sustainability, security*, edited by C. W. Slaughter and N. Berg, 37–50. Proceedings of the Ninth Biennial Watershed Management Council Conference, November 3–7, 2002, Stevenson, WA. Center for Water Resources Report No.107. Riverside, CA: University of California.

Marcot, B. G., and C. H. Sieg. 2007. System-level strategies for conserving rare or little-known species. In *Conservation of rare or little-known species: Biological, social, and economic considerations*, edited by M. G. Raphael and R. Molina, 165–186. Washington, DC: Island Press.

Marcot, B. G., and M. Vander Heyden. 2001. Key ecological functions of wildlife species. In *Wildlife-habitat relationships in Oregon and Washington*, edited by D. H. Johnson and T. A. O'Neil, 168–186. Corvallis, OR: Oregon State University Press.

Margules, C. R., A. O. Nicholls, and R. L. Pressey. 1988. Selecting networks of reserves to maximise biological diversity. *Biological Conservation* 43:63–76.

Margules, C. R., and R. L. Pressey. 2000. Systematic conservation planning. *Nature* 405:243–253.

Margules, C. R., and S. Sarkar. 2007. Systematic conservation planning. Cambridge: Cambridge University Press.

Marmorek, D. R., D. C. E. Robinson, C. Murray, and L. Greig. 2006. *Enabling adaptive forest management.* Final Report prepared for the National Commission on Science for Sustainable Forestry. Vancouver, BC: ESSA Technologies Ltd. Accessed May 20, 2010. http://ncseonline.org/CMS400 Example/uploadedFiles/NCSSF/.

Marsh, G. P. 1864. *Man and nature.* New York: Charles Scribners.

Martin, J. L., A. J. Gaston, and S. Hitier. 1995. The effects of island size and isolation on old growth forest habitat and bird diversity of Gwaii Haanas (Queen Charlotte Islands, Canada). *Oikos* 72:115–131.

Martín-López, B., E. Gómez-Baggethun, P. L. Lomas, and C. Montes. 2009. Effects of spatial and temporal scales on cultural services valuation. *Journal of Environmental Management* 90:1050–1059.

Mass, K. M., P. E. Bittenbender, and J. C. Still. 1995. *Mineral investigations in the Ketchikan mining district, southeastern Alaska, 1990–1994.* BLM-Alaska Open File Report 11–95. Anchorage, AK: USDI Bureau of Land Management.

———. 1996. *Mineral investigations on Baranof and Chichagof Islands, and vicinity, southeast Alaska, 1995.* BLM-Alaska Open File Report 60. Anchorage, AK: USDI Bureau of Land Management.

Matsuda, B. M., D. M. Green, and P. T. Gregory. 2006. *Amphibians and reptiles of British Columbia.* Victoria, BC: Royal BC Museum.

Matthews, E., and I. Fung. 1987. Methane emission from natural wetlands: Global distribution, area, and environmental characteristics of sources. *Global Biogeochem. Cycles* 1:61–86.

Mazza, R. 2003. *Hunter demand for deer on Prince of Wales Island, Alaska: An analysis of influencing factors.* General Technical Report PNW-GTR-581. Portland, OR: USDA Forest Service.

McCabe, T. T., and I. M. Cowan. 1945. *Peromyscus maniculatus macrorhinus* and the problem of insularity. *Transactions of the Royal Canadian Institute* 25:117–215.

McCarthy, M. A., C. J. Thompson, and H. P. Possingham. 2005. Theory for designing nature reserves for single species. *American Naturalist* 165:250–257.

McClellan, M. H. 2008. Adaptive management of young stands on the Tongass National Forest. In *Integrated restoration of forested ecosystems to achieve multi-resource benefits: Proceedings of the 2007 National Silviculture Workshop*, edited by R. L. Deal, 225–232. General Tech. Report PNW-GTR-733. Portland, OR: USDA Forest Service, Pacific Northwest Research Station.

McClellan, M. H., and P. E. Hennon. 2005. Maintaining old-growth features in forests used for wood production in southeast Alaska. In *Balancing ecosystems values: Innovative experiments for sustainable forestry*, edited by C. E. Peterson and D. A. Maguire, 127–133. General Tech. Report PNW-635. Portland, OR: USDA Forest Service, Pacific Northwest Research Station.

McClellan, M. H., D. N. Swanston, P. E. Hennon, R. L. Deal, T. L. De Santo, and M. S. Wipfli. 2000. Alternates to clearcutting in the old-growth forests of southeast Alaska: Study plan and establishment report. General Tech. Report PNW-494. Portland, OR: USDA Forest Service, Pacific Northwest Research Station.

McClory, J., and T. Gotthardt. 2008. Non-native and invasive animals of Alaska: A comprehensive list and select species status reports; final report. Anchorage: Alaska Natural Heritage Program, University of Alaska.

McCullough, D. A. 1999. *A review and synthesis of effects of alterations to the water temperature regimen freshwater life stages of salmonids, with special reference to Chinkook salmon*. EPA 910-R-99-010. Seattle, WA: US Environmental Protection Agency, Region 10.

McCurdy, S. 2008. *Production of coho salmon from the 2005 smolt migration from Chuck Creek in southeast Alaska*. Alaska Department of Fish and Game Fisheries Data Series No. 08–04. Anchorage, AK: Alaska Department of Fish and Game.

McDowell Group. 1989. *Alaska seafood industry study—a technical report: An economic profile of the seafood industry in Alaska*. Unpublished report. Juneau, AK: McDowell Group, 416 Harris Street, 99801.

———. 1991. *Alaska's visitor industry: An economic profile*. Unpublished report prepared for Alaska Division of Tourism, Department of Commerce and Economic Development. Juneau, AK: McDowell Group, 416 Harris St., Suite 301, 99801.

———. 1998. *Cruise industry impacts on local governments in southeast Alaska: An assessment of the effects of the cruise industry on local government revenue and expenditures*. Juneau, AK: Southeast Conference, 213 3rd Street, Suite 124, 99801.

———. 2002. Southeast Alaska and the new Alaska traveler's survey. Presented at the conference *Working together: Tourism in southeast Alaska*. Juneau, AK: McDowell Group, 416 Harris St., Suite 301, 99801.

———. 2008. *An assessment of the economic impact of forest restoration efforts in southeast Alaska*. Report prepared for The Nature Conservancy. Juneau, AK: McDowell Group, 416 Harris St., Suite 301, 99801.

———. 2011. *Alaska visitor statistics program VI: Interim visitor volume report, summer 2010*. Report prepared for State of Alaska, Department of Commerce, Community, and Economic Development, Division of Economic Development. Juneau, AK: McDowell Group, 416 Harris St., Suite 301, 99801.

McGuire, A. D., C. Wirth, M. Apps, J. Beringer, J. Clein, H. Epstein, D. W. Kicklighter, *et al.* 2002. Environmental variation, vegetation distribution, carbon dynamics and water/energy exchange at high latitudes. *Journal of Vegetation Science* 13:301–314.

McGuire, A. D., M. Apps, F. S. Chapin III, R. Dargaville, M. D. Flannigan, E. S. Kasischke, D. Kicklighter, *et al.* 2004. Land cover disturbances and feedbacks to the climate system in Canada and Alaska. In *Land change science: Observing, monitoring, and understanding trajectories of change on the earth's surface*, edited by G. Gutman, A. C. Janetos, C. O. Justice, E. F. Moran, J. F. Mustard, R. R. Rindfuss, D. Skole, B. L. Turner II, and M. A. Cochrane, 139–161. Dordrecht, Netherlands: Kluwer Academic Publishers.

McKean, J. A., D. J. Isaak, and C. W. Wright. 2008. Geomorphic controls on salmon nesting patterns described by a new, narrow-beam terrestrial–aquatic lidar. *Frontiers in Ecology and the Environment* 6:125–130.

McNay, R. S. 1995. The ecology of movements made by Columbian black-tailed deer. PhD Dissertation, University of British Columbia, Vancouver, BC.

McNay, R. S., and J. M. Voller. 1995. Mortality causes and survival estimates for adult female Columbian black-tailed deer. *Journal of Wildlife Management* 59:138–146.

McNeely, J. A., H. A. Mooney, L. E. Neville, P. J. Schei, and J. K. Waage, editors. 2001. *A global strategy on invasive alien species*. Gland, Switzerland, and Cambridge: IUCN.

McRae, B. H., N. H. Schumaker, R. B. McKane, R. T. Busing, A. M. Solomon, and C. A. Burdick. 2008. A multi-model framework for simulating wildlife population response to land-use and climate change. *Ecological Modeling* 219:77–91.

Mech, S. G., and J. G. Hallett. 2001. Evaluating the effectiveness of corridors: A genetic approach. *Conservation Biology* 15:467–474.

Mehrkens, J. R. 2009. *Tongass budget analysis 1991–2009*. Author's private collection, Juneau, AK.

Meidinger, D. V., and J. Pojar. 1991. *Ecosystems of British Columbia*. Special Report Series 6. Victoria, BC: Research Branch, British Columbia Ministry of Forests.

Mendenhall, V. M. 1992. Distribution, breeding records, and conservation problems of the marbled murrelet in Alaska. *Proceedings of the Western Foundation of Vertebrate Zoology* 5:5–16.

Millar, C. I., N. L. Stephenson, and S. L. Stephens. 2007. Climate change and forests of the future: Managing in the face of uncertainty. *Ecological Applications* 17:2145–2151.

Millennium Ecosystem Assessment. 2003. *Ecosystems and human well-being*. Washington, DC: Island Press.

Miller, J. n.d. Alaskan Tlingit and Tsimshian. University of Washington, Digital Collections. Seattle, WA. http://content.lib.washington.edu/aipnw/miller1 .html.

Miller, R. D. 1973. *Gastineau channel formation: A composite glaciomarine deposit near Juneau, Alaska*. USGS Bulletin 1394-C. Washington, DC: Government Printing Office.

Millien, V. 2006. Morphological evolution is accelerated among insular mammals. *PLOS Biology* 4:1863–1868.

Millien-Parra, V. and J.-J. Jaeger. 1999. Island biogeography of the Japanese terrestrial mammal assemblages: An example of a relict fauna. *Journal of Biogeography* 26:959–972.

Milner, A. M., C. L. Fastie, F. S. Chapin III, D. R. Engstrom, and L. C. Sharman. 2007. Interactions and linkages among ecosystems during landscape evolution. *BioScience* 57:237–247.

Minshall, G. W., K. W. Cummins, R. C. Petersen, C. E. Cushing, D. A. Bruns, J. R. Sedell, and R. L. Vannote. 1985. Developments in stream ecosystem theory. *Canadian Journal of Fisheries and Aquatic Sciences* 42:1045–1055.

Minshall, G. W., R. C. Petersen, K. W. Cummins, T. L. Bott, J. R. Sedell, C. E. Cushing, and R. L. Vannote. 1983. Interbiome comparison of stream ecosystem dynamics. *Ecological Monographs* 53:1–25.

Minteer, B. A., and J. P. Collins. 2010. Move it or lose it? The ecological ethics of relocating species under climate change. *Ecological Applications* 20:1801–1804.

Mitchell, A. K., R. Koppenaal, G. Goodmanson, R. Benton, and T. Bown. 2007. Regenerating montane conifers with variable retention systems in a coastal

British Columbia forest: 10-year results. *Forest Ecology and Management* 246:240–250.

Mitchell, R. J. 1995. A synopsis of windthrow in British Columbia: Occurrence, implications, assessment, and management. In *Wind and trees*, edited by M. P. Coutts and J. Grace, chap. 25. Cambridge and New York: Cambridge University Press.

Mitchell, S. J., and W. J. Beese. 2002. The retention system: Reconciling variable retention with the principles of silvicultural systems. *Forest Chronicles* 78:397–403.

Mitchell, S. J., T. Hailemariam, and Y. Kulis. 2001. Empirical modeling of cut-block edge windthrow risk on Vancouver Island, Canada, using stand level information. *Forest Ecology and Management* 154:117–130.

Mitchell, S. J., N. Lanquaye-Opoku, H. Modzelewski, Y. Shen, R. Stull, P. Jackson, B. Murphy, and J. C. Ruel. 2008. Comparison of wind speeds obtained using numerical weather prediction models and topographic exposure indices for predicting windthrow in mountainous terrain. *Forest Ecology and Management* 254:193–204.

Montgomery, D. R. 1994. Road surface drainage, channel initiation, and slope stability. *Water Resources Research* 30:91–109.

Montigny, M. K., and D. A. MacLean. 2006. Triad forest management: Scenario analysis of forest zoning effects on timber and non-timber values in New-Brunswick, Canada. *Forest Chronicles* 82:496–511.

Moffett, A., and S. Sarkar. 2006. Incorporating multiple criteria into the design of conservation area networks: A minireview with recommendations. *Diversity and Distributions* 12:125–137.

Moodie, G. E., and T. E. Reimchen. 1973. Endemism and conservation of stickleback populations of the Queen Charlotte Islands. *Canadian Field-Naturalist* 87:173–175.

Moore, K. 1991. *An inventory of watersheds in the coastal temperate forests of British Columbia*. Vancouver, BC: Earthlife Canada Foundation and Ecotrust/Conservation International.

Moritz, C. 2005. Overview: Rainforest history and dynamics in the Australian wet tropics. In Tropical rainforests. past, present, and future, edited by E. C. Bermingham, W. Dick, and C Moritz, 313–321. University of Chicago Press.

Morrison, M. L., B. G. Marcot, and R. W. Mannan. 2006. Wildlife-habitat relationships: Concepts and applications. Third edition. Washington, DC: Island Press.

Morse, K. 2000. *Responding to the market demand for Tongass timber*. R10-MB-372. Juneau, AK: USDA Forest Service, Alaska Region.

Moss, M. L. 2008. Outer coast maritime adaptations in southern southeast Alaska: Tlingit or Haida? *Artic Anthropology* 45:41–60.

Moss, M. L., J. M. Erlandson, and R. Stuckenrath. 1989. The antiquity of Tlingit settlement on Admiralty Island, southeast Alaska. *American Antiquity* 54:534–543.

Mote, P., D. Canning, D. Fluharty, R. Francis, J. Franklin, A. Hamlet, M. Hershman, *et al.* 1999. *Impacts of climate variability and change in the Pacific Northwest.* Seattle: JISAO Climate Impacts Group, University of Washington.

Muhar, S., and M. Jungwirth. 1998. Habitat integrity of running waters—assessment criteria and their biological relevance. *Hydrobiologia* 386:195–202.

Murcia, C. 1995. Edge effects in fragmented forests: Implications for conservation. *Trends in Ecology and Evolution* 10:58–62.

Murphy, D. D., and B. R. Noon. 1992. Integrating scientific methods with habitat conservation planning: Reserve design for the northern spotted owl. *Ecological Applications* 2:3–17.

Murphy, M. L., J. Heifetz, S. W. Johnson, K. V. Koski, J. F. Thedinga. 1986. Effects of clear-cut logging with and without buffer strips on juvenile salmonids in Alaskan streams. *Canadian Journal of Fisheries and Aquatic Sciences* 43:1521–1533.

Murphy, M. L., and K. V. Koski. 1989. Input and depletion of woody debris in Alaskan streams and implications for streamside management. *North American Journal of Fisheries Management* 9:427–436.

Nagorsen, D. W. 1994. Endangered mammals in British Columbia. In *Biodiversity in British Columbia: Our changing environment,* edited by L. E. Harding and E. McCullum, 143–151. Ottawa: Environment Canada, Canadian Wildlife Service.

———. 2004. Canada's endemic mammals at risk: Recent taxonomic advances and priorities for conservation. In *Proceedings of the species at risk 2004: Pathways to recovery conference, March 2–6, 2004,* edited by T. D. Hooper, 1–2. Victoria, BC: Species at Risk 2004 Pathways to Recovery Organizing Committee.

Nagorsen, D. W., and G. Keddie. 2000. Late Pleistocene mountain goats (*Oreamnos americanus*) from Vancouver Island: Biogeographic implications. *Journal of Mammalogy* 81:666–675.

Naiman, R. J., R. E. Bilby, and P. A. Bisson. 2000. Riparian ecology and management in the Pacific coastal rain forest. *Bioscience* 50:996–1011.

Naiman, R. J., R. E. Bilby, D. E. Schindler, and J. M. Helfield. 2002. Pacific salmon, nutrients, and the dynamics of freshwater and riparian ecosystems. *Ecosystems* 5:399–417.

Naiman, R. J., P. Bisson, R. Lee, and M. Turner. 1997. Approaches to management at the watershed scale. In *Creating a forestry for the 21st century: The science of ecosystem management*, edited by K. Kohm and J. Franklin, 239–253. Washington, DC: Island Press.

Naske, C. M., and H. E. Slotnick. 1979. *Alaska: A history of the 49th state*. Grand Rapids, MI: Wm. B. Eerdmans Publishing Co.

National Academy of Sciences. 2002. *Riparian areas: Functions and strategies for management*. Washington, DC: National Academy Press.

National Research Council. 2007. Progress toward restoring the Everglades: The first biennial review—2006. Washington DC: National Academy Press.

Neal, E. G., E. Hood, and K. Smikrud. 2010. Contribution of glacier runoff to freshwater discharge into the Gulf of Alaska. *Geophysical Research Letters* 37:LO6404.

Neiland, B. J. 1971. The forest-bog complex of southeastern Alaska. *Vegetation* 22:1–64.

Neilson, R. P. 1993. Transient ecotone response to climatic change: Some conceptual and modelling approaches. *Ecological Applications* 3:385–395.

Nel, J. L., D. J. Roux, G. Maree, C. J. Kleynhans, J. Moolman, B. Reyers, M. Rouget, and R. M. Cowling. 2007. Rivers in peril inside and outside protected areas: A systematic approach to conservation assessment of river ecosystems. *Diversity and Distributions* 13:341–352.

Nelson, E. W. 1887. *Report upon natural history collections made in Alaska between the years 1877 and 1881*. Arctic Series of Publications, US Signal Service, III.

Neuheimer, A. B., and C. T. Taggart. 2007. The growing degree-day and fish size-at-age: The overlooked metric. *Canadian Journal of Fisheries and Aquatic Science* 64:375–385.

New York Times. 1959. "Indians in Alaska win U.S. land suit." October 7.

Newmark, W. D. 1987. A land-bridge perspective on mammalian extinctions in western North American parks. *Nature* 325:430–432.

Newton, R. G., and M. L. Moss. 2005. *Haa Atxaayi Haa Kusteeyix Sittee, Our food is our Tlingit way of life, excerpts from oral interviews*. R10-MR-30. Juneau, AK: USDA Forest Service, Alaska Region.

Ngoc, Q. T. K. 2010. Creation of marine reserves and incentives for biodiversity conservation. *Natural Resource Modeling* 23:138–175.

Nichols, J., and B. Frenette. 2003. *Final report on the road condition and fish passage monitoring project.* Douglas, AK: Alaska Department of Fish and Game, Division of Habitat and Restoration.

Nicholson, E., and H. P. Possingham. 2006. Objectives for multiple-species conservation planning. *Conservation Biology* 20:871–881.

Nicholson, E., M. I. Westphal, K. Frank, W. A. Rochester, R. L. Pressey, D. B. Lindenmayer, and H. P. Possingham. 2006. A new method for conservation planning for the persistence of multiple species. *Ecology Letters* 9:1049–1060.

Nickelson, T. E., J. D. Rodgers, S. L. Johnson, and M. F. Solazzi. 1992. Seasonal changes in habitat use by juvenile coho salmon (*Oncorhynchus kisutch*) in Oregon coastal streams. *Canadian Journal of Fisheries and Aquatic Sciences* 49:783–789.

Nie, M. 2006. Governing the Tongass: National forest conflict and political decision making. *Environmental Law* 36:385–480.

Nilsson, C., and F. Götmark. 1992. Protected areas in Sweden: Is natural variety adequately represented? *Conservation Biology* 6:232–242.

Noble, I. R. 1993. A model of the responses of ecotones to climate change. *Ecological Applications* 3:396–403.

Noon, B. R., and J. A. Blakesly. 2006. Conservation of northern spotted owls under the Northwest Forest Plan. *Conservation Biology* 20:288–296.

North, M. P., and W. S. Keeton. 2008. Emulating natural disturbance regimes: An emerging approach for sustainable forest management. In *Patterns and processes in forest landscapes—multiple use and sustainable management*, edited by R. Lafortezza, J. Chen, G. Sanesi, and T. R. Crow, 341–372. Netherlands: Springer.

Norton, H. H. 1981. Plant use in Kaigani Haida culture: Correction of an ethnohistorical oversight. *Economic Botany* 35:434–449.

Nowacki, G. J., and M. G. Kramer 1998. *The effects of wind disturbance on temperate rain forest structure and dynamics of southeast Alaska.* PNW-GTR-421. Portland, OR: USDA Forest Service, Pacific Northwest Research Station.

Nowacki, G., P. Krosse, G. Fisher, D. Brew, T. Brock, M. Shephard, W. Pawuk, J. Baichtal, and E. Kissinger. 2001. Ecological subsections of southeast Alaska and neighboring areas of Canada. Tech. Publ. No. R10-TP-75. Juneau, AK: USDA Forest Service, Alaska Region.

Nunn, P. D. 2004. Through a mist on the ocean: Human understanding of island environments. *Tijdschrift voor Economische en Sociale Geografie* 95:311–325.

Nyberg, J. B., and D. W. Janz, editors. 1990. *Deer and elk habitats in coastal forests of southern British Columbia.* Special Report Series No. 5. Victoria, BC: BC Ministry of Forests, BC Ministry of Environment.

Oberg, K. 1973. *The social economy of the Tlingit Indians.* Seattle, WA: University of Washington Press.

Olson, D. M., and E. Dinerstein. 1998. The global 200: A representative approach to conserving the Earth's most biologically valuable ecoregions. *Conservation Biology* 12:502–515.

Olson, R. L. 1967. *The social structure and social life of the Tlingit Indians in Alaska.* Anthopological Records Vol. 26. Berkeley and Los Angeles: University of California Press.

O'Neil, T. A., D. H. Johnson, C. Barrett, M. Trevithick, K. A. Bettinger, C. Kiilsgaard, M. Vander Heyden, *et al.* 2001. Matrixes for wildlife-habitat relationships in Oregon and Washington. CD-ROM in *Wildlife-habitat relationships in Oregon and Washington,* edited by D. H. Johnson and T. A. O'Neil. Corvallis, OR: Oregon State University Press.

O'Neill, R. V., D. L. DeAngelis, J. B. Waide, and T. F .H. Allen. 1986. A hierarchical concept of ecosystems. *Monographs in Population Biology 23.* Princeton, NJ: Princeton University Press.

Orr, J. C., V. J. Fabry, O. Aumont, L. Bopp, S. C. Doney, R. A. Feely, A. Gnanadesikan, *et al.* 2005. Anthropogenic ocean acidification over the twenty-first century and its impact on calcifying organisms. *Nature* 437:681–686.

Osher, L. J., and C. T. Flannagan. 2007. Soil/landscape relationships in a mesotidal Maine estuary. *Soil Science Society of America* 71:1323–1334.

Otis, A. T., W. D. Honey, T. C. Hogg, and K. K. Lakin. 1986. The Forest Service and the Civilian Conservation Corps: 1933–42. FS 395. Washington, DC:, USDA Forest Service.

Ott, R. A., and G. P. Juday. 2002. Canopy gap characteristics and their implications for management in the temperate rainforests of southeast Alaska. *Forest Ecology and Management* 159:271–291.

Outerbridge, R. A., and J. A. Trofymow. 2004. Diversity of ectomycorrhizae on experimentally planted Douglas-fir seedlings in variable retention forestry sites on southern Vancouver Island. *Canadian Journal of Botany* 82:1671–1681.

———. 2008. *How do different levels of green tree retention affect the survival of ectomycorrhizae on the southern coast of British Columbia.* Progress report prepared for the BC Forest Science Program. Victoria, BC: Canadian Forest Service.

Ovaska, K., L., Chichester, and L. Sopuck. 2010. Terrestrial gastropods from Haida

Gwaii (Queen Charlotte Islands), British Columbia, Canada, including description of a new northern endemic slug (Gastropoda: *Stylommatophora arionidae*). *The Nautilus* 124:25–33.

Ovaska, K., and L. Sopuck. 2008. *Terrestrial gastropods as focal species for monitoring ecological effects of variable-retention logging practices*. Final report to Western Forest Products and the BC Forest Science Program. Sidney, BC: Biolinx Environmental Research Ltd.

Pahlke, K. A. 2005. Escapements of Chinook salmon in southeast Alaska and transboundary rivers in 2003. Fishery Data Series No. 05–20. Juneau, AK: Alaska Department of Fish and Game.

Paine, R. T., J. J. Tegner, and E. A. Johnson. 1998. Compounded perturbations yield ecological surprises. *Ecosystems* 1:535–545.

Palik, B. J., R. J. Mitchell, and J. Hiers. 2002. Modeling silviculture after natural disturbance to maintain biological diversity in the longleaf pine (*Pinus palustris*) ecosystem: Balancing complexity and implementation. *Forest Ecology and Management* 155:347–356.

Palmer, M. A. 2009. River restoration, habitat heterogeneity and biodiversity: A failure of theory or practice? *Freshwater Biology* 55:1–18.

Paquet, P. C., C. T. Darimont, R. J. Nelson, and K. Bennett. 2004. A critical assessment of protection for key wildlife and salmon habitats under the proposed British Columbia Central Coast Land and Resource Management Plan. Rainforest Conservation Society. http://www.raincoast.org/files/publications/reports/CCLRMP-final-analysis.pdf.

Parker, K. C., C. Robbins, and T. Hanley. 1984. Energy expenditures for locomotion by mule deer and elk. *Journal of Wildlife Management* 48:474–488.

Parmesan, C. 2006. Ecological and evolutionary responses to recent climate change. *Annual Review of Ecology, Evolution and Systematics* 37:637–699.

Paul, W. P., Sr. 1979. My family came to claim this land. In *Alaska's Native people*, edited by L. Morgan, 230–235. *Alaska Geographic* 6:230–235.

Peacock, E. 2004. Population, genetic, and behavioral studies of black bears *Ursus americanus* in southeast Alaska. Unpublished Dissertation, University of Nevada, Reno.

Peacock, E., M. M. Peacock, and K. Titus. 2007. Black bears in southeast Alaska: The fate of two ancient lineages in the face of contemporary movement. *Journal of Zoology* 271:445–454.

Pearsall, I. A. 2008. *Study to assess the efficacy of ground beetles (Coleoptera: Carabidae) as ecological indicators in two variable-retention experimental sites: A temporal comparison.* Progress report to Western Forest Products and the BC Forest Science Program. Nanaimo, BC: Pearsall Ecological Consulting.

Pearson, A. 2010. Natural and logging disturbances in the temperate rain forests of the Central Coast, British Columbia. *Canadian Journal of Forest Research* 40:1970–1984.

Peck, C. E., Sr. 1986. *The tides people.* Juneau, AK: Juneau Indian Studies Program.

Pemberton, M. 2009. Forest restoration helps heal Tongass' scars. *Seattle Times*, September 7. http://seattletimes.nwsource.com/html/localnews/2009954179_apakforestrestoration.html.

Perakis, S. S., and L. O. Hedin. 2002. Fluxes and fates of nitrogen in soil of an unpolluted old-growth temperate forest, southern Chile. *Ecology* 82:2245–2260.

Perault, D. R., and M. V. Lomolino. 2000. Corridors and mammal community structure across a fragmented, old-growth forest landscape. *Ecological Monographs* 70:401–422.

Perera, A. H., L. J. Buse, and M.G. Weber, editors. 2004. *Emulating natural forest landscape disturbances: Concepts and applications.* New York: Columbia University Press.

Person, D. K. 2001. Alexander Archipelago wolves: Ecology and population viability in a disturbed, insular landscape. PhD Dissertation, University of Alaska Fairbanks.

———. 2009. Habitat use and survivorship of Sitka black-tailed deer in southeast Alaska: A regional meta-analysis and synthesis. Federal Aid in Wildlife Restoration Final Report W-33-3. Juneau, AK: Alaska Department of Fish and Game.

Person, D. K., T. J. Brinkman, F. S. Chapin III, K. Hundertmark, and W. P. Smith. 2009. *Developing a method to estimate deer abundance on Prince of Wales Island, Alaska.* Alaska Dept. Fish and Game Final Research Report to USFS Wildlife Information System, Ketchikan, AK 99901.

Person, D. K., M. D. Kirchhoff, V. Van Ballenberghe, G. C. Iverson, and E. Grossman. 1996. The Alexander Archipelago wolf: A conservation assessment. General Tech. Report PNW-GTR-384. Juneau, AK: USDA Forest Service.

Person, D. K., and A. L. Russell. 2008. Correlates of mortality in an exploited wolf population. *Journal of Wildlife Management* 72:1540–1549.

———. 2009. Reproduction and den site selection by wolves in a disturbed landscape. *Northwest Science* 83:211–224.

Pess, G. R., D. R. Montgomery, R. E. Bilby, A. E. Steel, B. E. Feist, and H. M. Greenberg. 2002. Landscape characteristics, land use, and coho salmon (*Oncorhynchus kisutch*) abundance, Snohomish River, Washington State, USA. *Canadian Journal of Fisheries and Aquatic Sciences* 59:613–623.

Petersen, K., and J. Bruns. 2005. Prince of Wales Island: Hot bed for small sawmill operators bent on value-added commodities. *Alaska Business Monthly* 21:70.

Petit, S., L. Griffiths, S. S. Smart, G. M. Smith, R. C. Stuart and S. M. Wright. 2004. Effects of area and isolation of woodland patches on herbaceous plant species richness across Great Britain. *Landscape Ecology* 19:463–471.

Phillips, E.J. 1996. Comparing silvicultural systems in a coastal montane forest: Productivity and cost of harvesting operations., FRDA Rep. 247. Victoria, BC: BC Ministry of Forests.

Phillips, S. J., and M. Dudik. 2008. Modeling of species distributions with Maxent: New extensions and a comprehensive evaluation. *Ecography* 31:161–175.

Piatt, J. F., and R. G. Ford. 1993. Distribution and abundance of marbled murrelets in Alaska. *Condor* 95:662–669.

Pickett, S.T.A., and J. N. Thompson. 1978. Patch dynamics and the design of nature reserves. *Biological Conservation* 13:27–37.

Pickett, S. T. A., and P. S. White. 1985. *The ecology of natural disturbance and patch dynamics.* New York: Academic Press.

Pimentel, D., L. Westra, and R. F. Noss, editors. 2000. *Ecological integrity: Integrating environment, conservation, and health.* Washington DC: Island Press.

Pojar, J., K. Klinka, and D. V. Meidinger. 1987. Biogeoclimatic ecosystem classification in British Columbia. *Forest Ecology and Management* 22:119–154.

Pojar, J., C. Rowan, A. MacKinnon, D. Coates, and P. LePage. 1999. *Silvicultural options in the Central Coast.* Victoria, BC: British Columbia Environment and Land Use Committee.

Pollock, M. M., R. J. Naiman, and T. A. Hanley. 1998. Plant species richness in riparian wetlands—a test of biodiversity theory. *Ecology* 79:94–105.

Porter, B. 2007. Unit 2 deer management report. In *Deer management report of survey and inventory activities 1 July 2004–30 June 2006*, edited by P. Harper, 30–40. Juneau, AK: Alaska Department of Fish and Game.

———. 2008. Unit 2 black bear management report. In *Black bear management report of survey and inventory activities 1 July 2004–30 June 2007*, edited by P. Harper, 66–91. Juneau, AK: Alaska Department of Fish and Game.

Possingham, H. P., H. Grantham, and C. Rondinini. 2007. How can you conserve species that haven't been found? *Journal of Biogeography* 34:758–759.

Post, D. M., M. W. Doyle, J. L. Sabo, and J. C. Finlay. 2007. The problem of boundaries in defining ecosystems: A potential landmine for uniting geomorphology and ecology. *Geomorphology* 89:111–126.

Poulin, J. F., M. A. Villard, M. Edman, P. J. Goulet, and A. M. Eriksson. 2008. Thresholds in nesting habitat requirements of an old forest specialist, the brown creeper (*Certhia americana*), as conservation targets. *Biological Conservation* 141:1129–1137.

Powell, J., D. V. D'Amore, T. Brock, R. Thompson, P. Heuberth, and M. T. Walter. 2003. *Guidebook for the hydrogeomorphic assessment of riverine and slope river proximal wetlands in southeast Alaska.* Alaska Department of Environmental Conservation. www.dec.state.ak.us/water/wnpspc/wetlands/hgm approach.htm.

Power, M. E., and W. E. Dietrich. 2002. Food webs in river networks. *Ecological Research* 17:451–471.

Pressey, R. L., C. J. Humphries, C. R. Margules, R. I. Vane-Wright, and P. H. Williams. 1993. Beyond opportunism: Key principles for systematic reserve selection. *Trends in Ecology and Evolution* 8:124–128.

Preston, M. I., and R. W. Campbell. 2009. *Monitoring birds for sustainable forest management: Species-habitat associations and population trends for the southwest coast of British Columbia, 2000–2008.* Final report to Western Forest Products. Victoria, BC: Westcam Consulting Services.

Preston, M. I., and A. S. Harestad. 2007. Community and species responses by birds to group retention in a coastal temperate forest on Vancouver Island, British Columbia. *Forest Ecology and Management* 243:156–167.

Price, K., R. F. Holt, and L. Kremsater. 2007. How much is really enough? Informing old growth targets with threshold science. http://www.veridianecological.ca/publications/How_much_is_enough_DRAFT.pdf.

Price, K., A. Roburn, and A. MacKinnon. 2009. Ecosystem-based management in the Great Bear Rainforest. *Forest Ecology and Management* 258:495–503.

Price, K., J. Pojar, A. Roburn, L. Brewer, and N. Poirier. 1998. Windthrown or clearcut: What's the difference? *Northwest Science* 72:30–33.

Pringle, C. 2001. Hydrologic connectivity and the management of biological reserves: A global perspective. *Ecological Applications* 11:981–998.

Pritzker, B. M. 2000. Barry M. Pritzker, A Native American encyclopedia: History, culture, and peoples. Oxford: Oxford University Press.

Province of British Columbia. 1993. *A protected areas strategy for British Columbia.* Victoria, BC: Queen's Printer.

Prugh, L. R., K. E. Hodges, R. E. Sinclair, and J. S. Brashares. 2008. Effect of habitat area and isolation on fragmented animal populations. *Proceedings of the National Academy of Sciences* 105:20770–20775.

Puettmann, K. J., K. D. Coates, and C. Messier. 2009. *A critique of silviculture: Managing for complexity.* Washington, DC: Island Press.

Quinn, T. P., S. M. Carlson, S. M. Gende, and H. B. Rich. 2009. Transportation of Pacific salmon carcasses from streams to riparian forests by bears. *Canadian Journal of Zoology* 87:195–203.

Rakestraw, L. 1981. *A history of the United States Forest Service in Alaska.* Anchorage, AK: Alaska Historical Commission, USDA Forest Service, Alaska Region.

Ramsey, C. L., P. A. Griffiths, D. W. Fedje, R. J. Wigen, and Q. Mackie. 2004. Preliminary investigation of a late Wisconsinan fauna from K1 cave, Queen Charlotte Islands (Haida Gwaii), Canada. *Quaternary Research* 62:105–109.

Raphael, M. G., and R. Molina, editors. 2007. *Conservation of rare or little-known species: Biological, social, and economic considerations.* Washington, DC: Island Press.

Redhead, S. A. 1994. Macrofungi of British Columbia. In *Biodiversity in British Columbia: our changing environment,* edited by L. E. Harding and E. McCullum, 81–89. Ottawa: Environment Canada, Canadian Wildlife Service.

Redman, E. 1986. History of the Juneau gold belt 1869–1965: Development of the mines and prospects from Windham Bay to Berners Bay. Open File Report 91–86. Anchorage, AK: USDA Bureau of Mines.

Rehfeldt, G. E. 1989. Ecological adaptations in Douglas-fir (*Pseudotsuga menziesii* var. *glauca*): A synthesis. *Forest Ecology and Management* 28:203–215.

Reimchen, T. E. 1989. Loss of nuptial color in threespine stickleback *Gasterosteus. Evolution* 43:450–460.

———. 1994. Predators and evolution in threespine stickleback. In *Evolution of the threespine stickleback,* edited by M. A. Bell and S. A. Foster, 240–273. Oxford: Oxford University Press.

Reimchen, T. E., and A. Byun. 2005. The evolution of endemic species in Haida Gwaii. In *Haida Gwaii: Human history and environment from the time of the loon to the time of the iron people,* edited by D. W. Fedje and R. W. Mathewes, 77–95. Vancouver, BC: University of British Columbia Press.

Reimchen, T. E., D. Mathewson, M. D. Hocking, J. Moran, and D. Harris. 2003. Isotopic evidence for enrichment of salmon-derived nutrients in vegetation, soil and insects in riparian zones in coastal British Columbia. *American Fisheries Society Symposium* 34:59–69.

Ribe, R. G. 2005. Comparing changes in scenic beauty produced by green-tree retention harvests, thinnings and clearcuts: Evidence from three Pacific Northwest experiments. In *Balancing ecosystems values: Innovative experiments for sustainable forestry*, edited by C. E. Peterson and D. A. Maguire, 131–147. General Tech. Report PNW-635. Portland, OR: USDA Forest Service, Pacific Northwest Research Station.

Richardson, J. S., and R. J. Danehy. 2007. A synthesis of the ecology of headwater streams and their riparian zones in temperate forests. *Forest Science* 53: 131–147.

Ricklefs, R., and E. Bermingham. 2008. The West Indies as a laboratory of biogeography and evolution. *Philosophical Transactions of the Royal Society B* 363:2393–2413.

Rigby, P., J. McConnaughey, and H. Saviko. 1991. Alaska commercial salmon catches, 1878–1991. Regional Information Report No. J91–16. Juneau, AK: Alaska Department of Fish and Game, Division of Commercial Fisheries.

Ripple, W. J., and B. van Valkenburgh. 2010. Linking top-down forces to the Pleistocene megafaunal extinctions. *BioScience* 60:516–526.

Rodrigues, A. S. L., S. Andelman, M. Bakarr, L. Boitani, T. Brooks, R. Cowling, L. Fishpool, *et al.* 2004. Effectiveness of the global protected area network in representing species diversity. *Nature* 428(6983): 640–643.

Rodrigues, A. S. L., H. Akcakaya, S. Andelman, M. Bakarr, L. Boitani, T. Brooks, J. Chanson, *et al.* 2004. Global gap analysis: Priority regions for expanding the global protected-area network. *BioScience* 54:1092–1100.

Roemer, H. 1994. Rare and endangered vascular plants in British Columbia. In *Biodiversity in British Columbia: Our changing environment*, edited by L. E. Harding and E. McCullum, 91–95. Ottawa: Environment Canada, Canadian Wildlife Service.

Rogers, G. W. 1960. Alaska in transition: the southeast region. Baltimore: Johns Hopkins Press.

Rogers, R. A., L. A. Rogers, R. S. Hoffmann, and A. Martin. 1991. Native American biological diversity and the biographic influence of ice age refugia. *Journal of Biogeography* 18:623–630.

Rollerson, T., C. M. Peters, and W. J. Beese. 2009. *Variable retention windthrow monitoring project: 2001–2009*. Final report to Western Forest Products, BC Forest Investment Account, Proj. No. 6746006. Vancouver, BC: Golder Associates Ltd.

Rosenvald, R., and A. Lõhmus. 2008. For what, when and where is green-tree retention better than clearcutting? A review of the biodiversity aspects. *Forest Ecology and Management* 255:1–15.

Rudis, D. D. 2001. *Kensington mine area baseline contaminants study, Alaska*. Technical Report SEES-TR-01–01. Juneau, AK: US Fish and Wildlife Service.

Rudolph, S. 1990. Ancient forests as genetic reserves for forestry. In *Ancient forests of the Pacific Northwest*, edited by E. A. Norse. Washington, DC: Island Press.

Ruhl, J. B., S. E. Kraft, and C. L. Lant. 2007. The law and policy of ecosystem services. Washington, DC: Island Press.

Ryan, M. W. 1996. *Bryophytes of British Columbia: rare species and priorities for inventory*. Working Paper 12. Victoria, BC: Research Branch, BC Ministry of Forests, and Wildlife Branch, BC Ministry of the Environment, Lands, and Parks.

Sauer, J. R., J. E. Hines, and J. Fallon. 2008. *The North American breeding bird survey, results and analysis 1966–2007*. Version 5.15.2008. Laurel, MD: USGS Patuxent Wildlife Research Center.

Saunders, D. L., J. J. Meeuwig, and A. C. J. Vincent. 2002. Freshwater protected areas: Strategies for conservation. *Conservation Biology* 16:30–41.

Scenarios Network for Alaska Planning. 2009. *Statewide climate projections: Decadal averages for summer and winter*. http://www.snap.uaf.edu/down loads/statewide-climate-projections-decadal-averages-summer-and-winter.

Scheffer M., S. R, Carpenter, J. A. Foley, C. Folke, and B. Walker. 2001. Catastrophic shifts in ecosystems. *Nature* 413:591–606.

Scheffer M., S. H. Hosper, M. L. Meyjer, B. Moss, and E. Jeppsen. 1993. Alternative equilibria in shallow lakes. *Trends in Ecology and Evolution* 8:275–279.

Scheuerell, M D., J. W. Moore, D. E. Schindler, and C. J. Harvey. 2007. Varying effects of anadromous sockeye salmon on the trophic ecology of two species of resident salmonids in southwest Alaska. *Freshwater Biology* 52:1944–1956.

Schindler, D. E., M. D. Scheuerell, J. W. Moore, S. M. Gende, T. B. Francis, and W. J. Palen. 2003. Pacific salmon and the ecology of coastal ecosystems. *Frontiers in Ecology and the Environment* 1:31–37.

Schindler, D. E., R. Hilborn, B. Chasco, C. P. Boatright, T. P. Quinn, L. A. Rogers, and M. S. Webster. 2010. Population diversity and the portfolio effect in an exploited species. *Nature* 465(7298):609–612.

Schindler, D.W. 1998. Sustaining aquatic ecosystems in boreal regions. *Conservation Ecology* 2:18. http://www.consecol.org/vol12/iss2/art18/.

Schoen, J. W. 1990. Bear habitat management: a review and future perspective. *International Conference on Bear Research and Management* 8:143–154.

Schoen, J. W., and D. Albert. 2007. Southeastern Alaska conservation strategy: a conceptual approach. In *The coastal forests and mountains ecoregion of* southeastern Alaska and the Tongass National Forest: A conservation assessment and resource synthesis, edited by J. Schoen and E. Dovichin, chapter 10. Anchorage, AK: Audubon Alaska and The Nature Conservancy. http://www.conserveonline.org/workspaces/akcfm.

Schoen, J. W., and E. Dovichin, editors. 2007. *The coastal forests and mountains ecoregion of southeastern Alaska and the Tongass National Forest: A conservation assessment and resource synthesis.* Anchorage, AK: Audubon Alaska and The Nature Conservancy. http://www.conserveonline.org/workspaces/akcfm.

Schoen, J. W., and M. D. Kirchhoff. 1985. Seasonal distribution and home range patterns of Sitka black-tailed deer on Admiralty Island, southeast Alaska. *Journal of Wildlife Management* 49:96–103.

———. 1990. Seasonal habitat use of Sitka black-tailed deer on Admiralty Island. *Journal of Wildlife Management* 4:371–378.

———. 2007. Sitka black-tailed deer. In *The coastal forests and mountains ecoregion of southeastern Alaska and the Tongass National Forest: A conservation assessment and resource synthesis*, edited by J. Schoen and E. Dovichin, chapter 6.1. Anchorage, AK: Audubon Alaska and The Nature Conservancy. http://www.conserveonline.org/workspaces/akcfm.

Schoen, J. W., M. D. Kirchhoff, and J. H. Hughes. 1988. Wildlife and old-growth forests in southeastern Alaska. *Natural Areas Journal* 8:138–145.

Schoen, J. W., O. C. Wallmo, and M. D. Kirchhoff. 1981. Wildlife-forest relationships—is a reevaluation of old-growth necessary? *Transactions of the North American Wildlife and Natural Resources Conference* 46:531–544.

Schofield, W. B. 1989. Structure and affinities of the bryoflora of the Queen Charlotte Islands. In *The outer shores Queen Charlotte Islands*, edited by G. G. E. Scudder and N. Gessler, 319–327. Skidegate, BC: Museum Press.

———. 1994. Rare and endangered bryophytes in British Columbia. In *Biodiversity in British Columbia: our changing environment*, edited by L. E. Harding and E. McCullum, 71–75. Ottawa: Environment Canada, Canadian Wildlife Service.

Schoonmaker, P. K., B. von Hagen, and E. C. Wolf, editors. 1997. The rain forests of home: Profile of a North American bioregion. Washington, DC: Island Press.

Schrader, B., and P. Hennon. 2005. Assessment of invasive species in Alaska and its national forests. Anchorage, AK: USDA Forest Service, Regional Office. http://akweeds.uaa.alaska.edu/pdfs/literature/Schrader_R10_Inv_Spp_Assessmt.pdf.

Schroeder, R., L. Cerveny.and G. Robertson. 2005. Tourism growth in southeast Alaska: trends, projections, and issues. In *Social conditions and trends in southeast Alaska*, edited by R. Mazza and L. E. Kruger, 45–91. General Tech. Report PNW-GTR-653. Portland, OR: USDA Forest Service, Pacific Northwest Research Station.

Schroeder, R., and M. Kookesh. 1990a. *The subsistence harvest of herring eggs in Sitka Sound, 1989*. Division of Subsistence Technical Paper 173. Juneau, AK: Alaska Department of Fish and Game.

———. 1990b. *Subsistence harvest and use of fish and wildlife resources and the effects of forest management in Hoonah, Alaska*. Division of Subsistence Technical Paper 142. Juneau, AK: Alaska Department of Fish and Game.

Schwartz, C., and A. Franzmann. 1991. Interrelationship of black bears to moose and forest succession in the northern coniferous forest. *Wildlife Monographs* 113.

Schwartz, M. K., L. S. Mills, Y. Ortega, L. F. Ruggiero, and F. W. Allendorf. 2003. Landscape location affects genetic variation of Canada lynx (*Lynx canadensis*). *Molecular Ecology* 12:1807–1816.

Schwartz, S. E. 2011. Feedback and sensitivity in an electrical circuit: An analog for climate models. *Climatic Change* 106:315–326.

Scientific Panel for Sustainable Forest Practices in Clayoquot Sound. 1995. *Sustainable ecosystem management in Clayoquot Sound: planning and practices*. Report 5. Victoria, BC: Cortex Consultants. http://www.cortex.bc.ca/Rep5c3.pdf.

Scott, E. E., S. S. Perakis, and D. E. Hibbs. 2008. 15N patterns of Douglas-Fir and red alder riparian forests in the Oregon Coast Range. *Forest Science* 54:140–147.

Scott, J. M., F. Davis, B. Csuti, R. Noss, B. Butterfield, C. Groves, H. Anderson, et al. 1993. Gap analysis: A geographic approach to protection of biological diversity. *Wildlife Monographs* 123:1–41.

Scott, J. M., F. W. Davis, R. G. McGhie, R. G. Wright, C. Groves, and J. Estes. 2001. Nature reserves: Do they capture the full range of America's biological diversity? *Ecological Applications* 11:999–1007.

Scott, J. M., M. Murray, R. G. Wright, B. Csuti, P. Morgan and R. L. Pressey. 1991. Representation of natural vegetation in protected areas: Capturing the geographic range. *Biodiversity and Conservation* 10:1297–1301.

Scott, R. E., and S. J. Mitchell. 2005. Empirical modelling of windthrow risk in partially harvested stands using tree, neighbourhood, and stand attributes. *Forest Ecology and Management* 218:193–209.

Scudder, G. G. E. 1996. Terrestrial and freshwater invertebrates of British Columbia: Priorities for inventory and descriptive research. Victoria: British Columbia Ministry of Forests, Research Branch.

Scudder, G. G. E., and N. Gessler, editors. 1989. *The outer shores.* Skidegate, BC: Queen Charlotte Islands Museum Press.

Sedell, J., and C. Maser. 1994. From the forest to the sea: The ecology of wood in streams, rivers, estuaries, and oceans. Delray Beach, FL: St. Lucia Press.

Sedell, J. R., J. E. Richey, and F. J. Swanson. 1989. The river continuum concept: A basis for the expected ecosystem behavior of very large rivers? In *Proceedings of the International Large River Symposium,* edited by D. P. Dodge, 49–55. Canadian Special Publication of Fisheries and Aquatic Sciences 106. Ottawa: Le Ministere.

Sedjo, R. A. 1997. *The forest sector: Important innovations.* RFF Discussion Paper 97–42. Washington, DC: Resources for the Future.

Sgro, C. M., A. J. Lowe, and A. A. Hoffmann. 2010. Building evolutionary resilience for conserving biodiversity under climate change. *Evolutionary Applications* 4:326–337.

Shafer, C. L. 1990. Nature reserves: Island theory and conservation practice. Washington, DC: Smithsonian Institution Press.

Shank, C. C. 1999. The committee on the status of endangered wildlife in Canada (COSEWIC): A 21 year retrospective. *Canadian Field-Naturalist* 113:318–341.

Shaul, L., E. Jones, K. Crabtree, T. Tydingco, S. McCurdy, and Brian Elliott. 2008. Coho salmon stock status and escapement goals in southeast Alaska. Special Publication No. 08–20. Juneau, AK: Alaska Department of Fish and Game.

Shearer, K. D., T. Åsgård, G. Andorsdöttir, G. H. Aas. 1994. Whole body elemental and proximate composition of Atlantic salmon (*Salmo salar*) during the life cycle. *Journal of Fish Biology* 44:785–797.

Shephard, M., L. Winn, B. Flynn, R. Myron, J. Winn, G. Killinger, J. Silbaugh, et al. 1999. *Southeast Chichagof landscape analysis.* General Technical Report R10-TP-68. Juneau, AK: USDA Forest Service.

Sheppard, S. R. J., and M. J. Meitner. 2005. Using multi-criteria analysis and visualization for sustainable forest management planning with stakeholder groups. *Forest Ecology and Management* 207:171–187.

Sherley, G., editor. 2000. Invasive species in the Pacific: A technical review and draft regional strategy. Apia, Samoa: South Pacific Regional Environmental Programme. http://www.issg.org/database/species/ reference_files/ SPREP.pdf.

Shifley, S. R., F. R. Thompson III, W. D. Dijak, and Z. Fan. 2008. Forecasting landscape-scale, cumulative effects of forest management on vegetation and wildlife habitat: A case study of issues, limitations, and opportunities. *Forest Ecology and Management* 254:474–483.

Short, J. W., G. V. Irvine, D. H. Mann, J. M. Maselko, J. Pella, M. R. Lindeberg, J. R. Payne, W. B. Driskell, and S. D. Rice. 2007. Slightly weathered Exxon Valdez oil persists in Gulf of Alaska beach sediments after 16 years. *Environmental Science & Technology* 41:1245–1250.

Silverman, J. L., D. E. Benson, and S. E. Smith. 2009. For the rights of all: Ending Jim Crow in Alaska. Anchorage, AK: Blueberry Productions. Film documentary: 57 min.

Simberloff, D. 1988. The contribution of population and community biology to conservation science. *Annual Review of Ecology and Systematics* 19:473–511.

———. 2002. Introduced species: Fundamental ecological studies, science and management. In *Lessons from the islands: Introduced species and what they tell us about how ecosystems work*, 10–11. Conference Summary. Skidegate, BC.

Simenstad, C. A., M. Dethier, C. Levings, and D. Hay. 1997. The terrestrial/marine ecotone. In *The rain forests of home: Profile of a North American bioregion*, edited by P. K. Schoonmaker, B. von Hagen, and E. C. Wolf, 149–187. Washington, DC: Island Press.

Sisk, J. 2007. The southeastern Alaska timber industry: Historical overview and current status. In *The coastal forests and mountains ecoregion of southeastern Alaska and the Tongass National Forest: A conservation assessment and resource synthesis*, edited by J. W. Schoen and E. Dovichin, chapter 9.4. Anchorage, AK: Audubon Alaska and The Nature Conservancy. http://www.conserveonline.org/workspaces/akcfm.

Slocombe, D. S. 2001. Climate and other sources of change in the St. Elias region. In *Global change and protected areas*, edited by G. Visconti, M. Beniston, E. Iannorelli, and D. Barba, 61–69. Dordrecht, Netherlands: Kluwer Academic Publishers.

Small, M. P., K. D. Stone, and J. A. Cook. 2003. American marten (*Martes americana*) population structure across a landscape fragmented in time and space. *Molecular Ecology* 12:89–103.

Smith, J. 2005. Seral stage, site conditions, and the vulnerability of understory plant communities to forest harvesting. Masters Thesis, Simon Fraser University, Burnaby, BC.

Smith, M., and A. Sterritt. 2007. From conflict to collaboration: The story of the Great Bear Rainforest. http://www.forestethics.org/section.php?id=19.

Smith, N. J., and W. J. Beese. 2012. Effects of low levels of dispersed retention on the growth and survival of young, planted Douglas-fir. *Forests* 3: 230–243. doi:10.3390/f3020230.

Smith, W. P., J. V. Nichols, and S. M. Gende. 2005. The northern flying squirrel as a management indicator species of north temperate rainforest: Test of a hypothesis. *Ecological Applications* 15:689–700.

Smith, W. P., and D. K. Person. 2007. Estimated persistence of northern flying squirrel populations in temperate rain forest fragments of southeast Alaska. *Biological Conservation* 137:626–636.

Smith, W. P., D. K. Person, and S. Pyare. 2011. Source-sinks, metapoplulations, and forest reserves: Conserving northern flying squirrels in the temperate rainforest of southeast Alaska. In *Source, sinks, and sustainability*, edited by J. Liu, V. Hull, A. T. Morzillo, and J. A. Wiens, 399–422. Cambridge: Cambridge University Press.

Smith, W.P., and P. A. Zollner. 2005. Sustainable management of wildlife habitat and risk to extinction. *Biological Conservation* 125:287–295.

Smithwick, E. A. H., M. E. Harmon, S. M. Remillard, S. A. Acker, and J. F. Franklin. 2002. Potential upper bounds of carbon stores in forests of the Pacific Northwest. *Ecological Applications* 12:1303–1317.

Snepenger, D. J., and R. T. Bowyer. 1990. Differences among nonresident tourists making consumptive and nonconsumptive uses of Alaskan wildlife. *Arctic* 43:262–266.

Solomon, S., D. Qin, M. Manning, Z. Chen, M. Marquis, K. B. Averyt, M. Tignor, and H. L. Miller, editors. 2007. *Contribution of the working group I to the fourth assessment report of the Intergovernmental Panel on Climate Change.* Cambridge: Cambridge University Press.

Sorensen, F. C. 1983. Geographic variation in seedling Douglas-fir (*Pseudotsuga menziesii*) from the western Siskiyou Mountains of Oregon. *Ecology* 64:696–702

Soulé, M. E., editor. 1987. *Viable populations for conservation.* Cambridge: Cambridge University Press.

Soulé, M. E., and D. Simberloff. 1986. What do genetics and ecology tell us about the design of nature reserves? *Biological Conservation* 35:19–40.

Southeast Conference and Central Council of Tlingit and Haida Indian Tribes of Alaska. 2006. *Southeast Alaska comprehensive economic development strategy: 2006–2011.* Prepared for the United States Department of Commerce, Economic Development Administration. Juneau, Alaska.

Southeast Regional Timber Industry Task Force. 1997. Planning for a viable timber industry in southeast Alaska. Draft report prepared for Alaska Governor Tony Knowles. Juneau, AK: author's private collection.

Southwick Associates, W. J. Romberg, A. E. Bingham, G. B. Bingham, and R. A. Clark. 2008. *Economic impacts and contributions of sportfishing in Alaska, 2007*. Professional Publication No. 08–01. Anchorage, AK: Alaska Department of Fish and Game.

Spies, T. A. 2004. Ecological concepts and diversity of old-growth forests. *Journal of Forestry* 102:14–20.

Spies, T., and J. Franklin. 1988. Old growth and forest dynamics in the Douglas-fir region of western Oregon and Washington. *Natural Areas Journal* 8:190–191.

Sprugel, D. G. 1991. Disturbance, equilibrium, and environmental variability: What is "natural" vegetation in a changing environment? *Biological Conservation* 58:1–18.

Stanford, J., and J. Ward. 1992. An ecosystem perspective of alluvial rivers: Connectivity and the hyporheic corridor. *Journal of the North American Benthological Society* 12:48–60.

Stankey, G. H., R. N. Clark, and B. T. Bormann. 2005. *Adaptive management of natural resources: Theory, concepts, and management institutions*. General Tech. Report PNW-GTR-654. Portland, OR: USDA Forest Service, Pacific Northwest Research Station. Steadman, D. W. 2006. *Extinction and biogeography of tropical Pacific birds*. Chicago: University of Chicago Press.

Stem, C., R. Margoluis, N. Salafsky, and M. Brown. 2005. Monitoring and evaluation in conservation: A review of trends and approaches. *Conservation Biology* 19:295–309.

Steventon, J. D. 2011. Retention patches: Windthrow and recruitment of habitat structure 12–16 years after harvest. *BC Journal of Ecostems and Management* 11:18–28.

Still, J. C., P. E. Bittenbender, K. W. Bean, and E. G. Gensler. 2002. *Mineral assessment of the Stikine Area, central southeast Alaska*. BLM-Alaska Tech. Report 51. Anchorage, AK: USDI Bureau of Land Management.

Suring, L. H., D. C. Crocker-Bedford, R. W. Flynn, C. L. Hale, G. C. Iverson, M. D. Kirchhoff, T. E. Schenck, L. C. Shea, and K. Titus. 1993. A proposed strategy for maintaining well-distributed, viable populations of wildlife associated with old-growth forests in southeast Alaska. Juneau, AK: USDA Forest Service, Alaska Region.

Swanson, F. J., T. K. Kratz, N. Caine, and R. G. Woodmansee. 1988. Landform effects on ecosystem patterns and processes. *BioScience* 38:92–98.

Swanson, M. E., J. F. Franklin, R. L. Bescheta, C. M. Crisafulli, D. A. DellaSala, R. L. Hutto, D. B. Lindenmeyer, and F. J. Swanson. 2011. The forgotten stage of succession: Early successional ecosystems on forest sites. *Frontiers in Ecology and the Environment* 9:117–125.

Swanston, D. N. 1969. A late-Pleistocene glacial sequence from Prince of Wales Island, Alaska. *Arctic* 22:25–33.

———. 1997. Controlling stability characteristics of steep terrain with discussion of needed standardization for mass movement hazard indexing: A resource assessment. In *Assessments of wildlife viability, old-growth timber volume estimates, forested wetlands, and slope stability*, edited by K. R. Julin, 44–58. General Technical Report PNW-GTR-392. Portland, OR: USDA Forest Service.

Swanton, J. R. 1909. *Tlingit myths and texts*. Bureau of American Ethnology Bulletin 39. Washington, DC: US Government Printing Office.

Swarth, H. S. 1936. Origins of the fauna of the Sitkan District, Alaska. *Proceedings of the California Academy Science* 223:59–78.

Szepanski, M. M., M. Ben-David, and V. Van Ballenberghe. 1999. Assessment of salmon resources in the diet of the Alexander Archipelago wolf using stable isotope analysis. *Oecologia* 120:397–335.

Szumigala, D. J., R. A. Hughes, and L. A. Harbo. 2008. *Alaska's mineral industry 2007*. Special report 62. Fairbanks: Alaska Department of Natural Resources, Division of Geological and Geophysical Surveys, Office of Economic Development and Division of Mining, Land, and Water.

Szumigala, D. J., and D. B. Werdon. 2010. *Rare-earth elements: A brief overview including uses, worldwide resources and known occurrences in Alaska*. Information Circular 61. Fairbanks: Alaska Department of Natural Resources, Division of Geological and Geophysical Surveys.

Tappeiner, J. C., and P. B. Alaback. 1989. Early establishment and vegetative growth of understory species in the western hemlock–Sitka spruce forests of southeast Alaska. *Canadian Journal of Botany* 67:18–326.

Taylor, A. H. 1990. Disturbance and persistence of Sitka spruce (*Picea sitchensis* [Bong] Carr.) in coastal forests of the Pacific Northwest, North America. *Journal of Biogeography* 17:47–58.

Tecklin, D., D. DellaSala, F. Luebert, and P. Pliscoff. 2011. Valdivian temperate rainforests of Chile and Argentina. In *Temperate and boreal rainforests of the world: Ecology and conservation* , edited by D. DellaSala, 132–153. Washington DC: Island Press.

Templeton, A. R., R. J. Robertson, J. Brisson, and J. Strasburg. 2001. Disrupting evolutionary processes: The effect of habitat fragmentation on collared lizards in the Missouri Ozarks. *Proceedings of the National Academy of Sciences* 98:5426–5432.

Theberge, J. B. 1989. Guidelines to drawing ecologically sound boundaries for national parks and nature reserves. *Environmental Management* 13:695–702.

Thomas, C. D., A. Cameron, R. Green, M. Bakkenes, L. Beaumont, Y. Collingham, B. Erasmus, *et al.* 2004. Extinction risk from climate change. *Nature* 427:145–148.

Thornton, T. F. 1998. *Traditional Tlingit use of Sitka National Historical Park.* Sitka, AK: National Park Service.

———. 2008. *Being and place among the Tlingit.* Seattle, WA: University of Washington Press and Sealaska Heritage Institute.

Thorsteinson, F. 1950. *Statistics of the southeastern Alaska salmon fishery.* Fisheries Research Institute Circular No. 3. Seattle: University of Washington.

Tiegs, S. D., D. T. Chaloner, P. Levi, J. Ruegg, J. L. Tank, and G.A. Lamberti. 2008. Timber harvest transforms ecological roles of salmon in southeast Alaska rainforest streams. *Ecological Applications* 18:4–11.

Tingley, A., and W. Davidson. 2008. *Overview of the 2008 southeast Alaska and Yakutat commercial, personal use, and subsistence salmon fisheries.* Fishery Management Report No. 08–57. Anchorage: Alaska Department of Fish and Game, Division of Sport Fish, Research and Technical Services.

Tomimatsu, H., and M. Ohara. 2006. Evaluating the consequences of habitat fragmentation: A case study in the common forest herb *Trillium camschatcense. Population Ecology* 48:189–198.

Tongass Timber Act of 1947. 61 Stat. 920.

Tongass Timber Reform Act of 1990 [TTRA]. Public Law 101–626, 104 Stat. 4426.

Topp, C. M., and K. Winker. 2008. Genetic patterns of differentiation among five landbird species from the Queen Charlotte Islands, British Columbia. *The Auk* 125:461–472.

Traill, L. W., C. J. A. Bradshaw, and B. W. Brook. 2007. Minimum viable population size: A meta-analysis of 30 years of published estimates. *Biological Conservation* 139:159–166.

Trewick, S. A., and R. H. Cowie. 2008. Introduction. Evolution on Pacific islands: Darwin's legacy. *Philosophical Transactions of the Royal Society B* 363 (1508):3289–3291.

Trofymow, J. A., J. Addison, B. A. Blackwell, F. He, C. A. Preston, and V. G. Marshall. 2003. Attributes and indicators of old-growth and successional

Douglas-fir forests on Vancouver Island. *Environmental Review* 11(Suppl. 1): S187–S204.

Trombulak, S. C., and C. A. Frissell. 2000. Review of ecological effects of roads on terrestrial and aquatic communities. *Conservation Biology* 14:18–30.

———. 2005. Landscape ecology: What is the state of the science? *Annual Review of Ecology and Systematics* 36:319–344.

Turner, N. J. 1995. *Food plants of coastal First Peoples.* Royal British Columbia Museum Handbook. Vancouver, BC: UBC Press.

———. 2004. *Plants of Haida Gwaii.* Winlaw, BC: Sono Nis Press.

Tussing, A. R., S. Comitini, H. J. Gellert, I. Inukai, A. Iwasaki, and M. R. Massie. 1968. *Alaska-Japan economic relations: A study of the potential contribution of trade with Japan to Alaska's economic development.* Fairbanks, AK: Institute of Social Economic and Government Research.

US Congress. Senate. Subcommittee on Territorial and Insular Affairs. 1956. Statement of Cyrus Peck. 84th Congress, 1st Session, pursuant to H. Res. 30, Part 4, Serial No. 27. Washington, DC, p. 108.

US Congress. 2009. Southeast Alaska Native Land Entitlement Finalization Act. Senate Res. 881. 111th Congress, 1st Session. GovTrack.us (database of federal legislation). http://www.govtrack.us/congress/billtext.xpd?bill=s111–881.

USDA Forest Service. 1985. *Status of the Tongass National Forest, 1985.* Juneau, AK: Alaska Region.

———. 1992. *Channel type user guide, Tongass National Forest Southeast Alaska.* Technical Paper 26. Juneau, AK: Alaska Region R10.

———. 1997a. *Tongass land and resource management plan.* R10-MB-338dd. Washington, DC.

———. 1997b. *Tongass land management plan revision. Final environmental impact statement. Part 1.* Summary, Chapters 1–3 (Physical and biological environment), R10-MB-338b. Washington, DC.

———. 2000. Timber supply and demand, 1999. Report to Congress, ANILCA section 706(a.) Juneau, AK: Alaska Region.

———. 2001. *Forest roads: A synthesis of scientific information.* General Technical Report PNW-GTR-509. Portland, OR: Pacific Northwest Research Station.

———. 2002. *A summary of technical considerations to minimize the blockage of fish at culverts on the national forests of Alaska.* General Technical Review. Juneau, AK: USDA Forest Service R10.

———. 2006. *Draft timber supply and demand: 2001 to 2005.* Report to Congress, ANILCA 706 (a). On file with USDA Forest Service, Regional Economist, Ecosystems Planning, Juneau, Alaska.

———. 2008a. *Tongass land and resource management plan amendment: Final environmental impact statement and record of decision.* R10-MB-603a. Juneau, AK.

———. 2008b. *Tongass National Forest, land and resource management plan.* R10-MB-603b. Juneau, AK.

———. 2008c. *Tongass land and resource management plan, final environmental impact statement. Vol. 1.* R10-MB-603c. Juneau, AK.

———. 2008d. Tongass young-growth management strategy. Juneau, AK: Tongass National Forest, Region 10.

———. 2009. Civilian Conservation Corps. Tongass National Forest. http://www.fs.fed.us/r10/tongass/districts/admiralty/heritage/ccc.shtml.

———. 2010. Alaska Region harvest. USDA Forest Service, Alaska Region. http://www.fs.fed.us/r10/ro/policy-reports/for_mgmt/.

Van Hees, W.W. S. 2000. *Forest resources of southeast Alaska, 2000: Results of a single-phase systematic sample.* PNW-RP-557. Portland, OR: USDA Forest Service, Pacific Northwest Research Station.

Vannote, R. L., G. W. Minshall, K. W. Cummins, J. R. Sedell, and C. E. Cushing. 1980. The river continuum concept. *Canadian Journal of Fisheries and Aquatic Sciences* 37:130–137.

Veblen, T. T., and P. B. Alaback 1996. A comparative review of forest dynamics and disturbance in the temperate rainforests in North and South America. In *High latitude rain forests of the west coast of the Americas: Climate, hydrology, ecology and conservation*, edited by R. Lawford, P. Alaback, and E. R. Fuentes, 173–213. Berlin: Springer-Verlag.

Verburg, P. H., J. van de Steeg, A. Veldkamp, and L. Willemen. 2009. From land cover change to land function dynamics: A major challenge to improve land characterization. *Journal of Environmental Management* 90:1327–1335.

Vincent, P. 1990. *The* biogeography *of the* British Isles*: An introduction.* London: Routledge.

Voller, J., and S. Harrison, editors. 1998. *Conservation biology principles for forested landscapes.* Vancouver, BC: UBC Press.

Vyse, A., A. K. Mitchell, and L. de Montigny. 2005. Seeking alternatives to clearcutting in British Columbia: The role of large-scale experiments for sustainable forestry. In *Balancing ecosystems values: Innovative experiments for sustainable forestry*, edited by C. E. Peterson and D. A. Maguire, 155–163. General Tech. Report PNW-635. Portland, OR: USDA Forest Service, Pacific Northwest Research Station.

Wallace, A. R. 1869. *The Malay Archipelgo: The land of the orangutan, and the bird of paradise.* New York: Harper.

———. 1876. *The geographical distribution of animals: With a study of the relations of living and extinct faunas as elucidating the past changes of the earth's surface.* New York: Harper and Brothers.

———. 1880. *Island life, or the phenomena and causes of insular faunas and floras.* London: Macmillan.

———. 1902. *Island life.* Third edition. London: Macmillan.

Wallmo, O. C., and J. W. Schoen 1980. Response of deer to secondary forest succession in southeast Alaska. *Forest Science* 26:448–462.

Walter, R. A. 1984. A stream ecosystem in an old-growth forest in southeast Alaska: Part II, structure and dynamics of the periphyton community. In *Fish and wildlife relationships in old-growth forests,* 57–69. Juneau, AK: American Institute of Fishery Research Biologists.

Walters, C. J. 1986. *Adaptive management of renewable resources.* New York: McGraw-Hill.

———. 1997. Challenges in adaptive management of riparian and coastal ecosystems. *Conservation Ecology* 1:1. http://www.ecologyandsociety.org/vol1/iss2/art1/.

———. 2007. Is adaptive management helping to solve fisheries problems? *Ambio* 36:304–307.

Weaver, J. L., P. C. Paquet, and L. F. Ruggiero. 2002. Resilience and conservation of large carnivores in the Rocky Mountains. *Conservation Biology* 10:964–976.

Weckworth, B. V., S. Talbot, G. K. Sage, D. K. Person, and J. Cook. 2005. A signal for independent coastal and continental histories among North American wolves. *Molecular Ecology* 14:917–931.

Whitney, F., and M. Robert. 2002. Structure of Haida eddies and their transport of nutrient from coastal margins into the NE Pacific Ocean. *Journal of Oceanography* 58:715–723.

Whitney, F. A., W.R. Crawford, and P. J. Harrison. 2005. Physical processes that enhance nutrient transport and primary productivity in the coastal and open ocean of the subarctic NE Pacific. *Deep-Sea Research II* 52:681–706.

Whittaker, R. J., and J. Fernández-Palacios. 2007. *Island biogeography: Ecology, evolution, and conservation.* Second edition. Oxford: Oxford University Press.

Wigen, R. J. 2005. History of the vertebrate fauna in Haida Gwaii. In *Haida Gwaii: Human history and environment from the time of the loon to the time of the iron people*, edited by D. W. Fedje and R. W. Mathewes, 96–116. Vancouver, BC: UBC Press.

Wilderness Society, The (TWS). 1986. *America's vanishing rainforest: A report on federal timber management in southeast Alaska*. Washington DC: The Wilderness Society.

Williams, J. C., C. S. ReVelle, and S. A. Levin. 2005. Spatial attributes and reserve design models: A review. *Environmental Modeling and Assessment* 10:163–181.

Willson, M. F., S. M. Gende, and B. H. Marston. 1998. Fishes and the forest: Expanding perspectives on fish–wildlife interactions. *BioScience* 48:455–462.

Willson, M. F. and K. C. Halupka. 1995. Anadromous fish as keystone species in vertebrate communities. *Conservation Biology* 9:489–497.

Willson, M. F., and K. M. Hocker. 2008. American dippers wintering near Juneau, Alaska. *Northwestern Naturalist* 89:24–32.

Wilson, A. G., P. Arcese, and F. Bunnell. 2009. The status of genetic biodiversity in British Columbia. Biodiversity BC Technical Subcommittee Report. http://www.biodiversitybc.org.

Winchester, N. N. 1997. The arboreal superhighway: Arthropods and landscape dynamics. *Canadian Entomologist* 129:595–599.

Winchester, N. N., and R. A. Ring. 1996. Northern temperate coastal Sitka spruce forests with special emphasis on canopies: Studying arthropods in an unexplored frontier. *Northwest Science* 70:94–103.

Wind, E. 2008. *Pre- and post-harvest amphibian and small wetland study: 4-year results*. Progress report to Western Forest Products and Island Timberlands, Unpublished report. Nanaimo, BC: E. Wind Consulting.

Wipfli, M. S. 2005. Trophic linkages between headwater forests and downstream fish habitats: Implications for forest and fish management. *Landscape and Urban Planning* 72:205–213.

Wipfli, M. S., and J. Musslewhite. 2004. Density of red alder (*Alnus rubra*) in headwaters influences invertebrate and detritus subsidies to downstream fish habitats in Alaska. *Hydrobiologia* 520:153–163.

Wipfli, M. S., J. S. Richardson, and R. Naiman. 2007. Ecological linkages between headwaters and downstream ecosystems: Transport of organic matter, invertebrates, and wood down headwater channels. *Journal of the American Water Resources Association* 43:72–85.

Wittenberg, R., and M. J. W. Cock. 2001. Invasive alien species: A toolkit of best prevention and management practices. Wallingford, Oxon, UK: CAB International.

Wolf, E. D., A. P. Mitchel, and P. K. Schoonmaker. 1995. The rain forests of home: An atlas of people and place. Interrain Pacific. http://www.inforain.org/rainforestatlas/.

Woodall, C. W., and G. C. Liknes. 2008. Relationships between forest fine and coarse woody debris carbon stocks across latitudinal gradients in the United States as an indicator of climate change effects. *Ecological Indicators* 8:686–690.

Woodby, D., D. Carlile, S. Siddeek, F. Funk, J. Clark, and L. Hubbert. 2005. *Commercial fisheries of Alaska.* Special Publication No. 05–09. Anchorage: Alaska Department of Fish and Game, Division of Sport Fish, Research and Technical Services.

Wood Products Industry Advisory Committee (WPIAC). 2006. *Report to BC Competition Council, March 31, 2006.* Victoria, BC: BC Competition Council, PO Box 9327, Stn Prov Govt 7th Floor, 1810 Blanshard Street.

Woodroffe, R., and J. R. Ginsberg. 1998. Edge effects and the extinction of populations inside protected areas. *Science* 280:2126–2128.

World Wildlife Fund Canada. 1990. Conservation strategy for large carnivores in Canada. Toronto, Ontario: World Wildlife Fund Canada.

Worrall, F., R. Harriman, C. Evans, C. Watts, J. Adamson, C. Neal, E. Tipping, *et al.* 2004. Trends in dissolved organic carbon in UK rivers and lakes. *Biogeochemistry* 70:369–402.

Yanity, B. 2009. Transmitting development strategies. *International Water Power and Dam Construction* 61(8):32–37.

Yeo, J. J., and J. M. Peek. 1992. Habitat selection by female Sitka black-tailed deer in logged forests of southeastern Alaska. *Journal of Wildlife Management* 56:253–261.

Zbicz, D. C. 2003. Imposing transboundary conservation: Cooperation between internationally adjoining protected areas. *Journal of Sustainable Forestry* 17:21–38.

Zedler, J. B. 2007. Success: An unclear, subjective descriptor of restoration outcomes. *Ecological Restoration* 25:162–168.

Zielke, K., B. Bancroft, K. Swift, and J. Turner. 2008. British Columbia's coastal forests: Variable retention decision aid for biodiversity habitat and retention. *BC Journal of Ecosystems and Management* 9:1–4. Accessed 1 September 2012. http://www.forrex.org/publications/jem/ISS48/vol9_no2_art1.pdf.

PAUL B. ALABACK

Paul Alaback, professor emeritus of forest ecology at the University of Montana, is a leading authority on the ecology and conservation of temperate rainforests and the author of numerous technical publications and a book. He did his graduate work at Oregon State University, specializing in forest ecology and botany. He has been studying the ecology of temperate rainforests throughout the Americas for the past 30 years. He has been particularly interested in how climate controls the function and diversity of these forests and how they respond to both natural and human-caused disturbances, including restoration activities. He also has been involved in translating ecological research into policy and applications. He was a research scientist with the Pacific Northwest Research Station of the USDA Forest Service for 8 years, and then joined the faculty of forestry at the University of Montana in 1993. Currently he is an ecological consultant and conducts research on forest and grassland ecology, and he actively promotes public participation in science and natural history education.

WILLIAM J. (BILL) BEESE

Bill has over 30 years of experience in coastal British Columbia in research, environmental consulting, and policy development with several forest companies. He now teaches forest ecology and integrated resource management at Vancouver Island University. He has an international reputation for practical implementation of innovative forestry practices. His research has focused on silvicultural systems, prescribed fire, regeneration, and biodiversity. His leadership helped to phase in variable retention harvesting as part of a strategy that received the Ecological Society of America's Corporate Award for 2001. Bill coauthored two chapters in *For-*

estry and Biodiversity (published by UBC Press in 2009). He has served on numerous advisory groups on research, old-growth forests, and ecosystem-based management.

FRANCES BILES

Frances Biles is a geographer at the Forestry Sciences Laboratory with the Pacific Northwest Research Station. Frances received a BA in geography from California State University, Chico. At the University of Georgia she pursued her interests in biogeography and statistics, receiving a master's degree in geography in 1995. After 3 years as a GIS research coordinator at the University of Georgia, she moved to Juneau, where she has worked for the Pacific Northwest Research Station for the last 13 years. She enjoys trying to understand the ecological processes of the North American coastal temperate rainforest through the application of geospatial and statistical methods. Contact her at PNW Research Station, USDA Forest Service, Juneau, AK 99801.

TODD J. BRINKMAN

Todd Brinkman, PhD, is a research assistant professor in the School of Natural Resources and Agricultural Sciences at the University of Alaska, Fairbanks. Todd conducts integrative research on the changing interactions among wildlife, humans, and the environment. More specifically, Todd spends much of his time studying large-mammal hunting systems in the arctic and subarctic.

JOSEPH A. COOK

Joseph Cook is a professor of biology and the director and curator of mammals and genomic resources of the Museum of Southwestern Biology at the University of New Mexico (UNM). He held faculty and curatorial positions at the University of Alaska, Fairbanks, for a decade and then was chair of biology at Idaho State University prior to joining UNM in 2003. His research focuses on conservation, molecular evolution, and systematics of mammals and associated parasites. He cofounded ISLES, a museum-based field project aimed at understanding the biogeography of the Alexander Archipelago. He has instructed in Uruguay, Paraguay, Bolivia,

Costa Rica, Belize, Panama, and Mongolia and is director of the Undergraduate Opportunities Program at UNM, pairing underrepresented students with graduate students and faculty members in research projects. He also chairs the AIM-UP! Research Coordinating Network, which is exploring new ways to incorporate museum collections and their databases into educational initiatives.

LISA K. CRONE

Lisa received her BA in economics from the University of Montana and her PhD in economics from the University of Wyoming. She was an assistant professor at Weber State University in Utah from 1992 to 1995, before joining the USDA Forest Service in 1996. Lisa has worked for the Pacific Northwest Research Station in Oregon, Washington, and Alaska. She also worked on a Forest Service enterprise team headquartered in Montana for three years. Before rejoining the PNW Research Station in 2007, she spent a year in Anchorage working as a research economist for The Wilderness Society. Most of her research has focused on providing the best available scientific information to planners, managers, government officials, interest groups, and the general public. Currently, she is investigating opportunities to conduct research on the Chinese economy.

DAVID V. D'AMORE

Dave D'Amore is a research soil scientist with the Pacific Northwest Research Station in Juneau, Alaska. He received an MS in soil science from Oregon State University in 1994 and a PhD in natural resources and sustainability from the University of Alaska, Fairbanks, in 2011. He has worked in southeast Alaska for 17 years on soils and forestry projects related to nutrient cycling. His recent research work has examined the interaction between terrestrial and aquatic ecosystems, with a focus on restoration and carbon cycling.

RICHARD T. EDWARDS

Rick Edwards a research aquatic ecologist at the Forestry Sciences Laboratory with the Pacific Northwest Research Station. He received a BS in biology from the University of South Carolina in 1976 and a PhD in aquatic ecology from the University of Georgia in 1985. He worked at the Water Studies Centre at Monash University in Australia and at the University of Washington before moving to Juneau to work for the Forest Service in 2000. His research interests include stream ecosystem ecology, nutrient cycling, microbial ecology, hyporheic processes, and trophic ecology. Since moving to Juneau he has worked on a variety of issues centered around the effects of management and natural disturbance on land and stream interactions, with special emphasis on riparian zones, floodplains, and wetlands. He is currently the lead scientist of the recently established Héen Lateeni experimental forest near Juneau.

JERRY F. FRANKLIN

Dr. Franklin is professor of ecosystem analysis at the College of Forest Resources, University of Washington, in Seattle, where he has taught and conducted research since 1986. He received his PhD in botany and soils from Washington State University. He also served as chief plant ecologist for the USDA Forest Service's Pacific Northwest Research Station from 1975 to 1991. His areas of specialization include (1) structure and function of natural forest ecosystems, especially old-growth forests; (2) effects of changing environmental conditions, such as global climate change, on forest processes; (3) application of ecological principles to management of natural resources; and (4) theory and practice of landscape ecology. Jerry has served on many national and international panels dealing with forest ecology and has published over 400 articles.

KEN P. LERTZMAN

Dr. Ken Lertzman is interested in a broad range of topics related to ecosystem dynamics, conservation, and management. His research has focused on how natural disturbance regimes and management interact to produce pattern and dynamics in forest stands and landscapes. Dr. Lertzman has an ongoing interest in how changing climate drives ecosystems and the landscapes and resources available to people who live in them— and how people respond to those changes. Increasingly Ken's work focuses on understanding the complex dynamics and resilience of coupled social-ecological systems. This is being applied in his collaborative, multidisciplinary work as director of the Hakai Research Network for Coastal

People, Ecosystems, and Management. Ken's current research examines climate change impacts, adaptation, and mitigation; alternative silvicultural systems and forest management strategies; analysis of forest light environments; ecological restoration; forest fire risk analysis; analysis of forest tenures and stewardship; and First Nations' forestry and traditional ecological knowledge. Dr. Lertzman and his students work closely with researchers from other disciplines, as well as representatives of government agencies, First Nations, industries, and other nongovernmental groups, in applying their research to problems in ecosystem conservation, restoration, and management.

S. O. MACDONALD

S. O. MacDonald is a research associate and curator in the Mammal Division, Museum of Southwestern Biology, Albuquerque, and a research associate of mammals at the University of Alaska Museum of the North, Fairbanks. Stephen has been involved in a wide variety of field studies across southeast Alaska since the early 1970s and is coauthor of *Mammals and Amphibians of Southeast Alaska* (Museum of Southwestern Biology Special Publications, 2007) and *Recent Mammals of Alaska* (University of Alaska Press, 2009). He lives rurally with his wife in a small straw bale home in Gila, New Mexico.

ANDY MACKINNON

Andy MacKinnon is a research ecologist with the British Columbia Forest Service. He is responsible for ecosystem classification and mapping on BC's coast, and for a program of forest ecology research with focus on structure and composition of old-growth forests and their native plants, fungi, and lichens. Andy has also been involved in issues associated with conservation and land-use planning and management in coastal BC. Andy lives near Victoria, BC.

BRUCE G. MARCOT

Bruce Marcot is a research wildlife biologist with the Ecosystem Process and Function Research Program of the USDA Forest Service in Portland, Oregon. He participates in applied science research and technology application projects dealing with old-forest management, specifically on modeling of rare and little-known species, assessment of biodiversity, and ecologically sustainable forest management. He has served on numerous regional assessment teams, including the Interior Columbia Basin Ecosystem Management Project and the Forest Ecosystem Management Assessment Team, and has worked on forest biodiversity conservation and ecology research projects in India, Congo, Canada, Russia, China, Bolivia, and elsewhere. He received a BS in natural resources planning and an MS in wildlife management at Humboldt State University in Arcata, California, and a PhD in wildlife science at Oregon State University, in Corvallis. He serves as adjunct professor at several universities.

JOSEPH R. MEHRKENS

Joe Mehrkens is a retired forest economist with 35 years of experience in southeast Alaska. He has held positions with the USDA Forest Service, Alaska State Department of Commerce and Economic Development, Alaska Department of Law, and The Wilderness Society. He has commercially fished and manages private nonindustrial timber lands in Minnesota. He was recently a consultant to The Boat Company and represented their interests on the Tongass Futures Roundtable. He continues a part-time consulting business: Environmental Economics Alaska.

ERIK NORBERG

Erik Norberg has 10 years of research experience in southeast Alaska evaluating the chemical, physical, and biological structure of streams and rivers. He received a BS in biology from the University of Alaska, Southeast, in 2004. His research interests are focused in the area of watershed-scale biogeochemical processes, with a particular focus on the role of hyporheic zones in the storage and processing of carbon and nutrients derived from spawning salmon. He is currently working for the state of Alaska.

GREGORY J. NOWACKI

Gregory Nowacki is currently the regional ecologist for the Eastern Region of the USDA Forest Service. His interest in temperate rainforests and old growth stems from his past exploits as regional ecologist in the Alaska Region (1993–2001) and as an old-growth forest ecologist with The Nature Conservancy (1991–1993). Through his profession, Greg strives to aid land managers in applying ecological principals to resource management, especially through the use of ecological map products and application of disturbance ecology for restoration purposes.

GORDON H. ORIANS

Gordon Orians is professor emeritus of biology at the University of Washington in Seattle, where he taught and conducted research for 35 years. He received his PhD in zoology from the University of California, Berkeley. He was elected to the National Academy of Sciences in 1989 and to the American Academy of Arts and Sciences in 1990. Gordon's research interests are wide ranging and include behavioral ecology, population dynamics, plant–herbivore interactions, and community and ecosystem ecology. Gordon is not a stranger to Alaska: he has chaired two National Research Council reviews in the state, including "Wolves, Bears, and Their Prey" and "Cumulative Effects of the Oil and Gas Activities on Alaska's North Slope." Many biologists know Gordon for his landmark work on blackbird behavior.

DAVID K. PERSON

Dr. David Person is a research wildlife biologist with the Alaska Department of Fish and Game. He obtained degrees from the University of Alaska, Fairbanks; University of Vermont; and University of Maine at Orono. Dave's main interest is learning how landscape and habitat changes affect the dynamics of ecological communities, particularly predator-prey systems. He is also very interested in how spatial and temporal scales affect our ability to understand those dynamics. Dave currently lives with his border collie, Bella, in Ketchikan, Alaska.

SARI SAUNDERS

Sari Saunders is a research ecologist with the BC Ministry of Forests, Lands, and Natural Resource Operations out of Nanaimo, BC. She is a researcher and consultant on the provincial biogeoclimatic ecosystem classification system and on forest and landscape ecology within the coast area of the province. Dr. Saunders' interests and previous research areas included forest vegetation dynamics, land-use and land-change assessment and modeling, old-growth structure and dynamics, avian communities, multiscale process-pattern relationships, and disturbance ecology (e.g., fire, wind) in the Pacific Northwest, Midwest and Alaska.

JOHN W. SCHOEN

John Schoen is a retired wildlife ecologist living in Anchorage, Alaska, where he continues to explore his interests in conservation and photography. He formerly served as senior scientist for Audubon Alaska, where he led Audubon's Tongass science program. Prior to joining Audubon, John worked throughout Alaska for 20 years with the Alaska Department of Fish and Game as a wildlife researcher and conservation biologist. His research has included studies on the ecology of brown bears, black-tailed deer, and mountain goats in old-growth forests. John has also served as an affiliate professor of wildlife biology at the University of Alaska, Fairbanks, and is a fellow of The Wildlife Society. He received his PhD in wildlife ecology from the University of Washington's College of Forest Resources.

INDEX

Annette Island, Tsimshian settlement, 91

APC (Alaska Pulp Company), 102, 104, 105–6

archipelagos. *See* Alexander Archipelago; island *entries*

Argentina, 13, 74

Army Corps of Engineers, 111

Audubon Alaska-TNC, 141*f*

Australia, 7, 10, 13, 74

avalanches, 75, 261–63

Banks Island, aerial view, 128*f*

Baranof Island, shrew populations, 33–34

barite production, 111

baskets, 90, 94

bear populations: indigenous uses, 96; island distribution, 23, 34, 36; photos, 130–31*f*; in terrestrial-marine interactions, 53–54. *See also* predator-prey community, clear-cutting effects

beavers, 75–76, 96, 149–50, 152

Beese, William J.: biographical highlights, 361–62; chapter by, 227–52

beetle populations, effects of variable retention harvesting, 248–49

Big Sur River, development status, 195

Biles, Frances: biographical highlights, 362; chapter by, 43–72

biodiversity corridor, defined, 183

biodiversity effects, variable retention harvesting, 246–49

Biogeoclimatic Ecosystem Classification, 202

biogeographic patterns, research needs, 274

bird populations: clear-cutting effects, 166; climate change impact, 66–67; conservation biology example, 171;

effects of variable retention harvesting, 232–33, 234, 246–48; extinction vulnerabilities, 281; indigenous uses, 96; island lineages, 31; in terrestrial-marine interactions, 53–54, 66–67

bogs. *See* peatlands

Bokan Mountain, mining activity, 113

bottom-up pathways: clear-cutting effects, 155–60; terrestrial-marine interactions, 54

bridges, inadequacies, 151

Brinkman, Todd J.: biographical highlights, 362; chapter by, 143–67

British Columbia, coastal region characterized, 19–20. *See also specific topics, e.g.,* disturbance patterns, natural; island environments, biotic communities; variable retention harvesting

brownwater streams, 69

buffer requirements, riparian areas, 57, 58

Butterweed, Newcombe's, 129*f*

cable yarding, costs, 236

Callitropsis nootkatensis, 85, 94–95, 109–10, 228, 263

canneries, fish, 114

canopy gaps, 76–80, 127*f*, 133*f*, 147, 260–61. *See also* predator-prey community, clear-cutting effects

carbon, terrestrial-marine interactions, 52–55

carbon dynamics, research needs, 275

carbon storage, 6, 63–64, 286

caribou, Dawson, 26

carrying capacity, deer recruitment relationships, 156–57

Castor canadensis, 75–76, 96, 149–50, 152

continental drift, impact, 9–10

Cook, Joseph A.: biographical highlights, 362–63; chapter by, 19–42; comments on, 256; with team members, x*f*

copper, 97, 111

corridor, defined, 183

cost factors: electric power, 122; road building, 108–9, 221–22; timber harvest systems, 108–9, 236–37; timber products, 105–7, 110–11

cougars, 160

Court of Claims, U.S., 99

crabapple, western, 95

Cracker Jack, mining activity, 113

Craig, heating systems, 108

creeper, brown, 248

Crone, Lisa K.: biographical highlights, 363; chapter by, 89–126

cruise ships, 118, 119, 121, 135*f*

culverts, inadequacies, 60, 151

cutblock, defined, 229

Dall Island, 91, 134*f*

D'Amore, David V.: biographical highlights, 363; chapter by, 43–72

data gaps, summary, 124, 175, 274–79, 288–89

decay fungi, in gap dynamics, 76–77

deer, Sitka black-tailed: forage patterns, 147–49, 156; indigenous uses of, 96; island lineages, 23; logging impacts, 83–84, 156–60; as natural disturbance, 75; predation of, 152, 154; road-building impact, 155; succession debt problem, 156–60

deermouse populations, island environments, 23, 26, 31

degree-day accumulations, climate change impact, 65–67

DEMO study, 241, 244, 249

dipper, American, 52, 66

discharge patterns, climate change impact, 61–70. *See also* drainage patterns, road-building impacts

disease, indigenous people, 92, 99

dispersal corridor, defined, 183

dispersed retention, example, 229*f*

dissolved organic carbon (DOC), 46, 51, 62*f*, 63–65, 68–69

distance factor, island communities, 31–34

disturbance patterns, natural: biogeographical context, 74–76, 262; climate change interactions, 84–86, 262–64; as conservation strategy, 86–87, 202–3; cumulative effects, 260–61; gap dynamics, 76–81, 260; logging disturbances contrasted, 73–74, 80–84, 264–66; management scale considerations, 259–66; research needs, 278; in reserve design, 202–3, 207–9, 211, 212–13, 217; understory vegetation, 83–84

diversity criteria, for reserve content assessment, 201–2, 209–12

DOC (dissolved organic carbon), 46, 51, 62*f*, 63–65, 68–69

dogma watchlist, 183–84

Douglas-fir, 109–10, 220, 228, 245–46

drainage patterns, road-building impacts, 59–60, 108–9, 150–51

Duke Island, mining activity, 113

Duncan, William, 91

eagle, bald, 53–54

earthquakes, 75, 260, 262

ecological integrity measures, for emergent properties assessment, 207–9, 220–21

First Nations-British Columbia, land use planning, 11, 92, 100–101, 173–74, 287

fish populations: commercial harvests, 114–17, 121, 135*f*, 140*f*; indigenous uses, 94, 95–96; research needs, 274–75; road-building impacts, 150–51; sport-related harvests, 120, 121*f*

floating fish traps, 114, 115

flooding events, 67–68, 75

floodplain reaches, 49–50, 67–68. *See also* riparian zones

flycatcher populations, 247, 248

focal scale, in ecological studies, 256–57

food sources, indigenous people, 94, 95–97

Forest and Range Evaluation Program (FREP), 239

Forester Island, indigenous uses, 91

fox, arctic, 21

fragmentation, defined, 183–84. *See also* island *entries*; predator-prey community, clear-cutting effects

Franklin, Jerry F.: biographical highlights, 364; chapters by, 3–18, 253–91

FREP (Forest and Range Evaluation Program), 239

frog populations, effects of variable retention harvesting, 249

functional connectivity. *See* connectivity; riparian zones; transboundary *entries*; variable retention harvesting; watershed-based reserves

fungi, 76–77, 249

GAP analysis, species distribution, 171, 173, 186, 187

gap dynamics, 76–80, 127*f*, 133*f*, 147, 260–61

gastropod populations, effects of variable retention harvesting, 248

genetic corridor, defined, 183

genetic variability, maintaining, 210–11. *See also* island environments, biotic communities; metapopulation dynamics; watershed-based reserves

glacial dynamics, 21–22, 24–26, 74, 128*f*, 258, 259

glacial-type watershed, climate change influence, 61–66

Glacier Bay National Park, 11, 128*f*, 199

Glaucomys sabrinus griseifrons, 35

globalization challenges, timber products industry, 13–14

global scale, biogeochemical cycle examples, 256

goat, mountain, 23, 96

gold, 111–13

Great Bear Rainforest, 173–74, 189, 195

Greens Creek Mine, 111, 113

group retention, timber harvest example, 229*f*

group selection with reserves, timber harvest example, 229*f*

growth studies, variable retention harvesting, 245–46

habitat, defined, 184

habitat islands, 9–10, 258–59

Haida eddy, Gulf of Alaska, 55–56

Haida Gwaii: bird populations, 281; Butterweed plant, 129*f*; conservation biology example, 171; mammal populations, 21, 26; natural disturbance patterns, 75, 78; Ninstints village, 134*f*; ownership patterns, 11; protected areas, 189; variable retention harvest study, 244, 247. *See also*

island environments, biotic communities
Haida people: arrival of, 90–91; loss of territories/resources, 97–99; natural resource use, 93–101, 134*f*; socioeconomic structures, 91–93
Haines area, 100, 113, 122
Haliaeetus leucocephalus, 53–54
halibut, Pacific, 96
Hawaii, extinction patterns, 7
headwater riparian zones, 47–49. *See also* watersheds
heart rot decay fungi, 76–77
heating products, sawmilling industry, 108
Heceta Island, 146*f*
helicopter logging, costs, 236–37
hemlock, mountain, 109–10, 228
hemlock, western: aerial view, 131*f*; commercial value, 109–10; fungi infection effects, 76–77; indigenous uses of, 95; presence of, 228; understory vegetation, 83; variable retention harvesting effects, 245–46; windthrow effects, 79–80
hemlock-spruce, aerial view, 127*f*
herbivores, reserve size requirements, 207
herring, Pacific, 96
Hippoglossus stenolepis, 96
hoe-forwarding, costs, 236
Hoonah basketry, 94
house groups, indigenous people, 92–93, 97
household items, indigenous people, 93–95, 97
Huchsduwachsdu Nuyem Jees/Kitlope Heritage Conservancy, 142*f*
hunting activity, modern, 152–55, 158–60
hydropower, 100, 121–22, 124

IAR (Incremental Adaptive Restoration), 272–73
Icy Strait, aerial view, 127*f*
Iisaak company, 239
implementation monitoring, adaptive management, 238–42
Incremental Adaptive Restoration (IAR), 272–73
independent tourists, 118–19
indie-package tourism, 118–19
indigenous people: arrivals of, 90–91; land claims activity, 99–100; loss of territories/resources, 97–99; natural resource use, 93–101, 123, 134*f*; socioeconomic structures, 91–93
industrial development. *See* economic activity; timber products
insect populations, 66–67, 259
interaction element, riparian zones, 44–45
International Union for Conservation of Nature (IUCN), 197
intertidal areas, 51–52
invertebrate populations: canopy environments, 259; climate change effects, 66–67; effects of variable retention harvesting, 248; indigenous uses, 96, 98; in riparian nutrient dynamics, 48, 51–52
iron, 65, 97–98
island biogeography, rise of, 9–10, 23–24
island environments, biotic communities: aerial views, 128–30*f*; connectivity patterns, 34–36; distance factor, 31–34; distribution of, 19–20; evolutionary expectations, 26–27; extinction vulnerabilities, 28–29, 281; genetic framework, 22–23; habitat fragmentation problem, 35–36; influence of glacial

ments, biotic communities; predator-prey community, clear-cutting effects; *specific species*

mapping species distributions, 171

maps: glaciation, 22*f*, 25*f*; mammal populations, 34*f*; North Pacific coastal rainforests, 4*f*; southeast Alaska, 20*f*

Marcot, Bruce G.: biographical highlights, 365–66; chapter by, 168–88

marine-derived nutrients (MDN), 53–55

marine eddies, Gulf of Alaska, 55–56, 65

marine environments, research needs, 276–77

marking practices, variable retention harvesting, 237–38

marmot populations, 26, 96, 160

Marsh, George Perkins, 270

marten populations, 23, 37–38, 166

MARXAN models, 187

Massett, Haida people, 92

MASS project (Montane Alternative Silvicultural Systems), 244–45

mass wasting events, 60, 75, 151, 261–63

MDN (marine-derived nutrients), 53–55

measurement standards, variable retention harvesting, 237–38

medicine sources, indigenous people, 93–95, 96–97

Megin River, 199

Mehrkens, Joe R.: biographical highlights, 366; chapter by, 89–126

metapopulation dynamics: conservation biology's role, 182–83, 185; island environments, 34–35; in scale considerations, 255–56

methane releases, 69

Microtus spp., 23, 34

migration patterns: climate change effects, 85, 176; deer, 147–49, 158

minerals/mining, 97–98, 111–13

minimum dynamic area, defined, 203

mink populations, 53–54

Misty Fjords National Monument, 111, 179*f*

Mitkof Island, shrew population, 34

mixed retention, timber harvest example, 229*f*

moieties, indigenous people, 92

molybdenum mining, 111

monitoring elements, variable retention harvesting, 238–42

Montane Alternative Silvicultural Systems (MASS) project, 244–45

moose populations, 23, 96

Mount Andrew, mining activity, 113

Mount Fairweather, aerial view, 127*f*

multiagency relationships, 38–40

muskegs. *See* peatlands

Native corporation lands, timber harvesting, 11, 104–6, 145, 169, 239

nematodes, marten populations, 37–38

Neovison vison, 53–54

network, defined, 184

New England Fish Company, 121

newt populations, effects of variable retention harvesting, 249

New Zealand, 5, 13, 74, 262

Nie, Martin, x*f*

Nii Luutiksm/Banks Conservancy, aerial view, 128*f*

Ninstints village, 134*f*

nitrogen, terrestrial-marine interactions, 52–55

nonequilibrium hypotheses, development of, 9–10

Noon, Barry, x*f*

Norberg, Erik: biographical highlights, 366; chapter by, 43–72
Northern Rocky Mountains Park, 198
Northwest Forest Plan, 178
Nothofagus spp., 75
Nowacki, Gregory: biographical highlights, 366–67; chapter by, 73–88
nutrient dynamics, windthrow effects, 80. *See also* riparian zones

oceanic islands, land bridge islands compared, 24–26
Odocoileus hemionus sitkensis. See deer, Sitka black-tailed
oil spills, ecosystem recovery variability, 270
old-forest environment, defined, 184
old-growth forests: aerial views, 127–28*f*, 136*f*; bird abundance, 248; canopy gap characteristics, 76–80, 127*f*, 133*f*, 147, 260–61; as habitat islands, 259; harvest design recommendation, 288; research needs, 274–75; reserves establishment, 145–46, 162–64; understory vegetation patterns, 83. *See also* riparian zones; timber harvesting; watershed-based reserves
Oncorhynchus spp. *See* salmon populations
Oreamnos americanus, 23, 96
Orians, Gordon H.: biographical highlights, 367; chapters by, 3–18, 253–91; with team members, x*f*
otter populations, 53–54, 96

Palmer, mining activity, 113
parks, in BC's protected areas, 197–200
partnerships, resource management, 40–41
passive adaptive management, 180, 271

Pearse Island, 179*f*
peatlands: aerial views, 127–28*f*, 131–32*f*; connectivity functions, 46; headwaters, 48–49; McGinnis Creek area, 47; plant species, 85, 265
Peck, Cyrus, Sr., 114–15
peripheral species, role of conservation biology, 171–72
permits, fishing, 116
persistence of species, as reserve design goal, 201, 207–9
Person, David K.: biographical highlights, 367; chapter by, 143–67
Petersburg area, 100, 122
Petrel Island, indigenous uses, 91
phosphorus, 52–55, 64–65
phylogenetic systematics, impact, 9–10
Picea sitchensis. See spruce, Sitka
pine, lodgepole, commercial value, 109–10
population statistics, indigenous people, 99
population viability measures, for emergent properties assessment, 206–7, 217–20, 269
Porcupine Creek, 51, 52*f*
Port Houghton, 141*f*
Port Snettisham, mining activity, 122
precipitation patterns: climate change expectations, 61–63, 85–86, 176, 262–63; distribution estimates, 45
predator-prey community, clear-cutting effects: overview, 145–47; bear populations, 154–55, 156–60; beaver populations, 149–50; deer populations, 147–49, 156–60; human hunting, 155, 158–59; management implications, 161–66; salmon populations, 150–51, 158; succession debt problem, 144, 155–60; wolf populations, 151–54, 156–60

virtual islands, 9–10, 258–59
vole populations, 23, 34
Vulpes lagopus, 21

warbler populations, 247
watershed-based reserves: acreage
study opportunities, 87–88, 189,
193–95, 277–78; arguments for,
189–90, 221–26, 267–68; British
Columbia case study, 196–200, 202,
215; content criteria, 191, 192*t*, 200–
204, 209–15, 267–68; context criteria, 191, 192*t*, 200–201, 204–6, 215–
17; design perspectives, 192–93;
emergent properties criteria, 191,
192*t*, 200–201, 206–9, 217–21; evaluation categories, 190–92, 200–
201; scale considerations, 266–69;
tradeoff considerations, 195–96,
204
watersheds: aerial views, 127–28*f*, 130–
32, 138–39*f*, 141–42*f*; climate change
effects, 61–70; harvest moratorium
recommendation, 223, 288–89;
research needs, 277–79, 288–89.
See also riparian zones
wealth distribution, indigenous
people, 92–93
weir stakes, radiocarbon dating, 90
Wells Gray Park, 198
Western Forest Products (WFP), 230–
31, 235–36
wetlands, distribution of, 45. *See also*
riparian zones
Weyerhauser, 230, 241
wilderness designations, 56
wildlife-habitat relationships, modeling, 170–71

Wildlife Tree Retention Areas, 231
winds, Chile, 75
windthrow disturbances, 76–78, 79*f*,
80–81, 264
windthrow hazards, variable retention harvest planning, 235, 244–45,
246
Woewodski Island, mining activity,
113
Wolf Island, indigenous uses, 91
wolf populations, island environments, 23, 34. *See also* predator-
prey community, clear-cutting
effects
wood products industry. *See* timber
products
woody debris: in adaptive management monitoring, 239; for channel
restoration, 59–60; clear-cutting
effects, 83, 87, 150; in headwater
watersheds, 190; as old-growth
forest characteristic, 78, 83; in
restoration project planning, 87;
in variable retention study, 243
Wrangell area, 100, 122
Wrangell-St. Elias National Park, 199
wren, winter, 247

Yakutat eddy, Gulf of Alaska, 55–56
Yakut basketry, 94
yarding systems, costs, 236
yew, Pacific, 95
Yukon Territory, Tlingit settlements,
91

zinc, 111
zoning framework, variable retention
harvesting, 235–36